PLEDGED

The Secret Life of Sororities

ALEXANDRA ROBBINS

MJF Books
New York

Published by MJF Books
Fine Communications
322 Eighth Avenue
New York, NY 10001

Pledged
LC Control Number: 2013948089
ISBN 978-1-60671-192-7

QF   10 9 8 7 6 5 4 3 2 1

Dedicated with love to

MISSY, ANDREW, JO, IRA, IRVING, RACHEL, MARTY, SEENA,

AND DAVE

PLEDGED

PROLOGUE

———

IT IS BID DAY at Southern Methodist University in the late 1990s, the January day when hopeful rushees find out which sorority has accepted them. As throngs of students, families, and alumnae line the quaint suburban Dallas streets outside the Hughes-Trigg Student Center, hundreds of girls fidget nervously inside, agonizing about the important but barely discernible item practically burning a hole beneath their jeans like the pea beneath the princess. An hour earlier, these underclassmen, wearing the required Bid Day uniform of white shirts and denim, were ushered into the auditorium and handed their bid envelopes, each containing a name that many in Texas believe will either carve or destroy the paths of a young woman's life. Since then, the girls have been sitting on the envelopes, as instructed, while enduring a series of lectures by administrators and guest speakers about the sorority system, women's issues, and how to become more involved at SMU—similar to the speech a varsity coach gives to his tryouts before announcing his final cuts.

After anxiously squirming and sweating through the speeches, knowing all the while that the product of a semester's worth of schmoozing and image-polishing is just under their behinds, they practically shoot out of their seats when a speaker announces that now, all at once, they are allowed to open their envelopes. For a few moments, the room is full of five hundred girls (most of whom have been assigned a house, if not their house of preference) crying, laughing, and screaming, hugging each other in groups or slipping quietly away to a corner to weep alone. But there isn't time to linger.

Immediately, the girls are herded out of the auditorium, up the stairs, and out the student center doors for the SMU annual tradition called "Pigs' Run." Together, the girls (or "pigs"), squealing and cheering, must sprint from Hughes-Trigg to the newly revealed sorority house that has chosen them, through about five blocks' worth of car-less streets blockaded by police officers at every corner. On the way, they are jostled through an onslaught of fraternity brothers who line the paths with water guns and hoses, drenching the sisters until long after their mandatory white shirts turn transparent. The girls who do not get into the house of their choice run regardless, crushed and sobbing, through the gauntlet until they reach the houses, where the rushees are feted by cheering sorority sisters who slide a sorority jersey over their wet clothes and welcome them boisterously. The heartbroken girls must don their happiest face and adopt their most sycophantic tone—quickly, before their sisters spot their regret or reluctance.

The mothers, gathered with their families, friends, and, in many cases, their own sorority sisters, stand near the houses they expect their daughters to join. Many of these families are from Highland Park, the upscale neighborhood that hosts the ritzy SMU, which has been referred to as Southern Millionaires University and a "college in country club clothing." But others have traveled great distances to watch this event. An alumna of one sorority waits at her former house, draped in her sorority's colors and waving balloons and flowers as she scans the crowd for her daughter, whom she expects to continue the legacy. She stands with her family, anxiously searching the faces of the Pigs' Run participants flying by. And continues to wait. When the last of the stragglers careen toward the crowd, this legacy family rushes through Pigs' Run in reverse, clamoring into the student center, through the auditorium doors, where they find their baby-faced daughter bawling and refusing to leave the building because she has not been accepted at the sorority of her—and her mother's—choice. "Sororities are a completely different world," one of the Pigs' Run girls tells me. "But especially in the South, you don't even question the tradition. You just do it."

Pigs' Run, a custom carried out under different names (such as "Running of the Bulls" or "Squeal Day") at many schools across the country, distributes the girls into distinct social networks they believe will inevitably determine the trajectories of their college careers and perhaps their lives beyond. It is a dash away from anonymity on a college campus and toward the optimistic embrace of a smaller, more intimate community. Many rushees believe that Pigs' Run or its various other epithets represents the end of a journey through which they have sought identity through association, the culmination of their arduous and intense quest to belong. But truly, the quest has only just begun.

INTRODUCTION

—

"Delta, Delta, Delta, Can We Help Ya, Help Ya, Help Ya?"
(or, So Do They Really Have Topless Pillow Fights?)

BECAUSE I'VE NEVER BEEN a member of any girl-only group other than sports teams, I didn't know much about sororities when I started researching this book. Actually, I was slightly afraid of them. We outsiders, who can only envision what goes on behind sorority house walls and inside sorority girls' heads, merely have movies such as *Revenge of the Nerds*, *Animal House*, and *Legally Blonde* to inform our views about sororities. Those of us with the more salacious of imaginations—or the more B-movie of tastes—might associate with sororities the topless pillow fights that must inevitably occur when fifty estrogen-laden creatures gather for a sleepover (or so men everywhere fervently pray). Or perhaps a *Heathers*-inspired coldness might come to mind as we visualize the vicious hair-tearing, earring-twisting catfights between sororities clamoring for the most popular fraternity to escort them to Homecoming. Or our image of sororities (as was mine) is the tamer, more relatable version: the popular group of girls from high school—cooler, prettier, wealthier, multiplied by ten, living under one roof, and recognized officially by their college as a clique.

I don't think I realized the extent to which I was an outsider, however, until I found myself smack in a bustling epicenter of sorority life—a "Greek boutique" at a conference for sorority and fraternity representatives. The room was swathed in the hyperprecise sorority colors: not blue and yellow but "Old Blue" and "Café Au Lait" (Sigma Delta Tau); not green and white but "Olive Green" and "Pearl White" (Kappa Delta). I was surrounded by sorority letters, colors, and symbols stamped on, drawn on, embossed on, engraved in, carved into, or welded onto such a variety of objects that it felt as if I had arrived in a Disney gift shop for "Sororityland." As I watched sorority sisters in expensive-looking clothes try on kitschy jewelry they likely wouldn't deign to wear if it didn't bear their sorority letters, I wondered what possessed them to feel such passion for objects I obviously didn't understand. Here, on table upon table of items divided neatly by individual sororities and their corresponding colors (sororities also have certain mascots, symbols, jewels, and flowers, such as Delta Phi Epsilon's "Lovely Purple Iris"), the sisters had their pick of sorority emery boards, money pouches, picture frames, bottle openers, and refrigerator magnets. Lips feeling dry? Try the boutique's "Sorority Lip Balm"! Bathroom not smelling sparkly clean? Here's a sorority air freshener! Crave a more elegant hygienic experience? How about sorority bath crystals? Gesundheit! Have a sorority tissue.

In the long line at the cash register, sorority girls fussed and "fabulous!"ed over the souvenirs, twittering in italics about such foreign jargon as rush crushes, cold dorms, and prefs. I was officially entering Sorority World, a world of High Priestesses, Temples, and secret handshakes, a world so entirely different from my non-Greek experience that it had a name for people like me, people unaffiliated and unlettered. "Oh . . . ," one girl drawled in a honeyed southern accent. "You're a GDI." A GDI? "A God-Damn Independent." Oh.

Clearly, this wasn't going to be your everyday reporting assignment. In order to understand this world so fully that I could portray it fairly and accurately, I realized I needed to have so engulfing an experience that I would be living, breathing, and shopping sorority. My first plan was to try to follow a sorority throughout the 2002–2003 academic year, to become such an ever-present fixture in the house that I would be treated as something like an honorary member. I canvassed several campuses in search of an appropriate group to shadow: a national group, affiliated with a "historically white" national sorority organization—white and black sororities are still largely segregated. (The sororities illustrated in this book are "historically white" unless otherwise noted.) Finally, a sister invited me to observe her group, a popular sorority at a school whose Greek system had been under fire in recent years because of several hazing-related deaths.

The day I was to visit the house, I agonized over my outfit, blow-dried my hair straight, put on more makeup than usual, and dug my spikiest ankle boots out of the recesses of my closet. Admittedly, because not many of my friends were sorority sisters, I was nervous about entering an entire house full of them. The more I learned about sororities, the more bizarre their world seemed. As I tottered up to the porch, I suddenly didn't feel like a twenty-six-year-old investigative reporter preparing to dig into another project about secret group behavior. I felt like the kid I was in junior high school, wearing sweatpants and soccer sandals, hoping to please everyone but at the same time trying hard to pretend not to care.

Later that afternoon, I was curled up on a bunk bed and chatting with two of the sorority girls. Sometime during the emotional story one sister shared about how a sorority rivalry destroyed her relationship with her longtime best friend, I flashed back to my camp counselor days and had visions of serving as a kind of resident big sister to these girls. It hit me then that when I attended overnight camp, my teenaged bunk acted in ways that were somewhat similar to sororities. We traveled in packs, had rivalries with other bunks, pressured each other to break rules, and even fought over the same guy (who, coincidentally, eventually became the president of his fraternity at the school where I now sat). Here at the sorority house was a group that similarly provided selected college girls an automatic sense of belonging, no talent or niche required—a built-in social network to accompany a girl to bars, parties, sporting events, and study sessions. This comparison caused me not only to wonder if sorority girls were so different from the rest of us, but also to think that had I attended a larger college, maybe I would have been a sorority girl, too. But when the girls gave me a tour of the house, they told me about their sisters' diet pill addiction, their pride in the fact that they hazed new girls, and their "drug room," which displayed a bong, several bottles of pills, and some suspicious-looking white powder (some of the girls regularly did cocaine). If I had joined a sorority, I asked myself, would I, like the girls I met, inevitably have fallen into the kind of herd mentality among sororities that can encourage conformity, cliquishness, and compromising morals? At that initial point in my research, I didn't know.

After several days of observing this major national sorority, I was approached by the adviser of the house. A stern, heavyset sorority alumna who looked much older than her twentysomething years, she led me into the "scholarship room"—a small room with computers and a large file cabinet full of notes, tests, and papers from various classes offered at the school. She told me to sit down, and locked the glass door. Girls peered in quizzically as they walked by, but a quick glare from the adviser sent them scurrying on.

"You shouldn't have been given permission to be here," she said gruffly. She interrupted herself by cursing under her breath and yelling in her deep voice at the girls she could see through a window who were smoking cigarettes on the front porch. "You're not allowed to smoke in front of the house! It doesn't look good!" The girls reluctantly slinked away.

The adviser turned back to me. "You need to get permission from the national office, which is probably not going to give it to you." She paused again. "And if for some reason they do, I simply cannot allow you to write about the drugs."

When I got home, I called the sorority's national office and explained what I was doing, figuring this process of obtaining official permission was just a formality. The executive director, however, said otherwise. MTV had just aired a show called *Sorority Life*, which followed the six-week pledge process of a California sorority (a "local" sorority, which meant it was independent and unaffiliated with any national organization). The show had infuriated sororities nationwide, who believed that MTV had overly sensationalized life in a sorority house and concentrated only on the girls' drinking and catty fights. "Because of the MTV show," the executive director told me, "all of the national sororities have decided on a blanket policy not to cooperate with any members of the media. It's just not appropriate at this time." With that, I was suddenly completely closed off from a group of several dozen sorority girls I had already started to like.

Realizing that I wouldn't be able to openly observe a sorority house unless I received permission from its national office, I called other national sorority headquarters to state my case. One by one, every national office I talked to shut me out of their houses, even as I told them I was presenting a truthful—not necessarily negative—account of what sorority life is really like. "We're gun-shy," said one. "We've gotten several media calls even this week and we're turning them all down," said another. The twenty-six member groups of the National Panhellenic Conference, which was established in 1902 to oversee the historically white national sororities, had laid down the law.

I didn't understand the panicked responses of the national offices, which claim to instill within their sororities "individuality, . . . togetherness, . . . [and] friendships," according to the web site for Alpha Epsilon Phi, whose motto is "Many Hearts, One Purpose." They promote goals such as Delta Delta Delta's, to "develop a stronger and more womanly character, to broaden the moral and intellectual life, and to assist its members in every possible way." They foster, like Kappa Kappa Gamma, "friendship rooted in a tradition of high standards." These aspirations seemed laudable, these institutions beneficial. One would assume the real-life sororities, therefore, have so much to offer that their positives would far outweigh their negatives. But when one school's Panhellenic adviser attempted to blacklist me on her campus for writing this book, she insisted she must "protect our women." The question was, protect them from what?

Ω   Ω   Ω

BECAUSE NO SORORITY WOULD KNOWINGLY LET ME tail its sisters for the year, it became necessary for me to fly under the radar of both the national offices and the sorority girls themselves. I sought out individual sisters who were willing to risk their sorority membership by letting me into their lives for an entire academic year, knowing that they could not tell anyone—their sorority sisters, their friends, their families—who I really was. I can't divulge how the four girls I chose, who knew they would be the main characters in a book I was writing about sororities, introduced me to their sisters, who did not know; and I can't disclose the disguise I wore or role I played when spending time with these groups (suffice it to say, I can pass for nineteen). To further protect the four girls, who could be ostracized and even thrown out of the Greek system if their identities were revealed, I have given pseudonyms to them, their school, and their school's Greek groups, and have changed identifying details. But their dilemmas, emotions, interactions, and dialogues are real. (The girls didn't know I also monitored their Instant Messenger away messages, which they changed sometimes as frequently as once an hour. Away messages are bulletins that IM users post online so that friends can see what they are up to. Like many college students, the girls used their away messages to convey their state of mind or broadcast their whereabouts.)

In order to provide a balanced view of sororities, I selected good-hearted girls who were members of "normal" sororities not known on campus as extreme stereotypes. I also chose these girls on the basis of their diverse attitudes toward and roles in their sororities. These sisters, one of whom was a sorority officer, are largely the kind of girls whom the national offices would be proud to have represent them, had the national offices been willing to allow themselves to be represented. The two juniors and two sophomores all attend a school I'll call State University, a campus on which Greek life is considered important but not essential.

It turned out that "going undercover" gave me more candid access to the sororities than I would have had openly as a reporter. Because I played the role I did, the sisters didn't know to censor their behavior in front of me, and my four main subjects tended to view me more as a friend than a journalist. With that said, however, I would not presume that the experiences of these four sisters alone could accurately represent a sorority system of millions. Many of the posts on Greek system message boards constantly remind readers that it's not right to let a few renegade sisters, or even chapters, represent the image of the entire sorority system. I took this message to heart. My four girls aren't renegades; nevertheless, I have supplemented my observations of them with visits and interviews with scores of other sorority girls. By the time I finished writing *Pledged*, I had spoken with or met with several hundred girls. Essentially, I got to return to college and experience the path I had not taken the first time around (and had a far better time than I did when I was actually enrolled in college). When a sorority girl needed a date to a Date Party, I went; when sisters went shopping together, I joined them; when new members danced exuberantly on Bid Day, so did I. Though I couldn't incorporate all of the hundreds of interviews in this book, the sisters' frank assessments of sorority life shaped my observations.

In writing this book, the surprise for me—and this may delight many readers—was that the notions of those topless pillow fights may not have been so far off base after all. In the back of my mind, I don't think I ever really believed that sororities were quite as campy as their conventional image. But at about the time I heard about traditions like "Naked Party" and "Boob Ranking," I had to reconsider. I learned that many of the rumors (as well as the fantasies) about sororities are indeed staggeringly true, including those concerning loyalty, sex, conformity, drugs, violence, verbal abuse, mind games, prostitution, racism, forced binge drinking, nudity, cheating, eating disorders, rituals, "mean girls," and secrecy. But not all sororities encompass these experiences; and of the sororities that do, not all consist of girls one would necessarily consider "bad."

Much of sorority life espouses noble purpose, and the friendships and philanthropy encouraged by these organizations can enhance a girl's college experience, boost her self-esteem, and better her character. But the prevalence of the aforementioned litany, which still occurs on several campuses nation-wide in the name of tradition, speaks volumes about larger issues concerning women, higher education, and female group dynamics. Even halfway into the year, I was plagued by questions. Why are twenty-first-century women still so eager to participate in such seemingly outdated, ritualistic groups and activi-ties? What is the purpose of sororities and what does membership truly require of the sisters? How does a sisterhood change the way a girl thinks about herself? Do sororities cause women to fall further behind in the gender wars or are they instead women's secret weapon? My challenge, then, in writ-ing Pledged, was how to reconcile the unexpected discovery of a dark side to sorority life with the observation that many of the girls who participate in it and continue to join it in droves are "normal" girls, girls who are sweet, smart, successful, and kind both before and after they join. Girls—and this puzzled me—who by year's end no longer intimidated me. Girls who would be surprised to read how their sororities appear from an outsider's point of view.

AUGUST

The sorority becomes one of life's great forces in teaching the beauty of self-sacrifice. Leadership under the spell of this great power must be magnetic. Self-confidence, then, is creative, self-control restrictive, self-sacrifice persuasive.

—*The Sorority Handbook,* published in 1907

Manicured nails are of paramount importance for the finished look.
—*Ready for Rush: The Must-Have Manual for Sorority Rushees!* published in 1999

Ω   Ω   Ω

AUGUST 17
VICKI'S INSTANT MESSENGER AWAY MESSAGE
missing my california crew. can i come home yet?

ON SORORITY ROW, SORORITY girls stepped cheerily into their houses, many of them followed by fathers loaded up with boxes or, in the exceptionally good-looking cases, towing beefy undergrad boys just barely able to see over the duffel bags full of clothes and stuffed animals they dutifully hefted. As quickly as the men nailed extra shelves into the bedroom walls, the girls lined them with Michael Kors perfume, Juicy Couture tees, and rows of designer sunglasses. (One sister dissolved into peals of loud laughter because she'd lost the case to her Gucci sunglasses and as a result had stored them in a Calvin Klein case instead.)

At State U, it wasn't too difficult to distinguish which girls belonged to which of the eighteen houses. Sisters of the largest house on campus were tall and brunette, seemingly all of them slender with dancers' grace. Members of the most obnoxious sorority were almost uniformly dressed in white tank tops, or as they called them, "wife beaters," slim black sweatpants, and either white socks and sneakers or black platform flip-flops. The Alpha Rhos, whose girls were known as laid back but also, as some put it, "sexually relaxed," were slightly more haphazard in tanks, jeans, flip-flops, and bandannas. A few sisters of Beta Pi, Alpha Rho's biggest rival and a group considered to be princesses, trotted back and forth with their boyfriends across the Row in short shorts, tight tees, and platform shoes.

When the silver Lexus, its gleam wavering in the August humidity, pulled in front of the Beta Pi house, the Beta Pis watched with interest as a deeply bronzed leg cautiously stepped from the back door. Their boyfriends' eyes traveled up the length of the slender limb to where the natural tan, unfaded, met a pair of chic but modest designer shorts. The Beta Pis instinctively glanced downward, raising eyebrows when they noticed unpainted toenails curled in flat flip-flops. When a summer-blond head finally appeared, large green cat eyes fixed on the curb, the Beta Pis recognized the girl as "the one with potential" who had so far disappointed them. The sisters had invited the naturally pretty sophomore to join Beta Pi in the spring of her freshman year, thinking that with her dot-com-millionaire parents and her West Coast upbringing, she was a savvy California surfer girl who would fit right into the sisterhood. But so far, Vicki had turned out to be a dud. She was a painfully quiet small-town girl less interested in partying with new friends than spending hours on the phone with old ones from back home. The Beta Pis and their boyfriends shrugged and continued across the Row.

Vicki took a deep breath and reluctantly followed her parents inside Beta Pi. One of the most impressive homes on the Row, Beta Pi was a four-story white frame Victorian mansion with a classic wraparound porch, a rolling back lawn, and a spacious veranda spiked by long white columns. Inside, a massive fresh flower arrangement graced a polished oak table at the foot of the broad front staircase. To the right of the entry hall, Vicki could see women in white uniforms setting up a spread of cold cuts, chips, and petite cakes for the sisters and their families.

"Hi Vicki!" The president, thin and blond like most of the Beta Pis, smiled widely and effusively greeted Vicki's parents, who immediately tried to prod their daughter into a conversation.

"Um, hi," Vicki practically whispered in her childlike voice. She hunched her tall frame so she seemed closer to the president's height. "I'm, like, going to go unpack?" The president nodded and chattered at Vicki's father while he headed outside to unload the car.

Vicki heard her mother clamoring over the welcome banners festooned across the entry hall but tuned out the comments as she lost herself in her bewildered second thoughts. Compared to the noise of the street, the house was much quieter; Vicki could hear their footfalls echoing up the stairwell. When the rest of the girls streamed in later in the afternoon, the mansion would be a madhouse, with girls screeching and hugging after a summer of scattered sisterhood. Cringing, she could hear them already—"I haven't seen you in fo'-EVA!"—squealing the way seventh graders sign yearbooks. And now, as she passed bedroom doors decorated with handmade, gold-glittered names she barely recognized, it finally hit her that she was moving into a sorority house, that she was part of a sorority, and yet she had no idea what that meant.

Over the summer, Vicki hadn't thought about most of the girls in her pledge class, the group with whom she had rushed and been initiated, and now it was difficult to imagine actually living, eating, sleeping, studying, and partying with them. Instead, she had spent her summer doing what she had done every year since she could remember: watching television, listening to music, and eating takeout with her two best friends and her boyfriend, a caring boy who wanted to marry her. The only difference this year was that none of the other three could stop talking about how ridiculous it was that Vicki had joined a sorority in the spring. Vicki explained that she forced herself through the rush process to be part of a more intimate community within State U, to make a large university seem smaller. She had tried so hard to fake a sorority attitude during rush that she had painted her fingernails with clear polish so she wouldn't chew them. When she received her invitation, she was shocked and proud. But her girlfriends, who attended the local community college back home, didn't understand the point of being Greek, and her boyfriend, who had followed her to State U, worried that sorority life would mean they would have less time together. Now that she was back on campus, these Beta Pis were going to be her new best friends—they had to be, she had no choice—and she didn't really know them.

On the fourth floor, the sophomores' floor, Vicki headed to the tiny room she would be sharing with three roommates from her pledge class: loud Olivia; gorgeous Morgan, who resembled a Barbie doll; and Laura-Ann, who, with her springy red hair, seemed even more of an outsider than Vicki. Wary of the other, unfamiliar sisters, Vicki planned to stick closely to her roommates whenever she was in the house, particularly to Olivia. Olivia, a party girl who wore coats of thick black eyeliner and a spicy perfume, was an unlikely companion, but she had taken Vicki under her wing when they pledged Beta Pi together. Vicki had warmed to her when Olivia admitted that she had bleached her dark hair blond before rush so she would look like a Beta Pi.

"This is fantastic! Every student should live like this," her mother exclaimed as she drew out the standard Beta Pi burgundy-and-cream curtains and plunked a suitcase on one of the room's two bunk beds. The room was small, but it had sparkling hardwood floors and large, open windows. "Two cleaning ladies, a House Mom, a cook, and—oh, feel that air-conditioning—Vicki, this is great!"

Vicki grunted in response. She was close to her parents, but she wished they would stop trying to coax enthusiasm out of her. Vicki's parents had been surprised when Vicki had announced that she was joining Beta Pi, but they were thrilled that their daughter was branching out. They knew Vicki wasn't quiet when she was with her family or her friends back home; the difficult step for her was reaching that comfort level within a new group. When Vicki was a freshman, days, sometimes weeks, would go by between her social events. She hadn't gotten to know many people because she hadn't felt the need to; she was one of the few girls on her hall with a steady boyfriend. But now, because of the sorority, she would constantly be meeting people and, theoretically, had an automatic houseful of friends. The spring had been a whirlwind of pledging and social events involving frequent but fleeting visits to the house. This year would be different, it slowly dawned on Vicki as she helped her mother unpack the designer dresses, sleek tops, and accessories she had purchased specifically for sorority functions. Living in the house would be an entirely new level of commitment.

When her parents left in the evening, Vicki was relieved at the chance to catch her breath. All day it had been, "Vicki, we need to get you your books!" "Vicki, we should get shelf liner!" in a flurry of back-to-school errands and last-minute rearranging when Vicki was already overwhelmed by the house and the steady flow of female strangers flooding inside. Under the pretense of "getting settled," while her eighty-six new housemates mingled in the mess-hall-like dining room in the basement, Vicki stayed in the safe corner of her room, feeling disoriented and faintly claustrophobic, wondering why she had agreed to live in a house that seemed as if it would never feel like home.

One week later, Vicki was still in culture shock. There were so many girls everywhere—the house appeared to be infested with them, draped over the couches in the living room, huddling over magazines in the "gentleman's parlor" on the main floor, blow-drying their hair in the bathroom, gossiping in the halls—that Vicki felt like she was in a nursery rhyme. She had suddenly become diffident to an extreme and was uncomfortable leaving her room when her roommates couldn't accompany her. Occasionally she'd peek into the dining room, spot dozens of sisters chattering over their food, and duck back out before anyone saw her. Rather than sit with them over dinner and forced conversation, Vicki would either take a tray from the kitchen back to her room to eat alone or escape the house to lounge with her boyfriend in his dorm, their usual social activity. She couldn't even bring herself to join the sisters to watch *American Idol* unless Olivia agreed to go with her. In fact, she rarely ventured into the television room at all, even though it was the gathering spot where sisters socialized with each other. This didn't feel like a horizon-broadening college experience. It felt like junior high.

Even when the sisters in the house went out together on their frequent field trips to one of the campus bars, Vicki sensed a chasm. Her fake ID, purchased in anticipation of these regular inebriated bonding sessions, was enough to get her in the door. But once inside, the sisters, clotted in a corner, checked out the fraternity brothers in the room and plotted to set each other up at parties while Vicki sat quietly, feeling too guilty about her boyfriend to participate in the ogling and ignored by the sisters because they knew she had no interest in being set up. Eventually the sisters would meet back at the house for their post-hookup gossip sessions in the television room. At one of these sessions, a Beta Pi noticed Vicki sitting silently on the outskirts of the room. "You know, Vicki," she said coyly, "it would be so much more fun for us if you'd just break up with him."

"I-I couldn't," Vicki stammered. She blew her wispy too-long bangs out of her eyes.

The sisters nearby jumped into the conversation, their faces lit up. "It's so true! College is the only place where you're going to be with so many cute guys your age," they insisted. "It's not like you guys are going to get married, so it's better to break up with him now and have fun instead of waiting four whole years and missing out."

"Oh my God, you've been together since seventh grade!" Olivia exclaimed. "You've never been a single woman."

Vicki politely demurred. She wouldn't dream of breaking up with her boyfriend. They were one of those generally tolerated college couples who were in love but careful not to flaunt their distance from singledom with gooey-happy displays. Although he had no interest in the Greek system, he had stuck by Vicki and supported her even through the hectic eight-week pledge process, a period usually incomprehensible to outsiders. Despite her sisters' shared opinion, she could comfortably see herself with him for the long term and had no intention of jeopardizing that possibility.

But as she continued to spend her days with her boyfriend instead of at the house, the nagging sense of being out of a loop that was moving on without her grew into a serious worry. One night she came back from dinner with him to find Olivia, Laura-Ann, and Morgan in the middle of a screeching fight. Laura-Ann was yelling about how upset she was that the roommates weren't spending much time together as a unit and accused Olivia and Morgan of shooting her dirty looks whenever they came into the room. Eventually, they managed to mollify Laura-Ann by promising to spend more time with her. But Vicki couldn't help thinking that she was away from the house more than anybody because she had a boyfriend.

A few nights later, on a sorority outing at a nearby club, Olivia and a few other sisters introduced Vicki to William, the extremely attractive and well-liked president of Iota, Beta Pi's favorite fraternity. Olivia had slept with

William a few times in the spring and thought he and Vicki would get along well. Vicki was shy at first, despite her inebriation, which was due to her habit of sharing an entire bottle of Grey Goose vodka with her three roommates before every Greek social function, as well as a water bottle full of gin and tonic on the cab ride over. But when she saw beautiful Morgan draping her Barbie body over William on the dance floor, Vicki approached him, inspired by jealousy. As they danced for the rest of the night, Vicki's cornsilk hair nestled just under William's chin, Vicki wrestled with her conflicting feelings. In her drunken haze she could tell she liked him and she was struck by a conquering feeling when she realized he was interested in her. But she felt guilty about even entertaining the idea.

Nonetheless, she had apparently made an impression. At dinner in the house the following day, a horde of sisters joined Vicki and her roommates for dinner. They told her that William had just announced to several Beta Pis that he was mesmerized by Vicki. Within minutes, the sisters were circling Vicki; suddenly, everyone seemed to know who she was, especially now that a boy who met with the sisters' approval—the president of Iota!—had taken an interest in her.

"You and William?" the sisters hounded her.

"Do you like him?"

"Are you into him?"

"Are you going to see him again?"

"Um, no," Vicki kept replying, her delicate features slightly contorted in annoyance. "I mean, I'm really not interested."

The commotion lasted for a few hours before dying down when the girls realized that Vicki wasn't going to give them any grist for the gossip mill. But Vicki couldn't get her sisters' reaction out of her head. Having a boyfriend was obstructing her relationship with Beta Pi. The next day, when she tearfully told her roommates she was thinking about breaking up with him, they told her she was doing the right thing.

"I'm being so bitchy to the love of my life, you know?" Vicki sobbed.

"Oh my God, you *have* to do what makes you happy. If he really loves you, he'll understand," Olivia said. "Do what your heart tells you to do!"

Even as Vicki told the devastated boy on the flagstone patio in front of the Beta Pi house that "now just isn't a good time," she had misgivings.

"I didn't mean to hold you back from your sorority," he said. "I want you to be happy. I love you."

Vicki hesitated, her eyes swollen from crying, but she thought of her sisters. "I just . . . I just need to be single right now," she responded, and went back into the house to be with her fellow Beta Pis. Vicki would continue to cry for days.

Joining the Crowd

AUGUST 19

SABRINA'S IM AWAY MESSAGE
That was definitely not something I needed to see.

ON THE TWENTY-MINUTE RIDE FROM SABRINA'S PARENTS' apartment to the Alpha Rho house, Sabrina's Oldsmobile Cutlass spluttered down the interstate that divided her town's demographics in two. This was the third year Sabrina, a junior, had driven this solo back-to-school trip, but she still felt the same pride she had the first year. When she spotted the clusters of bright pink and purple crape myrtle trees, Sabrina knew she was nearing State U, the beacon that had pulled her to ace every class in high school, to the delight of her parents, who hadn't gone to college. They loved hearing stories about the philosophical discussions Sabrina had with her dormmates, loved watching her light up beneath the widow's peak that framed her small heart-shaped face as she recounted debates she had in seminars and interesting factoids she learned from friends. Sabrina had wanted to go to State U ever since she was old enough to read the local newspaper, which was constantly plastered with State U news. Now that she was halfway through her college career, Sabrina looked forward to another year of intellectual challenge to share with her parents.

When Sabrina got to her room in the Alpha Rho house, the first thing she heard was Bitsy.

"It's important to know the difference between a clitoris and a hood," Bitsy was telling a few sisters. "Oh, hi Sabrina." Sabrina raised a dark arm in response. The flighty redhead, who had a large bust and a penchant for talking about it, turned back to her small audience. "Think of a turtle hiding its head . . ."

Sabrina resignedly shook her long, no-fuss cornrows and set her two small suitcases on her bed. This was going to be a long year.

Sabrina hadn't intended to live in the house. She preferred to do her own thing, which wasn't always acceptable in a house governed by more rules than there were sisters. But sorority dues were expensive. Sabrina had struggled last semester to pay the $650, even as the sorority's bursar had done her a favor by letting her sign over occasional paychecks instead of making the usual onetime prepayment. Sometimes Sabrina could afford to give her $150, sometimes $50, but eventually she was able to pay for the entire semester. After two months of waitressing over the summer, however, Sabrina realized she wouldn't have enough money this year to cover dorm life, plus tuition, plus Alpha Rho dues for the next year. If she lived in the Alpha Rho house, on the other hand, dues were included in her room and board and the total cost was several hundred dollars less than if she lived elsewhere on campus. There was no question Sabrina would do what it took to stay in her sorority. She had rushed as a way to force herself to make connections, and she would remain a sister in order to be able to network in an elite sector of the white world that was otherwise untouchable to a black girl like her. Any stepping-stone Sabrina could find, she was going to leap to without hesitation.

She had signed up at the last minute for the remaining spot in the Alpha Rho house: squished in the side of the "Penthouse," the chilly, low-ceilinged room spanning the entire top floor of the house that was technically supposed to hold twenty-six girls, their beds, desks, clothes, computers, posters, shoes, and accessories, divided either not at all or by flimsy curtains. Every year, the "Pents" usually stuck together in a clique made exclusive not necessarily because they actively tried to alienate the other fifty-five girls living in the house, but rather because the girls who lived on the lower floors were usually too lazy to walk upstairs. But Sabrina would be spending most of her free time in the second-floor wing, where her favorite sisters, Amy and Caitlin, lived across from each other in a two-room double suite.

Meanwhile, Sabrina's main goal was to finish unpacking. Unless she unpacked soon, she would continue to procrastinate for days and probably end up living out of her suitcases when the other sisters snatched her closet space. The funny thing was that her sisters had ten times as many things as Sabrina did, but she happened to have the biggest dresser (a trade-off for having the smallest area in the room). The Pents each had two dressers and a closet in one of the assigned third-floor "sitting rooms"—small, sunny rooms with futons that served as studies and escapes for the girls stuck in the Penthouse. Sabrina couldn't believe how, for most of the girls, two dressers and a closet still weren't enough. She hoped they wouldn't realize that she wore her single pair of designer jeans several times before washing them.

A few afternoons later, Bitsy marched into the dining room in a tiny miniskirt to announce that she was going to get a clitoris ring. She had traipsed through the house collecting sisters to join her and now, with a trail of eight sisters behind her, was focusing on Sabrina and Alpha Rho's president, Charlotte, a conservative senior who constantly tried to blend in with her sisters.

"You should totally come and get something pierced, like your nipple!" Bitsy said to Charlotte. "I'm getting a clitoris ring, but they're"—she gestured to the girls behind her—"getting belly-button and nipple rings."

"Well," Charlotte chewed her lip. "I *have* contemplated getting my nipple pierced." Sabrina snorted, her nose in her book, doubting very much that the thought had occurred to Charlotte.

Another Pent came downstairs. "What are you guys talking about?"

Sabrina rolled her eyes. "Bitsy's talking about her chach again," she said. "Now she's trying to persuade Charlotte to get her nipple pierced."

"Don't do it, Charlotte!" the new Pent said. "That would be such a rash decision."

"Do it, do it," Bitsy goaded. "It won't hurt, really. And if I'm getting my hood pierced, you can get your nipple pierced. It's really not a big deal."

Charlotte looked uncertainly from sister to sister. Amused, Sabrina decided to weigh in. "A lot of the sisters got pierced over the summer," Sabrina encouraged, wondering if prudish Charlotte could be convinced. "They all did it together on a group piercing trip."

"It's the coolest thing ever!" Bitsy exclaimed.

Charlotte took a deep breath and closed her eyes. She exhaled loudly. "Okay, I'll go."

The group turned to Sabrina, who attempted to look engrossed in her chemistry textbook. "Come on, Sabrina, come with us!" said Bitsy.

"No thank you. I have work to do."

"But the semester just started," whined another sister.

"Have fun," Sabrina waved as the girls left.

Most of Sabrina's sisters couldn't comprehend why Sabrina spent so much time studying. Sabrina, however, didn't think she worked diligently enough. She wasn't proud of her time-management skills; for some reason, she was rarely able to get assignments done ahead of time, a problem that had gotten worse each year. She couldn't fathom how some of her sisters went out every night and still managed to keep up their grades. She would have loved to be able to party most nights, but she was afraid that her grades would slip. This weighed on her more than it might have on her sisters, because Sabrina had a creeping fear that she would never escape poverty. For nearly her entire life, her parents had earned a combined total of approximately $25,000 a year. At times during her childhood, Sabrina's family had survived on welfare and food stamps. Her mother had sacrificed necessities to make sure that Sabrina had suitable clothes so the other kids in school wouldn't make fun of her. And now Sabrina was working her own way through college in order to succeed enough to provide for herself and for her parents. It was her parents' dream to own their own home. Eventually, Sabrina hoped, she would be able to buy that place for them.

This was something that Sabrina's Alpha Rho sisters weren't able to understand. Sabrina constantly grappled with the difficulty of belonging to a house of girls more accustomed to Tiffany than Target. None of these girls knew what it was like to miss a meal unless they were dieting. Even Sabrina's close friends in the house were extraordinarily wealthy. Amy's father was a multimillionaire real estate mogul with houses in at least four cities. Caitlin, the daughter of a New York political figure, had a grand four-story brownstone in Brooklyn Heights and a summer house in the Hamptons. Sabrina's family lived in a small apartment in the projects. So yes, Sabrina studied hard. Someday she was going to be a wealthy doctor. And then she'd finally be able to stop worrying.

That evening, the Penthouse was full of sisters getting ready to go to an Omega Phi fraternity party when the piercing field trip returned. "How did it go?" Sabrina asked Bitsy, barely glancing up when Charlotte, obviously proud of herself, galloped by, whipping up her shirt and yelling, "Look at my nipple!"

"Fine," Bitsy responded, also ignoring Charlotte. "I'm about to show everybody if you want to see."

"Um." Sabrina didn't have a burning desire to look at that particular part of Bitsy. "Okay."

A crowd of two dozen Pents parted when Bitsy walked across the Penthouse to her corner. She lay down on her bed, rolled up her skirt, pulled down her underwear, and maneuvered herself so the beaded ring was easily visible. The sisters stared. A few sisters tried to play it casual: "Whatever, I've seen a vagina before. No big deal," one said. Sabrina wrinkled her nose and returned to examining the day planner at her desk. Most of the others gasped, unable to look away, and whispered some version of "Ow."

"It wasn't as bad as I thought it would be," Bitsy said, her head held high and heroic.

From across the room, Fiona, whose bed was next to Sabrina's, huffed. She was sitting at her desk with her boyfriend, an Omega Phi brother who was peering in Bitsy's direction but couldn't see through the mass of sisters. "Bitsy's gonna get a little more attention at our party tonight because of that ring," he told Fiona.

This upset Fiona, who thought highly of herself despite what Sabrina considered a lack of intelligence and unremarkable looks. "That's gay," Fiona fumed. "Forget it. I don't want to go to the party if Bitsy'll be there."

Just another typical day in the Penthouse, Sabrina thought, wondering how long it would be before Fiona went out and got something pierced, too. As she exchanged you-know-how-she-is looks with the other Pents nearby, Sabrina felt a sense of camaraderie despite her lack of pierced unmentionables.

The feeling didn't last long. Later that night, Fiona, who had positioned herself among the juniors as something of a Penthouse gang leader, held a group of Pents' rapt attention as she expounded on what she saw as the recent trends in Alpha Rho. "You know," she said, eyeing Sabrina, who wasn't a part of the conversation but who was studying close enough to the group that she could hear every word, "it's getting so that every pledge class in the house has a black girl. The sophomores have C.C. and the juniors have Sabrina." The other girls glanced sideways at Sabrina, then hurriedly focused their attention back on Fiona.

Sabrina only chuckled and said lightly, "Yes, that's me." But inwardly she cringed. To many of the girls in Alpha Rho, she would always be the "token black"; to some of them, apparently, that would be her only role.

Ω   Ω   Ω

Peer Pressure

THE BEGINNING OF THE ACADEMIC YEAR CAN BE AN UN-certain time for any student, but for girls in sororities—which exist mostly in the United States and Canada—the stakes are often higher. Especially for sisters who move into the house, the first few weeks of school are a crucial period as the girls jockey for social position among old and new members and struggle to gain acceptance and approval at the same time as they must quickly learn the attitudes and attributes the sorority prioritizes. Does the group eschew steady boyfriends, as did Beta Pi? Are Gucci sunglasses—or pierced privates—the statement of the season?

Urban legend dictates certain stereotypical characteristics that many people apply to all sorority girls; I would spend several months attempting to sort out the accuracy of this and other supposedly tall tales. As Vicki confided to me, "Generally, I thought sorority girls were bitchy, princessy, slutty girls who cared only about themselves and went out with frat boys," which contributed to her insecurity. But what I learned fairly quickly was that within the sorority system lies a broad subset of stereotypes to which the sisters themselves are sharply attuned. Sorority houses tend to have different reputations on different campuses, with nearly every house exhibiting a strong stereotype—and members of each house often feel pressured to conform to that stereotype to keep with the sorority's image.

Sorority "types" are inevitable; in many mainstream sororities, the women all look and act the same. At one Texas school, the Chi Omegas are the "grounded hippie chicks," the Delta Gammas are the fast girls who wear the tightest tank tops, the Alpha Chi Omegas are the sweet girls, and the Tri-Delts are "the marrying kind." The Thetas at an Arizona school are the promiscuous girls, and Pi Phis at a Missouri school are "the marrying kind." An Indiana university's Tri-Delts are fun and crazy partyers. At a Pennsylvania school, the Tri-Delts are the prettiest—and also the cattiest. The Chi Omegas there, too, are the hippies who smoke a lot of pot and many of them have unusual names, like Summer or India. ("One girl was really unattractive," an alumna said, "but she had a weird name so she got in.") Within the Greek system at these sorts of schools, the stereotypes lead to unflattering nicknames, such as Alpha Delta Pi's "Eighty-Pound Thighs" or "I ate a pie," Gamma Phi Beta's "Gamma Vibrator," Alpha Phi's "All for Free," Phi Sigma Sigma's "Phi Piggy Piggy," Zeta Tau Alpha's "Zits, Tits, and Armpits," or Kappa Delta's "Klan's Daughters."

At each school, certain sororities are deemed the "prettiest" or the "coolest"; every girl I asked could tick off the "top five" or "top three" sororities at her school, ranked in order of prettiness and coolness. When I asked girls about the criteria for determining the coolest houses, they said they change with every pledge class, but generally, the best looking and most extroverted sororities cement the top spots. Connections to prominent alumni help, as does background. In Texas schools, if many members of a sorority are from the same area in Texas, they are perceived to be cooler than less Texas-oriented houses. It is as if sororities are collective extensions of high school yearbook superlatives—as if some girls just couldn't let go.

Ready for Rush: The Must-Have Manual for Sorority Rushees!, published in 1999, delineates the many "types" of sororities. According to the authors, both sorority alums, each school has a "Wealthy Wanda," the old-money house containing the kinds of girls who park "BMWs up close to the front door [so] when rushees approach the house, they are either impressed or intimidated." There's "Beautiful Barbie," a house at which the sisters "don't meet up with friends on a Saturday night. If they don't have a date, they don't go out. They may stay at home with their other dateless Cinderella sisters, work out with their recently purchased exercise equipment, order in low-fat takeout (never pizza), and relax to music while trading pedicures and facials." There's "Fit Frannie," for athletes; "Perky Pamela," the only house the manual specifically says "participates in endless charities throughout the year"; "Natural Nancy," the hippies; the "Partying Patty" house, which "could be just the place for you"; "Academic Annie" ("Armed with ambition and brains, these no-nonsense intellectuals have little time for television"); and "Mixture Molly," "the sorority that thrives on diversity." Interestingly enough, the only two "types" the authors caution against are (a) the smart girls: "If words are used that you don't understand and political conversations float around your head leaving you dizzy and speechless, get out"; and (b) the diverse girls: "With so many personality types under one roof, it can be a hotbed for controversy."

Brooke, a native Texan sorority alumna who graduated a few years ago, always knew she was going to join a sorority like her mother and her two older sisters. A sincere girl from an old-money family that nonetheless taught her to appreciate the value of a dollar, Brooke, a debutante, was well aware that sororities in the South were an inevitable and often necessary part of college life. When she was accepted at a Texas school in the late 1990s, sorority membership was a foregone conclusion. Texas sororities, in particular, are like the Extreme Sport of the Greek world: astonishing, death-defying, and while not entirely in tune with the rest of the crowd, one heck of an interesting ride.

"Sorority life in Texas is like live or die. You know that if you're born from a sorority, you're going to be in a sorority," Brooke said. "And in the South, you don't know anything different, so you automatically think you're going to be a Greek. I mean, socially, at my school, you *had* to go Greek." In the South, Brooke explained, sororities are a major identifier, even for women half a century out of college. "Women who went to schools like Ole Miss, the University of Georgia, Auburn, and Clemson associate themselves with their sororities. You will never hear a southern lady say, 'She was a communications major at the University of Mississippi.' You'll hear, 'Oh, honey, she was a Delta Gamma at the University of Georgia, so she'd be a *great* Junior Leaguer.'"

As soon as she arrived on campus, Brooke realized that the girls in her class had known since high school which sorority they wanted to join and already knew many of the girls in that sorority. For advice, she called a male friend who had recently graduated from her college. "He told me that one group was the school leaders, another had brunette, athletic wild-children, and a third sorority was cute and southern but they were all blondes," Brooke said. "I mean, isn't that pathetic? That you know a house by their hair color?"

Actually, it's common. Within individual sororities, the tendency to adapt to and perpetuate a house standard is typical. The Tri-Delts at one large mid-Atlantic university, for example, are known to be extremely beautiful. "They'd take new girls and within a month, they all looked the same, with really straight hair and the same makeup," said a girl from a rival sorority. As a result, there is often a relentless pressure at these houses to fit in—a pressure that can be particularly dangerous in such groups because they focus so intently on looks. Several girls at the house I originally had hoped to follow were anorexic and/or took Xenadrine, laxatives, and diet pills. "My house," Brooke reflected, "was the king of eating disorders." True to another popular urban legend, plumbers had to come to Brooke's sorority house at least once a month to clean out the pipes, which would be clogged with vomit. (An alarming number of girls from other sororities and other schools told me that the plumber was a frequent visitor to their houses for the same reason.) Because the house's five cooks didn't work on the weekends, on Fridays Brooke's chapter House Mom collected from the sisters lists of their top ten favorite foods and did a massive two-hour grocery shopping trip. Weekends became "comfort eating days." The House Mom loaded up the kitchen with enough food to last through the weekend, but the girls gorged themselves as soon as she left. Then, after dinner, they disappeared into the bathrooms—a regular weekend binge trend.

The trend, it appears, is national. At a State U Panhellenic Council meeting (most campuses with sororities have a central sorority governing body, usually called Panhellenic Council or Panhellenic Association), representatives from all eighteen sororities said their houses had a problem with eating disorders. A recent midwestern Gamma Phi Beta alumna said her sisters "used to have puking contests after dinner." A Delta Zeta from a large East Coast school told me she blames her sorority for her own eating disorder. Having never been exposed to eating disorders before college, she didn't even know what bulimia was until she pledged her sorority. The Delta Zeta estimated that out of the 120 people in her sorority, about a third of them had eating disorders. During her first year in the sorority, five out of forty of the sophomore sisters left the university permanently because of eating disorders. "I would never have thought about starving myself to get thin. Then I saw other people doing it and they got kind of crazy, but it was catchy," the Delta Zeta said. "Everyone had done it, and since sororities revolve around looks, starvation became an acceptable thing to do."

In the spring of 1996, a sorority president at a northeastern university noticed that hundreds of plastic sandwich bags were disappearing from the sorority's kitchen. When she looked into the matter, she discovered the bags filled with vomit in one of the house's bathrooms. Their pipes, too, would be replaced because of erosion due to gallons of stomach acid. "It made sense" because her sisters were vocal about their extreme weight concerns, she told *People* in 1999 for an article about eating disorders. "It was like a competition to see who could eat the least. At dinner they would say, 'All I had today was an apple,' or 'I haven't had anything.' It was surreal." A 1990s study reported that a whopping 80 percent of college women who frequently self-induced vomiting were sorority sisters. Other sorority girls have said that the pressure to look good in their group was so intense that they turned to plastic surgery to better fit in.

Ω   Ω   Ω

Somebody to Lean On

AUGUST 24

CAITLIN'S IM AWAY MESSAGE
Sleeping . . . (alone)

BETWEEN HER DEVOTION TO THE STATE U WOMEN'S CLUB lacrosse team and her position as Alpha Rho vice president, Caitlin didn't have the energy to deal with the usual melodrama of her sorority sisters, which was why she was so surprised when she managed to churn up some of her own. Caitlin's yearlong relationship with Chris, "the love of her life" since she had met him during Freshman Orientation, had been defined by explosive fights and passionate reconciliations, but the argument they had one night in late August left her devastated.

During a screaming bout, she accused him of treating her badly. "You ignore me when it's convenient for you and you fucking disrespect me in front of my friends. And I'm not the only one who thinks that!" she yelled, her low, husky voice cracking.

"Oh, oh, your *sisters* think that?" he sneered. "The ones that would"—he made quotation-mark gestures—"'support you through anything'? That's why you pay them, right? So they'll support you while you get jealous or nag me?"

Caitlin, who rarely cried, struggled not to as her freckled face grew hot. "Look, I thought you were the kind of boyfriend I'd been waiting for," she said quietly. "The kind of guy who wants to do everything possible to make the other person happy. I thought that's who you were."

"Well," he said, "you have too many problems and they don't concern me, so I'm not dealing with them anymore. It's over."

Caitlin wasn't quick to ask for help or support; she was usually hesitant to open up, choosing instead to socialize from behind a sarcastic veneer that she thought made her seem tougher than she was. As a sophomore from New York, she didn't yet know any of the mostly southern Alpha Rho sisters besides Sabrina and Amy well enough to turn to them for consolation. The semester before, the only reason she had even so much as considered a sorority was because her spoiled roommate had begged Caitlin to rush with her. The roommate had planned out the girls' rush strategy so that they would concentrate on only the three sororities with the best reputations. At the open house rush events, the roommate was in her element while Caitlin hung back, disgusted by the sisters' phony airs and stuck-up attitudes. Caitlin thought the girls were telling her exactly what they thought she wanted to hear, even as they squinted haughtily at the inch of midriff between Caitlin's sporty top and shorts. It was common knowledge that certain sororities were trained to convince each rushee they loved her.

Caitlin perked up when they reached the Alpha Rho house, where she already knew Sabrina and Amy. Because her roommate clearly didn't want to be seen in a sorority that was considered just below the top tier, Caitlin, more confident than at the other houses, did most of the talking. She was surprised to find that the sisters she spoke with were mellow and able to have "real" conversations—and that a few of them were athletes with six-packs as chiseled as hers.

When invitations to the next round of rush events were delivered, Caitlin received a letter from Alpha Rho. Her roommate didn't get asked back to any of the houses. Regardless, Caitlin didn't see anything wrong with continuing the rush process; at the least she might meet a new friend. Before long she had accepted Alpha Rho's bid, and suddenly she was a sorority pledge, then a sister, and now the chapter's vice president.

A few days after the breakup, Caitlin was sitting alone late at night, fingering her cell phone in the Alpha Rho study when her "Big Sister," or sorority mentor, walked in. Caitlin's Big Sister sat down next to her and soothingly stroked her chestnut ponytail.

"I heard about you and Chris," she said.

"Whoa, it's gotten around the house that fast?" asked Caitlin. "I only told Sabrina and Amy."

"I overheard Chris's friends talking about it," said her Big Sister, a junior. "I'm really sorry. I know how hard this must be on you." Caitlin appreciated that her Big Sister didn't say what she was sure the rest of the sisterhood was thinking: good riddance. The sisters, sensing that Chris was intensely anti-Greek and hearing stories about how he treated Caitlin, had never approved of him the way her mother did. It didn't seem to make a difference to them, as it did to Caitlin, that Chris had been such a rock of support for her the year before. Or that her mother considered him Caitlin's best achievement to date.

Caitlin's Big Sister glanced at the name highlighted on Caitlin's cell phone display. "You're thinking of calling him, huh," she said.

Caitlin's pale blue eyes looked down. "I told him I wouldn't be able to talk to him, even as a friend, for a month so I could get over him, but I don't know if I can."

"You can," her Big Sister said gently, and took the phone. "I'll keep this for tonight."

Balancing

AUGUST 30

AMY'S IM AWAY MESSAGE

o no, not another one! i think i'm about to cry

AT THE START, THE NIGHT LOOKED PROMISING. AMY LEFT an Alpha Rho "Summer in the City" mixer with Spencer, a Mu Zeta Nu brother. Because she had been friends with Spencer for so long, she hoped this hookup would turn into something slightly more substantial than a random rendezvous. She was tired of those; for every sorority function over the last year and a half, she had brought a fling, never a boyfriend, as a date, which made her feel less attractive than her boyfriend-toting sisters.

After fooling around in Spencer's bed in the Mu Zeta Nu house for a while, Amy paused, her kind violet eyes twinkling.

"I never thought you'd be lying in my bed," Spencer mused.

"I never thought I'd be lying in your bed, either, honey," she said in her Mississippi drawl.

"I like you in my bed."

Amy's dimples deepened. "I have to get back to my place."

"No, stay. I'm too drunk to drive you anyway."

"I'll call Caitlin to pick me up," she said, popping a breath mint. "Do you want to come over?"

"I want you to stay."

Amy had a trump card. "My bed's bigger, sweetie."

"True."

"And I can make you breakfast in the morning."

"Deal."

Alpha Rho, like the other sororities at State U, prohibited male visitors after 1:30 A.M., but Amy had learned soon after becoming a sister that Alpha Rho house protocol was to ignore that rule. Nonetheless, Amy and Spencer pretended to sneak through a gauntlet of sleeping sisters on their way to the small suite she shared with Caitlin. Once in her bedroom, Amy kicked off her peach stilettos and flicked her matching purse to a corner. She flounced on her ruffled, pink canopy-style bed, tossed aside her stuffed swan—the Alpha Rho mascot—and smiled up at her Alpha Rho wooden paddle, a traditional sorority gift decorated by her Little Sister, which hung from her ceiling. It didn't take long for Amy and Spencer to pick up where they had left off.

"You're right," Spencer groaned. "This is much better." When he was nearly inside her, she pulled back.

"Do you want to?" he asked.

"No, we can't do this. It's wrong. If it's going to happen, it's going to happen when we're sober."

Spencer persisted. "Please? Pleeeease?" He pushed closer to her smooth, creamy skin.

"Don't try to make me do stuff I don't want to do." She held up a manicured hand.

"Okay, okay."

"Why can't you wait a day?" she asked.

"What's a day going to do?"

"A lot can happen in a day."

"Like what?"

"I'd just rather this work," Amy purred with her velvety southern charm. "I don't want this to be a one-night thing."

"So you do see this going somewhere?"

"I sure do."

Spencer smiled and kissed her. "Me, too."

But the next morning, Spencer only pecked Amy on the forehead and left without a word. Amy sighed and slid aside her frilly white drapes to glance out the broad, arched window at the sun-drenched State U campus, which was considered by many to host one of the best-looking student populations in the region. Guests would come from all over the area and pay the guest admission fee to the State U rec center for the sole purpose of watching girls in sports bras and hot pants sweat on the StairMasters. Gym attendance was such a given among sorority sisters that "gymming" had become a popular gerund, as in, "I need to go gymming if I eat this cookie." Amy knew that if Spencer didn't call her within the next few days, she would be at the gym, too. She tended to force herself to diet and exercise whenever things went wrong with a boy. Amy was no slouch, though. Her long, coal black hair, so shiny it looked lacquered, cascaded down her back in shampoo-commercial curls, and the former cheerleader had the kind of curves that made men flock to her at clubs whenever she shook her groove to what she liked to call "the ass songs."

Despite her looks, Amy hadn't had a steady boyfriend since her identical twin died the month before freshman year began. The pain had since subsided slightly, but back then Amy had felt as if she had lost half of herself, and she had wished she could have been the one to get leukemia instead. Her sister's death left her as the only daughter in a house with three brothers and a meek mother. Her father couldn't understand why a girl who had had steady boyfriends since she hit puberty—and who was so compassionate to everyone she met—would suddenly have trouble with boys in college. He bought her tickets to concerts, offered her limousine rides, and dangled expensive dinners to which she could bring potential boyfriends, but Amy usually ended up taking friends and sisters with her instead. The boys, meanwhile, would date her and they would sleep with her, but they were rarely interested in more. She hated when guys told her that she would "make the perfect girlfriend," because no one seemed to be taking her up on it. Instead, they would spend the night with her and disappear. She hoped that wouldn't happen with Spencer. She had spent too much time doubting herself because of her boy trouble, wondering if the constant attraction-then-rejection was because of the way she looked, the way she approached the situation, or the guys she chose. She had vowed that junior year would be different.

Amy cheered up quickly, though (her secret Alpha Rho name was "Mirth" for good reason), as she spotted her friend René waving at her through the window. Alpha Rho was not one of those sororities that frowned on sisters befriending non-Greeks, but René, a non-Greek, was still too intimidated to come inside the house. René had participated in sorority rush with Amy and Sabrina during spring of freshman year. On Bid Day, Amy and Sabrina were invited to join Alpha Rho while René was turned down by every sorority. René was furious with Amy, claiming that Amy wouldn't be her friend anymore now that she had Alpha Rho. "How can you say you like me and are friends with me and that those girls in your sorority are so nice, but they don't like me?" she accused. Amy was so upset at the prospect of losing one of her best friends that she considered "de-pledging," or disaffiliating, from Alpha Rho.

René got over the snub eventually, after Amy assured her that she wasn't going to turn into a different person because of her sorority membership. Amy became even more determined not to let the sorority change her when she noticed that the other sisters in her pledge class immediately began to cling to each other, ignore their non–Alpha Rho friends, and volunteer for additional Alpha Rho responsibilities. Amy preferred to ease into the sorority so it wouldn't take over her life. As she patiently explained to René, "I want to make of it what I want to make of it and not let it make me."

But gradually Amy sensed the pressure to "be more Alpha Rho," even though she wasn't entirely sure what that entailed. She had chosen Alpha Rho for its relative diversity compared to some of the other State U sororities, in which the sisters all majored in the same subject, had the same interests, or, like the rival Beta Pis, looked alike. The Alpha Rho house was more of a ragtag bunch, but the new pledges nonetheless tried hard to earn the older sisters' approval. As the spring of her freshman year wore on, Amy became increasingly attuned to Alpha Rho politics and protocol. She learned the hierarchy of the sorority officers. She picked up on the Alpha Rho views of which sororities on campus were acceptable and which were not to be associated with, which fraternities Alpha Rho could be seen with for November's Greek Week, and how Alpha Rho was in the process of "raising its status."

Amy tried not to get caught up in those superficialities. She was just glad to be forming connections with a group of girls, which was the reason she had rushed in the first place. Joining a sorority, Amy had hoped, would provide a chance to build a new female support system. Joining a sorority, she hoped, would re-create a sisterhood.

Ω   Ω   Ω

Politics and Protocol

THERE ARE THREE STAGES OF SORORITY LIFE: ON BID DAY, when a girl accepts her "bid," or invitation to join a sorority, she becomes a "pledge" of that group. When she is initiated, usually after a several-week pledge period, the girl becomes a sister, or "active" member. When she graduates, she becomes a sorority alumna. As soon as students become pledges they have a mass of particulars to learn about the source of their new allegiance. One of the first lessons pledges learn is to respect the hierarchy of the house. Most sorority houses are managed by the sisters who comprise the executive board, or "exec board," of the chapter. (A chapter, also referred to as a house, is a college branch of the sorority's national organization.) These elected officers usually include a president, a vice president, and officers who monitor the house's finances, public relations, scholarship, fraternity relations, standards, and pledges. Below these officers in the hierarchy, several girls serve as chairs of various committees. The social chair of a sorority is in charge of lining up frequent social events, usually mixers with fraternities. The rush chair leads the recruitment period, the song chair teaches the sisters their song collection and writes new songs for activities such as "serenading" (see the next chapter), and some sororities have an alumnae chair, a philanthropy chair, and others.

Sorority politics and protocol are a lot to get used to. As the girls moving into the house settle in, carefully arranging their rooms and belongings to reflect themselves, they also consider how to reflect themselves properly within the context of the larger group. This navigation of their housemates and their notions of their individual identities extends from room arrangement to social strategy. Within a sorority house, cliques form quickly, particularly when the newest pledge class initiated in the spring moves into the house in the fall for the first time. Amy watched her pledge class coalesce—and drop their non–Alpha Rho contacts—immediately upon entry into the sorority as they tried to gain favor with their new sisters. Even Amy, who was determined to maintain her current character, tried to, as she put it, become "more Alpha Rho." This attitude, common among sororities nationwide, is an early step toward the process of assimilation into the group.

To help the new girls become acclimated, sororities traditionally assign each girl a Big Sister to assist her through the process. When a pledge gets a Big Sister, she officially becomes a member of a "family" within the sorority; the succession of Big Sisters means that a new girl could have a Big Sister and a Grand Big Sister (the Big Sister's Big Sister). Often, as for Caitlin, there is a sense of kinship within a family that goes beyond the usual sorority sister relationship. (The relationships aren't always permanent. A midwestern Tri-Delt told me how her sorority-diehard Big Sister disowned her after she decided to spend a semester abroad rather than run for a chapter officer position for which she was a shoo-in.)

If a girl doesn't invest enough time in August constructing a place for herself within her sisterhood, she can fall behind in the group's kaleidoscopic bonding progression and, in some cases, never catch up. Many girls told me that when they devoted too much time to outside activities or academics during this period, by the time they were ready to prioritize the sorority it was too late. The cliques had already formed and they were branded an outsider, a tough label to overcome.

At her Texas school, Brooke was "terrified" that she wouldn't know how to incorporate all the right things in order to fit in. To begin with, she was a redhead aiming for a sorority of brunettes. The sisters, who all shopped at the same upscale store, had flawless makeup and wore certain strappy sandals, short black skirts, tiny linen tops, and silver Texas jewelry. So Brooke started shopping at that store. "You had all these different girls who were very put together," Brooke said. "They all looked perfect. You know when you see someone put together, it's like she just came back from a great interview? They'd get dressed up, and they'd walk out of the sorority house saying, 'Time to go rush the freshmen!' and then find us and go, 'Oh my gosh, how *are* you?' in the kind of voice that told you that they knew they looked perfect. It was overwhelming."

The urge to fit in can be so petrifying, especially at the start of the year, that the new girls often go to great lengths to blend in as quickly and seamlessly as possible. This explains the rampant eating disorders, the group piercings, and the similar hair color and dating patterns of sisters in the same sorority chapter. If they don't make every effort to conform, the girls worry that even after being invited to join a sorority, they could be deemed unsuitable sister material and subsequently be cast out from the group.

As the beginning of the 2002–2003 academic year illustrated, some girls will do anything to avoid that pitfall. According to a private investigation, on an early September evening, two California State University students, Kristin High and Kenitha Saafir, participated in an Alpha Kappa Alpha sorority pledging activity with at least three AKA sisters and two other pledges. After running through sets of rigorous calisthenics on the sand at Dockweiler State Beach, Kristin and Kenitha, blindfolded and bound at the wrists, were led into fierce riptides and ten-foot waves, wearing all-black jogging clothes and sneakers. The girls, said their families, were already exhausted by the calisthenics and had lost sleep because they had performed chores for AKA sisters at late hours almost every night for the previous month. They had reportedly been locked out of their rooms, forced to act as "slaves" by braiding their sisters' hair and other activities, and allowed sisters to throw paint over them.

When police officers, summoned to the scene by a report of women scream-ing, arrived, they could see two bodies being pitched by the waves about fifty yards from the beach. They dragged Kristin and Kenitha to shore, but they were too late. The girls had pledged to their death.

Kristin's family accused Alpha Kappa Alpha of engaging in "a cover-up" and filed a $100 million wrongful-death lawsuit against the organization, the country's oldest African American sorority. The national AKA office claimed it had no chapter at that particular university; lawyers for Kristin's family said that AKA has a citywide Los Angeles chapter. A preliminary Los Angeles Police Department investigation—the inquiry is ongoing—ruled the deaths accidental and unrelated to the sorority. The truth behind these conflicting details may never surface: when Kristin's car was returned to her family, personal items, including a diary in which Kristin had recorded entries about the pledge period, were missing. But members of the Greek system have admitted both that forced calisthenics are a common ritual and that leading pledges blindfolded into the ocean, an activity that is intended to build trust as the new girls follow the sound of a leader's voice, is a popu-lar component of West Coast pledge periods.

Kristin's mother, who, following Kristin's death, founded the group Mothers Against Hazing, has asked Alpha Kappa Alpha to "stop these savage acts of passion in the name of sisterhood." Whether these acts are out of pas-sion or are seen within the sorority as a way to bind a set of girls motivated by a desperate desire to belong, the message of Kristin's mother rings clear. Across the country, in hundreds of sorority chapters, thousands of girls are willing to do just about anything to fit in—and they do so, sometimes risk-ing their lives, all in the name of sisterhood.

SEPTEMBER

The advantages of sorority life are not only immediate but can also reach far into your future. Who knows? You might meet your future husband on a blind date arranged by your big sister.

—*Ready for Rush: The Must-Have Manual for Sorority Rushees!, 1999*

Kappa Deltas should aspire to be popular with other groups, but never at the cost of personal reputation or group dignity. Note how many social invitations your chapter receives and how much fun your sisters have together!

—*The Norman Shield of Kappa Delta, "the guidebook for all new members," July 2003*

Ω   Ω   Ω

SEPTEMBER 13

VICKI'S IM AWAY MESSAGE

dancing for boys. remind me why i'm doing this again?

IT WAS CLOSE TO 10 P.M. when the front doors to Beta Pi burst open and several dozen sisters, their hair loose down their backs, sashayed down the stairs into the glow of the streetlights. The ceiling inside the doorway was blanketed with balloons, and two vases of roses on the buffet bookended a poster reading Delta Lambda ♥ Beta Pi. About a third of the sisters—the sophomores, including Vicki—were in little black dresses and strappy sandals, while the rest wore nice jeans and tight black tops. "Ready, girls?" rasped a confident-looking sister in a tube top; the question sounded less 1950s school mistress than 2000s dance queen. The sisters gathered closer together on the sidewalk and, at the instruction of the Tube Top, began stomping down the block yelling, "Beta Pi, Delta Lambda, Beta Pi, Delta Lambda" over and over again. Vicki shrank into the middle of the crowd, reluctantly muttering the chant under her breath. When they passed onlookers, Tube Top turned backward to face the throng and raised her arms almost evangelically as the girls' chant grew louder. As they approached the Delta Lambda fraternity house at the end of the block, the girls became more and more boisterous. When the first of the girls reached the front door, a roar erupted from inside the Delta Lambda house. The roar crescendoed as the girls crossed the threshold, and it dissolved into cheers once the last of the Beta Pis stepped inside.

"Beta Pi! Beta Pi!" the boys shouted excitedly. It was no wonder; Beta Pis looked good in tight clothing. The sisters congregated in the front room, flipping their mostly blond hair and holding out their song sheets. As the girls launched into a raunchy version of Britney Spears's "Slave 4 U," changing the lyrics so they praised Delta Lambda, the older sisters pushed Vicki and the other girls in dresses to the front and made them dance for the boys in Delta Lambda.

It was only September, but the Greeks routinely began their anachronistic courting rituals far in advance of November's Homecoming to ensure they wouldn't get stuck with "losers" during the most important week of the year. Rather than seek out individual dates, entire fraternities were expected to woo entire sororities so that the fraternities and sororities could match up appropriately; the coolest or best-looking fraternity paired with its sorority equivalent, and so on down the line. For the Greeks, the week preceding Homecoming—known at State U as Greek Week—involved dozens of scheduled activities, from daily contests to nightly parties. Each sorority attended all of these events with its escort for the week: a fraternity, preferably of equal or better popularity, alongside whom the sisters would compete and celebrate. The fraternity-sorority teams at State U were judged by a group of supposedly impartial Greek students who ranked the competitors on their spirit, participation, and event results. They competed in intra-Greek athletic events such as

Wiffleball and beach volleyball, Greek Olympics—which involved silly games like water-balloon tosses and Twinkie-eating competitions—a float-decorating contest, and the centerpiece of the week: a talent competition called Lip Sync, for which teams sewed elaborate costumes, built sets, and learned complex dance routines during which they would lip-sync to a popular song.

Ω   Ω   Ω

Unchained Melodies

BEGINNING AT ABOUT THIS TIME EVERY SEPTEMBER, SOROR-ities across the country assess themselves as they evaluate the slightly shifting hierarchy that determines their place in Greek life. (Some schools hold two of these event series: Homecoming in the fall and Greek Week in the spring.) If the girls' social status is on shaky ground, they must aim to match up with one of the impressive fraternities to raise their stock. If the girls are on top, then they can choose either to match with an equally prestigious fraternity or to grant a favor to a struggling but acceptable fraternity that would benefit from matching with them. Or the sisters can pick their Greek Week escort entirely on the basis of the quality of gifts they receive from the suitors that week. The campus buzzes for weeks about which houses match together. Doing well at Greek Week means more than the huge trophy and champi-onship shirts that are distributed at a ceremony or, in State U's case, at halftime of the Homecoming football game at the end of the week. Winning Greek Week catapults a sorority up the hierarchy so that the group has its pick of the fraternities at mixers and at the following year's Greek Week—unless the win-ner is a perennially unpopular group like State U's designated "loser sorority," which won Greek Week a few years ago only to find that no one cared.

Shannon, a recently graduated West Coast Delta Zeta, remembered this time of year fondly. During Shannon's tenure, several weeks before Home-coming, fraternities would call the Delta Zeta president and tell her they wanted to invite the sorority. As part of the courting process, each fraternity sent representatives to bring gifts and entertainment to the sorority. In front of the sorority membership, the men had to sing songs, read funny poems, or perform a skit, and bring ice cream or extravagant floral arrangements. Usually the Delta Zetas would have quite a few of these offers to sort through. But if a fraternity they considered beneath them courted them, they would laugh. "As soon as they left," Shannon said, "we'd say, 'Oh, how cute that they asked us. How sweet and pathetic. There's no way in hell we're going with them!' We would pick the fraternity by how cool it was, not by the gifts we got."

"Serenades" are a popular form of this kind of courtship: the fraternities are expected to sing to the sororities and vice versa. Some sororities take this opportunity to adopt a sweetly teasing tone, as do the girls who serenade with "Pink Pajamas":

> I wear my pink pajamas in the summer when it's hot,
> and I wear my flannel nightie in the winter when it's not,
> but sometimes in the spring time and sometimes in the fall
> I jump into the covers with nothing on at all.
> Don't you wish that you could be there,
> Don't you wish that you could be there,
> Don't you wish that you could be there,
> In the spring time and the fall (*clap, clap*)
> With nothing on at all (*clap, clap*)
> I'm sure we'd have a ball (*clap, clap*)
> With nothing on at all. (*clap, clap*)

Other groups opt for a more delicate, ladylike tone, such as that of an Alpha Sigma Alpha chapter's serenade:

> Take me up to a fraternity house,
> take me up to your room.
> Buy me some beer and vodka too.
> Get me drunk and I'll surely screw you,
> for it's grunt, grunt, grunt goes the Alpha Sig as the [fraternity name]
>   shoves it in.
> For it's one, two, three times a night, thanks for getting me laid!

Many sororities and fraternities use similarly sexual songs—the more boisterous, the better—and incorporate suggestive gyrations into the routine.

The Courting Fiasco

SEPTEMBER 14
AMY'S IM AWAY MESSAGE
longest meeting ever

AT STATE U, ALPHA RHO WAS ON SOLID GROUND THIS YEAR.
Last year the sisters had done Greek Week with Delta Lambda, always a fairly
strong house. This year, the girls expected to be courted by multiple groups,
so they weren't surprised when Omega Phi, a decent fraternity, stopped by
on Monday with a rose and a note for each of the 130 sorority members. On
Tuesday, Zeta Sigma came over and spelled out "Zeta Sig craves A-Rho" in
protein bars on the patio. By the time the boys left, they had also hung slop-
pily sketched posters saying "Zeta Sigma wants Alpha Rho!" on the columns
in front of the house. The girls were delighted—house chatter all week
revolved around the two fraternities vying for their attention.

Most of the Penthouse girls were rooting for Omega Phi. Fiona, the Penthouse gang leader, had a boyfriend in Omega Phi who was always visiting
the room. Bitsy, the pierced Pent, constantly reminded her sisters that she
had recently hooked up with an Omega Phi who was "so incredibly hot."
Even Charlotte, the president, had a crush on an Omega Phi. As a result,
Omega Phi was quickly becoming known as the "hot" house. Sabrina, Amy,
Caitlin, many of the juniors, and the girls living outside of the house were
leaning toward Zeta Sigma. Zetas' gifts were, as the sisters described with
their preferred adjective, "fabulous."

On Wednesday, Omega Phi sent over tubs of gourmet ice cream and boxes
of popsicles. Zeta Sigma delivered a gorgeous bouquet of two dozen red
roses, which the sisters proudly displayed in a Waterford crystal vase just
inside the front door. For the girls in the house, it was like the captain of
the football team and the student body president fighting over who would
take them to prom. Well, not quite—Omega Phi and the Zetas were probably
more like the baseball captain and the vice president. But the brothers
were nice, the gifts were flattering, and the girls were tickled by the attention.

By Saturday, the girls were jittery with excitement because of circulating rumors that they were going to be serenaded that night. Sororities were allowed to serenade fraternities first to invite their courtship, but Alpha Rho hadn't bothered because the sisters didn't think they needed to. If a fraternity serenaded them, it meant that the boys were officially asking Alpha Rho to match with them for Greek Week. If the girls sang back their chapter's official serenade—whether right away or later on at the fraternity house—it meant they accepted the offer. The vibe was that the house was split pretty evenly between the Zetas and Omega Phi, so the decision would come down to a vote in the house that evening after the serenades. The arguments about the two houses were growing so heated that Amy expected a blowup at the vote meeting that night.

At 9:15, Amy beamed and excitedly grabbed another sister's hand when she heard the Zeta brothers chanting: "Alpha Rho, Alpha Rho" from a block away. Fraternity serenades at State U, as at many schools, consisted of crude rewritten lyrics about sex, smoking, and drinking, sung to the tune of a non-melodically challenging pop song. To a Justin Timberlake song, the Zetas sang the lewdest lyrics Amy had ever heard—something about going down on the sisters—but the girls laughed and clapped along. Sometimes for the sisters, these serenades were like watching an embarrassingly bad episode of *American Idol* (featuring contestants reeking of beer), but the Alpha Rhos never laughed at the brothers as long as they made an effort. In this case, the Zetas were a good group of guys, friendly and funny, and though they couldn't hit the notes, they were clearly excited and sang happily about how attractive the Alpha Rho girls were. Flattered, the Alpha Rhos responded with a rousing cheer for Zeta Sigma.

About an hour later, dozens of Omega Phi boys chanted at Alpha Rho's door until Charlotte let them in. Inside, they clustered around the TV room and handed a cute, inexpensive necklace to each girl. Delighted that all of her sisters now had matching accessories, Amy began to ponder voting Omega Phi instead.

After Charlotte quieted the crowd, one brother formally stepped forward. "I am the president of Omega Phi."

Charlotte, cool and confident, her neck straight beneath her carefully arranged pearls—the symbol of refined sorority sisters everywhere—stepped forward. "I am the president of Alpha Rho."

Another brother stepped forward. "I am the Greek Week chair of Omega Phi."

Caitlin and her co–Greek Week chair stepped forward. "We are the Greek Week chairs of Alpha Rho."

The group clapped as the officers stepped back into the crowd. Omega Phi finished the presentation by singing Omega Phi lyrics to a Limp Bizkit tune. The brothers marched out in unison to the girls' cheers.

Afterward, the house had a meeting, attendance mandatory. The girls had a huge decision to make: they knew the fraternity they chose would affect how much fun they would have during what was supposed to be the most enjoyable week of the year—and how much of a chance they would have at winning the top Greek honor at State U. First, the song chairs taught the girls the song they would use when they went to the fraternity house and indicated their acceptance by serenading. It was their traditional song: sweet, Daddy's-girl lyrics about love under the stars.

Then came the drama. The girls, about equally divided, started to compare Zeta Sigma and Omega Phi.

A senior cleared her throat. "Let's not rule out Delta Lambda." The younger sisters were perplexed. Some of them snickered, thinking it was a joke. They had just done Greek Week with Delta Lambda last year.

But the other seniors backed her up. "Yeah, girls, we really need to go for Delta Lambda." Some of the underclassmen stopped smiling as they wondered if the seniors were serious. Nobody had so much as mentioned Delta Lambda all week.

Now Whitney, the most crotchety of the seniors, spoke sternly. "It would be awful," she said, "if our chapter thought that the best thing for us would be to choose a fraternity other than the Delts."

The room fell hushed for a few beats as the underclassmen's jaws dropped. Delta Lambda hadn't even registered on their radar that week. The Delts had serenaded Beta Pi, the Alpha Rhos' next-door neighbors, that evening, and Beta Pi hadn't sung back. Word was that Beta Pi had rejected the Delts for Kappa Tau Chi, a bigger, more traditionally popular house. Groups weren't allowed to serenade more than one house per night, so Delta Lambda was scrambling to find an acceptable house to sing to on Sunday. But the underclassmen hadn't realized until now that Alpha Rho would be the target of the Delts' desperation. Delta Lambda had called Charlotte a few minutes before the meeting to tell her that the boys wanted Alpha Rho. Until now, the president had shared this information with the seniors and no one else.

Now there was chaos as the juniors shouted at the seniors, and the sophomores looked on in bewilderment. "Delta Lambda didn't give us any gifts this week! They don't want us, so we don't want them!"

"Why would you drop this on us at the last minute?"

"We did Greek Week with the Delts last year!"

"They haven't even serenaded us!"

"Just because you're seniors doesn't mean you can do this!"

"Okay, everybody quiet!" Charlotte broke in, smoothing her Armani skirt and tossing her meticulously highlighted hair as she tried to drown out the girls' side conversations. "Seriously, everybody shut up!" The room quieted, though sisters still glared at each other. "We're going to have to two-two-one."

Known in some houses as "Dissension," 2-2-1 was the way many sororities across the country ran debates and discussions. Amy sat next to Sabrina and settled in for what she figured would be a long meeting. During a 2-2-1, five girls were allowed to speak their opinions, one at a time: two positive points (pros), then two negatives (cons), then a positive. But the president was the one who chose exactly which girls would get to speak—and Charlotte was known to play favorites. Amy knew Sabrina, who was busy examining her braids, wouldn't bother raising her hand. Charlotte never called on people like her.

First up was Delta Lambda. Amy waved her hand, newly painted nails flashing, but Charlotte pretended she didn't see her. Amy was good at these; and Charlotte must have known she would be a negative.

"Pro: According to Greek politics," one senior said as she stood up, "Delta Lambda is a stronger house than both Zeta Sigma and Omega Phi."

"Pro: Delta Lambda has more brothers than the others," said another sister.

"Con!" a junior shot back. "The Delts didn't show any appreciation or interest in the form of presents."

"Con," another junior said. "Beta Pi was clearly their first choice. Why would we want to be someone's second-choice house—especially when their first choice was Beta Pi, of all people?"

"Pro." A senior sneered at the junior. "All the seniors want the Delts for a reason. It will look better for Alpha Rho if we match with them. Obviously," the senior sniffed, "the most popular girl wants the most popular boy."

The room broke into pandemonium again. "This is *important*," the seniors whined. Amy, Sabrina, and Caitlin didn't worry much—there were only twenty-two seniors, by far the minority.

"Next round: Zeta Sigma," Charlotte said, and selected the next group.

"Pro: Zeta Sigma is just as strong as Delta Lambda and it is steadily climbing the ladder of popularity."

"Pro: They have a house near Sorority Row, and the Delts don't," said a sophomore.

"Con:"—the debate was rapid-fire now—"Some of the guys are rude. They could reflect badly on our chapter."

"Con: More of us are dating Omega Phis than Zetas."

"Pro: The Zetas did a lot for us this week."

"Last one, Omega Phi." Charlotte seemed to be getting weary. The juniors wondered whether she was going to vote with the seniors just to get this over with.

"Pro: Omega Phi is as strong a house as Zeta Sigma."

"Pro: Omega Phi did a lot for us with the gifts and are a very supportive house toward us," a sophomore said. "Shouldn't that be what matters?"

"No." The senior who spoke was getting angry that the other girls couldn't see the importance of choosing the biggest house possible. "You guys don't understand. Omega Phi was so small last year it had to double up with another fraternity for Greek Week. When a house first becomes big enough to not double up, it's matched with the worst sorority. That's not us."

"Listen," Whitney responded out of turn, "this is our last Greek Week, so out of respect for your older sisters, you should vote our way. We've all been here longer than you, so we know what's best for this house." She paused, found some uncertain wide-eyed faces staring back at her, and looked hard at them. "And if you want the seniors to be active sisters this year, you will do this for us." The underclassmen gasped.

Amy raised her hand again. She didn't want to cause trouble, but she hoped to raise the point that it would be generous of Alpha Rho to accept a lower-tiered fraternity as an escort, thereby raising the boys' status. While waiting to be formally acknowledged, she told this to the juniors around her. The seniors overheard her whispering and shifted their seats so they surrounded her. By drowning her out and blocking Charlotte's view of her, they made sure the president wouldn't allow her to speak. Frustrated, Amy said, "Y'all, can I say something real quick?"

The seniors shushed her. "Enough talk," one of them said. "We're voting now." Charlotte nodded and distributed the ballots. Discussion was closed. The executive board left the room to tally the votes.

Going Through the Motions

SEPTEMBER 15
VICKI'S IM AWAY MESSAGE
i mean does any of it really matter?

THE BETA PI HOUSE WASN'T NEARLY AS CONFLICTED AS Alpha Rho. All week the Delts had made it clear that Beta Pi was their first choice and heavily courted the sisters with notes and presents. Beta Pi considered the Delts to be only an "eh" house, but had serenaded them to be polite. The girls were much more enthusiastic about the biggest fraternities—last year they had gone with Iota, in their eyes the top fraternity, and now several girls were dating brothers in another popular group.

Frankly, Vicki didn't much care when, with little fanfare, Beta Pi ended up choosing Kappa Tau Chi, one of the top three houses, composed of guys who could keep up with the sisters at the bar. She hated the serenading, surviving it only by mouthing the lyric as far back in the crowd of sisters as possible. She wasn't much for events like Greek Olympics, either, which usually consisted of such scintillating displays of athletic prowess as the Guy Has Peanut Butter on His Face While Girl Chucks Cheerios at Him event. Especially at times like these, Vicki was embarrassed that she was a member of a sorority. She never wore her letters outside of the house. When non-Greeks asked Vicki where she lived, she told them she lived in an off-campus house without saying which house it was. If pressed, she sometimes admitted she was in Beta Pi, but only if she accompanied her confession with a face that let the inquirer know that she wasn't *really* a sorority girl.

Vicki spent most of her time in the house talking online or on the phone to her friends back home, whom she believed were more similar to her than her sisters were. After she begged them for several days straight, her parents reluctantly agreed to pay for a cell phone plan with enough minutes to cover her nightly calls to her friends.

Now that she was single and willing to date fraternity brothers, Vicki found that the sisters were friendlier to her, though they were perplexed by the way she was chatty on the phone to her friends from home yet reticent in the house. Vicki, who was particularly timid around the cliques of older girls, wasn't daunted so much by the fact that the Beta Pis were mostly pretty and thin—Vicki herself fell into those categories—as by their ease and comfort with sorority life. With a Screw Your Sister event coming up in a couple of weeks, the sisters were working hard to set Vicki up with the right date. The point of Screw Your Sister was to set a sister up on a blind date with a fraternity brother who was either terrible (screw her!) or terrific (get her screwed!). Because Vicki had just broken up with her boyfriend, her roommates were being overly sympathetic. Vicki hoped they were going to set her up with William, the Iota president whom she had met at the club.

The Escort Revealed

SEPTEMBER 15

SABRINA'S IM AWAY MESSAGE

Thank goodness for marijuana

WHEN THE ALPHA RHO EXECS RETURNED, THEY AVOIDED EYE contact, except for Caitlin, who shot Amy and Sabrina a worried look. "Omega Phi: forty-three votes," Charlotte read. "Zeta Sigma: forty-one votes." She paused. "Delta Lambda: forty-six votes. We will be matching with Delta Lambda."

The house was in an uproar. Girls were shouting, crying, and screaming at each other. "I can't believe this is happening!" a junior gasped.

"This is ridiculous!"

"We're Beta Pi's leftovers!"

"This is humiliating."

Whitney pumped her fist. "Yes, we won!"

A junior frowned at the senior. "This wasn't a competition," she said quietly.

"Oh, yes it was!" Whitney exhorted. The youngest sisters were shocked. They whispered to each other that had they known the seniors would be able to swing so many votes, they would have all voted for the Zetas instead of Omega Phi just to keep the Delts from winning. The general consensus among the juniors was that most of the Alpha Rho executive board members, wanting to suck up to the seniors, had voted their way. The seniors must have cajoled the other votes out of some of the weaker younger sisters. It was clear that as Alpha Rho president, Charlotte, looking around at her quickly self-destructing house, had no idea what to do.

The seniors gathered in the entry hall, celebrating, while the other sisters went upstairs and complained to each other about the power the seniors wielded and how Delta Lambda had come out of nowhere. On her way upstairs, a sophomore who had especially wanted Zeta Sigma broke down crying. When the seniors glanced at her and laughed, she cursed them out. "You don't say anything to the seniors," Caitlin said sarcastically as she led the sophomore upstairs by the hand. "Not the seniors. They're the oldest sisters in the chapter so they have to get whatever they want." The weeping sophomore decided to boycott every event held with the Delts.

Charlotte called the Delt president to promise him that when the Delts serenaded Alpha Rho on Sunday, the girls would sing back. Later that night, the Delts scattered on the Alpha Rho patio red roses and a huge platter of brownies. From the veranda upstairs, Sabrina spotted the platter on the porch and crept down the back stairs of the house. The seniors hadn't yet noticed the gifts. When the seniors in the entry hall moved their victory party into the TV room, Sabrina snuck out to the porch, grabbed the platter (no small feat—in typical overstated Delt fashion, it was rather large for tiny Sabrina), and sprinted upstairs to Caitlin and Amy's suite. "This is for us," Sabrina said, "and we're not sharing!" The girls stuffed themselves with as many brownies as they could cram in. To make sure that the seniors wouldn't benefit, the girls, doubling over with laughter, then defaced the remainder of the brownies, mashing their hands in them until they looked too gross to eat. Caitlin, who was particularly incensed at the way the vote had gone, brought the platter of ruined brownies downstairs and left it in the kitchen.

The next night, only forty girls—not even all of the girls who had voted for Delta Lambda—dressed in their traditional A-line sundresses (white with thick, ruffled straps and a tiny flowered pattern) and halfheartedly warbled their serenade to Delta Lambda in the Alpha Rho entry hall. The rest stayed upstairs in protest. Later, the Delts hosted a keg party in honor of their new dates. Sabrina and Caitlin decided that because Caitlin was Greek Week co-chair and they still wanted to have fun during Greek Week, they might as well participate, despite their distaste for the Delts. Only a few of the under-classmen sisters bothered to be courteous to the fraternity, neglecting the sorority's goal of maintaining good relations with all other Greeks on cam-pus. Therefore, Sabrina and Caitlin made a show of valiantly offering to "take one for the team" and to represent the honor and dignity of their largely reluctant sorority; at least for that night, they volunteered to be in charge of "keeping up relations" between the two houses by spending time with the boys of Delta Lambda.

Actually, they'd heard the Delts had weed.

During the next few days, the Delts sent e-mails to each individual sister: "Delta Lambda loves you." "We can't wait for Greek Week." "We think you're so hot." It still took about a week for the Alpha Rhos to get over the fiasco.

Ω Ω Ω

Framed by Fraternities

MUCH OF THE DRAMA IN SORORITY HOUSES REVOLVES around fraternity issues. Because so many of the official sorority activities— Greek Week, bar nights, "mixers" (theme parties)—involve their male coun-terparts, a sorority's standing among fraternity brothers often determines its status in the Greek system. Sororities resemble high school cliques, vying for the attention of the most attractive boys to boost their standing among the popular girls.

Surprised that Alpha Rho, a relatively low-key sorority, emphasized the fraternity hierarchy so strongly, I asked Amy why it mattered so much. "Every house wants to 'look good,'" she explained, her dark plum eyes sincere. "As much as we're laid back, we still want to appear to be wanted and more popular among the Greek community. About half of Alpha Rho cares about being the popular house, and the other half doesn't. I think that's why we always fight over everything."

Granted, Alpha Rho doesn't represent the extreme. Social chairs of other sororities and fraternities planning mixers have been known to match up individual sister-brother dates between the groups by age, looks, or personality. At many sororities, sisters monitor fraternity relations so closely that they encourage members to date brothers in only one or two specific fraternities. Girls who disobey by dating a brother from the wrong fraternity can be ostracized. Even when the sorority sisters approve of an individual guy, his fraternity affiliation can taint his overall image—as well as the image of his girlfriend.

Brooke, the Texas redhead, met her boyfriend Johnny a few weeks into their freshman year at Texas College. He was sweet, gregarious, and extremely attractive. When Brooke fell for him, the ten girls on her dormitory hall—all of whom were preparing to rush in January—swooned. "He's so adorable!" they cooed. "You're so lucky!" As the semester progressed and the girls got to know the sisters in the sororities they preferred, they gravitated toward the "It" fraternities accepted by those sororities. Eta Gamma, for example, was "married" to the Delta Lambdas that year. As a result, the ten girls started dating Delts or freshmen who planned to become Delts, in the hopes that their relationships would improve their chances to get into Eta Gamma. Johnny, who was also rushing, had narrowed his choices down to two: Delt (to Brooke's relief) and Mu Zeta Nu, a low-tiered fraternity considered to be composed of nice guys who unfortunately also happened to be geeky.

On Bid Day, as Brooke celebrated with her new Eta Gamma sisters outside the house, she nervously wondered which letters Johnny had chosen. The girls on her hall, who had all made Eta Gamma, were surrounded by Delt boyfriends lavishing them with roses and bear hugs under the approving eyes of the Eta Gamma sisters, mothers, and alumnae, and the rest of the Bid Day Party onlookers, practically a Who's Who of Texas Greeks. When Brooke spotted Johnny bounding toward her in his new Mu Zeta Nu jersey, her heart sank. She tried not to show how upset she was, but she couldn't believe her boyfriend had gone "MuNu." When Johnny leaned over for a kiss, Brooke turned away. As a new Eta Gamma pledge, she couldn't be seen kissing a MuNu. "All of a sudden you become a snob," Brooke said to me. "If you're an Eta Gamma, you think you're the bee's knees."

She could see the reaction in the Eta Gammas' faces when they asked about Johnny. "Oh my Lord, he's a MuNu?" they said with disgust. Brooke understood why Johnny had chosen MuNu—several other amiable freshmen had joined— and she loved him too much to break up. But that didn't matter to the more die-hard Eta Gammas and the girls in Brooke's pledge class who insisted on adhering to the status quo. Over the next semester, Brooke watched helplessly as her fellow pledges pulled away from her, treating her differently because of Johnny. When the ten girls, all still dating Delts, wanted to hang out with their boyfriends and the other brothers, they would bring their sisters along to the fraternity house (proper sororities didn't allow boys to hang out in their houses). But the sisters and the Delts wouldn't invite Brooke because she was dating a MuNu. As Brooke missed out on all of these bonding sessions, the ten girls from her hall, who had rapidly become the most popular girls in her pledge class, grew even tighter.

Ω Ω Ω

Placing Blame

SEPTEMBER 20
CAITLIN'S IM AWAY MESSAGE
I am a survivor

CAITLIN AND AMY WERE AT A POOL PARTY WITH STATE U'S Mu Zeta Nu fraternity, sitting on the lap of their friend Jake. Because they were the only two people at the party who knew he was gay, they helped him conceal that fact from his fraternity brothers by flirting with him ostentatiously. Jake was terrified that if Mu Zeta Nu found out, his brothers would alienate him. Outside of Caitlin, Amy, Sabrina, and a few others, Jake was closeted among straight students. While it was difficult to keep any secret quiet in the Greek community, homosexuality was an exception. In both the fraternities and the sororities, there was a clear but unspoken don't-ask-don't-tell policy. Mostly, people didn't question because they didn't want to know.

It figured that the one time in her life when Caitlin couldn't bring herself to find other guys attractive, they were suddenly drawn to her. At the MuNu party, Caitlin met Taylor, a seemingly sweet junior with dark floppy hair who compared biceps with her and made sure her cup of Jungle Juice—Hawaiian Punch and grain alcohol—didn't run empty. They spent some time talking in that faux-philosophically self-analytical way that Jungle Juice tended to encourage.

"I have a reputation in the house," he said.

"For what?" she asked, her voice even smokier than usual as her speech slurred.

"Being a male slut." He didn't realize Caitlin had already heard that about him. Most Greeks knew him as a "player." "A lot of it is just speculation. It's more reputation than actual truth."

Taylor wasn't around, though, when the room started spinning and Caitlin, her sinewy legs buckling, had to get outside for air. Amy and Jake spotted Caitlin taking off alone and quickly elected Jake chaperone for the night. The two of them walked around campus for an hour, with intermittent stops for Caitlin to vomit in gutters strewn with fallen crape myrtle petals. While they were gone, Amy told her friends later, she overheard some of the brothers talking—impressed with Jake, they assumed he was hooking up with Caitlin.

"Man," one said, "that guy gets around." Jake was becoming known at Mu Zeta Nu for being a ladies' man. Granted, his dark hair, deep brown eyes, football-player build, and chiseled jaw would have lured the ladies anyway, had he been seeking them.

"Caitlin smokes weed, plays lacrosse, watches pro sports, and she's hot," the MuNu president said. "What a great combination." They liked Caitlin's sky blue eyes and auburn-streaked ponytail. They liked the taut stomach muscles just visible beneath her cropped rugby shirt. Taylor seemed particularly interested.

It was too bad Caitlin wasn't looking. Caitlin's avowed monthlong hiatus from Chris had lasted about a week and a half. And now she spent too much time debating with Chris the possibility of a future relationship. "I don't know what I want," Chris had said to Caitlin. "But I don't want to not be with you at all."

Caitlin told him she had made a big enough impact on his life that he ought to know by now whether he missed her or missed having a steady relationship.

Chris had pondered this. "If you're in my life and we're hanging out, then I'm a lot more likely to get back with you than if you're totally out of my life," he told her. So she had agreed to start hanging out with him again, as friends. Well, friends with privileges. Caitlin knew how Amy felt about this; they had already had a few concerned discussions on the topic. Amy didn't think Chris should be so easily forgiven, if at all, because of the way he had hurt Caitlin. But Amy didn't understand just how much Chris's support had meant to Caitlin over the past year.

Part of the sorority pledge process involved attending "pledge parties"—mixers with pledge classes in other sororities and fraternities. When Caitlin had pledged in the spring of her freshman year, she had gone to as many events as she could to get to know the girls who were going to be her sisters. One night they had a pledge party with Kappa Tau Chi's pledge class at a satellite house where some of the brothers lived. (Satellite houses are off-campus houses or apartments where alcohol violations are less likely to be spotted by Greek officers.)

Caitlin was having such a good time that when her ride left, she decided to stay at the party a while longer. At 1 A.M. a few Kappa Tau Chi brothers offered to walk Caitlin and some other Alpha Rho pledges home. Caitlin lagged behind with one brother, bantering about Major League Baseball stats. When she stopped to check her watch, Caitlin realized the others were far ahead.

"Whoa, let's catch up to the group," she said.

"Okay," the brother said. "My car's parked over there. We can drive to meet them."

The brother drove a block or so before Caitlin realized he wasn't heading in the right direction. "Wait, no—everyone else went the other way!" Caitlin tried to squirm out of her seat belt, suddenly losing the free and easy feeling of her buzz. As they reached an empty parking lot, he stopped the car, shoved her into the backseat, and slid his hands down her pants.

"Get off of me, asshole," Caitlin angrily insisted. "I need to get back." There was nothing she could do. He overpowered her.

As he raped her, Caitlin kept quiet, afraid that if she yelled he would get violent. When he let up, Caitlin scrambled out of the car to a lit area. She hurried to her dorm, the brother not far behind.

"Let me walk you back!" he shouted.

"No, it's fine," Caitlin whispered, scurrying faster, keeping close to streetlights. "I'm fine." He followed. As she reached her dorm, Caitlin, trying to stay close to the building, passed a large bush. This time when he grabbed her ponytail and tried to shove her down again, she caught him off guard and pushed him to the ground. Shaking, she ran upstairs and found Chris. At Chris's insistence, Caitlin called the police from the emergency phone outside.

The police met her in front of the dorm and told her she needed an ID and a change of clothes. Chris ran upstairs to get them as Caitlin, wide-eyed, whispered, "Not the fake one!" While Caitlin was being examined, Chris wrote love poems for her in the hospital waiting room. When the doctor reached in to retrieve evidence, Chris heard her screams through the walls.

The next night Caitlin called her father, who insisted she fly home for the weekend. She was terrified to tell her mother about the rape. Caitlin's mother was a strict, controlling woman who insisted that Caitlin adhere to the image befitting the daughter of a New York state-level politician. Because she was campaigning for reelection that season, Caitlin's mother was even more on edge than usual. Caitlin's athletic success at her exclusive Brooklyn private high school had looked good for her mother's political image. But since she had arrived at State U, it seemed nothing she did pleased her mother, who considered sorority membership an unproductive use of time, club lacrosse not as prestigious as the varsity team for which Caitlin had refused to try out, and drinking and partying an insult to the parents who raised her. After a semester of disappointing her mother, Caitlin was trying to turn the corner. She let her mother choose her political science classes—even though Caitlin would have preferred to take art courses—and diligently called her twice a week, on schedule, during her mother's hairstyling appointments. But so far it seemed that the only thing Caitlin had done right was to attract Chris, whom her mother adored because of his clean-cut image and the fact that he came from a genteel, old-money southern home. His family and its network could help her greatly if her political ambitions ascended beyond the state level. In the company of Caitlin's mother, Chris was unfailingly polite and charming. Her mother would never believe that he drank even more often than Caitlin did.

At home, Caitlin argued with her parents, who didn't want her to return to school, let alone the sorority. Realizing the information would come out if the case went to trial, she admitted to her mother that she drank in college and that she had slept with four other guys. The night of the rape, her blood-alcohol level had been above the legal limit. Her mother, enraged, blamed Alpha Rho. "You don't understand what's happening to you," her mother said. "It's all the sorority's fault. You would never have been in that situation if not for the sorority. It's the Greek system's fault you were drinking." Caitlin felt bad for her mother. She was only trying to find somebody to blame. "I put my child in their care," she said softly. Caitlin sobbed as her parents told her she had to quit Alpha Rho. She suddenly realized she was more upset about leaving her new sorority than anything else. Sorority membership would give her a chance to be a leader among her peers—she was planning to run for vice president—an opportunity that she didn't think she would otherwise have. And she loved the few Alpha Rhos she had gotten to know well.

"Look, it's my life and you can't tell me what to do," she said, her jaw set. "I'll pay my own dues. Then you can't stop me from joining Alpha Rho." Finally, they worked out a compromise. Caitlin could go back to school and continue with the sorority on two conditions: if her schoolwork suffered she would drop Alpha Rho, and she would only attend events where there was no alcohol. If alcohol appeared, then Caitlin was to leave immediately.

"I have ways of checking up on you," her mother claimed.

Back at school, Caitlin's new sisters were there for her the remainder of the year—even as she refused to attend parties out of fear that her mother would find out. When she was elected vice president, she welcomed the routine of the regular meetings and administrative tedium, which gave her a sense of purpose beyond rape recovery. Chris was there for her, too, offering her steady support and constant companionship as she battled with depression and worked through sexual issues. It warmed her that Chris was so protective of her, in an "I want to kill him and keep you safe" way, as she put it.

He made himself available at any time, day or night, to meet her or pick her up because he vowed she would never have to walk anywhere alone again. He called her mother regularly to let her know how Caitlin was doing. Chris, Caitlin knew, would never hurt her.

Other than the police, Caitlin refused to tell anybody the rapist's name, because she assumed Chris would assault him; and if Kappa Tau Chi brothers recognized Chris, they might identify her. When detectives tracked the boy down, he insisted the sex had been consensual, but to no avail. Kappa Tau Chi pulled his pin—kicked out a brother who had already been initiated—and he transferred schools. Since then, the Kappa Tau Chi brothers, who knew the girl involved was a member of Alpha Rho, refused to seek out Alpha Rho for mixers and, the sisters heard, had gotten into arguments over whether individuals could date Alpha Rhos. But as far as Caitlin knew, none of the brothers knew her identity. She hoped that wouldn't change.

$$\Omega \quad \Omega \quad \Omega$$

When Sex Turns to Scandal

WHAT HAPPENED TO CAITLIN IS HARDLY UNCOMMON. Several studies have found that rape and sexual assault are particularly prevalent at Greek events and houses. Out of the four State U sorority sisters whom I chose to follow throughout the academic year, two turned out to have been raped by fraternity brothers after Greek functions: Caitlin by a new acquaintance and Amy by a friend (I didn't know about these incidents when I chose the girls). It would be irresponsible, though, to suggest that these kinds of episodes, however common, characterize the Greek system as a whole or that they occur only in the Greek system. Yet it is still important to explore the sexual side of fraternity-sorority relations because of its broader statements about the image and function of sororities and the power distribution within them.

In the Greek system, sex, whether assault or affair, rarely remains an issue between the participating individuals alone. At one university, sorority sisters convinced a sister who was raped at a fraternity party not to report the rape because if she did, the fraternity brothers would "hate" them and wouldn't invite them to parties anymore. In Caitlin's case, the rape caused a lasting rift between the entire sorority and the entire fraternity. When I asked Caitlin why, after her experience, she would still want to be a part of this system, she told me that what happened to her could have happened at any party. When I asked her why she fought to return to Alpha Rho, she said that besides the chance to hone leadership skills, she had by then also already forged a connection with her pledge class. "In high school, I bounced a lot between groups and was kind of a loner. So in Alpha Rho, it felt really good to feel like I was part of a group. Since we had to be at the house several days a week for pledging, I'd already spent so much time with these girls," she told me. "I was so proud of myself because I had gotten into my first-choice house. I couldn't see cutting that out of my life." In fact, because the rape had occurred within the Greek system, Caitlin said she felt more protected than if she and the rapist had not been Greek. "I know Kappa Tau Chi can't do anything because there are enough people who know about it. There's a 'They can't touch me' mentality," she said. "But it's still awkward at functions when the sisters are wearing letters and standing with their house and the brothers are wearing letters and standing with their house. I'm standing in my letters with my sorority and I'm sure they look at me and think I'm evil."

Several sororities have rules that seem to discourage sex; some, if not most, have a strict bylaw forbidding men from venturing upstairs in the house. Many sororities impose a curfew on male guests and forbid sisters from hosting them overnight. During one mid-Atlantic sorority house meeting I attended at the beginning of the year, the adviser instructed the sisters that they even had to "escort male guests to the bathroom." But that hardly deterred the girls; that mid-Atlantic house was known as one of the most promiscuous houses on campus. State U's Alpha Rho and Beta Pi both utterly ignored the no-overnight-guest rule. Some of Brooke's Texas Eta Gamma sisters blatantly defied it by regularly sneaking boys into the supposedly secret chapter room to have sex.

But the real problem isn't one of sorority sisters hustling boys into a no-guy zone under cover of bunk bed. The more interesting issue is the sorority system's contradictory perspectives about sex. On the one hand, the girls are reminded of the need to appear chaste and ladylike; on the other hand, they are pressured to find dates for a multitude of events and are encouraged to go to fraternity formals, which often include an overnight hotel stay. This paradoxical view can confuse new members, who then look to the older sisters to lead by example. An interesting power structure ensues, on two levels. From the fraternities' perspective, sororities generally consist of attractive girls who have already been prescreened through the rush process. These girls have dates to offer because they need escorts to the many Greek system functions. So a sorority can afford to be a selective group, which is why it is the sororities who usually have control over the Greek Week escort process and can choose the highest bidder (or most generous suitor) from among the fraternities. But the sexual power structure within sororities is even more fascinating. When girls are put in charge of other girls—younger girls who don't yet understand the political landscape within the house—sex can become a commodity and a way to establish dominance within the sisterhood.

In 1997, a sorority girl came forward to announce that her sorority had ordered her pledge class to sleep with an entire fraternity. The pledge class was sent to stay at a fraternity at another college, where the girls were told to have sex with the brothers. "You have to sleep with the brothers here in order for you to cross over," the pledges were told. "You have to sleep with them . . . That's your duty." At first, the girl thought it was a joke. But when she again was told that her pledge class had to have sex with the fraternity brothers as well as the fraternity's pledges, she refused and depledged.

Other university groups have attempted to capitalize on sorority sisters' sexuality. One of the biggest sex scandals to hit the sorority system allegedly occurred at Southern Methodist University in the late 1970s and early 1980s. SMU boosters reportedly set up a student-run network that paid sorority sisters to have sex with athletic recruits to persuade them to play for the SMU Ponies (the boosters also supposedly bribed university secretaries to alter course grades for athletes and paid other students to take tests and write papers for football players). Under the supervision of the boosters, an SMU law student known as "King Rat" worked with four other students to pay about a dozen sorority girls $400 per weekend to seduce recruits. They gave the sisters a booster's credit card, a fur coat, and a Mercedes-Benz to use to entertain the athletes. The girls were instructed to sleep with the recruits both to convince them to come to SMU (with promises of continued sex if they did) and to get information about what other schools were illegally offering the high school athletes. The sorority sex network, which began in 1979, ended in 1985 when the sorority sisters became too frightened by the emergence of AIDS to continue sleeping with strangers. These and other allegations led the NCAA to impose its first "death penalty" on a football program when it prohibited SMU from playing football in 1987.

The SMU sex scandal, which the media dubbed "Ponytail Gate," seemed to involve consenting sorority sisters who were willing to sell sex as something of a fund-raiser (as an alternative to, say, bake sales). But other sorority women have stepped forward since then to claim that they were expected to provide similar services despite their unwillingness to participate. One evening in 1988, a sorority girl who was a little sister to the Pi Kappa Alpha fraternity at Florida's Stetson University attended a punk-themed mixer. At the "Pike" house, the little sister, wearing a denim miniskirt, black stockings, and black shoes, went to the bar area and drank a couple of rum runners. She went into another room where she had an "upside-down margarita": she lay down with her mouth open while three brothers poured three kinds of alcohol down her throat. Eventually she passed out on the dance floor. When she came to, she was being gang-raped by fraternity brothers, who scattered when she started to scream. "How could they do this to me?" she shouted. "I've done so much for them." The next day, the little sister returned to the Pike house and resigned. She later found out that while she lay semiconscious and stripped of her skirt, stockings, and shoes, several of the brothers poked and slapped her and poured shampoo over her body as they laughed and pointed. She also learned that the event had been a "spectrum"—a fraternity term for sex as spectator sport; while some brothers raped her, others stood outside on top of a bicycle rack to peer through a window at the scene. A former Pike later admitted that the house held spectrums twice a month. The little sister dropped out of school.

Fraternity chapters started the little sister programs (a different group from the Little Sisters within sororities) in the 1960s, but by the late 1980s universities had begun to abolish fraternity little sisters because of claims that the fraternities were sexually exploiting the girls. In 1988, the Association of Fraternity Advisers resolved that the program treated the women as "subservient or 'second-class' status." At the University of Missouri-Columbia, which suspended its little sisters program after a spate of sexual assaults in

1989, some of the girls were forced to drink alcohol and read sexually explicit material before meeting their "big brothers." The University of South Florida terminated its program in 1990 because of complaints of sexual harassment. And a 1994 report from the University of Rhode Island discussed how fraternity brothers referred to little sisters as "freshmeat" and held parties where some female students were denied entry because their breasts were too small.

But experts told me that these organizations continue to exist, both openly and underground, even though neither the National Panhellenic Conference nor the Interfraternity Council condones little sisters. According to the 1985 book *Rush: A Girl's Guide to Sorority Success*, little sisters are generally defined as a group of between eight and twenty girls, often sorority members, chosen by fraternity brothers to "help the fraternity plan and hold parties and have money-raising projects to buy the fraternity expensive gifts." Little sisters often pay dues and attend weekly dinners and little sister meetings at the fraternity house. The relationships often become far more complex.

Many fraternities also expect the little sisters to be their cheerleaders at athletic events, to cook for them, to clean up after parties, and to serve as trophy dates to help them recruit new brothers by flaunting their sexuality to rushees. Fraternity brothers use pictures or slide shows of their little sisters to lure recruits and suggest that joining the fraternity will give them sexual access to these girls. The pictures have ranged from charts explaining the number of beers it took to seduce each little sister to glossy, full-color centerfold advertisements of the sisters in bathing suits accompanied by the explanation, "Chosen on the basis of beauty, charm, and loyalty to [this fraternity], they remember our birthdays, host parties for us, and generally take pretty good care of the brothers."

"Take pretty good care" is quite the euphemism. Several little sisters have admitted that their membership included sex with many of the brothers, with gang rape a distinct possibility. Studies of these programs have shown that a girl is often expected to have sex with most of the brothers in order to be accepted as a little sister in the first place. Indeed, there have been cases when little sisters who refused to have sex with a brother were kicked out of the program, or "had their jersey pulled." Even girls who have merely broken up with a boyfriend in the fraternity—or who have dated a member of a different fraternity—have had their jerseys pulled. But fraternities have also kicked out sisters who became too promiscuous, leaving a blurry line between what is considered appropriate little sister sexual behavior and what is shunned.

At one little sister initiation ceremony, the girls had to touch their breasts while simulating oral sex on a banana. They still would not receive their little sister pins unless they French-kissed the other little sisters sexily enough to meet with the brothers' approval. Some fraternities auction off their sisters in an annual fund-raiser known as "Slave Auction." As the little sisters are encouraged to drink and "hump the pole" on a stage, brothers bid on their "services," including baking, cleaning, and driving.

Competition to become a little sister is intense. When a fraternity selects a little sister, the brothers might take her for a limousine ride or give her roses. "They . . . sing and put you on their lap and lean on one knee," one little sister told then-doctoral student Mindy Stombler, who studied the programs. "It was seen as a big honor," another sister said. "It feels good that so many guys have picked you. When they came and got me, I was so light-headed that I almost fell over." The perceived prestige is partly why the girls accept this kind of treatment—and may similarly explain sorority sisters' devotion to the importance of fraternity relations. A little sister told Stombler, "Something that made me so mad was that they would tell us to go up to the would-be pledge and make sure that he is having a good time . . . [The brother would say] 'You know, dance with him or give him a drink or something or walk outside with him,' " she said. "I wouldn't stand up at a little sister meeting and say, 'They're using us.' I didn't feel like I had the power to do that."

OCTOBER

Clothes are the first thing sororities will notice about you. You must dress appropriately. Proper attire does not necessarily mean expensive designer clothes. (But wearing them can't hurt!) Rather, your clothes should fit into your personal style while expressing a sorority girl image.

—Rush: A Girl's Guide to Sorority Success, 1985

Big and little sisters exchange presents on every holiday (Christmas, Valentine's Day, St. Patrick's Day, Halloween, Easter, and so on). Birthdays are expensive gift-giving times. Popular gifts are handcrafted or specially made objects that represent the sorority's symbol, crest, colors, or Greek letters. Needlepoint is very popular, as are hand-painted wooden and acrylic objects. Fresh flowers are a must.

—Rush: A Girl's Guide to Sorority Success, 1985

Ω   Ω   Ω

OCTOBER 6

SABRINA'S IM AWAY MESSAGE

if i'm going to waste time, i'm going to do it right.

FOUNDERS DAY, OCTOBER 6, was one of the few occasions when all thirteen Alpha Rho alumnae advisers—a general supervisor and an adviser for each executive board position—showed up at the house. On each anniversary of the founding of Alpha Rho, the girls were required to dress in "badge attire," which meant they had to wear their gold, bejeweled Alpha Rho pins, or "badges," and dress as if they were going to church or synagogue: no denim, no sneakers. Usually the unofficial dress code in the house was dictated only by what most girls happened to be wearing that season. But badge attire was ordered for alumnae functions, certain events, and one chapter meeting—the "formal meeting"—each month.

Sabrina padded downstairs in jeans at 3 P.M., when the girls had been instructed to come down to the entry hall. Sabrina wouldn't have to mingle for long; when Caitlin came back from her lacrosse scrimmage, she was supposed to take Sabrina to a campus bar to watch a National Football League game. As the sisters gathered on the front stairs to sit and sip iced lemonade while waiting for the alumnae to show up, they eyed the crystal-fringed dining room, where fancy trays sported finger sandwiches, berries, and coffee cake cubes. Fiona, the event chair, had announced to the group that no one could eat anything until the alumnae arrived.

About two dozen alums walked in the door—women ranging from their twenties to their seventies. By 3:30, the girls were finally allowed to converge on the tables. Immediately, Fiona made a beeline for Amy and another sister, who, at size 10, were the largest girls in the sorority (though by no means portly). "Make sure you don't take too much food," Fiona hissed. She didn't warn any of the other girls, who piled their plates high.

After the group mingled, Fiona ushered the girls into the chapter room for speeches. Every year on Founders Day, the returning alumnae spoke to the sisters about what it was like to be in Alpha Rho, what Alpha Rho had done for them, and how the sorority had remained a part of their lives since graduation. As the room hushed, there was a loud knock at the chapter room door. Fiona opened it a crack, and the entire room turned to look at Caitlin, their vice president.

"You can go in and sit down," Fiona whispered. "She's getting ready to speak."

"Oh, I'm just picking up Sabrina and passing through," Caitlin whispered back. Sabrina, relieved, slipped out the door while Fiona watched, mouth agape.

"But this is *Founders Day!*"

"Yep," Caitlin said, laughing, and she and Sabrina, braids flying, scampered out of the house.

Despite the occasional outing, Sabrina was working harder than she had in previous semesters. Accustomed to getting a 4.0, she had received Bs on a few papers already this term and had resolved to work harder. Part of the problem was that she had added shifts to her waitressing schedule and she was taking more course credits than usual. On the first day of classes, she had checked out a creative writing class just to hear what the class was about. She hadn't planned on taking it; she didn't need the credit. But Professor Stone, a good-looking man in his late thirties, had interesting things to say and seemed like such an engaging teacher that Sabrina decided to cram his course into her schedule.

Now that Sabrina lived in the Alpha Rho house, where she was constantly barraged by reminders of Alpha Rho commitments, she was having a difficult time balancing her heavy courseload with the sorority. When she had accepted Alpha Rho's bid as a freshman, she hadn't foreseen the scores of obligations that would come with it. Nor had she expected membership to be so expensive. It didn't seem to bother the rest of the Alpha Rhos that there were a multitude of less obvious sorority costs in addition to the dues. For instance, sisters were supposed to buy Alpha Rho–lettered clothes in blue and green, the sorority colors. When Little Sisters were assigned in early March, each Big Sister had to buy gifts: food, Alpha Rho clothes, Alpha Rho trinkets, jewelry. For Greek events, sisters had to purchase tickets and were strongly encouraged to buy the party favors and T-shirts the sorority inevitably created to go along with every event—in addition to new dresses, shoes, accessories, jewelry, and limousines for every semiformal and Formal. They were also constantly being asked to donate to various charity and sorority fund drives. This was on top of the cash needed for the frequent casual sorority outings to bars, clubs, or restaurants. Most sisters didn't think twice about the money. Sabrina couldn't get it out of her mind.

Ω   Ω   Ω

Moneyline

THE FINANCIAL COMMITMENT A SISTER MUST MAKE TO HER sorority can be enormous. In fact, many girls cite this as one reason why candidates who wouldn't be able to withstand the financial drain of sorority membership simply won't be accepted to the sorority in the first place. Wealth becomes a prohibitive prerequisite. (At Syracuse, one Greek newspaper boasts that, as at many schools, "Social Greeks tend to be the wealthiest and most mobile segment of the SU student population, pledging a social life and bringing a large disposable income.") When sororities evaluate candidates during rush, the rushees' financial status, which sororities determine partly by assessing the rushees' wardrobes and asking what their parents do for a living, plays a major role. If a sorority doesn't believe that a girl will be able to pay sorority dues—which can range from a few hundred dollars to $2,500 a semester—it's not likely to accept her as a member. (Sabrina had made clear to the sisters that she would take on enough hours waitressing to afford her dues.) Sorority dues cover the costs of sorority functions as well as fees paid to the campus Panhellenic association and the chapter's national office.

Sorority chapters also impose fines on members who miss meetings or house events; Brooke's Texas house fined its girls up to $50 if they let their grades slip, skipped sorority study hall, or missed activities such as decorating the Homecoming float. The emphasis on finances can partly be explained away by the reality that sororities are run like businesses. Each campus chapter is expected to contribute a certain amount of money both to the national organization and to the national organization's philanthropic cause.

Moreover, in certain houses, there is an image to uphold. State U's Alpha Rho was not so homogeneous that any sister who didn't conform to certain fashion standards was necessarily shut out; Sabrina wasn't shunned because she couldn't afford the Louis Vuitton bags that her sisters clutched. But once as we walked from a restaurant to her house, passing a pack of designer-clad sorority girls giggling loudly, Sabrina said quietly to me, "Sometimes it feels like I'm the only one who's not wealthy." She wasn't bitter about the stark line between her and her sisters, though I occasionally caught her wondering what might have been had money not played such a large role in these girls' lives. "It's natural that people gravitate toward people more like them, and I'm not a lot like them. I can't buy a new Formal dress every semester," she said. Sometimes Sabrina tried to blend in: she'd see her sisters carelessly spending money at malls and bars and convince herself that since everyone else was splurging she would, too. But she always ended up regretting her indulgence and secretly returning the items later.

Ω   Ω   Ω

Obligation

OCTOBER 11

VICKI'S IM AWAY MESSAGE
my life has officially been taken over

VICKI AND OLIVIA WERE SHOPPING IN THE CITY WHEN their Beta Pi sister Ashleigh, a sweet though oversensitive girl who tended to wear hot pink, called to warn them. Tonight was Dance Marathon—a popular nationwide fund-raiser—but many of the sisters who were supposed to represent Beta Pi had left for the weekend for a fraternity semiformal at a lakeside resort and waterpark. As a result, the Beta Pi president was calling the remaining sisters to assign times to dance throughout the night in a hotel ballroom. "If you see a strange number on your cell," Ashleigh told Vicki, "don't answer it. The only sister she's excusing from Dance Marathon is Laura-Ann because she has major period cramps."

Vicki groaned. The last thing she needed was another last-minute Beta Pi commitment. If she had been told ahead of time that the sorority needed her to dance that night, she would have done it because she knew the money raised was for a good cause: a neonatal care unit at a local hospital. But now? Forget it. Of all of the inane sorority rules Vicki was expected to follow, she couldn't see why she should have to prioritize last-minute dancing in the middle of the night.

Vicki was afraid to go back to the house, where the sisters might see them, but the girls had to drop off their things and shower and change before going out that night. They parked a few blocks away, where Olivia's car would not be noticed, spit-wiped Olivia's wrists free of her telltale perfume, and sneaked inside the back door. When they heard people talking on the main staircase, Olivia quickly led Vicki up the back stairs, the girls stifling their laughter as they managed to slip unseen into their room. Once inside— relieved that Morgan and Laura-Ann, their roommates, weren't there—they didn't turn on the lights and play music as they usually did when they were getting ready to go out. Instead, they whispered and tiptoed back and forth between closets as they arranged their clothes for the night. "We're, like, so shady!" Vicki murmured giddily.

Vicki and Olivia peeked out of the room to see if anyone was around and, when the hall was empty, sprinted in their towels and shower shoes to the bathroom. While showering, they kept their towels with them inside the stalls so other sisters couldn't identify them. As they crept back to their room they heard voices complaining downstairs. "There are girls hiding in their rooms upstairs so they don't have to dance, and that's not fair." Vicki and Olivia looked at each other wide-eyed and, muffling their laughter, shimmied back into their room. While Olivia applied her usual thick coat of eyeliner, the two were plotting how to escape the house unnoticed when Olivia's cell phone rang—its distinctive tune, to Pink's "Get the Party Started," easily recognizable to the sisters down the hall. With a sigh, Olivia picked up to hear the Beta Pi president asking her to come downstairs. The sisters who had been in the house that afternoon while Olivia and Vicki were shopping had grabbed the most convenient dance shifts: 5–7 P.M. or 7–10 P.M. The only ones left for Vicki and Olivia, the president told them, were 2–5 A.M. or 5–9 A.M.

"Oh. My. God. Just because we weren't here doesn't mean we should get stuck with the worst shift," Olivia fumed. Vicki slouched quietly by her side.

"There's nothing we can do about it," the president said.

"It's not our fault the fund-raising chair didn't do her job." The president relented and allowed Olivia and Vicki to split the 5–9 A.M. shift.

After joining Olivia at a bar to drown their frustration in Amaretto Sours, Vicki managed about an hour of sleep that night before she had to get to the ballroom. Although each sorority was required to have girls dancing at all times, sisters could get away with standing and making mild gestures, if necessary. Vicki spent her shift folded in a corner for two hours, hiding behind her wavy blond bangs and grumbling to herself about the pointlessness of being there as she waited for Olivia to relieve her. She couldn't even spend the time talking to her friends back home because they didn't stay up that late. That night the sororities that participated in Dance Marathon raised tens of thousands of dollars.

Ω   Ω   Ω

Pancake Philanthropy

DANCE MARATHON, A COMMON GREEK FUND-RAISER, UN-derscores a sentiment I observed in many sorority houses: community service, widely publicized as a cornerstone of sorority life, often revolves more around donations than actual service. The level of commitment to community service varies widely by the chapter. Some chapters do nothing. Only on occasion did I come across a sorority that in fact exhibited a regular commitment to service rather than philanthropy, such as the groups that signed up for "Adopt-a-Grandmother" at a local senior center, cleaned up trash around a riverbed, tutored, or visited a children's hospital to give young female patients manicures and accessories to make each feel like a "Queen for a Day." Many chapters, however, merely profess a commitment to community service, spending no more than an hour a semester making and distributing arts and crafts or holding an annual party and donating the proceeds.

Because what I'll call "event philanthropy"—a once-a-semester or yearly function for charity, like Dance Marathon—is so popular, I spent an October evening with a West Coast university Tri-Delt house to observe the annual traditional fund-raiser of many Tri-Delt chapters: a middle-of-the-night, all-you-can-eat pancake buffet party.

It was 12:30 and the Tri-Delt house was packed. After paying the $10 cover and getting the Tri-Delt triangle drawn on my hand in permanent marker to prove I had paid, I wove my way through the students, around the all-male a cappella group serenading a pack of swooning sisters wearing identical T-shirts designed for the party, and past a table heaped high with small pancakes, slices of coffee cake, and Krispy Kremes. Many of the Tri-Delt sisters were taking shifts in a satellite house, where they were frantically flipping pancakes and rushing them back to the Tri-Delt house.

Munching on a chocolate chip pancake, I spotted Riley, a junior who had agreed to let me shadow her for the evening of philanthropy (she told her sisters I was "a friend from home"). Riley had the 1–2 A.M. pancake-making shift, so we headed to a satellite house where Tri-Delts were carelessly flipping pancakes that were oddly shaped, blackened, and occasionally oozing. Fifteen sisters were crowded around a stove, sliding in oil spills and batter droppings while attempting to maneuver a pan on every burner. Having run out of key ingredients like milk, the girls were tossing whatever was handy into the pancake batter. A few girls carried a tray of pancakes out the fire door as they dashed to the Tri-Delt house. "These pancakes are horrendous," Riley said. "But the people at the party will eat them anyway."

The girls chatted loudly as they neglected the pancakes. Philanthropy didn't enter the conversation, which revolved around boys, weddings, other sisters, and *Dawson's Creek*. One sister danced in from another room wearing a teased wig. The other girls doubled over in hysterics.

"We're going to be white trash for Halloween," Riley explained to me.

When I returned to the party at the on-campus Tri-Delt house, most of the crowd was crammed either at the pancake table or in front of a student cover band, where partygoers bounced to the music and watched the Tri-Delt sisters dancing on the furniture. Just before 2 A.M., the Tri-Delts had sent sisters into the bars to advertise the pancake buffet. The tactic worked—the crowd was much thicker now that students from the bars and other parties had filtered in. Edging toward the door, I saw Riley arriving from the satellite house, holding a pancake tray over her head. As I shifted to make room for her, she caught my eye and grinned. "They're all alcohol now!" she yelled over the din to me as she squeezed by. "Don't eat the pancakes!"

By the end of the night the Tri-Delts would tally a few thousand dollars— the only philanthropic activity they would perform all year.

Ω Ω Ω

Going Out Greek-Style

OCTOBER 16

AMY'S IM AWAY MESSAGE

trasjhed andq goin to bedj :-P

THE DAY OF THE CRUSH PARTY, THE FIRST BIG GREEK social event of the year, Amy and Caitlin spent a few hours "doing a fashion show" for each other, trying on dozens of clothes—their own and each other's—and, in particular, trying to figure out which bras went best with which shirts. "Man, I love living with girls," Caitlin remarked to no one in particular, as she tightened a push-up bra she found in the midst of a pile of Amy's lacy lingerie on the floor. "We never would have done this in the dorms."

Crush Parties at State U were themed parties to which each Greek party-goer could invite five "crushes"; this party's theme was "Fire and Ice." The sororities and fraternities that sponsored the event rented out a bar or club and charged students for tickets to get in. Because it was still early in the year, Amy and Caitlin had decided to invite friends, rather than crushes, and arranged to meet them at the bar.

As Amy waited for Caitlin to get ready, she started to pre-game. Before nearly every Greek event, Alpha Rho sisters, like many sororities nationwide, would pre-game—that is, get a buzz going before the actual activity started, sometimes with their house, sometimes with a fraternity. Pre-gaming was like tailgating a party. This way they saved time, since they didn't have to spend the first hour of an event getting drunk (having arrived already inebriated), and money, because they wouldn't have to pay for too many additional drinks at overpriced bar costs. Tonight the pre-game beverage of choice was a jug of wine that someone had left in the kitchen.

A couple of sisters stopped by the suite when Amy was on her third glass of wine. "What are you drinking?" one asked.

"Grape wine," Amy said cheerfully. "Y'all want some?"

"What do you mean, grape wine?"

"It's grape!"

"You dumbass," Caitlin said from the bathroom, "what other kind of wine is there?"

"Um," Amy paused. "There's red . . . there's white . . ."

"They're all grape. That's where wine comes from. How much have you had, anyway?"

"But it says it on the bottle—grape wine!"

The girls investigated. The bottom of the label did indeed say, "100% grape wine."

"Ha!" Amy laughed and the sisters couldn't help but smile—Amy's laugh was infectious. Amy launched brightly into an Alpha Rho fight song and proceeded to belt out Alpha Rho tunes for five minutes.

Amy had no idea what her status was with Spencer, the Mu Zeta Nu brother whom she had nearly slept with in August. She still hoped for a relationship with him, but she hadn't seen him outside of the few times he accepted her regular invitations to cook dinner for him. She knew he wouldn't be at the Crush Party because he had to study for an early midterm, but just in case, she had done an extra hour on the StairMaster that afternoon. Amy wondered how many other "mishaps" she would run into. Amy had made an effort to remain friendly to all of the boys with whom she had had dalliances during sophomore year, an active year for her—and even to those whom she had turned down. She endured polite small talk with a boy her sisters called "Ugly Dork," who stalked Amy and repeatedly told her they were meant to be together. While the other Alpha Rhos mocked him, Amy would deftly deflect his overtures with her southern charm before continuing on her way.

But while the Alpha Rhos couldn't fathom why Amy "wasted breath" on Ugly Dork, they were absolutely mystified by her refusal to be rude to the fraternity brother who had date-raped her during her sophomore year Greek Week. Two nights after she had drunkenly fooled around with Nathan, a Mu Zeta Nu brother, Nathan had spiked Amy's drink at a party so he could sleep with her. Amy woke up the next morning, realized the ceiling didn't look familiar, rolled over, saw Nathan lying in his bed next to her, looked back at the ceiling, looked down, saw she was naked, and yelled "Oh Lord!" before dashing out of the room, clothes in hand. Amy was devastated that she had been date-raped and withdrew to her room for days. When she told her gay friend Jake what had happened, he wanted to confront Nathan, but Amy wouldn't let him say anything because she didn't want to "rock the MuNu brotherhood boat." When Amy's close friend Greg asked her why she was missing Greek Week, she told him, crying hysterically, why she felt degraded and taken advantage of.

Greg, unlike Jake, looked perplexed. "What do you want me to do? He's my fraternity brother."

FINALLY, CAITLIN EMERGED, WEARING A MIDRIFF-baring halter top that matched her azure eyes, tight white pants, and one of Amy's gold butterfly clips at the top of her ponytail. The girls then produced small Alpha Rho thermoses and filled them with Bacardi rum.

"Hey, we're Alpha-holics," Caitlin smirked as they slipped the thermoses into their dressy handbags. At eleven, they left the house, an hour later than they had planned. They walked a block before Amy, rummaging through her purse for breath mints, remembered she had left the Crush Party tickets on her bed. Caitlin made fun of her all the way back home, until she realized she had left her ID on her desk.

It was a breezy night in the low seventies, typical October weather for State U. As they waited for the bar to open, dozens of girls huddled in circles, divided according to sorority and, within those groups, by pledge class. Most of the girls were drunk by now (pre-gaming for an hour would have that effect). Amy and Caitlin headed straight for the Alpha Rho circle in the middle of the lawn. Squeals and hugs ensued.

A tall, thin blonde in Amy's pledge class lurched toward them, catching her arms around Amy's neck as she fell. "So great to see you!" Her exaggeratedly drunken expression suddenly drooped into stern concentration. "But," she spoke haughtily now, "we get to go in first, because we've been waiting so much longer than you."

The herd of girls jostled their way toward the door of a club near campus. They spotted the two policemen checking IDs and swiftly rearranged their purses and their hair—shoving the thermoses down underneath their cosmetics and pulling their hair back to best resemble the photos of the other people on their IDs. Tonight Amy was a twenty-three-year-old from Montana and Caitlin was a twenty-one-year-old from Maine. The officer glanced at the birth date on Amy's ID and snorted. "Ri-ight," he said, flicking the ID back to her as he nonetheless stepped aside so she could continue into the bar. "Bring a better one next time." Amy and Caitlin laughed and continued inside.

By eleven-thirty, the crowd was still mostly girls. The fraternities knew the sororities' routine: pre-game, arrive, drink some more, dance—so they preferred to get to Greek events later, when the girls were at their most inebriated. Amy and Caitlin headed to the bar, where Amy paid for their drinks: a Cosmopolitan for Amy, a Jim Beam and Coke for Caitlin. After a few sips, they poured the rum from their thermoses into their cups. Amy made a face after trying her new concoction, then downed the drink.

The DJ played Nelly's "Hot in Herre." "Man, I love this song!" Caitlin rasped above the din. It was the most animated she had been in a long time, given her angst over her breakup with Chris. "We have to dance!"

The dance floor was packed with girls in low-rise pants and tight tops—halters, tubes, spaghetti straps, red, white, and silver, in keeping with the Fire and Ice theme—dancing with a drink in one hand and a purse slung over the other arm. Midriffs shone with newly applied shimmery moisturizer. The brothers who were starting to trickle in sat on couches that ringed the dance floor and peered at the girls gyrating scandalously with each other.

In the middle of the hardwood circle, Amy and Caitlin made their way to Alpha Rho, the biggest horde on the floor. For half an hour the group shouted lyrics at each other and danced in each other's arms to Ja Rule, J.Lo, and Missy Elliott's "Work It" (to which each girl sang different garbled lyrics because nobody could decipher some of the lines). When the DJ yelled over the music, "I have a shout-out for one of our hosts, Alpha Rho!" the center of the dance floor whooped.

On the way to the bar, Caitlin bumped into a friend who happened to be in Kappa Tau Chi, the fraternity of the boy who had raped her. He asked if he could buy her a drink. As they sat at the bar and chatted, Caitlin noticed a group of guys slowly moving toward them, almost surrounding them at the bar. One of the brothers approached them. "She's a slut. You can't buy her a drink," he said loudly. Others at the bar turned and stared.

The brothers pulled Caitlin's friend away from the bar. As they left, Caitlin could hear what they hissed to her friend.

"She fucked over the fraternity," one said.

"She screwed over one of my best friends," said another. "She changed her mind after they had sex."

Caitlin, done for the night, disappeared. Kappa Tau Chi had finally placed a face with a name. Soon afterward, Caitlin changed her phone number and kept it unlisted.

Screw Your Sister

OCTOBER 21
VICKI'S IM AWAY MESSAGE
another day, another dumb t-shirt

THIS YEAR'S BETA PI SCREW YOUR SISTER, THE EVENT DURing which sisters set each other up on blind dates, was to take place on a haunted hayride. The fraternity brothers were supposed to pick their dates up at the house, where the sisters stood, jittery, tapping their heels in the wide entry hall, except for Vicki, who felt silly waiting. The sisters, in their "Beta Pi Hayride to Hell: Screw or Be Screwed" spaghetti-strapped tank tops, congregated in clumps, glancing nonchalantly through the open door to monitor the boys' arrival. Vicki downed five shots of vodka in her room to try to calm her nerves. She barely even knew her sisters, let alone their taste in dates. She paced around the dining room, pretending she needed glasses of water or a few crackers, afraid to go outside and see whom her sisters had chosen for her. From the entry hall, Olivia called Vicki's cell to tell her that her date had arrived. Blowing her bangs out of her eyes, Vicki slowly pushed through the girls to the front door.

Vicki was surprised that the rest of the sisters had all managed to get ready on time. The bathrooms had been packed with girls lined up to do their hair. Vicki preferred to get ready in the privacy of her own room, where she had her own, less stressful space, though it didn't take her long. She simply brushed her blond shag, dabbed on some sheer lip gloss and then

IMed with a friend from home while she waited for Olivia, who spent ten minutes combing anti-frizz serum through her hair and spritzing her pungent perfume on the appropriate pulse points.

Outside, Olivia and her date stood next to William, the Iota president whom Vicki hadn't seen since the night in the club. He was "skater-boy cute," tall and stocky with unruly blond curls and a scruffy little goatee. Vicki smiled and hesitatingly took his hand when he offered it. She and William stayed close to Olivia during the haunted hayride, which took them from evergreens like those that bordered State U to thick rows of trees that were just starting to turn. As the sun began to set, matching the sky with the trees, William turned to her. "I remember that night at the club you blew me away. Then I found out you had a boyfriend. Everything came crashing down." Vicki was still trying to gauge his sincerity when he leaned over and kissed her.

For the next several days, as William regularly stopped by the Beta Pi house to see Vicki, she marveled at her good fortune. Vicki didn't so much care that William was the president of Beta Pi's favorite fraternity (though others did). But she found some measure of satisfaction that she was dating a guy who was the lust object of many a sorority girl.

Later that week, Olivia took Vicki to a party at Theta Theta, another fraternity house. When Olivia introduced Vicki to her friend Dan, a fraternity brother from Los Angeles whose deep tan matched Vicki's, Dan invited her to drink with him and some friends upstairs. Eventually the party dwindled and Vicki was left alone with Dan, whom she kissed a few times before starting to feel slightly uncomfortable. She had never dated two guys at the same time before. Olivia came in to say good-bye.

"I'm going home," Olivia said, winking in response to Vicki's "don't leave me!" gestures. "You stay here."

Vicki noticed William had left a message on her cell phone and scrambled off Dan's bed. "I'm going with you, okay?" She turned to Dan. "I have to take Olivia home but, um, I'll be right back."

On the way back to the Beta Pi house, Vicki explained to Olivia that although she liked Dan, she was more interested in William. Olivia, insisting Vicki should date both of them, sent her in the direction of the Iota house, where Vicki ended up staying the night with William.

The next day, at Olivia's prodding, Vicki called Dan to apologize. "Um,

Olivia got sick," she lied. "I'm sorry I didn't come back." Dan believed her, and was so understanding about the situation that Vicki felt guilty and agreed to see him the following weekend.

Moving On

OCTOBER 22

CAITLIN'S IM AWAY MESSAGE

"Is it worth it? Lemme work it."—Missy Elliott

CAITLIN AND AMY WERE OUTSIDE GETTING SOME AIR AFTER an Alpha Rho chapter meeting when they ran into Taylor, who stopped to chat. Caitlin's mood shifted from elation about a successful presentation she had given as vice president at the meeting to feeling ill at ease. The last time she'd seen Taylor—at the MuNu party—she hadn't exactly been sober.

"Yeah, so the MuNu Date Party is next week," Taylor said, brushing a lock of floppy hair out of his eyes.

"Really." Widening her dark eyes innocently, Amy pretended she hadn't known.

"Yeah. Hasn't anyone asked you guys yet?"

Amy explained her confusion over Spencer.

"How about you?" Taylor turned to Caitlin. "What's your deal?"

"I just broke up with my boyfriend and he was a frickin' jerk," Caitlin said lightly. "So I don't trust guys right now. It's a long story." The three of them flirted until Taylor had to leave for a MuNu meeting.

Later, Amy and Caitlin discussed the situation. "Honey, I bet Taylor will ask you to his Date Party," Amy said.

"Yeah, well, he hasn't really expressed any interest in getting with me," Caitlin said. "And he was very forthright about his reputation as a player. But yeah, I want to go to Date Party."

"Taylor could totally take you," Amy insisted. Caitlin went to her room to call her mother at their designated time. Her mother's first question was whether she had seen Chris since they last spoke.

When Taylor got back from his meeting, he IMed Amy. "So. Your suite-mate . . ."

"You should take her to Date Party, Taylor."

"I hate IM," Taylor backtracked. "Why don't you just call me."

Amy called. "If you ask her, she'll say yes."

"I never got that vibe."

"Caitlin, Taylor's on the phone! He wants to talk to you." Amy was deter-mined to make this work. She thought it would be good for Caitlin to see what it was like to go out with someone she considered a gentleman, for once.

"So I hear you wanted to ask me to Date Party," Caitlin said.

"Actually," Taylor replied, "I wanted to ask you to dinner first because I don't know you that well." Caitlin was impressed. She had underestimated him. They planned a date at a low-key restaurant for a few nights later.

The night of the date, Caitlin was nervous. She still wasn't over Chris, even though they were only "fuck buddies" at the moment. It didn't help that Chris came over the afternoon of the date, clearly rattled that Caitlin was going out with someone else. That night, he told Caitlin that during the week after their breakup, he had kissed another girl twice. Caitlin was heartbroken that he had moved on so quickly.

"No, wait," Chris said, trying to console her. "The only reason I'm telling you this is because the first kiss I didn't enjoy, and the second one made me realize I didn't enjoy it because she wasn't you," he said. "I love you so much." Before he left, he asked, "What are you going to do if Taylor kisses you?"

"Well, I don't know, Chris. We'll just see," she said. "If I kiss him, I'll probably be thinking about you anyway, but you made that decision for me. Look, everything that's happening is your doing. If it was up to me, we would never have broken up."

Caitlin wasn't sure if she liked Taylor, but this counted as her first date since her breakup with Chris. "I really hope he doesn't try anything," she said to Amy, who waited with her, smoothing Caitlin's ponytail as she fidgeted by the door. "I don't think I like him like that." But she tried to relax.

To Caitlin's relief, when Taylor brought her back home, he only leaned over in the car and asked her if she'd like to go to Date Party. When Caitlin got to her room, she took down her IM away message. Immediately, Chris called, livid with jealousy, and insisted she tell him everything about the date. During the next week, Chris slept over at the house every night. As she and Chris reconnected, Caitlin realized that she had accepted Taylor's invitation to the Mu Zeta Nu Date Party mostly because she wanted to go with Amy and Jake, not because she was interested romantically in Taylor. She had too much of a history with Chris to give up on him easily, and besides, if her mother discovered Caitlin was seeing a fraternity boy, she would be furious. Caitlin was already tempting fate by returning to her pre-rape relationship with alcohol and marijuana.

Hoping to be honest with Taylor, Caitlin IMed him: "Look, I'm in a complicated situation. So let's just go and have a good time. I still think it'll be fun." She decided she might as well get to know him as a friend. Date Party season was just beginning, and she would need dates to all of the Alpha Rho functions. If it worked out with Taylor, she would have someone to take other than Chris, whom many of her sisters didn't approve of. They agreed that Chris was extremely attractive, came from the "right" type of family, and could not have been a more caring boyfriend after Caitlin was raped. But sometime during the previous spring, the Alpha Rhos had sensed a change in him and became convinced that he treated Caitlin differently than before. Despite the obvious chemistry between Caitlin and Chris, her sisters constantly told her she was pretty enough to do better.

Barraged

OCTOBER 27

AMY'S IM AWAY MESSAGE

o no! Date Party! now accepting applications from all gentlemen who kno how to have a nite of fun ;-)

A FEW DAYS BEFORE MU ZETA NU'S DATE PARTY, AMY AT-tended a small birthday gathering at the MuNu house for Priscilla, the girl-friend of her close friend Greg. As usual, Amy was at the house as Jake's date.

Jake usually didn't look or act gay unless he was with his more gregarious gay friends, but with her flirtatiousness, Amy was good at keeping him in check, just in case.

A Gay-Lesbian e-mail petition for peace in the community had spread around the campus. A group of MuNu brothers huddled around a computer as they read through the list of names, assuming that anyone who signed the petition was officially coming out. Suddenly, the boys came across Priscilla's name on the petition. Delighted, they sashayed around the room, singsonging, "Priscilla's a dyke! Priscilla's a dyke!" Jake said nothing.

"A friend of mine is lesbian," Priscilla said. "She asked me to sign to show my support, so I did."

Amy looked at the MuNu brothers dancing around the couch. "Wouldn't y'all sign the petition if you had a gay friend and he asked you to?" The brothers looked disgusted.

"I would," Greg said.

"I wouldn't," Spencer said, and laughed.

Amy silently seethed for Jake, whose hand she grabbed and held tightly.

As the conversation shifted to money, Nathan, the brother who had date-raped Amy, lay down on the couch next to her. Stiffening as his leg grazed hers, she chattered to mask her discomfort and happened to mention a pair of shoes she planned to buy on a weekend shopping trip.

"Oh, with the credit card that Daddy pays for?" Nathan smirked. Amy was sensitive about financial issues. It was true she was well off—she was one of the wealthiest sisters in an already affluent sorority. But she tried not to let her money shape her personality, and for the most part she succeeded; because of her unpretentious attitude, most people were surprised when they found out that Amy was incredibly rich.

"Nathan, who pays for *your* room and board?" she retorted.

Nathan looked pleased to get a rise out of Amy. "So, babe, are you staying over here tonight or am I going over to your place?" he asked.

Amy's smooth skin flushed with anger. Instead of admitting that he had date-raped her, he pretended they had an ongoing flirtation. Spencer rescued Amy by calling her into the kitchen. As she walked away, Nathan called after her, "Let's have sex now. You know you want me."

"So," Spencer said when they were alone in the kitchen, "what's with you and Jake?"

"Oh, bless your heart, nothing's going on." Trying not to laugh, Amy patted his arm reassuringly.

"Well, then, what's going on with us?" he asked.

"You tell me."

"I don't want to lose your friendship, but there's something more going on here," Spencer said.

"Okay."

"But it's complicated," he insisted.

"Why is this so complicated?"

"I just don't know what to do," he said.

If that weren't enough, Amy's father called when she got home. He was trying to get her together with the son of one of his friends, whom she disliked. When she mentioned she was going to Jake's Date Party, her father grew angry.

"I know you think it's all fun and games, but I'm really sick of hearing about a different guy every week," her father said. Until she came to college, Amy had always had steady boyfriends. This was the longest she'd gone without a boyfriend, and her father wasn't pleased.

"It's just Jake! He's gay, Daddy!" she argued. That didn't help.

"I think you're pushing straight guys away. You hide behind your gay friends."

"Daddy, I'm trying." She told him the chronology of what had happened with Spencer.

"You must have done something wrong," said her father. Amy burst into tears.

AT THE ALPHA RHO CHAPTER MEETING THE NEXT night, Charlotte, the president, told the girls the date and place for December's Formal, and then added nonchalantly, "We're having a great Date Party pretty soon."

In addition to casual socials and mixers, Alpha Rho sisters had one Date Party—which was like a semiformal—one Formal, and one Date Dash each semester. For Date Dashes, sisters were notified four hours in advance that they would have to find a date and clothes for a party at a bar or club.

The sisters flipped their sorority calendars.

"When is it?" Normally the girls got at least three weeks' notice so they had enough time to cozy up to a potential date before springing an Alpha Rho function on him.

When Charlotte told them, the Alpha Rhos squawked: "That's too soon!" "I can't find a date!" "My boyfriend just broke up with me a week ago! Who am I going to take?"

The girls continued to grumble after the meeting about the short notice—this was more like a Date Dash than a Date Party. Within ten minutes, many of the sisters had put up IM away messages reading versions of, "If you want to go to Date Party, tell me!" The Alpha Rho Date Party announcement had left the girls hyperventilating about how to find an acceptable date in a short period of time. If she could just have one more weekend, Amy thought, maybe she could work things out with Spencer in time for Date Party. The sisters told her to wait and see how the MuNu Date Party went, because she was sure to see Spencer there.

Ω   Ω   Ω

Inside the Meetings

MANY SORORITY GIRLS CONSIDER THE HUNT FOR DATES TO various sorority events and activities an exhausting process. Not only do they have to find people to go with them in the first place, but they also often carefully weigh the acceptability of a potential date because the date reflects on the sister and the sisterhood. In some cases, as in Brooke's house, in order to gain the sorority's approval he must be an acceptable boy from an acceptable fraternity.

This aspect of sorority life frustrated Amy in particular. She was already having rough luck on the boyfriend front—and now, faced with numerous date events, she felt that her inability to keep a guy interested was being rubbed in her face. She tended to panic before Date Parties if she didn't have a date lined up far in advance. A couple of weeks before one date event, I asked Amy, who was still dateless, how she was feeling. Usually chipper, Amy was the most discouraged I had seen her yet. "It's so stressful, and there's even more stress for me because I don't like to ask boys out. I guess I'm old-fashioned and traditional that way. It's so much easier for girls who already have boyfriends," she said. "I have the pressure to find the perfect date. I've already spent too much time crying over dates." I asked her why she didn't let her sisters set her up. "Because if they didn't need to be set up and if they could meet someone normally, why can't I?" she said. Amy was determined to fix whatever was wrong with her so that she, too, could meet someone "normally." She was convinced that losing some weight would solve the problem.

Another huge sorority time drain is the meetings. There are usually weekly executive board meetings for the sorority officers, rush meetings before and during recruitment, weekly pledge meetings during pledge period, and occasional house meetings for the sisters who live there. Some chapter officers attend weekly Panhellenic meetings with the campus Panhellenic adviser and representatives from each of the other national sororities at the school. These pale in importance, however, compared to the weekly chapter meetings, which are sorority sacred ground. Every sorority holds these chapter meetings, governed by parliamentary procedure, which essentially are informational sessions that update the girls on national and local sorority news, business, and plans. Several girls deliver reports, and votes are conducted on important issues. In many houses, like Alpha Rho, there is one "formal" chapter meeting a month, during which the sisters come dressed in "badge attire" and are expected to behave sedately in a chapter room lit by candlelight. At informal meetings, the sisters like to do each other's hair and often arrive in their pajamas. At both kinds of meetings, sisters in most sororities are instructed to snap their fingers when they agree with something said.

When the Alpha Rhos walk one by one into the chapter room for a meeting, they are greeted at the door by the sister elected chaplain. To greet the chaplain, they have to place their right hand on the chaplain's left shoulder and say the sorority's secret word. The chaplain does the same and lets them pass. At "Meeting," the Alpha Rhos sit in straight-backed chairs, ordered alphabetically and by pledge class, so that the girls with the most seniority sit in the front of the room. The president conducts the opening ceremony, which is intended to remind the sisters of their values. She reads a passage from an Alpha Rho ritual book and the sisters read their response. At the end of the meeting, after the vice presidents and committee chairs have given their reports, the president conducts the closing ceremony ritual, consisting of another reading and the Alpha Rho secret handshake.

Some sororities run chapter meetings like a cross between strict business meetings and etiquette school. In some chapters, Kappa Deltas are not allowed to cross their legs at formal meetings—it is considered "unladylike"—unless they cross at their ankles. Before events in these houses, the Kappa Delta Vice President of Standards goes over proper etiquette and prayer with the girls to make sure they handle themselves with grace. ("One thing we were always reminded of was that we don't bite our bread. We tear pieces off and butter each piece individually," a Kappa Delta said.)

Chapter meeting—particularly the formal meeting—is one of the times when the sororities are most likely to perform secret rituals. One common custom, which is practiced at both State U and Brooke's school, is known as the "candlelight," a ceremony held when a sister plans to announce that she has been lavaliered (asked to be a girlfriend), pinned (pre-engaged), or engaged. The sister puts an anonymous note in the president's mailbox to request a candlelight at the next meeting. When the president announces the ceremony at the meeting, the sisters hold hands and form a circle. As the president lights a candle and passes it around the circle, the sisters sing their sorority's specific candlelight song. Details vary by house, but usually if the sister blows out the candle on its first trip around the circle, she is lavaliered, if it's the second trip, she's pinned, and the third means she is engaged.

A southern Kappa Kappa Gamma alumna who graduated recently recalled her chapter's candlelight ceremony wistfully. "It was my dream to have one, but it didn't come true," she said. "But I still sing the candlelight song all the time." As the girls passed around the candle, they would sing:

I found my man, he's a Kappa man,
He's my sweetheart forever more.
I'll leave him never, I'll follow wherever he goes.

"Then the girl showed her engagement ring to everyone and we all oohed and aahed and someone gave her flowers," the Kappa told me. "It was a way to announce your engagement. I remember being extremely jealous."

Attendance at chapter meetings is mandatory and girls are often fined for absences. At some schools, one girl said, "If you had to miss a meeting for class, you had to get a note from your professor. You're a senior, you're twenty-two, and you still have to get a note from the teacher." A former teaching assistant at State U told me that when she held labs on Tuesday nights— chapter meeting night—the sorority girls in her class wouldn't attend. One day she took the sorority sisters aside and told them that lab attendance was mandatory for her class. "We can't miss chapter," they said. "It's mandatory." The TA informed her students that if they continued to miss labs, they would fail the lab section of her class. She was disgusted to see the girls' seats empty over the following weeks; the girls chose to take Fs for their labs rather than miss chapter meetings.

Not all meetings, however, consistently follow a formal procedure. I sat in on an executive board meeting at a sorority at a large East Coast campus. (I could not attend executive board meetings at State U without the Alpha Rhos and Beta Pis becoming suspicious of my presence because I was not a sorority officer.)

The sorority adviser and several chapter officers lounged on couches and on the floor of the chapter room. The sisters, thin and beautiful, all wore tight sweatpants, tank tops, and straight, sleek ponytails. I watched in amusement as Emmy and Justine, two of the officers, grew increasingly frolicsome on a couch in the corner.

After discussing the situation of a sister who refused to pay her dues, the adviser informed the officers that the chapter was in financial trouble.

The president looked around at the room. "We can't rely solely on our dues for money. We do philanthropy for other people. I think we should start doing fund-raisers for ourselves." The other sisters nodded.

Meanwhile, Emmy and Justine were busy hitting each other with couch pillows. Justine slouched on the couch pulling her eyelids with her index fingers so that only the whites of her eyes showed. "Justine, ew!" one of the sisters cried.

"That's disgusting," Emmy said, bopping her with a pillow. "Will you put your eyeballs back in already?"

The president steered the conversation back to the chapter's lagging finances. "It's because we lost a lot of girls last year and didn't make it up," she said.

"Well, there's another girl we could get back if she could get reduced dues," a sister suggested.

"My personal goal for this semester is to do more philanthropy," the president said.

"World peace!" Justine yelled as the girls dissolved into laughter.

"Cure for cancer!" another sister yelled.

"Well," the president said, "we were thinking of an all-you-can-eat pasta dinner."

"Agh," Emmy yelled. "That's carbohydrates!" Growing rapidly more hyperactive, she paused while her sisters roared. Then she added, more meekly, "Do we have to *eat* the pasta?"

The adviser looked annoyed. "Can we get back on track? Think sorority. Let's talk about Preference Night." Preference Night, the last night of rush, is an event held for a sorority's top-choice candidates. "We have to make the girls feel really special this year. We have to make them want us."

"Can we give them gifts?" a sister asked. Emmy stood up, dramatizing with flair: "It is both a privilege and an honor to grant you . . . this new Prada clutch!" Justine doubled over in hysterics, then sniffed her armpits as if checking to make sure that whatever she smelled in the room wasn't emanating from her.

Emmy noticed what her friend was doing and began sniffing herself.

"We need to e-mail everyone that they need to bring their schedule and unofficial transcript to the chapter meeting," said the president.

Emmy piped up. "Why do my hands smell like vagina?"

"Because your hands were in your crotch the whole meeting!" Justine squealed. The meeting officially broke up.

"Next time Emmy comes to a meeting," the adviser muttered to the president, "she needs to take some Valium."

Afterward, Justine informed me that I had just witnessed a typical executive board meeting in her house.

Ω Ω Ω

Double Whammy

OCTOBER 30

AMY'S IM AWAY MESSAGE

playing dress-up is way more fun than studying

THE ALPHA RHO TRIO CHATTED WHILE AMY, IN A SATIN Victoria's Secret robe, and Caitlin, in a baby tee and boxers, got ready for the Mu Zeta Nu Date Party. Sabrina had come over with a chemistry textbook, hoping to get some work done while keeping her sisters company. Amy and Caitlin had tried to find Sabrina a MuNu date, but Sabrina wasn't all that interested. She had so much work to do—it was easier, she figured, to spend a few hours reading than to waste an entire night without getting any studying done.

Sorority events, even Date Parties, were basically double whammies. There was the event, but also there was the getting-ready-for-the-event, which in itself became an event. For the Alpha Rhos, getting ready usually included a fashion show, pre-game, and several hours' worth of hair-doing and makeup-applying. Beth, a nonsorority friend of the trio, walked into Amy and Caitlin's suite lugging a large bag full of hair products and accessories. She wasn't a professional, but she had voluntarily done so many sisters' hairstyles for these events that they considered her an expert. She got right to work on Amy, who shook her black curls from the pink towel turban that matched her robe. Beth ran through Amy's hair with a flatiron and twisted it on top of her head in various ways, holding the hair up with one hand as she stepped back with furrowed brow to judge her work.

Sabrina told the girls she was taking Beth to the following week's Alpha Rho Date Party because she claimed to have sworn off men. Well, not all men. She had been visiting Professor Stone during his office hours after the creative writing class. At first they had talked about her coursework, but after a few weeks they started discussing broader subjects, such as Greek life and graduate school. Professor Stone listened to her, and even better, he understood her because he had worked hard to rise out of poverty. Professor Stone was one of the few people Sabrina had met who had come from a similar economic background and reached a level of success. She admired him greatly. He had become, to Sabrina, almost like a friend.

Sabrina suddenly realized that she had ten minutes until her study group meeting and she hadn't prepared. She grabbed her book, shoved it into her bag, and ran out the door.

"Sabrina works really hard," Beth remarked. "She parties really hard, too."

Amy nodded. "I don't party as hard and I don't work as hard. I don't see the point of studying away all of college just to get a 4.0."

Caitlin changed into a skirt and Amy's green mesh tube top, which showed off her toned shoulders. Most of the sisters wore dresses to their own Date Parties, but when it came to fraternity semiformals, they almost always chose sundresses or skirts and heels. As Beth twisted Amy's curls into a top-knot, the conversation topic shifted to the differences among sororities. Amy and Caitlin rattled off the defining features for each sorority: Beta Pi wore Tiffany's jewelry; another sorority wore shorts with letters on their behinds.

"I wonder what Greg's girlfriend is going to wear to Date Party," Amy mused, and leaned forward to put her chin in her hands.

Beth pulled her back. "Shoulders back, please!"

"Y'all remember last party Priscilla was wearing her hair in a headband and pigtails?" Amy said, popping open a Tic Tac box. "When it's time to dress up, I actually take time to do my hair." Caitlin and Amy took bets on whether Priscilla would have her hair in a headband for Date Party.

"She's just tacky. She has no fashion sense whatsoever," Amy said.

Beth asked Caitlin to hold the tiny braids she had woven in Amy's hair while she rubbed a fruity-smelling product over Amy's crown. Beth then twisted the braids into the shape of what looked like two Princess Leia Danishes on top of Amy's head. When Amy got up to do her makeup, Caitlin took her place in front of Beth. Beth held up Caitlin's hair. "What do you think? Half up or up?"

"I always wear it up," Caitlin said, before pausing and cocking her head. "I don't do anything halfway." Amy snickered from the other room.

As Beth stuck Amy's pastel clips in Caitlin's hair, Amy rummaged through her purse. "Caitlin, should we ask the boys to bring something for the thermoses?"

Caitlin: "Taylor's bringing Smirnoff."

Beth: "Oh, Taylor's going, too?

Caitlin: "Taylor's a male slut."

Amy: "Taylor's obsessed with Caitlin."

Beth: "Caitlin's a pothead."

Caitlin: "We're not potheads. Me and Sabrina have been cutting back."

Beth: "To what?"

Caitlin: "We're down to four days a week."

As Beth continued to fuss over Caitlin's hair, Caitlin stared at the ceiling and sang a Missy Elliott song to herself: "Not on the bed, lay me on your sofa. Phone before you come, I need to shave my chacha." After about fifteen more minutes, Caitlin grew fidgety. "It's okay, I'll just wear it in a ponytail," she told Beth. "I only have ten minutes to do my makeup, anyway."

Beth picked up a curling iron and tried to put some waves in Caitlin's hair. After forty-five minutes, Beth announced that she had finished. Caitlin stood up looking exactly the same as when she had first sat down.

TAYLOR AND JAKE CAME TO PICK UP CAITLIN AND AMY and walk them to their frat house to pre-game. When the girls walked in, the Mu Zeta Nu brothers flocked to them. Amy spotted Priscilla across the room, glaring at the sorority girls for drawing attention. Amy subtly nudged Caitlin, pointed her chin toward Priscilla, and both of them burst into loud laughter. The boys assumed they were laughing because they had been drinking already. But that wasn't it. Priscilla was wearing a headband.

On a couch in the den, Taylor put his arm around Caitlin, lightly scratching the back of her arm. Caitlin froze—she hadn't let a boy other than Chris, who was gentle and considerate in bed, touch her since the rape—but tried to calm herself down. It helped when Amy came over with two shots of vodka and a beer for each of them. Caitlin knew Amy was keeping an eye on her and she appreciated it, but she also wasn't telling Amy everything. Amy, Caitlin believed, didn't give Chris a chance. Ever since he had broken up with Caitlin, Amy had made it clear she didn't like Chris. "Go for Taylor," Amy had told her. "Forget about Chris. Forget about your mama." But this was Caitlin's life, and how she felt about Chris was her own business. So she didn't tell her sister about how much time she and Chris had been spending together—he had even prepared a spaghetti dinner for her, even though he had never cooked before. She didn't tell Amy that he refused to get back together officially but he still had sex with her. Or that she was maybe starting to love him again, and that her mother was thrilled with her for giving Chris another opportunity.

Under different circumstances, Caitlin might have dated Taylor—it was because of Chris that she wasn't interested now. She could envision them meeting up again sometime later in college. "I wasn't sure why you asked me," she told Taylor, feeling guilty. "I don't do random hookups."

"As much of a reputation as I have among the sororities, a big part of me wishes I didn't have it, because it bites me in the butt," Taylor said. "I wanted to go with you because you're a cool person. You're intelligent, attractive, funny, athletic, and I'm interested in you. So I thought we'd have a good time."

"Okay," Caitlin replied—but she had one more thing she wanted to get off her chest. "Look, the next person I get involved with, he's going to have to work really hard because I'm not going to settle. I'm going to be swept away."

"Check please!" Taylor said. "Just kidding. Maybe we'll pursue something more, but we'll see." Caitlin felt better. After that conversation, there would be no way Taylor could possibly accuse her of leading him on.

On the bus to the bar, Amy and Jake happened to sit in front of Spencer and his date, a Beta Pi. Because the seats were staggered, whenever Amy wanted to turn around to talk to Caitlin, she had to look right past Spencer. As she was chatting with Caitlin, Amy saw Spencer's date pull Spencer toward her and pucker her lips. Spencer didn't kiss her. Amy turned around and shared some of her Alpha Rho thermos full of vodka with Jake.

"You're going to outdrink me tonight, aren't you?" Jake said, giving her a sympathetic look. Amy glanced at Spencer, who was still squirming out of his date's grasp. Spencer caught her eye but didn't change his expression.

Amy turned back around. "You know it." Then she lit up. "I don't want to deal with any more guy stress. Will you go with me to next week's Alpha Rho Date Party?" When Jake agreed, Amy was relieved. One less date to line up.

Caitlin and Amy started off the night with Kamikaze shots before Amy and Jake started freaking on the dance floor ("freaking" is the 2000s version of dirty dancing, but with more graphic sex simulation). Every time an "ass song" played, Amy playfully backed up into the brothers, who affectionately referred to her behind as "ghetto booty." Taylor and Caitlin, who by now had joined Amy on the dance floor, started a pool to guess how long it would take for Amy's breasts to pop out of her shirt.

Caitlin had loosened up and was having a good time with Taylor. She let him put his arm around her and even took his hand as they walked around, although she took it partly for balance. When they danced closely, slow dancing in the middle of a crowd of people bopping to a techno song, she purposely turned her head so he couldn't try to kiss her, but he didn't object. After a while, she gravitated toward Amy, who was upset about Spencer. They spent the rest of the night making fun of Spencer's date, who was putting on her best eye-batting, lip-plumping "I want you" look and hanging all over Spencer, who seemed embarrassed.

On the bus ride home, Amy and Jake ended up sitting across from Spencer and his date. Amy watched her try to pull Spencer into an embrace, attempting the same seductive look she'd been giving him all night—and smiled as Spencer fell asleep. Amy sighed, wondering what it was about her that was so horrible that she drove straight guys away. The bus was quiet, with couples either making out or sleeping. "Hey Amy, you still alive?" a drunken Caitlin yelled from somewhere in the back of the bus. Amy giggled as brothers shushed Caitlin.

About three seconds after Amy removed her away message that night, Nathan, the irrepressible date rapist, IMed her. "I thought you were going home with Jake!"

"Now why would you think that?"

"Because you guys were really working it on the dance floor."

Amy, feeling the half-dozen mixed drinks and beers she'd consumed at the party, laughed so hard she fell off her chair.

"I danced with most of the MuNu guys tonight."

"How come you didn't dance with me?"

"Because they came up to me and just started dancing."

"I can't believe I missed my chance! If I wasn't so tired, I'd come over now."

Amy raised an eyebrow and decided to tease him.

"Well, if you're not going to come over and play, then I'm going to sleep."

"Wait, you'd actually let me come over?"

"Good night, Nathan." Amy put up her bedtime away message.

Nathan was still typing. "Wait! Come back! Wait!"

The next morning, another MuNu brother asked Amy what was going on with her and Jake. Amy called Jake, laughing, to tell him. "Everyone thinks something happened between us last night!"

"What the hell? Can't we just be friends?"

Amy updated him on the evening.

"Oooh, I can't believe Nathan thinks he can get with you again."

"I'm done with Spencer."

"You should be," Jake said.

"Sweetie, if he starts dating this girl, I'm going to stop talking to him. He told me he wasn't ready for a relationship."

"You're right."

"And I'm so much cuter!" Amy said, but wondered.

"I know!"

Ω   Ω   Ω

Juggling

BETWEEN MEETINGS AND ACTIVITIES, FUND-RAISING AND date-finding, sorority membership can be as much of a commitment as a part-time job. Even attending a party can require more time than a girl might be willing to spend. At many schools, when a sorority rents out a bar or club and a bus to get there, every sister who attends must remain at the party for its entire duration, usually from about 9 P.M. to 2 A.M. Sabrina often bowed out of these mixers, which occurred on weeknights because the sorority couldn't afford the weekend rental rates. Sabrina couldn't rationalize partying for five hours on a weeknight when she had so much work to do—in addition to her waitressing job and a search for a summer internship.

What saddened her about missing not only these activities but also frequent casual outings with the sisters was that every night she couldn't afford to spend with her sisters added to the distance between them. "That's when people bond the most—through their experiences. Going out builds a sister-hood," Sabrina told me. "If I had been able to go out more, I definitely think I'd be more comfortable with more people in my house."

Because she was so busy—and was content with her few close friends in the house—Sabrina wasn't terribly upset that she had to miss some Alpha Rho events. It was her choice. In order to be allowed into an Alpha Rho social function, sisters had to accumulate "merit points" by attending at least 70 percent of Alpha Rho activities. (Many sororities use this merit or "loyalty" points system.) Sabrina was careful to go to as many of the shorter events as possible. "Speaker Events," which the State U Greek system held every few weeks, featured educational speakers who lectured for about forty-five minutes on topics such as drunk driving and eating disorders. Sabrina considered those to be easy points.

But it infuriated Sabrina when she learned that one of her sisters was prohibited from attending Alpha Rho's Date Party because, like Sabrina, she had to work a part-time job to pay her dues. "She's here in the house because she wants to be here, but she can't stay in the house if she can't pay her dues," Sabrina fumed to me soon after she heard that her sister didn't make the 70 percent cutoff. "To pay her dues, she has to work, like me. A lot of the executive board members don't accept that not everyone is Daddy's little girl and can have their parents pay for everything." Sabrina despised the sorority Catch-22, which applied only to the less privileged sisters: if a sister had to miss events in order to work to pay her dues, then she wasn't allowed to go to social functions, which were a main reason to pay the dues in the first place.

Over the course of hundreds of interviews, I heard several stories about sisters who missed important events because they either were told to or believed they had to attend sorority functions instead. Brooke, the Texan red-head, missed her sister's debutante ball to go to an Eta Gamma philanthropy function that she had signed up for to fulfill her philanthropy requirement. She told me she could have asked the president for permission to skip the event, but because she was only a sophomore and wanted to be, as she put it, "the perfect little EtaGam," she attended the philanthropy event without complaint. During initiation activities at Brooke's house, sisters were told outright that they could not miss sorority functions for any reason whatsoever. A sister at another sorority canceled a meeting with a sorority adviser on her birthday because she wanted to spend the day with her family. The adviser, who had missed her five-year wedding anniversary to attend a sorority meeting, responded, "Birthdays come and go; where do your sisters stand in all of this? I think you have your priorities out of order."

Several girls complained about the enormous time commitment of sorority life and its often seemingly contradictory expectations. Sororities expect their sisters to prioritize their sorority membership above other aspects of their lives. This leads many sisters to wonder how they are supposed to be able to afford acceptable sorority attire or tickets to Greek events when to do so means having to work at a job that will take their time away from the sorority. They are also supposed to maintain the sorority's minimum grade point average even as they must spend so much of their time doing sorority activities rather than studying. Most sororities, including those at State U, have grade requirements, both to get in and to stay in. The minimum GPA usually ranges from 2.0 to 3.2 on a 4.0 scale.

At the end of the East Coast sorority's executive board meeting I attended, the president reminded the girls that they had to bring their schedules and transcripts to the upcoming chapter meeting. This is a common sorority practice and one that illustrates how membership requires a tremendous sacrifice of privacy. Sisters' grades are constantly monitored by the sorority and/or by the school's Panhellenic Council, which often receives transcripts from the administration and distributes them to each sorority house adviser. (Rush candidates must sign a waiver that allows the administration to release their grades to these groups.) For the freshmen, this standard is based entirely on their first semester or high school grades, both of which can be marginal. When Brooke was a sophomore, one of her best friends rushed Eta Gamma. Brooke broke a rush rule by calling her friend to inquire about her GPA, which was a 2.6. Brooke then had to explain to her friend that she would automatically be cut, and there was nothing Brooke could do to change the rules.

At most sororities, if a sister's GPA drops below the requirement, she is put on "academic probation," which means she has to attend mandatory study hall sessions monitored by sisters throughout the semester, as well as, in some cases, to log every hour she spends studying. While sisters are taught that the sorority is their first priority, they also must figure out a way to reconcile that time crunch with the emphasis on grades. For this reason, I was told, many sororities give their members a little extra help. Scores of houses across the country expect each sister to contribute to their files the papers and exams they write for every class they take. As a result, the sororities have thorough "class files" for the exclusive use of their sisters. The files in Brooke's house weren't extensive, but the sisters were often able to persuade their boyfriends to bring them tests and papers from their fraternity's files. "We always did much better on tests when we had access to the files," Brooke said.

Laney, a former president of Alpha Sigma Alpha at a Nevada school, told me that her house has files that go back for years. "There was a fifty-fifty chance that you could find in those files exactly what you were looking for. It helped a lot, especially when one term my GPA was a 0.19," she said. "Every sorority had them, and we never got caught. I never had the guts to take a paper. But I did use some tests." Class files, a Greek system tradition, are often viewed as a deserved perk of sorority membership. "Test files are a part of the benefits of being Greek," a Kappa Kappa Gamma at Texas Christian University has said. "After all, we pay to be Greek."

NOVEMBER

Instead of being an undesirable thing as many pessimists would have us believe, the clique, as established by the sorority, is a most salutary arrangement for grouping college girls into congenial coteries. Promiscuous friendships, though democratic, are dangerous.

—*The Sorority Handbook, 1907*

What Sororities Girls Do in Their Spare Time: Watch soap operas, Go to happy hour . . . Go to the library to see people (not to study) . . . Shop for clothes, Bake their boyfriends cookies, Make presents for their big or lil sisters, Paint their nails.

What They Don't Do: Watch the news—it's too depressing and boring, Read the newspaper—for the same reason . . . Do extra-credit projects, Do laundry—it goes to the cleaners.

—*Rush: A Girl's Guide to Sorority Success, 1985*

Ω   Ω   Ω

NOVEMBER 1

CAITLIN'S IM AWAY MESSAGE

I think I'm old enough to know what I'm doing, thank you.

A FEW NIGHTS AFTER Mu Zeta Nu's Date Party, Taylor IMed Caitlin. "What are you doing this weekend?"

"Chapter meeting and working out," she wrote back.

"Sounds like you're pretty busy."

"I tend to overcommit myself."

"Maybe we could go to dinner or a movie," Taylor offered.

Caitlin was taken aback. Two or three minutes went by. "Amy," she yelled, "what do I say?"

Before Amy reached Caitlin's room, Taylor wrote back. "Okay, well, I'm going to the gym. You can call me later." He logged off.

As much as she liked him, Caitlin didn't want Taylor to keep asking her out, not when she was growing increasingly certain that she and Chris were meant to be together. Chris continued to sleep in Caitlin's room and talked about spending Thanksgiving break with her family, though he still insisted they weren't an item. Caitlin expected he would come around eventually, which was why she still agreed to have sex with him. That afternoon Chris even admitted to her that he wished they had never broken up.

"That sounds like a regret, and you pride yourself on not having regrets," she said.

"This is an exception," he said. Caitlin raised an eyebrow.

"No, seriously," he added. "I regret kissing those other girls, but I also needed to kiss them to realize how important you are to me."

Caitlin didn't accept that excuse, but she let it go. Instead, because it seemed as good a time as any to bring it up, she told him she didn't think it was appropriate to be having sex at this stage of their nonrelationship. "I know you're not using me for sex, but I feel like you expect things to happen," she said.

Chris scowled. "But I express things through the way I treat you physically."

"I'm not trying to force you to make a decision," Caitlin spoke cautiously, "but we're acting like we're together and we're not, and while I'm waiting we can't be this serious."

"But I like the way everything's going. Everything has to be running on all cylinders for us to get back together," Chris said.

"If you love me," Caitlin told him, "you need to show me through other ways. It's not fair to me because I'm getting more involved in this again."

"But sex is still more than just sex with you," Chris insisted. "It's not just a hookup." Before long, they were yelling fiercely at each other the way they used to.

When their argument died down, Caitlin lay on top of Chris. "I hate it when we fight," she said.

"I was out of line and I'm really sorry," he said.

Caitlin was pleasantly surprised that Chris really did seem to be coming around. "Whoa, you never would have said that before," she said. "You never would have admitted you were wrong."

"Can we just act like we're together?" Chris asked, drawing Caitlin closer with a tug on her ponytail.

"Act like it or be together?"

"Can we act like it and I'll get back to you?" Chris asked. Caitlin decided this was his way of saying he wanted to ease back into the relationship.

"I want to be with you," he said, "but I just need some time."

Even though it wasn't her designated time to call, Caitlin left a message on her mother's cell phone to tell her that she and Chris were getting back together. She hoped that the news would put a halt to her mother's constant threats of withholding tuition money unless Caitlin transferred to a New York school.

A few nights later, Chris and Caitlin were fooling around in Caitlin's room when Taylor called and asked her to come downstairs. Chris went downstairs and left the house first, pretending he didn't know Caitlin. Caitlin came down a few minutes later. When she let Taylor into the entry hall, Chris stood outside a window.

Taylor handed Caitlin a bouquet of tulips, the Alpha Rho flower. "This is to thank you for a really great time at my Date Party. I didn't want to bring you roses because I didn't know how you'd react."

Caitlin blushed through her freckles.

"Regardless of what happens, I thought you should have this because you deserve it," said Taylor.

Caitlin explained that she and Chris were possibly back together. "I don't deserve this," she said.

"Caitlin, you deserve a really great guy and someone who will treat you right, whether it's me or someone else," Taylor said. "I just hope you don't end up with an asshole. I want you to know you're worth it."

Caitlin blinked hard. She couldn't remember the last time a guy had said such nice things to her. She didn't know what to say. "In another time and place I'd definitely want to date you," she tried. During the conversation, she hugged Taylor several times.

Chris stood outside the window, watching intently.

After Taylor left, Chris came back up to Caitlin's room. "Who wants a tulip?" he said disgustedly to the sisters who were around.

"Cut it out," Caitlin warned.

"I'm a wickit dirty Yankee out to capsha yah haht," Chris poorly mimicked Taylor's Boston accent.

"Hey, I really don't appreciate that," Caitlin said. "You aren't being sensitive at all that it was a bad situation for me."

"Why is this hard for you?" Chris sneered.

"Because here's a guy going out of his way to do nice things for me and I'm with a guy who can't even decide if he loves me or not."

"Fine, don't be with me then, if you think you're getting shortchanged."

Caitlin clenched her jaw. "I want the fairy tale! I want someone who makes sure that I know I'm an important part of his life." For a moment, Caitlin considered ending the relationship for good. "Look, I'm not trying to force you to make a decision to be with me or not. This just makes me realize I want something more."

Later, Caitlin told a few sisters that she had gotten angry with him and picked a fight on purpose because he wasn't getting enough hints about their relationship. "We fight passionately and we love passionately," Caitlin told them. "That's just how we are."

Caitlin knew her sisters didn't approve of the way she was letting Chris back into her life. She saw them give Chris what she considered to be evil looks when they thought she wasn't watching. Even Amy, who had known

Chris back when he was "sweet as pie" in the beginning of the relationship, wasn't supportive enough for Caitlin's tastes. When Caitlin told Amy she wanted to take Chris to Alpha Rho's Date Party, Amy looked startled.

"What," Caitlin said expectantly.

"I just . . . am a bit surprised," Amy said. "Are you sure you know what you're doing?"

"Yes."

"Okay." Amy's brow furrowed. "I'm not delighted about your giving him a second chance, but I'll support you, whatever you decide, as your friend."

"Don't worry, if he hurts me again, I won't cry to you," Caitlin said.

"No, sweetie, I'm saying you *can* come to me—I'm your friend no matter what. I just don't think he's worth your time. I just don't want you to get hurt."

"Look, I know you don't always agree with what I do, but as my friend you're supposed to support me."

"I can do that."

But the next day, when Chris came into their suite, Caitlin heard Amy mutter to another sister, "Why is *he* here?"

Chris heard it, too. "You should tell her it's none of her business instead of creeping into a corner and letting her scold you," he said.

Caitlin was well aware that Chris loathed the way her sisters had gotten involved when he broke up with Caitlin in August. He accused her of paying for her friends—friends whom he suspected wouldn't support her if she got into some sort of trouble. In one sense Caitlin agreed with Chris that their issues weren't her sisters' concern. But her sisters had also been there to support her, whether or not she asked for their help. Besides, Caitlin thought, it was true that when Caitlin and Chris were together, they often picked on each other. These fights were the part of the relationship that her sisters saw most frequently; they didn't grasp that beyond the belligerence, which Caitlin merely attributed to opposite backgrounds, Chris could be a caring boyfriend. He was the kind of person who constantly made small, loving gestures, like slipping her love notes for no reason or surprising her with tickets to athletic events. He was the only person who went to every one of her lacrosse games. When Caitlin was feeling depressed in the aftermath of the rape, Chris once showed up at her door with a puppy he had borrowed from a friend to cheer her up. She had no doubt he loved her. Nevertheless,

Caitlin was careful not to invest too much in the relationship this time around. She would protect herself this time, she was sure. She just wished her sisters would trust that she knew what she was doing.

Saving Privacy

NOVEMBER 2
VICKI'S IM AWAY MESSAGE
absolutely miserable

BY NOVEMBER, VICKI HAD BEGUN TO DISTINGUISH WHICH girls she could be comfortable with and which girls she was better off avoiding; the problem was that one of the girls she was learning to dodge happened to be one of her roommates. She was still too shy, however, to wander into the television room to catch up with the sisters who lounged there. When she walked into the Beta Pi dining room, Vicki wouldn't sit with the older girls, who continued to intimidate her, but she was secure enough to eat alone rather than do what seemed like the loser takeout—scurrying away to her room with her food. The more Vicki went out to bars and parties with her sisters, the more her confidence within the group grew. In settings outside the house, the sisters seemed to feel more protective of each other—it was sorority versus sorority, us versus them, rather than the sisters against sisters controversies and cliques that often split the house. At Louie's, the Greeks' bar of choice, each sorority usually gathered in a different corner, where they eyed and gossiped about the other sororities across the room. Even though the comments were usually catty, those nights were the times when Vicki most felt like she belonged in Beta Pi, as if she were on a par with her sisters. Not to mention that the girls tended to be much friendlier to each other when they were drunk.

There were six juniors in particular whom Vicki had learned to steer clear of. The six rarely deigned to talk to the sophomores. Only when the seniors were watching did the juniors suddenly ooze kindness and cordiality to younger sisters. Once in a campus quad, Olivia had run into one of these juniors, who stopped to chat with her for fifteen minutes. But the next day, when Olivia and Vicki saw her in the kitchen, the girl didn't say a word to them. Vicki's strategy was simply to be as "sweet and cute" as possible to the juniors who openly snubbed her pledge class, so that even if they didn't like her, at least they wouldn't drastically turn against her and spark a new house drama.

For Vicki, the patterns of tension had flip-flopped since the beginning of the year. Now Vicki dreaded returning to her room in the house, while before it had been the closest thing she had to a sanctuary. She had started to notice that Laura-Ann, a legacy, was acting strangely (a legacy is a daughter, granddaughter, or sister of a sorority member). Laura-Ann constantly talked about how pretty the older sisters were. She had been telling the older sisters that she was a twin—but she wasn't. She had even managed to convince half the house that she had diabetes—but she didn't. And she was constantly snapping at her sisters. One night in the bathroom, Laura-Ann was rubbing lotion on her legs, and Vicki said sweetly, "Laura-Ann, that smells really good." Laura-Ann turned and gave her a nasty look, shook her red curls, and continued to rub in silence. Five minutes later, Laura-Ann huffed, "Thanks," as if she were furious at Vicki. Vicki couldn't understand her roommate's mood swings, which came without warning or apology. When Olivia was in a bad mood, by contrast, she would inform her sisters loudly, "I'm in a bad mood today, so if I'm bitchy, I'm sorry and I warned you."

The next night, when Vicki went to take a shower, she couldn't find her new bath towel. About half the sisters in the house—including Vicki, Olivia, and Morgan—had ordered extra-long, extra-fluffy, luxurious designer bath towels with the Beta Pi monogram. On warm days, the girls planned to take them out to the hill behind their house to sunbathe. But Vicki's was no longer hanging on the hook in her closet where she had left it.

"Um, this is so weird," Vicki whispered to Olivia and Morgan, who were giving each other French manicures on Morgan's bed. "My towel is gone."

The girls immediately glanced at Laura-Ann's empty bed. She had gone home for the weekend.

"What if Laura-Ann took my towel?"

"Oh my God," Olivia said, "she did say she was taking her towel home with her this weekend. She said she wanted to get it monogrammed at a less expensive store."

The next night, when Laura-Ann was back and all the girls were in bed,

Vicki asked no one in particular, "Did something happen to my Beta Pi towel? Because, I mean, I can't find mine?"

"Geez, why would you think that?" Laura-Ann immediately sniped. Vicki didn't have a tactful answer, so she didn't say anything further.

Not long afterward, Olivia and Vicki decided to try to switch to a double room for the spring semester. There were simply too many girls around. When one roommate was trying to nap, everyone else had to be quiet. When one wanted to be alone with a guy, she had to go to his place. And there was no way to get any studying done in that room. Vicki ached for a place of privacy, beyond the prying sisters who asked her things she didn't want to tell anybody about besides Olivia. To be part of a sorority, Vicki was learning, meant that sisters were constantly in her business. On the occasions when she managed to muster the courage to venture downstairs to the television room, she would get annoyed by the immediate inundation of inquiries from girls who asked her questions not because they cared but because they just wanted to know. She would be sitting in the den talking to a friend when a herd of sisters would rumble in, bellowing things like "Who are you talking about? Who, who, who?" "Is this about William?" "Does he know about Dan?" "Oh, are you still seeing Dan?" All Vicki wanted to tell them was "Shut up and go away," but she couldn't openly snub sisters like that, just as she couldn't say anything rude to the strange sister who seemed to live in the television room, where she would wait on the periphery for sisters to start conversing and then quietly repeat everything they said.

Olivia and Vicki went to Olivia's Big Sister for advice.

"We're afraid Morgan and Laura-Ann are going to freak out when we tell them we want a double," Vicki said.

"I don't care." Olivia threw up her hands. "Oh my God, I need to get out of that room. I can't live with three other people and I think they know that."

"If you want to make yourself happy, you should just do what you want to do. Don't worry what other people say," offered Olivia's Big Sister, a junior. "If this is what's going to be good for you guys, you can't worry about hurting their feelings."

"Maybe it's not really that bad," Vicki wavered. "It's just a lot of, like, girls." But she could tell it was getting to Olivia.

Ω   Ω   Ω

Cramped Quarters

NOT ALL SORORITIES HAVE ACTUAL HOUSES. BUT THOSE that do add a fascinating variable to these all-girl groups. Imagine the estrogen-fueled stress and chaos of, say, three biological teenage sisters sharing a bathroom. Now imagine one hundred sisters sharing four. The sorority environment is one that can pack practically grown women in triple bunk beds, six to a room, one hundred to a house, as if they were ten-year-olds at sleepaway camp. At the University of Missouri, some sororities own mansions that lodge up to 120 girls, many in triple bunk beds. Most sorority houses at the University of Washington have "sleeping porches": gigantic rooms in which all of the forty pledges must sleep. At half the houses at Purdue, girls are encouraged for bonding purposes to sleep in "Cold Air," an open room—large enough to hold more than one hundred girls—that is kept dark and cold, with the windows left open at all times.

Everyday life in a sorority house generally goes unsupervised. The only adult who lives there is the "House Mom," who usually has a private apartment with its own bathroom and kitchen. Depending on the sorority, the House Mom can be an alumna, a grad student, or, in some cases, a non-Greek woman from the local community. The degree to which she is involved with the house also varies by chapter. In State U's Alpha Rho and Beta Pi, the House Moms were older women who were unaffiliated with any Greek organization. They took care of house maintenance—calling technicians to fix lagging Internet connections, for example—but played no role in anything specifically sorority-related unless they were needed for safety or disciplinary reasons, as happened later in the year with Alpha Rho. The girls didn't want them to. They viewed them more as building administrators than as a part of the sorority.

Sororities with houses run them like a part of the business and often order members to live there a specific number of years. At Indiana University, sororities require sisters to live in the house for at least three years in order to be considered an active member. "Sororities have to make money," one alumna explained. In order to maintain the house, the sorority needs a certain quota of girls who will pay extra for the room and board. If chapters don't fill quota, Nationals have been known to shut them down. The houses are usually owned by a local House Corporation, a nonprofit board of local alumnae incorporated in the state. The House Corporation, which makes the financial decisions for the house, hires the cook, House Mom, and house-keepers out of the money the sisters pay in rent and a "parlor fee" charged to all members to help support the house. (This budget is separate from the chapter budget, which is run by an undergraduate sister acting as treasurer and covers parties and similar expenses.)

There is also a lighter, more innocuous side to life in a sorority house. In a houseful of dozens of young women, one of the most popular activities can be pulling pranks on the other sisters. One Sigma Delta Tau chapter had a house phone as well as individual lines for each bedroom. A common prac-tice was what the girls called "double lining"—they would dial a number on the house phone, put the call on hold, dial someone else from a room phone, and then connect the two calls together so that each recipient thought the other placed the call—while the girls listened in on the conver-sation. "We liked to connect two people who used to date and didn't talk anymore, just to see what would happen, or people who secretly liked each other but no one knew but us, or people who were in the middle of a huge fight. It was bad," said a Sigma Delta Tau. At her house, SDT pledges were expected to pull pranks on the older sisters. One year they stole all of the underwear of the forty girls who lived in the house and replaced it with tiny diapers. Meanwhile, they brought a trash bag full of the underwear to the fraternity house around the corner. Within minutes, the fraternity boys came tearing back around the corner and into the house with underwear on their heads and tossing panties at every turn. It took the sisters six hours to sort through the underwear, and hours longer to fight over the washing machine because no one knew exactly where their underwear had been. Another pledge group placed ads in the *Daily Texan* that advertised all of the older sis-ters' cars, exaggerating the amenities and reducing the price ("1997 black Toyota 4Runner, fully loaded, $3,000"). The house received more than 350 calls in twenty-four hours.

As many sisters told me, there is at least one undeniable benefit to life in a sorority house: "The clothes sharing was the best part," said Jordan, a midwestern Pi Phi. "There were so many different girls, you could always find something to wear."

Ω   Ω   Ω

Costumes and Masks
NOVEMBER 4

SABRINA'S IM AWAY MESSAGE

I will seduce and date Professor Stone and then he will fall in love with me and ask me to marry him. That is the plan.

ONE NIGHT IN EARLY NOVEMBER, SABRINA LOUNGED IN the Penthouse as the Pents got ready for an Alpha Rho "Masquerade Mixer." Aside from the costumes, it was a typical night in the house. Fiona pondered whether she would look better in a nurse costume or a French maid's outfit, both of which, for some reason, she owned. She pulled on the French maid dress, which barely covered her behind, and leaned forward in front of the mirror to pop her breasts slightly out of the low-cut top.

Two sisters at her side watched in the mirror. "Wait," one of them said, "I can see your bra through that." The dark bra showed easily through the practically transparent white top.

"I know." Fiona cupped a breast and pushed it up some more. "It's supposed to be that way."

"Um, it looks slutty," the other sister said.

"I know!" Fiona exclaimed happily.

Sabrina, absentmindedly twirling a braid, didn't pay much attention to the sisters. She was busy daydreaming about Professor Stone. Their office-hour meeting this week had extended into a coffee break, first to talk about academics and then to chat about anything that came to mind. He was a good listener and seemed truly to care about what she had to say. Sometimes she sent him e-mails, ostensibly to ask questions about class, but also just to say hello. He always responded, always professionally, but occasionally Sabrina noticed an extra line or two that seemed more like something from a friend than a teacher. Sabrina had already signed up for the class Professor Stone was teaching next semester. She was sure the course would be interesting anyway, but she also guessed that staring at Professor Stone's flecked hazel eyes and large biceps would make class time fly by. Because of him, Sabrina decided she wouldn't go to Alpha Rho's Date Party. She wasn't interested in college boys anymore.

IN HER PENTHOUSE AREA, BITSY WRIGGLED INTO A little red dress with a pitchfork pattern that was high on the bottom and low on top. She drew pointed arches on her eyebrows, lined her eyes with smoky shadow, and stuck on a two-pronged tail and horns. Then she came out into the middle of the Penthouse and struck a pose for no one in particular. No one noticed.

"I need boots!" she shouted. The sisters in the Penthouse turned and looked at her as she struck another pose. Sabrina rolled her eyes and continued talking to Amy, who had come upstairs for a rare Penthouse visit. Bitsy had been prancing around in the devil dress now for two days in anticipation of the Masquerade Mixer.

When no one responded to her, Bitsy turned to Amy. "Your boobs are looking good today," she said.

"Er." Amy didn't know how to react. "Thanks." She would later ask Sabrina if that meant on other days they didn't look so good.

"Now, my boobs," Bitsy continued, "they don't look right."

"Honey, that's because you don't wear a bra and your tops are too small."

Bitsy gazed down at her chest. "I'll take you to Victoria's Secret," Amy said to Bitsy, "and we'll buy you the right size bra and then you can wear shirts one size bigger."

"Oh yeah, I didn't think about that," Bitsy said. She put on a padded bra.

Bitsy reappeared in her devil costume downstairs, where some Alpha Rhos and fraternity brothers were watching television. At a commercial, she model-walked into the TV room and posed in front of the sisters until people noticed her.

"Nice, Bitsy!"

"Woohoo!"

"You working tonight . . . on the corner?" Bitsy seemed one exhale away from bursting out of her dress.

"Bitsy's not going to have to buy any drinks tonight because her boobs are going to be in everybody's face!" The room erupted into howls. The fraternity boys, embarrassed, tried very hard not to look at Bitsy's breasts.

Bitsy, oblivious, extended a leg and pointed her foot. "How do I look? I'm not sure about the boots."

"You need the hooker boots!"

"But they make me so ta-all," Bitsy whined. "The boys will come up to here!" She held her hand up to her chest.

"That's what they *want*, Bitsy, you idiot!" Bitsy smiled sweetly and sauntered back upstairs.

Twenty minutes later, as the group dispersed, Bitsy came downstairs, this time in a brown sweater, khakis, and more subdued makeup. She had a masquerade-style mask in hand. "Look, here I am in normal clothes!" she announced. No one asked her why she bothered to wear the devil dress, horns, and tail only to take them off before she went out for the evening.

Gossip

NOVEMBER 6

AMY'S IM AWAY MESSAGE

dancing with jake, my date of the month. don't wait up!

AMY AND CAITLIN WERE IN THEIR COMMON ROOM, PREPARing for the Alpha Rho Date Party. As Sabrina sat in a corner reading, Beth, their hairstyling friend, braided half of Amy's hair into a crown.

"Shake your head, is it coming loose?" Beth said. Amy shook her head as Beth focused intently on the braid.

"Shake harder!" Amy shook her head so hard it looked like she was trying to mosh sideways. The crown fell out.

"Shit." Beth retrieved the bobby pins that had fallen on the floor and started again.

Sabrina helped pick up the pins and headed back to her corner. "Oh Sabrina, I just realized you won't be there to dance to the ass songs with me tonight!" Amy said. Sabrina planned to work the late shift at the restaurant.

"There will be plenty of other drunken bitches there to dance to the ass songs with you," said Sabrina.

"But they don't have our ghetto booty, sweetie. They just have fupas!" Amy said while strapping on a stiletto. The girls laughed. Fupa, in their sorority lingo, stood for "fat upper pussy area," which the girls described as "the part that bulges over your pants when you sit down" (as opposed to the "food baby," which described a belly).

The sisters gossiped about other girls in the chapter. More than two months into the school year, a definitive hierarchy had developed in the house. Caitlin, Amy, and Sabrina mingled among various groups. Half a dozen sisters were on the most popular tier, as the "pretty" girls—the party animals who knew the most fraternity boys and could usually be found at the bars. Bitsy and a few others formed the boy-crazy clique. Charlotte and another sister were the house prudes, known by the way they strictly adhered to sorority rules, who spent time together because they weren't entirely accepted by the other cliques. One might have expected that as president, Charlotte would be accessible to every sister in the chapter, but Sabrina had discovered otherwise. Charlotte would say hello to some sisters, but never to Sabrina, whom she ignored completely. Other sisters flitted in and out of the house periphery, such as the three sophomore sisters who constantly flirted with each other. They liked to stalk each other throughout the house, lurking behind doors to scare and tickle each other. As far as the Alpha Rhos knew, however, the closest the girls had come to hooking up was their occasional wrestling bouts.

Fiona, Whitney, and Elaine were the bossiest sisters. Fiona, a junior with a superiority complex, wielded influence—or thought she did. Before a recent chapter meeting, Sabrina was in the Penthouse jotting down some homework assignments in her day planner before she headed downstairs to join the rest of the sisterhood. The other Pents had left just a minute before. Fiona came upstairs.

"Is someone up here?" she said.

"Me, I'll be down in a second."

"Are you going to Meeting?"

"Yes," Sabrina said.

"It's really important that you go down there right now," Fiona said.

On another night, when Sabrina was out, Fiona was spotted going through Sabrina's things and strewing them across the Penthouse, supposedly looking for something she had lost. When Sabrina returned, her bed had been moved, her sheets were loose, her furniture rearranged, and the pictures that she had been sorting for her sorority scrapbook were scattered on the floor. It took two days for Sabrina to put her area back together.

A few days before the Alpha Rho Date Party, Sabrina discovered that the bag of chocolates that Caitlin had given her for her birthday was empty. Watching her gasp in dismay, a nearby Pent confided to Sabrina that Fiona had eaten them. This time, Sabrina approached Fiona in the dining room.

"What happened to my chocolates?" Sabrina asked.

"Whitney ate them all," Fiona said without hesitation. Another Pent later related to Sabrina the conversation that ensued as soon as Sabrina had left the room. Guffawing, Fiona had plopped onto a chair next to Whitney.

"I just told Sabrina you ate all her chocolate," Fiona said to Whitney.

"You bitch, I did not," the senior responded, laughing. "Now she's going to be mad at me."

But Sabrina never said anything to Fiona, just as she never spoke up to Charlotte. She was stuck living in the house all year; better not to make waves by confronting people, she thought.

Whitney wasn't much better. Whitney, whose life seemed to revolve around Alpha Rho, rarely talked to a girl, even a sister, unless she decided that she needed to be friends with her for some reason. To everyone else, Sabrina pointed out to her friends, Whitney shot dirty looks.

"Well, people think Caitlin is giving them dirty looks," Amy cautioned, "but you just have to get to know her first."

"Whitney's different," Sabrina insisted. That week, a group of Alpha Rhos had been downstairs watching *Sex and the City* in the TV room. One of the youngest sisters in the house came downstairs, stood behind the couch, and timidly asked Whitney a question.

"Are you actually *talking* to me? While I'm watching *Sex and the City?*" Whitney scolded her in front of everyone and turned back to the television. Clearly upset, the young sister had run upstairs.

AFTER THEY FINISHED GETTING READY, THE GIRLS MET up at a satellite house to pre-game with a few other sisters and their dates. Amy went into a side room, where she whispered with Jake. Occasionally, sisters would duck in and quietly ask why Chris was there with Caitlin when they thought he had broken up with her. "I don't know," she told one. "Look asshole up in the dictionary and his picture's there."

At the bar, the bouncers gave all of the sisters over-21 bracelets and let them in but took most of their dates' IDs for the evening. Amy was thoroughly enjoying dancing with Jake, especially when he started to point out the dates he found attractive.

Then he thought better of it. "Uh-oh, someone will hear me." A guy jumped on top of a table in the corner of the room and yodeled like Tarzan as he beat his chest. The bouncers rushed over and threatened to throw him out.

"No one will care." Amy turned back to Jake. "This isn't your fraternity."

"Oh, true."

Amy gravitated across the bar to Fiona's date, a cute fraternity brother whom Fiona had seemingly abandoned. The brother, chatting affably, started dancing with Amy. As soon as Fiona spotted them, she hurriedly oozed over to her date. "Come dance with *me*!" she cooed.

Ω Ω Ω

Cliques and Hierarchies

JUST AS IMPORTANT AS THE BONDS AND ATTITUDES THAT form during the monitored house activities are the cliques and tensions that develop between the lines. Looks, wealth, bloodlines, connections, dates, friends—all of these can be major factors when sororities are deciding on which new members to accept. But even once these girls have been chosen, many told me, they continue to walk on eggshells. For some girls, the sorority experience involves a constant struggle to keep up with the trends and attitudes dictated by particular cliques within the sorority. Belonging to a house offers a sister a permanent affiliation, but it doesn't signify unconditional acceptance. As Vicki discovered, the "us versus them" shifts from sorority versus sorority outside the house to clique versus clique within the house. Inevitably, hierarchies develop between these cliques of sisters, the kinds of power plays that caused Vicki to be intimidated by the older girls, and Amy, Caitlin, and Sabrina to feel slighted by bossier sisters. These intra-sorority subgroups can divide by factors including looks, pledge class, and general attitude toward the sorority. Jordan, the midwestern Pi Phi, explained to me that there are, to generalize, two types of groups that can be found in sororities: "One is the die-hard, 'I'll-take-every-secret-to-the-death' type. The other is the 'This-is-ridiculous-but-I-guess-I'll-do-it-anyway' group." It is inevitable that these two factions routinely clash.

No sorority is without its subsorority divisions, often provoked by the die-hard group of girls that Jordan described—the kind that eschews anything that doesn't sustain the sorority's image and follow sorority policies to the letter. In many houses, if a sorority sister drastically changes her look, or dates or befriends the wrong person—or, worse, a person in the wrong fraternity or sorority—she could be ostracized by the rest of the group.

In Brooke's pledge class, the tight clique of ten girls rapidly became the popular group that determined who or what was "cool" and dismissed anyone who didn't fit the criteria. The bulk of Brooke's pledge class was, she said, an especially spoiled group. The sisters came from wealthy, cultured backgrounds; they were "trust fund babies" who were always driving the newest, slickest cars available. "My pledge class," Brooke said, "would tear down anything or anyone that wasn't 'cool.'"

The Ten, as the sisters eventually called these materialistic members, were a clique within a clique. They were girls who were so blindly into the sorority that all other activities and aspects of college life paled by comparison. They had the attitude, Brooke explained, that "If you're an EtaGam, you're an EtaGam through and through. You bleed blue and cream." These were the girls who unofficially controlled the Eta Gammas by deciding the homogeneous characteristics to impose on the group. The Ten had the power to "make your life hell," Brooke told me. "If you weren't hanging out with the

Delts, they made fun of you. They planned parties and wouldn't include you. They made you feel unimportant, like something was wrong with you. They had a 'You're not cool enough' attitude and would blow you off."

Most of the Ten were die-hard EtaGams, but one in particular led the group's push to institute "proper" Eta Gamma policy. An Eta Gamma legacy whose mother was intensely involved with the sorority's regional organization, this sister was constantly correcting the Eta Gammas: "Well, the EtaGams at my mom's school do it a better way," and "This is not the way the EtaGams do it." When she returned from the Eta Gamma national convention she attended with her mother, the scope of her criticism grew—she wanted to alter voting policies and raise the minimum GPA, among other changes—and the sisters voted for her proposals. They didn't doubt that she had Eta Gamma's best interests at heart; her room was like an Eta Gamma shrine, with an Eta Gamma bedspread, a large Eta Gamma mascot dangling from the ceiling, Eta Gamma poems tacked on the walls, and Eta Gamma pillows in every corner.

I asked Brooke why, in a sorority of seventy-nine girls, the sisters let a group of ten rule the chapter, mowing down other girls in the process. "They were the coalition. You wanted to be liked by them because there were so many of them, because it was easier to be in their inner circle than out of it," Brooke said. "Especially because they lived in the house: ten people in a house that accommodated thirty-five is a huge chunk of the house, so they had the influence over the rest of us."

That this kind of exclusivity is collegiately condoned makes the situation all the more intriguing: sororities themselves are cliques. Envision taking the groups of girls in high school who bond and exclude and formally recognizing their belonging to one group and not to another by assigning them letters, colors, and mascots. The blondes, the super-thin, the rich, the promiscuous, and the girls who smoke marijuana are separated and recognized as being distinctive, nonoverlapping groups. Once a girl is accepted into one of the groups, she can never affiliate with another. Each group is allotted certain areas of the high school building—a perch of lockers and a cafeteria table (decorated in their colors) from which they can observe the other groups. They are given secret rituals and an oath swearing allegiance to one another. The girls are encouraged to create and wear T-shirts and other clothing items that bear their letters and slogans about their group's superiority. They have their own rules that dictate what to wear, how to act, which groups are acceptable, and which to avoid. The high school sanctions a formal recruitment process by which the cliques can screen and reject potential additions to the group. But even if a candidate fits the external mold perfectly, if she doesn't make a noticeable effort to impress the group with the right outfit or attitude, she will be shunned, doomed to an invisible existence with the other, nonaffiliated high school castoffs.

In reality, high schools don't grant cliques letters and mascots or run a formal recruitment process. But the rest of the characterizations in the preceding paragraph constitute the kind of teenage-girl behavior that recently spawned a spate of poignant books and workshops aimed at teaching girls that these divisions can be dangerous and geared toward eliminating that behavior. This movement toward bridging the barriers between groups, whether they are Queen Bees and Wannabes or Alphas and Betas, has focused on girls in elementary through high schools. But I would argue that the cliquishness doesn't stop there. The foregoing descriptions, those same characterizations that have caused such an uproar among teens, parents, psychologists, and school administrators—including the letters, mascots, and formal recruitment—also accurately describe life in a sorority.

As noted in the first chapter, there are popular sororities, "loser" sororities, and sororities known for their promiscuity, drug use, body type, and hair color. These groups are extensions of the kinds of cliques formed in secondary schools, but with an added element of officialdom: with the blessing of the school and the cliques' national organizations, the groups' process of exclusion is both formal and final. It should come as no surprise that girls who are sometimes only four months out of high school continue the social behavior developed in their prior academic settings. A difference in the Greek system, however, is that this exclusivity is perpetuated even by college seniors—girls twenty-one and older—as well as condoned and even encouraged by the older women who run the sororities at the local, regional, and national levels. Critics may argue that group exclusivity is a fact of life: varsity athletic teams cut players, orchestras choose first and second chairs, drama directors cast leads. But sororities, like high school cliques, aren't groups formed according to a specific talent, such as how well a girl can debate an issue, speak Italian, or bake canapés.

It seems inevitable that girls who are encouraged to form cliques as sororities, to accept or reject people based on predetermined (and often shallow) criteria, will perpetuate that exclusive behavior even once inside the sorority. Sororities stereotypically seem to personify collectively certain "types" of girls. But there is, of course, the question of whether the girls create the sorority or the sorority creates the girls. As Rosalind Wiseman cautions in her book about cliques of young girls, cliques are "natural. Girls tend to have a group of girlfriends with whom they feel close, and often these friendships are great . . . But something in the way girls group together also sows the seeds for the cruel competition for popularity and social status." One can't help but wonder how distinctly college girls would segregate themselves into cliquish groups anyway, but the point is that universities formally recognize their exclusivity by slapping on Greek letters and a motto.

In a sense, sorority girls are in a clique for life. A sorority is more than an affiliation; it's a label that a girl can't simply unstick after school ends. A few years after graduation, Brooke attended the wedding of a Texas friend who was a member of another sorority. A thousand people circulated in the ballroom, starting their conversations with guests like Brooke not by asking what they did for a living but by inquiring which sorority they were in. "Oh, were you a Sigma with the bride, darlin'?" a genteel woman in southern finery drawled when she approached Brooke.

"No, ma'am."

"Reeeally." The speaker raised an eyebrow. "Well then, what sorority were you in?"

"I was an EtaGam, ma'am."

The woman smiled in approval and fanned herself as if in relief, because Eta Gamma was considered one of the top sororities and therefore an acceptable association.

In another part of the room, older women were aloof and patronizing to Brooke until she managed to slip into the conversation that she was an Eta Gamma. Suddenly, the women included her in their circle. "Oh, my cousin was an EtaGam!" one exclaimed.

"It's unreal in Texas and the South," Brooke mused now. "Even decades after you graduate, you're only accepted or not by what sorority you were in."

Ω Ω Ω

Clinging and Clashing

NOVEMBER 9

VICKI'S IM AWAY MESSAGE

i don't think i can take this anymore

VICKI WAS CHATTING WITH A GUY IN HER LITERATURE class before their midterm when he asked her where she lived.

"Oh, um, off campus."

"Where?" he pressed.

"Beta Pi?"

"I *knew* you were in a sorority," he said. Vicki was shocked. Even now, more than halfway into the semester, she didn't consider herself much of a sorority girl. Beta Pi wasn't intertwined with her identity; it was just a group she had happened to join to make the campus seem a little smaller. Vicki asked her classmate what it was about her that made him think she was Greek.

"I don't know," he shrugged. "I can't figure it out."

After the exam, he approached her again. "I know what it is now."

"What?"

"Your hair." Vicki had straightened her wavy shag that day so it was long and sleek. "Sorority girls know how to do their hair right."

Vicki didn't *feel* like a sorority girl. She was gradually growing more comfortable in the house, although she still spent much of her time on the phone with her friends back home. While Vicki could say hello to anyone in the house, she wouldn't approach most of the sisters or have an in-depth one-on-one conversation. She had come a long way, however, since she pledged in the spring, when she had circulated with the wrong people.

Nicole, who initially seemed friendly and open, was one of the first pledges Vicki had met. In a group full of strangers, it was comforting to have someone who so eagerly wanted to be Vicki's new friend. Vicki and Nicole were together constantly as they suffered through the pledge process. When

Nicole asked Vicki to room with her in the Beta Pi house for the fall semester, Vicki readily agreed. But after a few more weeks, Vicki regretted being so quick to form the friendship because Nicole wouldn't leave her alone. She told Vicki intensely personal stories about herself, disturbing things that Vicki thought girls shouldn't tell each other when they had just met. "Vicki, I'm sad," she would say, and then expect Vicki to listen attentively as she complained about her life. As Nicole grew increasingly clingy, Vicki began to notice that none of the other pledges were friendly with Nicole. So she tried to distance herself.

During the pledges' weekly Saturday night sleepovers in the house, Nicole regularly maneuvered her sleeping bag next to Vicki's and followed Vicki around the room as she tried to meet other pledges. But the more Vicki heard the other girls talking about Nicole—"Oh my God, what a weird girl," they said, "I can't believe she's in our house"—the more Vicki avoided her. At the last sleepover before Spring Break, when Vicki was chatting with Olivia, who was then another new friend, Nicole tramped across the room to whine, "Vicki, aren't you going to hang out with me tonight?" Olivia and some of the other pledges gave Vicki a strange look that seemed to say, "What are you doing with her?"

By the time Vicki returned from Spring Break, she had made up her mind that she was going to room with Olivia instead. Vicki waited until she was alone with Nicole to tell her. "I don't think it would be a good idea to live with each other," Vicki said as gently as she could. "I want to keep being your friend, and as friends we really wouldn't be able to live with each other, you know?"

"No," Nicole started crying. "What are you saying—that I'll be in your face all the time?"

"No, I'm not saying that." Vicki was getting really uncomfortable. "Um, I'm just saying I want to be your friend, but I think maybe you depend on me a little too much."

Nicole's eyes narrowed into slits. "What's that supposed to mean?" The girls didn't speak for the rest of the semester. But because she had latched on to Vicki, Nicole hadn't gotten to know any of the other pledges. Immediately after Vicki turned her down, Nicole asked another pledge to live with her. The pledge, backing away, looked horrified and said, simply, "No!" The rest of the sorority shied away from her.

When Vicki moved into the house in August, she bumped into Nicole, who was carrying things to her car. "I think I know the girl you're living with," Vicki said. "I saw your names on the list."

"No, I transferred," Nicole said coldly.

"Oh, you switched rooms?"

"No, I switched schools."

"Oh." Nicole was just there to get her things out of the house.

"I'm going to study art and be a painter," Nicole said.

Vicki brightened. "Oh, you can come paint my room!" As Nicole huffed and walked away, Vicki winced. Vicki hadn't intended to be mean—she meant to be funny and cute, but her response had come out mean. She decided she wouldn't dwell on it.

Now, however, the pattern of finding a sister increasingly repugnant seemed to be repeating itself with Laura-Ann. Laura-Ann borrowed Vicki's clothes without asking, dumped her papers on Vicki's desk, and, most recently, left her wet towel on Vicki's shopping bags, dampening the designer sundress she had bought for the upcoming Homecoming game. Inwardly, Vicki felt like she was going to spontaneously combust. She couldn't stand one of her roommates and it was only November. Vicki suspected that Laura-Ann was testing how far she could push her. "New rule," Vicki said to her roommates. "Anything that's on my bed, dresser, stuff, or desk that's not mine is getting thrown out." The others nodded, surprised to hear Vicki speak assertively.

What bothered Vicki the most was that she couldn't find peace in her own home. When she first moved in, Vicki had thought that, in a houseful of girls, at least her room would be her refuge. She thought wrong. Now Vicki found herself constantly trying to make excuses to get out of the room, usually to avoid Laura-Ann, who was always watching her intently and making comments. When Vicki banged her elbow on her dresser while leaving the room, Laura-Ann was off: "Oh geez Vicki are you okay that must have hurt are you all right?" Vicki's stomach churned in annoyance, though that didn't bother her nearly as much as Laura-Ann's favorite refrain. Laura-Ann was constantly pleading, "Don't be mad," as in, "I went to the supermarket and got juice for the room, don't be mad at me. I got a new potpourri, are you mad? Don't be mad, I thought you'd like it," and, more frequently these days, "Oh geez, I'm such a fuck-up, don't be mad."

Well, Vicki *was* mad. She woke up disgruntled every morning because she knew she would have to face Laura-Ann. One morning when Vicki looked out her window and saw Laura-Ann walking away from the house, she was flooded with a powerful sense of relief and joy, because if Laura-Ann was walking away it meant that even if just for a little while, she wouldn't be in the house. Olivia felt the same way about Morgan, whom she believed had latched on to her. After much discussion, Vicki and Olivia bought long navy curtains and hung them around their bunk bed so they would have a place to hide.

Reading Between the Lines

NOVEMBER 11

SABRINA'S IM AWAY MESSAGE
I might have just made progress.

IN PROFESSOR STONE'S CREATIVE WRITING CLASS, THE STU-dents were doing a ten-minute stream-of-consciousness exercise while the professor graded papers at the front of the room. Sabrina began writing but found she couldn't concentrate. From her seat in the middle of the class, she peeked through her braids at the professor. Professor Stone was looking right at her. Her skin reddening, Sabrina returned to her paper. A few minutes later, she looked up to find the professor staring again, with a barely detectable smile crinkling his face. This time, Sabrina stared back. The other students, still feverishly writing, didn't notice the change in tension in the room.

After class, Professor Stone suggested they hold their usual office-hour chat at a Starbucks on campus. Once there, after briefly discussing one of Sabrina's essays, they somehow got onto the topic of past relationships. They ended up talking for three hours. As they got up to leave, the professor quietly asked Sabrina if she would give him a few photographs of herself for a "project" he was doing. Flattered, Sabrina agreed and walked him to his car.

When he opened the car door, he told her, without making eye contact, that a few of the other professors had seen Sabrina with him at office hours regularly and had made some joking insinuations about the two of them. "It is a little awkward being your professor and being friends with you, because it isn't normal," he said as he eased into his Saab. "Although a lot of professors do end up marrying their students."

"I won't come by your office like that anymore," Sabrina agreed. But all she could think about was the professor's second sentence.

Friction Among Friends

NOVEMBER 12

CAITLIN'S IM AWAY MESSAGE

I have no idea what just happened

CAITLIN WAS AT A RESTAURANT CELEBRATING THE START OF a new relationship with Chris, who was officially her boyfriend again. After dinner, she planned to meet Amy and Sabrina, who were eating with Jake at the Mu Zeta Nu house, and walk with them to Alpha Rho in time for chapter meeting.

When Caitlin hadn't shown up by the designated time, Amy called her cell phone. "By the time you get here, we'll be late if we walk to meeting. Do you want to meet at the house? Or, since Chris is dropping you off, can he pick us up and take us back to Alpha Rho?" Amy asked. She heard Caitlin ask Chris but couldn't decipher his muffled response.

Caitlin came back to the phone. "Chris says he has plans and he doesn't have time . . . Whatever, we'll just call you when we get closer to you." Amy hung up the phone and told Sabrina what Caitlin had said, wondering why Caitlin wanted to hang out with Chris in the first place.

"That is bullshit," Sabrina said. "I'm calling Caitlin." Sabrina had a quick conversation, then told Amy, "They're coming to pick us up."

"I thought Chris had plans."

Sabrina sighed and tucked a few braids behind her ear. "Caitlin told me that Chris didn't want to come get us because you were the one who asked him."

Amy was beside herself. She had never been rude to Chris; in fact she had taken care to make small talk with him whenever he was in the suite. Tired of tiptoeing around confrontation, Amy waited until Chris dropped the girls off at the Alpha Rho house. As she and Caitlin sat next to each other in the chapter room, waiting for the meeting to begin, she spoke up.

"If Chris has such a problem with me, then I don't want him in our suite," Amy said.

"What are you talking about?" Caitlin looked confused.

"Sabrina told me what Chris said about picking us up."

"Chris didn't say anything."

"So Sabrina made it up?" Amy said, putting a smooth, manicured hand on her hip.

"Look, Chris has picked up on some tension between you. It's no secret you guys aren't best friends."

"I've been nice and polite to him. There have been times when I could have been a real bitch to him, but I wasn't."

"I could say the same thing about Chris," Caitlin said, her square jaw clenched.

"If he thinks that's how it is, then let's clear up all this tension. I don't want him in our suite again. Ever," Amy said. Caitlin walked away and wouldn't speak to Amy the rest of the evening.

Later, Amy commiserated with her Big Sister, who coincidentally that night had gotten into a fierce argument with her three roommates about a fraternity brother they all liked. After meeting, Amy's Big Sister came to Amy's room, crying. "They're supposed to be my best friends," the sister said. "Chicks before dicks." Amy gave her Big Sister a snack and pajamas to borrow so she wouldn't have to go back to her room. As they drifted to sleep in Amy's bed, they discussed Taylor, the Mu Zeta Nu who had given Caitlin the tulip bouquet. It wasn't that Amy thought Taylor was the perfect guy for Caitlin. But there was no doubt in her mind he would treat her better than Chris did. Amy had discussed this with Taylor, hoping Caitlin would come around. She decided not to bring up the Chris issue again with Caitlin.

In the morning, when Amy's Big Sister went back to her room, her roommates apologized. But Caitlin and Amy didn't reconcile so easily. Since the beginning of their friendship, this was the first time there had been "drama" between the two. Amy hated it.

Caitlin saw the situation differently. Unless Caitlin had to deliver a presentation, she and Sabrina usually smoked marijuana before meetings. By the time Amy confronted her, Caitlin was so high she couldn't think straight. Figuring there must have been some miscommunication and not knowing what else to do, Caitlin had walked away.

After the meeting, Caitlin and Sabrina went outside to smoke some more. They didn't "do drama," preferring not to gossip like the other sorority girls did. "What's going on here? Our entire house is falling apart tonight," Caitlin wondered as they smoked. "Is this just a girl thing? Is that their nature? Catty and dramatic and obsessive over stupid things?"

Days later, Caitlin and Amy hadn't said anything further about Chris. Both of them, it seemed, wanted to act as if the argument had never happened.

Ω Ω Ω

Mean Girls, Queen Bees, and Alphas

IS IT JUST A "GIRL THING"? MANY SORORITY SISTERS TOLD me about daily and ongoing dramas that constantly split the house. "When you get a hundred girls together," Laney, the Nevada Alpha Sigma Alpha, said, "there's no way they're all going to get along. It's not possible. Whoever says they can is lying. But thirty of those one hundred girls would have bent over backward to help me, without a doubt." Especially in houses in which sisters are loud, outspoken leader types, personalities clash almost daily. As an officer of the first house I visited remarked, "If you don't have some sort of [interpersonal] problem in this house, then there's something wrong with you."

The most common catalysts for cattiness in sororities are boy-related issues. As a newly initiated Alpha Sigma Alpha, Laney went out several times with Nick, an older fraternity brother. At one event Laney was greeted coolly by an older sister.

"What did you do today?" the sister asked loudly, in front of the entire sorority membership.

"Nothing, why?" Laney responded.

"Did you see Nick?"

"No, not today."

"Don't you think it's funny that you're fucking my boyfriend?"

Laney stood there, shocked and devastated—she had had no idea Nick was otherwise committed (and she hadn't had sex with Nick)—as the hisses ricocheted around the room: *"You're sleeping with a sister's boyfriend?"*

Laney later confronted Nick, who insisted the sister wasn't his girlfriend, but the sister was hostile to Laney for the rest of her college tenure. "It's bound to happen that a sister is going to date another sister's boyfriend," Laney said now.

Several factors associated with sororities create an atmosphere that provokes discord among the sisters. The race to get dates for sorority functions, especially when the acceptable pool is limited to one or two fraternities, as well as the often looks-based acceptance criteria, further a sense of competition among the sisters. Rosalind Wiseman—who discusses "how [young] girls' social hierarchy increasingly traps girls in a cycle of craving boys' validation, pleasing boys to obtain that validation, and betraying the friends who truly support them"—also points out that "girls' fights over boys are . . . one of the consequences of girls' social hierarchies." In addition, the grouping of dozens of girls in small living spaces and a "sister is forever" mentality ensure that they can't merely walk away from an antagonist. And the implicit and explicit hierarchies within the sorority distribute power unevenly so that sisters are never on equal ground. Between pledge class order and the executive board, there are always sisters or groups of sisters who have official power over other girls. In extreme cases, they assert this power by making other girls do things—like the Chi Omega sisters who allegedly arranged Kristin Verzwyvelt's date rape. In the more mundane cases, they verbally cut other sisters down to size, like Fiona's "go down there *right now*" or Whitney's "Are you actually *talking* to me?" It is fertile ground for what Wiseman calls the Queen Bees and others have called the Alphas or "the mean girls."

Many sororities, with their strict subdivisions, are the next obvious stop for the mean girls from junior high school and the popular groups from high school. They are the segue to the Junior Leagues, the country clubs, and the Hamptons-type cliques of young adulthood. In fact, several groups have a specific subsorority, a group of girls who set out to destroy selected sisters' psyches, supposedly out of devotion to the sorority. A sorority at one mid-Atlantic university in the late 1990s actually referred to its die-hard sisters as "the mean girls." The mean girls from the class above them had taken them under their wing by choosing them as Little Sisters and inviting them to join their clique. These new mean girls erupted after one of their sorority sisters agreed to wear her boyfriend's lavaliere. (At some schools, if a fraternity member gives a girl his lavaliere—a charm of his fraternity letters, usually fastened on a necklace—his fraternity hazes him terribly. The girl who receives this token therefore feels that "he loves me enough to get tortured by his fraternity.") The boyfriend was attractive, but the mean girls decided that he belonged to a "loser fraternity." They repeatedly harassed the girl to break up with him, even though the couple's one-year relationship had been going well. They pressured their sister so relentlessly that she did break up with him. After college, away from the girls, however, the couple got back together—and eventually married.

The mean girls often did what they called "slumming," or visiting a fraternity that was not considered cool. Because these girls were from one of the top sororities, the boys were excited and treated them like royalty—giving them their most expensive alcohol and falling over themselves trying to please them. After they left the fraternity house, however, the girls made fun of the fraternity, laughing at them and boasting to others about what they had done. "There were pockets of mean girls and it was really easy to get sucked in by them," a sister told me. "They'd get on a trend of 'Let's make her the outcast and make her feel unwelcome,' and since they were the cool girls, you didn't want to be on the outs with them. You wanted to stay on their good side. It was very, very, very junior high."

Once a girl is initiated into a sorority at one school, she automatically becomes a member of that sorority at any other school if she should transfer. This posed a problem when Mary, who had been a Delta Zeta at a small southern school at which the Delta Zetas were not a desirable sorority, transferred to a larger school, where Delta Zetas were considered the fun sorority, with pretty sisters (though not the "supermodels," a sister was quick to clarify). Mary was, two Delta Zetas told me, the nicest girl they had ever met—a compassionate, sincere, naïve girl who came from a small town where she was adored. But she had extremely thick glasses, sported a short, "monkish" haircut, and constantly wore a bright pink satin jacket with the Delta Zeta letters on the back. She wore matching outfits, like pink shirts and pink socks, and different glasses frames to match each getup. While she had supposedly been the most popular girl in her small hometown, her style didn't fit in with that of her new sisters. To her face, this sorority's mean girls wouldn't be outright hostile. But they left anonymous messages on her answering machine: "*Your sisters don't like you.*" "*Leave the sorority.*" One night the mean girls broke into Mary's dorm room and stole everything she owned that bore the Delta Zeta letters—sweatshirts, T-shirts, mugs, the pink satin jacket—because they didn't want a girl whom they considered a loser to be seen wearing their letters. Mary was heartbroken. She didn't return to the sorority and, at the end of the semester, left the school for good.

Just as appalling as the mean girls' actions is the fact that not one of the other sisters in the sorority—not one out of dozens of bystanders—stood up for Mary. Nobody was brave enough to speak out against the mean girls on Mary's behalf; nobody openly questioned whether the girls were getting carried away. I asked several sisters why they were reluctant to intervene when a clique of sisters targeted another girl. The girls who joined in spoke of what could be called a herd mentality. The girls who watched without comment said it wasn't their "place" to get involved, they didn't want to "get in the middle of things," or they didn't want to turn a drama between sisters into a full house war.

A June 2002 *Newsweek* article cautioned that the current popularity of "mean girl" books is based more on anecdotes than scientific study, that there are girls who fall in between the Queen Bee and Wannabe categories and are neither bullies nor victims, and who turn out just fine. The same could be said for sorority girls. But even for these middle women it is difficult not to get caught up in the social battles of the sisterhood. Amy, Caitlin, Sabrina, and Vicki were neither "mean girls" nor alienated targets, at least to the extreme of Mary's case; one of the reasons I chose to follow them was that each of them could be the sweet, sincere, cool girl next door. And yet all of them were involved in subtle scenarios that illustrated the power plays of sorority girls. Amy and Caitlin made fun of Priscilla, Greg's nonsorority girlfriend who wore headbands. Sabrina accepted being bossed around by other sisters, especially Fiona. And Vicki admitted that because Nicole considered her such a good friend, she must have played a large role in driving her out of State U.

Several times over the course of the academic year, I asked Sabrina, a disciplined, highly intelligent girl, why she put up with the condescending comments and behavior. She said she didn't want to confront any of her sisters because they would turn against her and make her life in the house uncomfortable, if not intolerable. "I know I should say something," Sabrina said. "I just don't have the energy to say anything and then have them attack me." I was surprised at first that Sabrina would have the courage to flirt with her professor but not to speak her mind to girls her own age, until she clearly articulated the undercurrents running through the sisterhood. A disagreement in a sorority house rarely stays between the sisters concerned. Instead it has a ripple effect as the girls in question seek their roommates for consolation and their Big or Little Sisters for help, and those sisters consult other sisters for advice. An argument between two sisters, therefore, is likely to become a housewide debate. Sabrina stayed silent to avoid conflict and drama, the same reason that Amy and Caitlin buried their feelings, the same reason Vicki was determined to act "sweet and cute" to escape her sisters' notice. It is this fear of confrontation that allows the mean girls' actions to continue unabated and without consequence. Sisters are already afraid they will be ostracized if they voice dissent; the added prospect of having to stand up to a clique of particularly aggressive girls who seem to control the sorority proves to be an intimidating deterrent.

It is important to note, however, that many sorority sisters simply choose to view this unofficial crash course in female sociology as real-world training. Some recent graduates told me that they have found the power plays and politics in a sorority house helpful in the end because they learned how to tolerate living in a woman's world, which the girls say is a crucial tool for dealing with future female colleagues and superiors. "Being friends with a woman is not easy, so when you're forced to be, it can be a valuable tool in learning how to deal with other women," one sorority alumna said. "You learn you're not the center of the universe. In the world of women, it's interesting to see how you form bonds—or not—with them."

But does that justify the strategies that better resemble fifth grade slambooks than corporate backstabbing? Many common sorority sister techniques to exhibit power over other girls seem like natural extensions of what researchers have called "social manipulation on the playground" or "relational aggression." At a Virginia school, at least one sorority's "pledge books"—books in which pledges record interviews with sisters—often turn into something entirely different. "One book went around and we had a page for everyone on which we'd get to write whatever we wanted," a pledge in this sorority told me. "For the girls we really didn't like we'd write 'Most Likely to Be a Lesbian.'" Each May, at one school's Alpha Epsilon Phi Formal, the girls distribute to each sister a pamphlet that they have assembled over the course of the month, a rag sheet that is not uncommon in sororities across the country. Each sister writes whatever she wants to about whichever members she chooses. The comments generally consist of "mean humor," the girls said. When they showed me the 2002 booklet, I saw what they meant. Hoping to drive a particular junior out of the sorority, they listed her as "Person We Most Want to Stay Abroad." When I asked if the junior planned to be involved with the sorority in the fall, one girl remarked, to her sisters' laughter, "Not after she sees this." These kinds of incidents shed light on a sentiment I heard repeatedly from sorority sisters—and one that surprised me because so many girls join sororities in search of comfort, support, friendship, and loyalty: "It's funny," Jordan, the Pi Phi, said to me, "how you can feel so lonely sometimes even in the big group of girls who have 'chosen' you."

GREEK WEEK

———

Don't wear faded or shabby clothes or clothes that have been perspired in. Be prepared to change clothes in the middle of the day if it's hot outside.

—*Rush: A Girl's Guide to Sorority Success, 1985*

The American professor is a boy at heart, he understands young men, but the pressure of work is severe both in and out of the classroom and there is a limit to human possibilities, to human endurance.

—*The Sorority Handbook, 1907*

Ω   Ω   Ω

NOVEMBER 15: LIP SYNC REHEARSAL
SABRINA'S IM AWAY MESSAGE (EARLY MORNING)
I love Professor Stone in multiple states of consciousness.

GREEK WEEK, THE LONG-AWAITED demonstration of sorority and fraternity spirit, was finally here. Every day this week, the sorority-fraternity teams would compete in events judged by Greeks who had volunteered to temporarily separate from their chapters. These supposedly impartial judges would determine the points each team would accumulate during the week's series of competitions: Greek Olympics, various intra-Greek athletic events, Float Decorating, and "Lip Sync," a talent show that was the week's highlight.

The judges, who could grant additional points for enthusiasm, would announce the results at halftime of Saturday's State U Homecoming football game.

This year's Greek Week theme, chosen by the campus Panhellenic Council and Interfraternity Council because of the expected war, was World Party, with each team assigned a country. As Australia, Beta Pi and Kappa Tau Chi members would wear green bandannas and T-shirts on which they had their letters printed next to the slogan "Come Down Under." Alpha Rho and Delta Lambda, representing Egypt, had yellow T-shirts with a graphic of a sexy genie emerging from a bottle to cozy up to King Tut, accompanied by the slogan "Rub Us the Right Way." Although this was a week intended to display Greek spirit to the rest of the State U campus, intra-Greek rivalries tended to heat up during the events. Beta Pi and Alpha Rho, sororities with perennially strong teams, were expected to duke it out for the trophy, which carried with it prestige and respect that would elevate the winner's status just in time for January's rush. Winning Greek Week was considered the most important honor a sorority could achieve, even more crucial than the status of the fraternity with which it matched. For the whole week, the sisters would devote themselves almost entirely to the performances, crafts, and athletics that could accumulate team points. For the whole week, sisters hardly thought about anything else.

On the afternoon before Greek Olympics, the first event that could garner a team points, Alpha Rho was holding a Lip Sync dance rehearsal in its basement. Most of the girls who weren't participating in the show were at the Delta Lambda house, where they were sewing costumes and helping the boys build sets. Sabrina, Caitlin, and Amy stretched in the basement with the other dancers as they waited for the Delta Lambda boys to show up for practice. About three dozen of the girls and several Delt brothers would rehearse their complicated dance performance several times during the week to prepare for Friday night's show. For busy sisters like Sabrina, participating was an easy way to accumulate merit points for attending Alpha Rho activities so that she would be able to go to Date Party and Formal.

"I would like smaller boobs," one of the dancers announced.

Breasts were a frequent topic of conversation among the girls in the house. Many of the girls named each half of their pair and occasionally talked directly to them. In fact, one of the more philosophical discussions the sisters had in the house this year was an entire debate about what life would be like if they had three breasts.

"Me, too, they get in the way."

"Then we could wear tube tops and skinny tanks," Sabrina said. She usually wore sleeved shirts that fully covered her ample cleavage.

"I want them to get smaller before they get saggy."

"I used to have big boobs," said Grace, the Alpha Rho treasurer.

"What happened?"

"I lost weight."

"You can lose weight in your boobs?"

Grace nodded sadly. "They were the first to go." Then she added, "And I was big into doing those exercises, too."

"What exercises?"

"You know"—Grace made the gesture somewhere between a chest fly and a chicken flap known by Judy Blume readers everywhere. "I said the words, too: 'I must, I must, I must increase my bust.' That was my mantra."

Someone laughed.

"Hey, it worked! Well, for a little bit, anyway."

The Delta Lambdas walked in and the conversation stopped. The girls appraised the boys, who slouched over to a couch and waited for further instructions. They seemed uncomfortable to be on the girls' turf, but they were also sneaking glances at the sisters, who were flexing and doing splits in their slim sweatpants, tight tanks, and white ankle socks. Most of the girls wore their hair down; a few had tied their hair in scarves that draped down their backs.

Now that the brothers were in the room, the girls' voices turned shrill.

"Let's go, everybody!" Elaine, one of the Alpha Rho choreographers, clapped her hands. "Listen up, we're starting now!"

The Delts seemed overwhelmed in the beginning, trying to do the moves as coolly and casually as possible. Each sister, however, was dancing full-throttle, bending over and shimmying her backside into her partner's pelvis. Other sisters lined the perimeter and cheered.

"Go, Amy!"

"Shake it, Caitlin!"

In between sets, with the music paused, Bitsy squatted and bent over in a dance move for no reason. The brother in back of her, dumbfounded, stared at her behind. The other girls discussed Beta Pi, which had beaten them at Lip Sync several years in a row because it had a dance major in the sorority.

"This could be the year we finally beat them," one sister said. Alpha Rho had more cheerleaders than in the past, which was helpful for Lip Sync dance routines.

"They beat us every year."

"They've dominated for the last three years."

"When does their dance major graduate?"

"This year."

"Thank God. I'm tired of second place."

By the last run-through, the brothers were comfortable enough that when the sisters shook their rears in front of them, the brothers gripped their hips.

Back in the Penthouse, Sabrina received an e-mail from Professor Stone, thanking her for dropping off the photos of her that he had requested. "I am pleased that you are in the class and that I have an opportunity to work with you," he added. "I hope that we continue to talk about our class, your other classes, and your plans for the future. I will also help in any way that I can. Professor Stone."

Sabrina wrote him back immediately.

He responded within minutes. "Thank you for your kind words. I will always have time for you. Professor Mike Stone."

Sabrina called her mother to tell her about the exchange. "We're meeting again next week," Sabrina said.

"You marry this one," her mother responded. "This one's a keeper." Sabrina's mother fervently hoped that a man like Professor Stone, who was already settled with a stable, middle-class career, could help raise Sabrina to a higher social class.

"I know, Mom." Sabrina could envision a long-term relationship with Professor Stone for reasons other than economic advantage. Smart, attractive, ambitious, and a good conversationalist, he was everything she would look for in a husband.

Bitsy overheard Sabrina talking. When Sabrina hung up, Bitsy came over to sit on her bed. Sabrina chided herself for talking about the professor in the sorority house. If the sisters found out, Sabrina would be the subject of Alpha Rho gossip for far longer than she could tolerate. The only sisters she trusted unconditionally were Amy and Caitlin, and even they didn't know everything.

"I think he's hot for you," Bitsy said.

"I hope so."

"How old is he?"

"He is sixteen years older than me."

"Wow, that's old."

"When I'm seventy-one, he'll be eighty-seven. That's not so bad."

"Yeah," Bitsy said, "but when you're thirty, he'll be forty-six and you'll be like 'I want to get married' and he'll be like 'I broke my hip!' " Bitsy stood up. On her way back to her area of the Penthouse, she loudly asked the Pents who were around, "Hey, anybody have batteries?" Sabrina made gagging noises as Bitsy, catching a pack a Pent tossed at her, grabbed a vibrator from her underwear drawer and went to a sitting room for privacy.

The Drive to Drink

NOVEMBER 15: GREEK WEEK KICKOFF SOCIAL EVENT
VICKI'S IM AWAY MESSAGE
olivia told me to work now, play HARD later!

THE NIGHT BEFORE GREEK OLYMPICS, EACH TEAM HELD A kickoff event so the teammates could get to know each other. Most of these events involved alcohol. Beta Pi and Kappa Tau Chi planned a Chug-Off, during which teammates paired up and, tied at the wrists, had to drink two pitchers of beer before they were allowed to untie themselves. The first three teams to finish wouldn't have to pay for their drinks for the rest of the week's nightly parties. Because this was an activity specifically forbidden by the State U Greek system, the chapter officers were careful to watch for the campus "Greek Police," students paid by the Panhellenic and Interfraternity Councils to find Greeks committing alcohol violations and report them to the councils.

At shortly after 10 P.M., Beta Pis and Kappa Tau Chis filled the second-floor bar area of Yakamoto, a Japanese restaurant a few minutes' drive from

Sorority Row. Some of the other students in Yakamoto, clearly not sorority types, hastily paid their checks and left. Vicki sat with Olivia and Morgan at the back of the bar, where they preferred to watch the scene with interest rather than buy "warm-up drinks" like their sisters.

The Kappa Tau Chis, almost uniformly dressed in untucked button-downs and khakis, guzzled drafts and crunched fried noodles as they watched football on the fuzzy television in the corner. The girls, all wearing low-rider jeans or tight black pants, sexy tops showing skin, and excellent makeup jobs, were seated, legs crossed, chests out, stomachs in, as they drank daiquiris and exotic-looking pastel cocktails. When a few of the sisters in revealing clothing, like a girl in a red backless top, attempted to distract the boys from the television, Morgan joined them.

From the spot where she was folded in the corner of a booth, Vicki watched, amused, as the Beta Pi president ran around gesturing, frantically ordering restaurant staffers to move the tables, change the music, and bring out more drinks. By ten-thirty, the boys ventured outward to flirt with the girls holding the biggest drinks. The girls were getting tipsy and starting to lean on each other for support, kissing each other's cheeks and wrapping their arms around each other's waists, forgetting now to keep legs crossed, chests out, and stomachs in. At eleven, the last three Kappa Tau Chi stragglers entered the restaurant wearing baggy pants and T-shirts. These stoners moved slowly, lackadaisically, and with effort. One of them walked into the wall. By now the girls had switched to beer and, having had two to four drinks already, most of the sisters who weren't smoking cigarettes before were smoking now.

The president pulled the girl in the backless top out of the bar area and whispered to her. They nodded and walked outside to the president's car. The two grabbed fistfuls of green Beta Pi–Kappa Tau Chi Greek Week bandannas out of the backseat and hustled back into the restaurant, tripping on the top stair. As Backless stumbled around handing bandannas to the boys, Olivia led Vicki (Olivia's perfume leading both of them) into the crowd.

After a few minutes, the Kappa Tau Chi president stood on the bar. "Yo, everybody hush up!" The assembled, now tied in pairs, looked at him expectantly. "Yo yo, everybody, yo. We just heard the Greek police are coming down to check this place out"—there was a groan from the room—"so put your bandannas away. Please have a good time, but just put the bandannas away. We'll do Chug-Off another week."

"Nope, we can't have any fun at this school!" muttered a Kappa Tau Chi. Resigned to a normal bar night, most of the group left, slowly weaving out the door in a drunken mass. Many of the drivers hadn't begun to sober up, but they drove off anyway. No bondage, no bar.

Ω   Ω   Ω

Alcohol's Role

I FIND MYSELF HESITANT TO RAIL AT LENGTH AGAINST ALCOhol use in sororities, a common non-Greek media activity. Alcohol abuse is not an activity limited solely to Greek students. Nonetheless, several studies have been done to illustrate that it is prevalent enough in the Greek community to warrant at least some discussion here.

A 1996 Harvard University College Alcohol Studies Program report found that 76 percent of female non-binge drinkers in high school become binge drinkers in college when they live in a sorority house. (The researchers defined binge drinking for women as consuming four or more consecutive drinks during the two weeks preceding the study.) Only a quarter of girls who are not affiliated with a sorority become binge drinkers in college. "Virtually all fraternity and sorority members drink," the report stated. "The single best predictor of binge drinking in college is fraternity [or sorority] membership . . . Fraternity and sorority house environments appear to tolerate hazardous use of alcohol and other irresponsible behaviors . . . this directly contradicts the claim that the members of fraternities and sororities that belong to a national organization exhibit more responsible behavior than groups that are not affiliated with such organizations. Such behavior is decried by national fraternity leaders though they seem powerless to do anything about it." In 2003, Penn State University released a survey revealing that 94 percent of students in fraternities and sororities drink alcohol, as opposed to 81 percent of non-Greeks. Drug use is also prevalent: in 1992 the Journal of Alcohol and Drug Education reported that 98 percent of the Greeks studied drank alcohol every week, while nearly half used marijuana or cocaine within the thirty-day period preceding the study. Six years later, the *Journal of Higher Education Management* stated, "All types of casual drug use, especially marijuana usage, seem to be escalating on college campuses within the Greek community."

These drug and alcohol assertions are supported by my own observations. It was clear that just about every State U Greek activity involved drinking: all Date Parties, Crush Parties, Date Dashes, and Formals were expected to have alcohol, and when the sisters got together for virtually any Greek event, they made a point of pre-gaming. During the 2002–2003 academic year, several sorority sisters at State U had to be rushed by ambulance to the hospital for treatment for alcohol poisoning. Other girls across the country told me of similar experiences with alcohol and drugs, particularly during the pledge period, when forced alcohol consumption is a common hazing activity. Brooke's Texas pledge class, for example, was taken to a bar where every girl was required to down an entire pint of Jack Daniel's. If the pledge next to you passed out or vomited before she could finish her glass, you had to finish it for her. Brooke, perhaps wisely, passed out. At other schools, ID-swapping is a long-standing tradition in which older girls hand down their IDs—real or fake—to younger girls with similar hair and eye colors. In 1985, a Kappa Alpha Theta pledge at the University of Colorado fell to her death at a sorority party after drinking so much that her blood-alcohol level was three times the legal limit. (It is important to note that many sororities prohibit pledges from drinking; instead, pledges at several schools must serve as the sisters' designated drivers.)

Fraternities frequently run contests for sororities, such as relay races in which each girl on a sorority team must finish a pitcher of beer in less than five minutes. They also have parties at which they set up several stations around the house that serve different specialty drinks. A partygoer is expected to stop at each station. "You were cooler and more fun the more you drank," one girl told me. "The day after any event, conversations were always about who had the funniest drinking story the next morning. A lot of the girls wet the bed." On Bid Night at some schools, fraternities hold parties and hand each sister her own full bottle of champagne as she walks in the door. It is expected that she will finish the bottle quickly.

Sororities' pressure to conform can also lead otherwise straight-arrow girls to experiment with drugs. In one house I visited, the "house dealer"—the daughter of a clergyman—provided her sisters with drugs including cocaine and the prescription drug Adderall, a form of speed. Shannon, the Delta Zeta from a West Coast school, confessed that one of the reasons her sorority was considered "the fun girls" was because they were heavy drug users. She remembers pressuring younger girls to smoke marijuana and to do mushrooms and acid. "It wasn't part of a formal event, but if a fraternity we were tight with had a party, most of the sorority would go upstairs and do bong hits with the guys. I really liked it and I thought it was cool. I was definitely guilty of encouraging the other girls to smoke," she said.

In a review of twelve hundred claims against fraternities between 1987 and 1995, an insurance company discovered that "alcohol was involved in 90% of all claims, whether they be falls from roofs, sexual abuse, or automobile accidents." National Greek organizations and universities, swayed in part by their increased liability, have considered alcoholism such a problem that many have taken strong measures to combat it. All sorority houses are now supposedly "dry houses," with alcohol banned from the premises. (Each of the girls I followed broke the dry house rule on numerous occasions.)

Fraternities and sororities at several schools agreed in the 1990s to ban alcohol from their parties. Many followed policies similar to those set by the University of Missouri in 1989: fraternities were required to hire off-duty police officers to check IDs, close the house bar at 1:30 A.M., limit each guest to one beer per trip to the bar, and participate with the sororities in a mandatory alcohol-education program. (Other schools also prohibited beer kegs and required a guest list registered with the university's Greek office to prevent open parties.) Violation of the policies resulted in a fine for the first offense and, for future offenses, the risk of losing university recognition as a chapter.

The catch? At Missouri, the policies were supposed to be enforced by "student members of the Greek Community Board." At many of the schools I visited, the role of the "Greek police" and the responsibility of enforcing strict antialcohol rules on the Greek community lay on the shoulders of the Greeks themselves. At one university in Virginia, I chatted with a sorority sister who had considered becoming an "AGC" or Assistant Greek Coordinator.

"Why would you want to be part of the Greek police?" I asked her.

"Because it's a paid job," she said. "You get paid to patrol all of the parties one night each weekend. I decided not to do it because I didn't want to lose a weekend night every week."

"Wouldn't your sisters dislike you for getting them in trouble?" I wondered.

"Oh, no," she laughed. "Everyone knows that an AGC tends to 'overlook' when her own sorority commits an offense."

From what I saw over the course of a year, it appears that these policies simply aren't working. While it is true that the sorority houses themselves were mostly party-free, that didn't stop girls like Vicki and her sisters from drinking alcohol in their rooms. The sisters who attended fraternity parties that followed the party registration rules brought their own extra thermoses of rum or vodka. When they found those parties too limiting, they drank (or pre-gamed) at off-campus satellite houses. And when, as happened during Beta Pi's Chug-Off, they were faced with the threat of answering to the Greek police, they simply drove away, still wildly inebriated.

Ω   Ω   Ω

Warming Up

NOVEMBER 16: GREEK OLYMPICS
AMY'S IM AWAY MESSAGE
let's go Alpha Rho and Delta Lambda!

IT WAS A CRISP SATURDAY AFTERNOON, AND A FEW GREEKS managed to tumble out of bed by twelve-thirty. Two sororities were warming up on the field in the middle of Sorority Row. Across the street, a group of fraternity boys stretched. Leftover jack-o'-lanterns carved with Greek letters, still sitting on the stoops of the sorority houses two and a half weeks after Halloween, had started to turn. Uniformed landscapers diligently pulled up the beds of summer annuals in front of the Alpha Rho house to plant pansies in their place. They muttered about how the sorority's last-minute request for the late planting would result in smaller flowers.

"Anyone who doesn't have a T-shirt, come get one now!" Greek Olympics were slated to start at one, but much of Alpha Rho wasn't moving. Amy and some of the other Alpha Rhos were growing anxious. Most of the sisters sat bleary-eyed in the dining room, trying to remember why they were eating breakfast so early in the day. Some were reluctantly responding to the sister with the cardboard box of bright yellow Homecoming shirts and matching bandannas.

"I look like a retard in this shirt," one girl grumbled. Amy checked her Gucci watch. "Y'all, everyone else is already heading over. Why aren't we moving?"

Charlotte, the Alpha Rho president, came downstairs in her pearls with an armload of posters. "Everybody take one!" The posters varied between the competitive ("We'll Raid Your Tomb"), the punned ("Cry for Mummy"), and the uninventive ("Pyramid Power"). Most of the girls chose double entendre signs that joked about rubbing a genie bottle.

"Now we have to come up with a fight song!" Charlotte tried to rouse the yawning crowd. A few girls tried chanting different permutations of "Alpha Rho, Delts," but the others, convinced they could come up with nothing clever, only leaned against the walls of the entry hall and attempted to wake up.

By 1 P.M., all of the girls were crowding into the entry hall—a swarm of yellow and ponytails. An excited sister pushed to the door and cleared her throat. "Come on, once before we go!" Then she made a sound that to the uninitiated could be described as a backward Doppler effect, and pumped her fist in a circle. The sisters joined in, building to a crescendo, and when the noise reached a feverish pitch, the house broke into the secret Alpha Rho rally cheer. Now fully awake and enthusiastic, they burst out of their house at once, cheering and laughing when one sister screamed, "Let's go kick some sorority *ass!*"

On their way out of the house, a few girls suddenly remembered that they had to compete alongside Delta Lambda. "I hate the Delts," one said. Another sister nodded emphatically; some sisters were boycotting several events that week to protest September's serenade fiasco. "Oh well"—she found a bright side—"at least I won't want to hook up with our team."

Amy and Caitlin reached the Row a few minutes ahead of the rest—and stopped short. A few Mu Zeta Nu brothers were standing at a car next to the field. "Oh no, it's Nathan!" Amy whispered. Caitlin spotted Amy's date rapist staring at them. "Why is he always wherever I want to go?"

A Beta Pi sister parked a Mercedes nearby and stumbled over to the MuNu brothers. "Look at me, I am the epitome of a drunk driver!" she cackled, swinging a large white plastic cup full of vodka as she hopped onto the trunk of the MuNu car and babbled. With Nathan distracted, Amy and Caitlin linked back up with the rest of their sorority.

As the teams arrived, the colorful field on the Row looked increasingly as if the Greeks were trying to put on a stadium show. Hundreds of sisters and brothers wore their assigned T-shirts and bandannas and huddled together—crimson with crimson, lavender with lavender. Rarely did the colors mix, except for an occasional bound across the field for a liplock. Many Greek couples had less time to spend together this week because their groups weren't matched for Greek Week; this was known to put a strain on relationships.

By the time the final team arrived, the field pulsated with energy (helped along by the Greeks' good friend Absolut). The groups yelled their cheers at each other, at themselves, at nobody in particular, and waved their signs in competitive fury. The judges, in head-to-toe khaki (an effort to be true neutrals), wove around the crowds, stopping to talk to friends. It was clear that no one was really in charge, even after the events started. The event lineup, consisting of water balloon tosses, Slip-'n'-Slide bowling, wheelbarrow races, tricycle races, and a Twinkie-eating contest, rendered the Olympics something of a drunken camp color war. The chants and cheers continued throughout the afternoon, getting louder whenever a judge stopped to count the posters the teams held up and to gauge a team's spirit. "Get your hands up! Here come the poster refs!" Alpha Rho and Beta Pi, both loud groups, stood next to each other and tried to outdo each other's several-minute-long screams of "Wooooo." Some of the Alpha Rho cheerleaders attempted to add kicky rhythm bits to the standard Alpha Rho cheer. The Delta Lambdas, not having practiced the cheers in the Alpha Rho house with the sisters, were busy shouting pretty much anything that came to mind, relevant or not, such as "Somebody grabbed my balls!" Members of one team raced around the entire inside of the circle yelling and waving their posters. Ten minutes later, not to be outdone, one lone representative of another team did the same, tripping drunkenly around the field as he galloped solo with his poster held high and his expression gleeful.

Amy milled around the yellow section, too short to see the Twinkie-eating contest over the Delts' heads. "Hey baby, what's your sign?" a Delt yelled and then belly-laughed, pointing to Amy's poster. Amy laughed demurely as he high-fived the surrounding brothers. The sisters who couldn't see the events looked at each other helplessly.

"Why are we here again?" one asked. The others shrugged. An Alpha Rho–Delta Lambda cheer began, and even the indifferent sisters yelled and clapped boisterously. When the cheer ended, their faces fell back into expressions of boredom. A few of the brothers in the back attempted to rap a few lines of Eminem's latest, getting the lyric order backward.

Snap back to reality, Oh there goes gravity . . .
His palms are sweaty, knees weak, arms are heavy,
There's vomit on his sweater already.

The girls nearby tuned in only to hear the last line and, not realizing the brothers were emulating Eminem, glared around disgustedly as if to avoid the dude who had puked on himself. It wouldn't have been a sight out of place here—except none of the brothers were wearing sweaters.

Priorities

NOVEMBER 19: GREEK WEEK SOCIALS
SABRINA'S IM AWAY MESSAGE
Wow.

ALPHA RHO'S SOCIAL CHAIR HAD WORKED HARD TO SET UP social events for Greek Week. All of the sororities participated, but each house had to commit a certain number of attendees by purchasing tickets. Tonight the social chair had enlisted several sisters to go clubbing in the city, but by the time the group had to leave, only four girls were gathered in the entry hall. She stormed upstairs to the Penthouse. "Come on, we're going to the club now!" The girls in the Penthouse looked at her blankly. Most of them were studying for midterms. At first the social chair tried yelling. When that didn't elicit a reaction, she tried to guilt-trip her sisters. "Why aren't you guys going?" She tried to look the girls in the eyes. "I put out a lot of money for tickets and only four sisters are going! You're not representing the house well." That pressured another girl to agree to go. Sabrina didn't budge. Not only was she scheduled to waitress tonight, but it was also the tail end of midterm season and a Tuesday night. Who went out on a Tuesday night? Sabrina understood that the social chair had fronted a sizeable sum of her chapter budget, but she hadn't actually asked the sisters if they wanted to go before signing up Alpha Rho for the event. The sisters had other priorities, too, and clubbing on a Tuesday night wasn't always at or near the top of the list.

Sabrina's computer dinged to let her know she had new mail. Professor Stone! Her heart raced. She abandoned midterm studying while she tried to decipher the meaning behind the e-mail:

"Sabrina, I would like to talk with you on Friday, so let's meet at 6:30. I have a few things that I want to speak with you about. Good things. Mike Stone." Sabrina wondered what "good things" meant. She hadn't turned in her paper rewrite yet, so he couldn't have been referring to that. Maybe he had heard of a job opening that he could help her with. But she didn't really think it was that, either.

Sorority Gigolo

NOVEMBER 20: FLOAT DECORATING
VICKI'S IM AWAY MESSAGE
too sick to care

VICKI DIDN'T MUCH CARE WHO WON GREEK WEEK, BUT SHE skipped her Wednesday classes to help the Beta Pis with the Float Decorating competition. The teams had a trailer and twelve hours to construct a float representing their theme. By noon, four hours into the competition, few of the teams had started; many of the Greeks were still in class or in bed. Vicki could see, however, that next door the Alpha Rhos had already erected on their trailer massive pyramids which some sisters were painting gold. An hour later, Sorority Row, packed with Greeks in their Greek Week tees and bandannas, echoed with the sounds of hammering, sawing, shrieking, and accompaniments blasting from various stereos. Vicki walked around the Row surveying the floats.

Two Beta Pi sisters in front of Vicki's house looked confused as they perused an instruction manual. "Umm, it says here we need a screwdriver?" pondered one. It would be a while before they built trees for their koalas. Vicki moved on. The England team worked diligently on a castle façade, Brazil constructed a rain forest, and Spain designed a bullfighting ring. The sorority and fraternity representing Holland were attempting to attach a line of pinwheels to a tall pole on their trailer. After an hour of work on precarious ladders to get the string fastened properly, a gust of wind blew the pinwheels to the ground.

"Ohhh myyy Gawwwd," a Holland sister groaned in an accent shared by most of her sisters.

"There goes that idea," said a fraternity brother on the ground. From the top of a ladder another brother muttered, "I quit."

Vicki passed the Iota house but she didn't go in to greet William. As much as Vicki liked him, she wasn't interested in having a boyfriend. She saw him every few days—usually to smoke marijuana in his room—and had taken him to the Beta Pi Date Party. But to make sure she didn't invest too much in him, she was also regularly spending time with Dan, the bronzed Theta Theta brother from Los Angeles. Vicki's closest sisters in Beta Pi were thrilled. They thought Dan was a nicer person than William, who had a reputation among the Greeks as a sorority gigolo—someone who cavorted with girls in several different sororities at once.

That afternoon, Vicki fell ill. She could do nothing all day but sleep and whisper on the phone to her friends in California. She had been sleeping for twelve hours straight when blond frizz poked through her bed curtain as Olivia slid her a tray with water, orange juice, and toast.

"Hi, I brought food. You have to eat," Olivia said. "And I brought a visitor!" Olivia pushed aside the curtain as Vicki blew her bangs out of her eyes to see Dan holding a bouquet of roses. Vicki brightened.

Later that night, when William stopped by with a care package, Vicki felt like royalty. But William had more on his mind than the chicken soup he offered her. "So just be my girlfriend already," he said, half smiling.

Vicki laughed, which led to banter that she later realized was half serious.

"Please, just be my girlfriend!" William begged, tickling her cheek with his goatee.

"No!"

"I'm going to call you that anyway."

"No!"

"Come home with me for Thanksgiving, then."

"No!"

Vicki didn't want her relationship with William to escalate into something serious, but her conscience was bothering her because neither he nor Dan knew about the other. The prospect of having a boyfriend again so soon scared Vicki. She now knew, however, that William wasn't interested in dating anyone else.

The next morning she called Dan and told him she couldn't see him so often anymore. "Um, I've started talking to my ex-boyfriend again, the one I broke up with in September?" she lied. "So you and I should probably take it easy for a while." Again, Vicki was struck by how graciously Dan handled her brush-off.

Two Faces of Talent

NOVEMBER 21: LIP SYNC
CAITLIN'S IM AWAY MESSAGE
Gyrating for the masses

THE GYM, SMELLING OF STALE COLOGNE AND FEET, WAS packed for Lip Sync. The Greeks were slightly more controlled now than during Greek Olympics, if only because they were assigned to certain sections of the bleachers (on which, inevitably, hung banners proclaiming their team's ultimate superiority). But again there were the chants, the poster waving, the spirit gauging, the yells and jeers ricocheting across the gym. Again the furtive meeting of warring colors—a brother in yellow, a pink-ribboned girl—that rendezvoused in the middle of the room for a quick kiss.

Most of the Greeks wore their T-shirts, except for the talent show participants, who were decked out in elaborate costumes sewn specifically for Lip Sync, including open kimonos revealing black lingerie; short, tight Dutch-girl dresses with platformed clogs; or practically nothing (that was Brazil). The Delt dancers were face-painted like King Tut, while the Alpha Rhos wore billowing pants, matching bikini tops, and veils below their eyes. The Beta Pis wore short, sexy skirts with kangaroo tails and the Kappa Tau Chis sported croc-hunter safari suits. Most of the girls wore an abundance of makeup, as if they expected theater lights. The gym resembled an R-rated version of "It's a Small World."

The twenty-one judges, again in khaki, chatting and waving at their friends, sat in folding chairs at a long wooden table in front of the stage, where they had the best view of the enormous constructed sets the teams had built. Some groups had consulted professional choreographers. Beta Pi had brought dry ice.

During each long stretch between dances, as students gave up trying to discern the emcee's unintelligible blather, the teams erupted into barely controlled pandemonium. Girls loudly sang along when a Britney Spears song came on the unsophisticated sound system. Brothers in the back of the gym played keep-away with another guy's skullcap. In the middle of the gym, a fat guy fell down. Although amid the chaos most of the Greeks didn't seem to notice, he nonetheless got back up again and immediately dove onto the hardwood floor, trying to make it look as if the first one had been on purpose, too. The teams did waves and practiced their dance moves, but mostly they screamed their dueling chants at each other from across the room, which caromed Greek-letter echoes off the walls.

Chris, his hands shoved into his jacket pockets, stood alone in the back of the gym, watching Caitlin interact in the bleachers, remove the T-shirt she wore over her bikini top, and then make her way to the stage with Amy and Sabrina. When Caitlin danced, her muscles rippling, Chris high-fived a neighbor. The routine went smoothly, to cheers from the audience and smiles from the judges. Caitlin met up with Chris and wrapped her arms around him. After a kiss, she playfully shoved him and he shoved back. They sat together on the floor in front of the Alpha Rho–Delta Lambda bleachers to watch the Beta Pis complete a similarly impressive dance routine.

. . .

LATER THAT NIGHT, THE BLACK GREEKS, WHO, AS ON many campuses across the country, did not participate in Greek Week, staged their own competition on the other side of campus: the university's annual "step show." At least two thousand spectators—not merely Greeks, as had been the case at Lip Sync—jammed the darkened auditorium and head-bobbed to the hip-hop music blasting from a high-end sound system as they waited for the show to begin. Neon spotlights danced across the faces in the crowd, illuminating a tiny smattering of whites among the black and Hispanic faces. The judges sat in semiformal clothes at an elegant table directly in front of the stage. There was an aura of respect about the crowd. Soon it wasn't difficult to understand why.

The step show was like a mix of dance and sport and something tribal, like Broadway's Stomp with fewer props and more emotional expression. Some of the acts were breathtaking. After the usual stomp-clap-and-chant opening, the sororities incorporated more perilous dance moves, tossing props by their heads. Their sounds were perfectly synchronized. Between acts, the sororities and fraternities in the audience "called" at each other. One fraternity made barking sounds. A sorority stood while sisters formed signs with their hands. A dozen or so fraternity brothers stood in a line and danced.

The crowd was already on their feet and applauding when the girls in the third step act, in time with the music, suddenly blindfolded themselves. The crowd gasped as the girls leapt over each other in stilettos, continuing to step as they sat on each other's laps and wove across the stage, unseeing. This was step at its finest and the crowd knew it. "No one can perform as good as this," an older woman in the audience whispered to another, who nodded emphatically.

Ω   Ω   Ω

The Meaning of Step Shows

STEPPING ORIGINATED IN THE MID-1900S AMONG BLACK sororities and fraternities as a way to express group identity and Greek loyalty. It is defined, according to dance historian Jacqui Malone, as "a complex multilayered dance genre [that] features synchronized, precise, sharp, and complex rhythmical body movements combined with singing, chanting, and verbal play. It requires creativity, wit, and a great deal of physical skill and coordination. The emphasis is always on style and originality, and the goal of each team is to command the audience with stylistic elements derived primarily from African-based performance traditions."

But neither that description nor mine can truly do the art form justice. Step is a performance of synchronicity and harmony that serves as a more striking display of group unity than perhaps any other Greek activity, black or white. It is marching, cheerleading, call-and-response, rap, tap dancing, martial arts, percussion, gymnastics, military drilling, singing, stomping, stamping, and slapping in one. When I attended the State U step show, I was awed by both the spirit and the talent—and that was before I learned about the meaning behind the sisters'—or, as black sororities refer to them, "sorors' "—intricate footwork.

Each of the four historically black national sororities has "signature" or "trade" steps that audiences are sophisticated enough to recognize, such as Alpha Kappa Alpha's "It's a Serious Matter" and Zeta Phi Beta's "Sweat." To distinguish the groups further, each sorority has a "sign," or hand signal, and a "call"—a verbal acknowledgment to indicate membership, whether during a step show or while walking across campus—often used to start and end steps (the audience also calls, to encourage the performers). Alpha Kappa Alpha's call is "skee-wee," Delta Sigma Theta's is "ooo-oop," Sigma Gamma Rho's is "ee-yip," and Zeta Phi Beta's is "ee-i-kee." (Black sororities also have a "stroll" or "partywalk," which is a choreographed series of dance steps that they perform in shows or fall into at casual parties.) During a step performance, a sorority will frequently include "salutes" or tributes to another sorority, or "cracks"—comical insults—by mimicking the other group's trade steps. Another type of step, called a "retrospect," tells the history of the sorority or the culture through dance.

Essentially, step shows are to black Greeks what Greek Week is to whites in terms of the immense amount of preparation and anticipation, the display of sorority spirit, and the crowning of a champion. But step is more than that: it is a form of solidarity and identity pride that lasts far beyond a performance. As one sister has explained, "The greatest feeling in the world is to meet a Soror that you've never met before from across the country, then you start singing, chanting, stepping, and partying together."

Ω   Ω   Ω

Connecting

NOVEMBER 22

SABRINA'S IM AWAY MESSAGE

Best night ever.

AFTER SABRINA FINISHED HER AFTERNOON SHIFT AT THE restaurant, Professor Stone picked her up in his Saab to take her to an out-of-the-way Starbucks rather than the one on campus. Sabrina, her heart pounding wildly, tried hard not to look at him. Good things, she thought to herself. He wants to talk about good things.

"I have a question for you," he said.

Sabrina, who hadn't had time to change out of her waitress uniform, daintily smoothed her green skirt and looked at him.

"What do you want in life?"

Sabrina pondered this. "Well, I would like a home and a job, to start with." She talked about wanting to escape poverty.

Professor Stone shook his head. "No, that's not quite what I meant."

Sabrina tried not to blush.

"I meant, what is it you want out of the relationships in your life?"

Wondering what the question implied, Sabrina thought her answer over carefully. "Well, I would like someone who is intelligent—that's really important."

"What else?" he urged.

"I guess I would like someone taller than me, even though that sounds silly." Professor Stone towered over her.

"What else?"

"Someone with ambition."

They parked at Starbucks, ordered coffee, and grabbed a table.

"And what else?" he urged again.

"All right," Sabrina exhaled. "I want someone who I can be myself with. I want to be able to be silly or mean or whatever I'm feeling at the moment and I wouldn't have to explain it and it wouldn't jeopardize the relationship. And I want someone who could support himself financially so I wouldn't have to do it for him."

Professor Stone nodded understandingly. He told her about how he was broke when he was in college, and that there were certain things a person had to be able to provide for himself. Sabrina grew bolder.

"So what else do you want?" she asked.

Professor Stone talked about other things he desired eventually out of life and out of his career.

"Yes, but," Sabrina swallowed, "what do you want in a relationship?"

Professor Stone looked into her eyes. "I want someone who is a good conversationalist," he began, and went on from there.

"Some friends of mine were at my place this weekend," he said, "and they noticed your photographs on my desk. They asked me what they were, so I showed them." Sabrina's mind whirled. She had left about a dozen photos for him. He had taken them home?

"I explained that I had asked you for a few photos. One of my friends was looking through them and commented, 'She didn't just give you a couple pictures—she gave you her whole life. She's beautiful!' " Sabrina's heart threatened to pulse out of her chest.

"Sabrina." Professor Stone cleared his throat. He grinned shyly and blushed. "You *are* beautiful." At the same time embarrassed and ecstatic, Sabrina alternated between listening to Professor Stone and to the voice in her head saying: "Sweet! Sweet victory is mine!" She finally knew for sure. She didn't say a word.

"I think a lot of you, Sabrina," Professor Stone continued. "It is really awkward teaching you because I don't see you just as my student. You mean a lot to me and you have taught me things." Sabrina subtly covered her mouth with her hand and let her braids fall forward so he wouldn't see that she was beaming. "I didn't think we would be having this conversation right now. I thought it could wait until after December twenty-third, when the term ends, but this just sort of happened. I noticed from the e-mails you sent me that there was a little something more to them than 'Will you look at my paper?' Am I right?"

"Yes, you are," Sabrina said.

"Okay, that's what I thought," said Professor Stone. "Well then, when I wrote that e-mail to you about talking about good things, this is what I meant." He didn't come right out and say, "Sabrina, I like you." But he made some gestures and shook his head emphatically as if to say, "You know what I mean so I don't have to actually say it, right?" Sabrina nodded, ecstatic.

"After the semester's over," he continued, "if this goes in the direction that I think it will, then I want to take you places over Winter Break and Summer Break. There are places we can see together, books we can read together . . . Once the semester is over, things will be able to take a natural course."

For the next few hours, they talked about their views of marriage, and about the first time they had had sex—Sabrina the year before, at nineteen, and Professor Stone, at eighteen, who spoke about losing his virginity much more graphically than Sabrina would have expected. Professor Stone never specifically said that they would have to be careful until the semester ended in a month, but Sabrina sensed it. He still had to grade her papers, and he said he was already having a difficult time with that.

"Thank heavens you are bright and doing very well in my class. If you weren't doing well, I'd have a very, very hard time grading your papers," he said. "So, what are you doing tomorrow afternoon?"

Sabrina couldn't think of anything she had to do. The Homecoming game didn't seem so important anymore.

"Good, I'll take you for coffee and you can meet my friends," he said. "And Sabrina? Please call me Mike."

When Sabrina got home late that night, she found an empty sitting room, shut the door, and called her mother, who was thrilled. Sabrina was so excited she was barely coherent. "I am the happiest, luckiest girl in the world!" she gushed—and Sabrina wasn't one to gush. She had hoped for this moment for more than a month, but she hadn't expected anything to happen because Professor Stone . . . Mike . . . was her teacher. She felt slightly strange, as if she were watching her date rather than experiencing it; this was like a scene from a movie—not something that actually would happen to her. She didn't mind the age difference, but she was shocked that she had found somebody she truly liked, respected, and appreciated when she was only twenty years old. She could already envision spending the rest of her life with him.

Sabrina made a note to make a gynecologist appointment the next day to talk about birth control options. She spent the rest of the night wondering what she was going to do about the Alpha Rho Formal. Clearly, she didn't want to go with anybody else.

And the Winner Is . . .

NOVEMBER 23: HOMECOMING GAME

AMY'S IM AWAY MESSAGE

sooo proud of my ALPHA RHOS!!!

BY THE TIME THE HOMECOMING GAME TAILGATES BEGAN AT noon, it was already eighty degrees and the parking lots were packed with thousands of students and alumni decked out in blue-and-white State U gear. Officials expected a sellout crowd. Old ladies wore blue-and-white shorts, babies sported blue-and-white tees, and middle-aged men cocked blue-and-white visors over their Wayfarers. Almost uniformly in denim cutoffs and tiny tanks, small packs of sorority girls milled around the various Homecoming booths, flashing their student IDs to get free frozen yogurt or blue-and-white flags. Local vendors set up sample stations, State U dining hall workers handed out small slices of pumpkin and apple pies, and Greek alums clustered around cars festooned with flags and roped with reunion banners. The Greeks had been tipped off to lie low because they heard the police planned to crack down on underage drinking at the game this year. Therefore, only the girls in what were generally considered the "dorkiest" sororities—the girls who wouldn't be drinking in daylight anyway—were wearing their letters.

Cheerleaders wove in and out of the booths, fixing their hair and chirping hellos. All of the sororities were represented on the squad—and most of the squad was represented in Amy's Tae Bo class. So she had heard the entire story about how Grace, the Alpha Rho treasurer and a cheerleader for two years, was told in the spring to drop out of the cheerleading squad because she was "too fat to be a cheerleader." She was a size 2.

At kickoff, Amy and her Big Sister were cheering in the Dome, wondering where the rest of the Greeks were. There weren't many of them in the stands. They hadn't set up their usual parking lot tailgates. What Amy and her Big Sister didn't know was that in the farthest corner of the most remote parking lot, in the woods beyond a set of off-campus buildings, in a small clearing, out of the earshot of alumni and out of the sight range of the police, there, singing and mingling around several kegs, were hundreds of Greeks.

By halftime, however, the Greeks had gathered in a room in the stadium for the Greek Ceremony. Amy and her Big Sister huddled together with the Alpha Rhos and listened intently to the announcer. The sisters whispered their predictions to each other. "We have to have placed in Lip Sync, and maybe Teamwork," said Amy's Big Sister. The girls around them agreed.

"We totally won Greek Week, y'all," Amy said.

"No we didn't," said another sister.

"Come on, girls, think positive!" Amy insisted.

"The Intra-Greek Athletic award goes to . . . ," the announcer started, "Beta Pi." Beta Pi erupted.

The announcer went down the list: Greek Olympics, Float Decorating, Teamwork. When he got to Lip Sync, Alpha Rho went silent.

"In Lip Sync, fourth place goes to . . . Sigma." Cheers from Sigma. The Alpha Rhos held their breaths. "Third place goes to . . . Alpha Rho." There were mixed reactions among the Alpha Rho sisters. Third place was fine, but the seniors had hoped to beat Beta Pi before they graduated; they believed this year's performance had far outdone that of their next-door neighbors.

Amy blamed the ranking on three of the judges. The judging committee could not socialize or compete with their respective chapters throughout the week. They were supposed to be unbiased. But these three judges, all Beta Pis, hated Alpha Rho. They had been close friends at the beginning of freshman year with Amy, Sabrina, and René, the girls' non-Greek friend. In the spring, the three judges joined Beta Pi while Amy and Sabrina chose Alpha Rho. The next year, when Caitlin and René rushed, they didn't even consider Beta Pi. Insulted, the judges now wouldn't speak to any of them and hated Alpha Rho as a whole.

The Alpha Rhos tallied up the placements while the announcer paused. Alpha Rho and Beta Pi had similar scores.

"I still think we won," Amy insisted.

The sisters looked skeptical.

"No, seriously. We had to place overall. Maybe we got fifth in the other events and we just don't know it."

"Third place overall . . . Epsilon!" The announcer tried to speak over the Epsilons' cheers.

"We're either first or second," Amy whispered in anticipation.

"Overall Greek Week Runner-up . . ." The Alpha Rhos fidgeted throughout the announcer's dramatic pause. "Beta Pi!"

"We won!" Amy shouted. The Alpha Rhos, screaming and stomping as they hugged each other tightly, nearly drowned out the announcer's confirmation that Alpha Rho and Delta Lambda had won Greek Week.

At the next chapter meeting, the president congratulated Caitlin and her co–Greek Week Chair on their hard work. It would be much easier to convince next semester's rushees to join Alpha Rho with the Greek Week trophy in the house's entry hall.

Whitney, the notoriously cranky senior, stood up. "I would just like to say that this week showed that you should never doubt the seniors," she said. Annoyed, the underclassmen looked up sharply. "Seriously," the sister continued, "in the future, trust that we seniors know what we're doing."

DECEMBER

The well-dressed sorority girl wears ironed or starched jeans, a jersey with Greek letters sewn on, a visor with Greek letters painted on, Greek jewelry, a headband, the most "in" sunglasses, a pearl necklace, expensive leather tennis shoes or penny loafers, and Lauren perfume. If it's after hours, she's donned her Lanz nightgown or a fraternity jersey and she's still wearing her pearls.

—*Rush: A Girl's Guide to Sorority Success*, 1985

Moral Conduct—Each member and pledge shall be responsible for her own moral conduct, realizing that her actions will reflect either credit or discredit upon her fraternity sisters. Behavior which brings discredit upon her fraternity sisters, the chapter or the national Fraternity may be cause for dismissal.

—*Pi Phi Forever*, the "Membership Manual" given to new members in the 1990s

Ω   Ω   Ω

DECEMBER 3
AMY'S IM AWAY MESSAGE
would've been better if all my girls were there

ONE AFTERNOON IN EARLY December, the Alpha Rhos learned that they were having a Date Dash, which meant they had four hours to find a date.

Caitlin called Chris. Amy wasn't sure whom to take. And no one had seen Sabrina in days.

As they got ready for Date Dash, Caitlin and Amy worried about Sabrina. "Okay, can I vent?" Caitlin asked, fastening an earring as she walked into the bathroom, where Amy was doing her makeup.

"Of course, sweetie."

"Sabrina's letting her professor influence her. She's changing her whole frickin' life because of him."

"I know it," Amy said. "She said she doesn't even want to go to medical school anymore. Now she wants to be a teacher like him."

"Everything's changing." Caitlin sounded sad.

Amy nodded as she powdered her already ivory nose. "Ever since I knew her, Sabrina wanted to be doctor."

"She spent the night with him last night," Caitlin said. "And she did more than kiss him. I asked her, 'Where were you last night?'

" 'In the city,' she said.

" 'Where in the city?' I said.

" 'His house.'

" 'Where in his house?' I go. 'Did you sleep on his couch?'

"She said, 'Yes, that's it,' and laughed." Caitlin sighed. "I'm going to have to be careful not to get too angry when I see her next."

"You're right," said Amy. "She'll blow you off and say, 'I'm happy.' "

Caitlin anxiously wrung her hands on her sweatpants. "It's not that he's so much older than she is. They're just at different points in their lives," she said. "And it's not that I don't get to see her because she wants to spend time with her man. I can definitely understand that. But she's changing her whole life around."

"I know. She's even been late to chapter meetings—and she didn't even come to tonight's," Amy said, and then her voice rose. "She told me that Alpha Rho is a *waste of time*. Why would she say that?"

"I don't know."

The other day, Amy told Caitlin, Amy and Sabrina had been shopping in a sunglasses store, where Amy had fingered a pair of purple-gold Guccis. She decided not to get them because she couldn't justify the $150 price tag.

"Why not?" Sabrina had asked. "You have the money."

"Honey, I'm not going to waste it," Amy replied.

"I'm sure your father will pay for them."

"No, he wouldn't. He only splurges to help me pay for dates," Amy had said, taking offense.

"She's never ever been like that before," Amy said to Caitlin. "And she's already listing the holiday gifts she wants to get her professor—two hundred dollars' worth of clothes that she can't afford."

Caitlin wearily rubbed her forehead. "Look, I'm not going to attack her. I'm going to hear her side," she said. "But it makes me question her. Because if she's being so sketchy, then is she really at the library tonight like she says, and that's why she's missing Date Dash, or is she hanging out with the professor? I have no reason to doubt her, but if she's going to be sketchy, like, 'I know what I'm doing, leave me alone,' then I wouldn't be surprised if she's not at the library."

"She swore off guys all semester," Amy groused. "She said, 'They're awful and I hate them.' "

Date Dash turned out to be a fairly typical Alpha Rho evening out. The sisters and their dates were carded on the way into the bar by a harried-looking bouncer who didn't bother looking at the IDs flashed in front of him as he slapped over-21 bracelets on at least a hundred wrists.

"I can't believe I got in!" one sister blurted a few steps beyond the checkpoint. "I'm only eighteen!"

Once in the room, which contained a bar, a dance floor, disco lights, a sushi station, and a few funky suede couches scattered in a neon-lit corner, everyone headed immediately to the bar, except for Grace, who knew she could dance, and Whitney, who thought she could. Other girls' dates leered over their drinks while the two gyrated together on the dance floor. Caitlin and Chris immediately found a loveseat in the darkest, most remote corner of the room, and collapsed on it. Amy and her date drank and mingled.

Amy and Chad, a low-key non-Greek senior, had hit it off and seen each other almost every day since Amy gave in and let her Big Sister set them up after Homecoming. But because Amy was determined not to ruin the progression of something that seemed to be working, she calculated that it would be too overwhelming to ask Chad to Date Dash. She planned to ask him to Formal and didn't want him to think she was coming on too strongly.

Not wanting to take a male friend, who might make Chad feel threatened, Amy had cautiously decided to take a girlfriend, figuring that at least she could drink, dance, and people-watch like the other sisters. Still, some of the sisters raised eyebrows at the pair of girls.

"Unbelievable," Whitney had said to Amy earlier when she glanced down the Date Dash Invitation List. "Some of the sisters are actually taking girls as their dates tonight. I mean, what's wrong with these girls that they can't find dates?! Some of the sisters are just bringing each other!"

Amy rolled her eyes. "Maybe people's boyfriends, or the guys they wanted to take, couldn't go on such short notice."

"But they had four whole hours to find somebody! There are sooo many guys at this school. Anyone who can't find a guy to go is retarded."

"What difference does it really make, Whitney, if they want to take girls?"

"Anyway," Whitney tossed her hair, "you obviously don't have to worry." She glanced at the name—Sam—next to Amy's. "At least you found a guy."

"Honey," Amy tried not to laugh, "Sam is a girl."

Whitney sniffed.

AMY AND SAM DANCED WITH THEIR FIRST AND SECOND drinks in hand, joining the half dozen or so girls—most in jeans and skimpy tops, some backless, a few in sundresses—who were on the dance floor already. The rest of the crowd was either eating sushi on the couches or shoved over on the side of the bar where the partygoers could watch the dancers and pretend to have deep conversations. It took half an hour (roughly three drinks) for the mass to shift from the bar to the dance floor. By eleven, dates were making out while freaking to a Christina Aguilera song and six girls had migrated to the DJ's platform, where they humped each other single file, one arm holding out a drink and the other grasping the girl in front of her. (Amy referred to this particular human configuration as "the booty train.") By midnight, Caitlin and Chris hadn't moved from the loveseat.

When the DJ played Missy Elliott, a girl came over to Caitlin to try to drag her to dance. "Come on, Caitlin, you love this song!"

"Maybe later," she replied. Chris sat expressionless, Caitlin on his lap.

By two, several of the sisters had passed out across the room, while Amy and Sam were still double-fisting Long Island Iced Teas on the dance floor, laughing about other sisters' dates. There was one date who had been to every Alpha Rho function Amy could remember—but with a different date each time. She referred to him privately as "the Alpha Rho manwhore." Amy and Sam laughed even harder about the sinfully unattractive fraternity brother who was Whitney's date.

Escaping

DECEMBER 3 (NIGHT)
SABRINA'S IM AWAY MESSAGE
out with mike

DECEMBER 4 (MORNING)
SABRINA'S IM AWAY MESSAGE
out with mike

DECEMBER 4 (NIGHT)
SABRINA'S IM AWAY MESSAGE
out with mike

SABRINA WASN'T AT THE LIBRARY.

The last week had been one of the best weeks of her life. The day after the Starbucks meeting, Sabrina was relieved that Mike showed a movie in class, so she didn't have to worry about looking at him. She was so determined not to be conspicuous that she didn't so much as sneak a glance at him through-out the entire class period. She didn't think the other students had noticed how often she had been meeting with Mike, but she didn't want to take any chances. (She had canceled plans to take Mike's class in the spring.) When they went out after class to talk in an off-campus diner, Mike gave her some pictures of himself that Sabrina had been staring at dreamily ever since.

The secret that Sabrina was keeping from everyone was that she had spent most nights this week at Mike's place. Because Amy and Caitlin didn't visit the Penthouse—Sabrina usually went to their rooms—they didn't realize she was missing at night. The girls in the Penthouse assumed she was working at the restaurant or studying at the library at night, and because she was an early riser, they also assumed she had left the house before them in the morning. It was a shame, Sabrina thought, that she had to hide her feelings and experiences from her sisters, who were supposed to be her support network. But she couldn't risk certain sisters discovering her secret. If they did, they could have her brought in front of the chapter's Disciplinary Board. Even worse, they could get Mike in trouble for dating a student. In Alpha Rho, dating an older man, let alone a professor, was considered taboo. But because so few Alpha Rhos had made the effort to get to know Sabrina, most of them would never guess her secret.

Sabrina relished going to Mike's as an escape from sorority life. At Mike's, an entirely separate, clandestine part of her life, she didn't have to worry about the daily dramas that beset the houseful of girls. And she could temporarily forget the barrier that sat unbudged between her and her sisters, the one that sharpened into focus at unexpected times, like when Amy had considered buying the Gucci sunglasses. Sabrina wasn't jealous of Amy or the other sisters, most of whom were ostentatious about their wealth while Amy was more subtle. But sometimes her sisters' inability to relate to her left her feeling isolated. Her sisters were largely spoiled girls who had had everything handed to them throughout their lives. They had no understanding of what it was like not to have food on the table or to anguish that their parents wouldn't be able to pay the rent.

Mike understood. He had been there, he had worked his way out of it, and already, he had told Sabrina he was in love with her. He had even given her a key to his apartment and cleared out some of his dresser drawers for her. (She guessed they weren't waiting until December 23 after all.) Sabrina was elated but overwhelmed as she tried to digest how her first—and, she hoped, only—adult romance had progressed so quickly. She supposed she could slow it down if she wanted to, but she wasn't sure what she wanted, or how to balance this relationship with the rest of her life. A few times she had already backed out on plans with sisters, even Caitlin, because she didn't want to leave Mike's apartment. It wasn't that sorority activities suddenly seemed juvenile now that she was dating a thirty-six-year-old. She wouldn't have minded going to Date Dash or to Formal, which was in a couple of weeks. But she was upset that she couldn't go with the date she wanted to take. Sabrina had briefly considered asking Mike to Formal. None of the other sisters knew who he was, and he had such a youthful look that he could pass for a grad student or one of her older friends from home. But she could only imagine the kinds of questions the sisters would throw at her about this new face. Mike told her to take someone else, but Sabrina had no interest. It was, however, getting increasingly difficult to hide from her sisters the real reason she didn't have a Formal date set up by now. Maybe she would take Beth. Or maybe she wouldn't go at all.

Keeping in Line

DECEMBER 5
VICKI'S IM AWAY MESSAGE
will someone please get me out of here?

VICKI'S ROOMMATE SITUATION WAS GETTING WORSE, THOUGH she didn't believe it could be possible. For instance, Morgan's "eccentricities," as Vicki politely referred to them, were becoming increasingly aggravating.

Morgan, who considered herself to be even more drop-dead gorgeous than she actually was, tended to flaunt her Barbie looks. When she walked into a bar, she sashayed in as if she were the most beautiful creature ever to enter the room. After a night at the bar a couple of weeks before Formal, one of Morgan's male friends sent her an IM to that effect.

"u r the hottest girl ever," he wrote. "damn ur a babe."

Morgan told Vicki about the message. "Vicki, I'm thinking about putting that in my IM away message, what do you think?"

"Um, sure, why not," Vicki answered. "I've done stuff like that." When one of Vicki's friends IMed her that she was "a total cutie," she had proudly posted it at the bottom of her IM away message for a day.

"Yes, but this is different from yours," Morgan insisted. "It's cute when you do it, but guys know I know how attractive I am."

Morgan frequently hinted that certain other sisters' looks weren't up to the Beta Pi par. Once Morgan picked up a miniskirt from the floor of the gentleman's parlor, examined it, and scowled.

"Laura-Ann, is this yours?" Morgan asked, holding up the skirt.

"Nope."

Morgan looked perplexed. "But it's a *medium!*" she said, as if Laura-Ann was the only sister who could possibly require a medium. Vicki made a mental note not to leave out the size-large sweatpants she had just bought.

While the younger members of the house looked up to Morgan and had elected her Alumnae Liaison, the older girls whispered about how they disliked her. They didn't appreciate her tendency to talk about herself and her male prospects in the television room for twenty minutes straight. They didn't like the way she used her position as a chapter officer to encourage the house to set up pre-games only with fraternities that had a brother she wanted to date. Vicki and Olivia agreed with the older girls. Because Morgan had several moles ("beauty marks," Morgan called them) on her ultrathin body, Vicki and Olivia privately referred to Morgan as "Spotty."

But Vicki didn't have enough energy to dwell on Morgan's appearance obsession because it was becoming even more unbearable to live with Laura-Ann. Laura-Ann was regularly leaving cigarette butts on the floor near Vicki's bed. She and Olivia confronted Laura-Ann about the cigarettes because the girls had a "No Smoking in the Room Except in Emergencies" policy.

"Oh my God, Laura-Ann, clean those up," Olivia said.

"They're not mine."

"Well, I don't smoke cigarettes," Vicki said, "so they're not mine."

"And Morgan and I don't smoke that brand," Olivia said, "so they're not ours."

Laura-Ann walked out in a huff.

The last straw came a few nights before Winter Formal, when Vicki was seeking advice from a friend from home about William, who would be her Formal date, though her interest in him was flagging. Olivia and Morgan were in bed, and Laura-Ann was puttering around the room, so Vicki went into a sitting room down the hall. She was five minutes into her call when she heard a rustling noise outside the door. She opened the door just enough to spot Laura-Ann crouched on the floor of the hallway, her ear pressed up against a vent.

The Beta Pis had discovered earlier that week that they could hear each other's conversations through the vents. One of the sophomores had been alone on the phone in her room when she mentioned one of William's attractive Iota brothers. That night in the kitchen, a junior repeated the conversation, word for word, as she made fun of the girl to the other sisters.

"She said she wanted to 'tap that ass!'" the sister howled. "I heard it through the vent!" Since then, the vents had become popular gathering spots. But because few of the girls in the house were awake at this hour, it was clear to Vicki that Laura-Ann was specifically trying to listen in on her conversation.

Sure enough, a few minutes later, Laura-Ann barged into the sitting room, interrupting Vicki, who was still on the phone. "I heard you curse and talk about staying over and smoking pot at a fraternity house."

Vicki looked at her in disbelief. "So?"

"So you're not representing Beta Pi the right way." Laura-Ann sat down directly in front of Vicki and stared at her.

"Uh-huh," Vicki said dryly. "Can you give me five minutes and I'll come talk about it with you?"

"Okay." Laura-Ann didn't move. She stared at Vicki, who was attempting to resume her conversation. Vicki was incredulous.

"Can you *move?*" Vicki yelled.

"Fine," Laura-Ann snapped, and left.

Vicki exploded. She sprinted down the stairs into the backyard, screaming and cursing into her cell. "I fucking hate her!" she vented to her friend. "She's a freak!" Vicki hated the way her roommates were changing her personality. Formerly mellow, Vicki now felt constantly wound up. If Laura-Ann was in the room—or even in the house—Vicki's mood soured. To try to console her, Olivia suggested they rearrange the room. When Laura-Ann and Morgan left for class the next day, Vicki and Olivia moved the furniture to separate themselves as far from Laura-Ann and Morgan as possible.

Ω   Ω   Ω

The Values of Nationals

AT FIRST I FOUND IT CURIOUS THAT WHITNEY WOULD CARE if her sisters brought girls as dates to sorority functions, that Sabrina would worry about her sisters' perception of her relationship with the professor, and that Laura-Ann would try to hold Vicki accountable to sorority standards. But gradually I learned that when a sister belongs to sorority letters, everything she says and does is perceived as reflecting back onto those letters. There is an image to maintain, and certain values and standards are expected to accompany it. As much as sisters may try to argue that their membership is diverse, their mentality laid back, and their members just "normal" students, they cannot circumvent the fact that belonging to a chapter of a national sorority inherently signifies fitting into a certain mold. They often assess themselves regarding how they measure up, and when the mold doesn't quite fit, sorority sisters can feel contrite or secretive as they tiptoe around its edges. At State U, Amy fit the Alpha Rho mold so confidently that she felt secure enough to snub it slightly by taking a girl as a date. Vicki was gradually learning to fit into the mold and was adjusting her lifestyle and demeanor accordingly. Sabrina so resented the mold that she began to defy it—and, unbeknownst to Amy and Caitlin, was considering dropping out of the sorority entirely.

To get a better sense of the source of the values and standards that compose such a mold, I attended the Northeast Greek Leadership Association Conference, an annual three-day program of workshops and lectures for hundreds of sorority and fraternity officers in the Northeast region. For the 2003 Conference, held at the Pittsburgh Hilton, the NGLA was trying something new: a "Values Institute" designed to honor, uphold, and impart the "four pillars" of Greek life: Leadership, Scholarship, Service, and Friendship for Life.

The keynote speaker, discussing Greek values and standards, began by telling his ballroom audience that "being Greek is a privilege." Then he asked the fraternity members to volunteer stereotypes of sorority sisters.

After several beats of silence, one brother offered, "Dumb."

"Yes!" the speaker shouted, trying to rile the crowd. "They're ditzy! Sluts! Sorostitutes and fraterniture!"

The brothers laughed loudly.

"Stuck up!"

"Yes!" the speaker pumped a fist. "Snotty bitches!"

Hands shot up around the room.

"Dramatic!"

"High maintenance!"

"On drugs!"

"Lushes!"

The speaker had worked himself into a frenzy egging the brothers on. "And whose alcohol do they drink?"

Practically in unison, hundreds of fraternity brothers yelled, "Ours!"

The room buzzed with laughter and chatter. Even the sorority girls—most in slim, tailored button-down shirts and skinny cigarette pants, or white pants and white sweaters, or winter shirts lined with collars of fake fur, flipping their freshly blown-out and flatironed hair—placed their designer purses on their laps and clapped.

The speaker waited until the ruckus died down before asking, "Why do we laugh?" When one brother responded, the speaker, his voice now close to a whisper, somberly repeated his answer as he scanned the sisters in the audience, who nodded as if they recognized themselves or their sisters in the descriptions. "Because some of them are true," the speaker said. "Because some of them are true."

Certainly, some of the stereotypes are true. Snobbery: Alpha Rho and Beta Pi, neither of which was considered a particularly snobby or dramatic house on campus, nonetheless had both snobs and dramatic moments. Promiscuity: Sabrina, Amy, Caitlin, and Vicki had few qualms about practicing casual sex as a means of getting to know someone. Flakiness: Laura-Ann and Bitsy, for example, didn't come across as the brightest pearls on the necklace. Wealth: Sabrina, who inadvertently revealed her frustration with her sorority sisters' wealth when she harped on Amy for considering Gucci sunglasses, regarded many of her sisters as ridiculously high maintenance; and they were far more affluent than the average college student. Drugs: When I chose the four girls to follow, I didn't know at the time that three of them smoked marijuana regularly. I could have guessed, however, that all of them would drink alcohol before and during nearly every social event they attended, but I would have guessed so not because they were sorority girls, but because they were college students. Looks: Morgan, thin and pretty, prioritized her beauty above all else and rebuffed the girls who, in her opinion, weren't on par aesthetically. And sorority-centered: Amy and Caitlin were miffed that Sabrina's relationship severely curtailed her devotion to Alpha Rho, which sisters expected her to prioritize.

All four girls believed their sororities were more moderate and more "normal" than other sororities and therefore defied the stereotypes. After a year of visiting sororities, I would agree that they had a less rigid image than many other groups across the country. But that didn't mean the stereotypes were irrelevant. As she distanced herself from Alpha Rho in the middle of the year, Sabrina pointed this out to me. "I'm not one to believe in stereotypes," she said, "but the stereotype of a sorority girl has to come from somewhere, and in Alpha Rho I'm starting to see where."

These were also some of the stereotypes portrayed on the MTV show *Sorority Life*, which had so incensed Greek communities across the country and caused Nationals to bar all sisters from talking to the media. I could understand that sororities were upset that MTV didn't paint a thorough picture of sorority life, choosing instead to focus on the stereotypes rather than on the "four pillars" (which undeniably would have made for less interesting television). But as far as I could tell, the "worst" things MTV's original *Sorority Life* girls did that could possibly raise Nationals' ire were to drink, catfight, and dance sexily with each other. Not only did these actions hardly seem scandalous, particularly because some of the girls were at least twenty-one, but also they are commonplace among sisters. (I have now seen that all-girl "booty train," of various lengths, at many a sorority function.)

It is perplexing, then, whether the Nationals' sorority media blackout is because Greek officials believe that the media depicts sororities untruthfully or because they believe that it exposes too much of the truth. One sorority official, decrying the media's coverage of sororities as "biased," even went so far as to warn an entire campus Panhellenic Council about me merely for writing on the topic. A professor at this school had kindly gone out of her way to tell some of her students about this book so that sorority sisters interested in contributing to my research could contact me. At least one girl tried to help me before her efforts were clamped down by the officers of her sorority. Subsequently, the campus Panhellenic adviser sent a note to the professor that included:

> *We have serious concerns about our women giving interviews for [Ms. Robbins']*
> *book and I would appreciate if you would contact me before contacting any more*
> *sorority women. The entire issue was brought up to our Panhellenic Council last eve-*
> *ning and the women know to be aware of being contacted. We would like to do what*
> *we can to protect our women and our Greek community.*

Angrily, the professor wrote back to the adviser that because the students involved "are free, rational adults, capable of deciding for themselves whether or not to speak to the press, there seems to me no reason to go through any intermediaries . . . While I understand and appreciate your concern for the Greek women of [this university], I believe my students to be intelligent, mature, and capable of self-determination, and therefore will continue to deal directly with them on all matters that concern them."

I was curious about sorority officials' vehement reaction to the media and their adamant insistence that the media is something against which the officials have to "protect our women" (our being an interesting choice of proprietary pronoun that perhaps would lead to too academic a discussion here). Thus I thought it might be amusing, as a member of the media myself, to sit in on a lecture at the NGLA Conference entitled "The Greek PR War Room." Confidently blending in (I thought) among several dozen sorority and fraternity members, I listened warily as the presenter began with, "Pay close attention and you may be able to wag the dog in your Greek community.

"There is bias in the media," he continued. "It's our general perception that journalists don't like Greeks. They don't give us enough credit."

Between the presenter's slides and his surly side comments, it occurred to me that his statement could be flipped: the alleged bias goes both ways. "Journalists are held to a professional code of ethics that requires them to be compassionate [and] respectful . . . (This is not always the case.)" read one of his slides. Another stated, "Journalists view themselves as public advocates (even when this may not be the case). This explains their desire to 'expose' organizations and individuals to the general public." While the students gazed at the projector screen, the presenter admonished, "They especially like secret organizations . . . Keep that in mind. They could be trying to expose you."

He went on to suggest ways that Greeks could improve their public image: pinpoint unfriendly journalists to "figure out how their mind works and read their past articles"; install a chapter public relations officer with the power to change chapter behavior; contribute to college newspapers by writing a Panhellenic column or letters to the editor; plant allies in the press by "bringing journalists into your organization"; create a Greek community newsletter; frequently circulate news releases to campus media relations officers; co-sponsor events; poll public opinion on Greek life; and, the suggestion that particularly raised my eyebrow, "Watch *Wag the Dog*."

"One death," the presenter explained, "takes ten thousand hours of community service to make up for the public relations aspect."

This slightly quieted the crowd, who had chosen this session not for suggestions on how to contribute to college publications but, rather, for lessons on damage control. A girl with delicate features from a Boston school raised her hand. "Two undercover reporters came into our formal recruitment. How do I handle that?"

The presenter's face contorted with anger. "If they're going undercover, that's unethical, that's attacking. Send a note to the society of professional journalists and expose their unethical behavior," the presenter fumed, his hand gestures bordering on wild. "That's ugly! That's not PR. That's ugly journalism! They shouldn't be doing that. It's like not having a search warrant. You don't fool people like that. Don't let a journalist fool you. If they do fool you, they are wrong."

Feeling slightly guilty as something of an undercover reporter in the middle of the room listening intently to a harangue against undercover reporters, I wondered what choice writers like me had, when faced with the national organizations' media blackout. I didn't have sinister intentions, didn't plan to write a book sensationalizing negative aspects of sororities; as I explicitly told national officials, my goal was to provide a truthful, balanced look at real sorority life. But as official after official countered, my intentions didn't matter. Reporters—all reporters—are threats. To sororities, the media is the enemy because there's a chance it might present the wrong "image." As the "Greek PR War Room" presenter said with disgust, "We do community service and they don't cover it. One person falls out of a window and every paper in town is there."

Well, sure. When in October 1998 Courtney Cantor, a Chi Omega pledge at the University of Michigan, plummeted through a window to her death following a Greek activity involving alcohol, that was news. When the Tri-Delts flipped pancakes for charity, that was not news. Frankly, with all of the focus on community service at the NGLA Conference, I was surprised to discover that in white sororities, service is much less a part of the organizations than Greeks would have outsiders believe. Moreover, the PR presenter implied that the point of community service was not to benefit the community but to balance public relations for the Greeks.

"The Values Institute," held on the second day of the conference, was comprised of a series of plenary and breakout sessions on the four pillars. I was assigned to a group of about twenty-five mostly white Greeks attending sessions run by two adult moderators: one a national officer of a sorority and the other the incoming president of an organization governing national fraternities. Throughout the day, the moderators led discussions and activities designed to inspire the student leaders to return to their chapters ready to instill and improve the proper Greek values.

During the session on service, the group discussed the differences between philanthropy (donating money) and service (spending time and energy). "White groups do more philanthropy, cultural groups do more service," one of the moderators explained. This statement was borne out by the responses when the moderators asked how often the participants' chapters did some form of community service. "Once a semester," mumbled a few people. "When we have a Panhellenic event," others agreed. One of two Latinos—the only nonwhites in the group—looked around the room in surprise. "We do it every single week. It's so important to us. It's a big part of our brotherhood," he said, as the Latina sorority sister nodded emphatically in agreement. The other participants seemed sheepish, though they offered some creative ideas. One white sorority sister later mentioned that her group had started a Girl Scout troop—an idea that was voted the top idea of the session.

The white Greeks were much more vocal during the conversations about the other three pillars. They had plenty of recommendations for how to improve the average GPA of their chapters, one of the official measuring sticks of a sorority's success in the eyes of its Nationals. Another session began, "What values are important in the Greek community?" The group came up with this list, which one moderator scrawled on a large sheet of paper with a Magic Marker: safety, trust, support, loyalty, personal and professional growth, unity, pride, ritual (the moderator refused to write down "ritual," explaining, "That's how we practice the integrity of our organization," and added "justice" instead), commitment, respect, service, responsibility, learning, excellence, and honesty.

The session on "Friends for Life" began innocuously enough, until the moderators wanted to discuss the differences between friendships inside and outside the Greek world. A brother who desperately wanted to discuss hazing—who had, in fact, asked at an earlier session, "Why isn't there a discussion about parties?"—answered, with support from other brothers, "Pledging—the fact that we've been through that together." Some of the other students tried to shift the topic. "With Greek life there are opportunities to expand on those friendships outside of and beyond school, through the sisterhood," one girl said. "People don't pledge organizations. People pledge people," said another. But the rest of the session turned into a heated debate over whether Greeks should be allowed to haze.

Overall, the lectures and sessions of the NGLA Conference did come across as inspiring. Along with stoking the pride of being Greek (in some cases, a pride that involved a sense of superiority over non-Greeks), many of the conference leaders offered genuine intentions and noble purposes. The theme of the conference, "Values-Driven Leadership: Back to Basics," encouraged participants to strive to emphasize the principles on which Greek-lettered groups had been founded in the nineteenth and twentieth centuries. But as an officer of a New England sorority pointed out to me during a break, "For every one of us here, there are at least fifteen girls back at the chapter who just don't get it. Those are people in my chapter I'd call my friends but not my sisters. This is preaching to the choir," which could explain why, by the last breakout session, more than a quarter of the participants in my group had disappeared.

During the breakout sessions, I wondered whether the stereotypes and the values of sororities were mutually exclusive. Here were the college chapter officers of sororities across the region from Maryland to Maine—student leaders chosen to attend this conference because of their commitment to developing within their chapters the proper values, as dictated by their national organizations, or perhaps because these individuals already adhered to the correct standards. And yet, these girls clearly exhibited many of the sorority stereotypes, such as conformism: girls from the same chapters often looked alike, with nearly identical clothes and similar hair colors and cuts (usually long and straightened); and being overly image-conscious: when I asked one sorority sister about the prevalence of eating disorders, she responded, "They're even here, this weekend. Everyone is watching what everyone else is eating and is trying to eat the same amount or less because none of the girls want to be the heaviest eater at the table."

But perhaps the most telling moment occurred in the first few minutes of the first breakout session, during an icebreaker activity. The moderators asked increasingly inclusive questions: "If you have a biological sister, stand up." "If you have brown eyes, stand up." And at the end, as they smilingly tried to rouse enthusiasm, "If you're proud to be Greek, stand up!" (Yes, self-consciously, I stood up with the rest of the room.) And finally, a joke intended to get the audience back into their seats and ready to begin discussions, "If you think MTV's *Sorority Life* is an accurate portrayal, stand up." To the moderators' surprise, two sisters stood.

There seem to be two sets of warring imagery at play. One is the image of the stereotypical sorority girl, embodying many of the traits attributed to them by outsiders; the other is the image of a different kind of stereotypical sorority girl, prude and proper, "wearing her pearls," a 1950s throwback that Nationals seemed to hope would soon displace the former image. Two sisters of different sororities at a midwestern school told me that their Nationals were working feverishly to change the composition of their chapters. "I picked this chapter because it's extremely diverse," said the Delta Zeta. "Now they're trying to tell us how we should be: we're supposed to conform to one mold."

Her friend chimed in, nodding furiously. "Nationals have a picture of what their ideal Tri-Delt is. But the personality of the house on the campus is why I chose it. The reason I went Tri-Delt is because the girls were personable, outgoing, and diverse. Nationals don't know how the girls are in the house, but they have their own mold. They don't want the Tri-Delts to be crazy and fun. But that's why I joined."

I asked the Delta Zeta to describe the mold. "Very old school, how it used to be when they were in sororities. Perfect, typical women."

The Tri-Delt broke in again: "Polite, definitely passive, reserved. They can't handle women with outgoing, strong personalities. Nationals are like PR—they look for groups of women who will represent the house. It doesn't matter if they're fake or real."

"The image they want us to have," said the DZ, "is a girl who's proper, prim, doesn't cuss, drink, smoke, have sex. Nationals just wants to look good! But we just want to recruit people we can live with."

"You know that commercial for MTV's *Sorority Life 2*?" asked the Tri-Delt. The commercial showed a wealthy, conservative-looking southern woman with an exaggerated drawl and teased, "done" helmet hair, extolling the virtues of her sorority and sincere sisterhood while fiddling with her pearls. "Yeah, that's what our Nationals is really like."

In her book *Torn Togas*, Esther Wright described how Nationals forced her chapter to kick out certain pledges. The sorority's national adviser arrived at the chapter to encourage the sisters to vote two pledges out of the group. "Ladies, I cannot stress just how important it is for you to let this girl go," the adviser said. "I know these girls are your sisters and friends, but if they are still in our sorority next semester, Nationals will probably not allow you to have all five of your exchange parties. You really have no other choice." The girls voted to drop the pledges.

Ultimately, Nationals seems to be trying to expand the scope of its control beyond sorority houses and into individual identity. These desperate-seeming reactions from sorority officials made me realize that being "pledged" to a sorority had a much deeper meaning than merely committing one's self to her newfound sisters. A sorority girl isn't just pledged to a house; she must also be pledged to the group of older women in the national office who control the sorority's activities and recruitment and watch over the house as the Big Brother—or Big Sister—of the sisterhood. Commitment to a sorority doesn't just obligate a member to socialize with a specific group of girls—it imposes on her a set of rules, regulations, and codes that in many cases are intended to supersede even those of her school and her family. (Indeed, many girls told me, as did a sorority sister from Bucknell, "If Nationals says no and Bucknell says yes, the university rules are superseded by Nationals'.") The danger of sororities, it became clear, is that instead of enhancing a girl's identity as she shifts from her formative years toward adulthood, the sisterhood could have a tendency to swallow that identity altogether.

At the first session of the NGLA Values Institute, a general session during which participants were supposed to discuss the four pillars with other students from their campus, I sat in front of a group of national representatives in their thirties through fifties, expecting to hear them expound on the values associated with the pillars, guided by their NGLA workbooks. Instead, the advisers were discussing thongs. "I could not *believe* what those girls were wearing when they were supposed to be wearing 'badge attire,'" said one, her nose in the air. "They were in tank tops and denim skirts with the badge *on the strap* of their tank tops!" The other women shook their heads and clucked knowingly. "I told them, 'If you can slide the badge up and down, that is *not* badge attire.'"

Another woman chimed in. "I keep telling the girls to buy beige thongs," she said. "Tan bodies, white thong, white dress—I can see it!" I wondered how sorority sisters managed to live in an environment in which they were constantly being judged by these women and their minions. "It's frustrating because when you're in the house you're under a looking glass at all times," Brooke told me later. "You're always getting judged. The only way I could get out of it was to go to my boyfriend's house, where I could be myself."

Sorority girls are often caught between having to conform to two different sets of standards: the unwritten codes of trends and styles within a house, and the standards that Nationals insist they are supposed to represent. Lissa, a western sorority sister, described a story that illustrates the consequences that can result when these two value sets collide.

"Even once you're in a sorority, it continues to be about your image, about maintaining a good stereotype," Lissa said. "We're a very respectable house on campus. So much goes into public relations, parties. We're the [Betas], so that means we're classy but we know how to party. We're smart but we're not nerds. We're wealthy and well dressed, but we're not snobs like the Kappas and we don't have perfect bodies and eating disorders like the Thetas and Pi Phis. The others are mostly smokers who have big parties. They're less like Daddy's perfect little girl."

"Is that what your sorority is?" I asked.

Lissa sighed. "Yeah. We try to fight against that image by partying. They tell the sophomores during rush, 'Don't talk about grades or that the house has the best GPA. Tell them we don't care what your GPA is.' The national office exerts control because they want [Beta] to be a good name everywhere. If Nationals weren't as involved, our experience would be less about stuff prescribed in the book, and image."

One year at a pre-game, one of Lissa's sisters collapsed after someone slipped a drug into her drink. When her sisters found her, they dragged her to another sorority house, dropped her, unconscious, on the stoop, rang the doorbell, and ran away. She was taken to the hospital to have her stomach pumped.

The chapter's behavior was akin to the cover-ups that some officials say occur when a university learns about a rape at a fraternity party. "Generally, what happens [is] the image of the university takes precedence over the well-being of the individual, and a cover-up ensues immediately," Claire Walsh, a former university official who now runs a rape-prevention program, told Stone Phillips of *Dateline* NBC. "I have been told of instances where the victim is convinced not to report, where she is blamed for what has happened to her, which of course is very devastating to the victim."

The next day, when the girl who had been drugged returned to the house, the chapter president called her in to see her. "This didn't happen," the president insisted. "You aren't allowed to tell anyone and you can't press charges."

"The president said this because she didn't want to get in trouble with Nationals," Lissa explained. "She didn't want anyone to know it was a [Beta]. One of the national rules, though we don't enforce it, is that you're not allowed to pre-game." The president was petrified that Nationals would find out that their chapter didn't measure up to the national image. "My sister was just floored," Lissa said. "She couldn't believe she had been treated this way. She had something totally traumatic happen to her and she was like, 'You don't even care about *me*?'"

Ω   Ω   Ω

The Fight

DECEMBER 7

CAITLIN'S IM AWAY MESSAGE

"To err is human, but to forgive, divine."

CHRIS WAS WALKING CAITLIN HOME FROM A PARTY WHEN they got into what began as a petty argument over whether Caitlin's lacrosse coach was playing favorites.

"You don't believe me?"

"No, Chris, I don't believe you." Caitlin teased him with a self-satisfied smirk, thinking they were just playing around.

Chris stomped onto the stoop of the Alpha Rho house. "You don't believe me?" Caitlin suddenly realized that Chris was angry—and drunker than she had thought.

"Chris, what just happened? I didn't do anything wrong. I—I'm sorry." She tread cautiously.

"You don't trust me?" He was yelling at her now.

"Whoa, why are you yelling at me—because you don't think I believe you?" Caitlin hoarsely raised her voice back at her boyfriend. "I said I was sorry." Chris, she could see, was furious. "I'm not doing this. Fuck you," Caitlin said, and went inside alone, still wearing Chris's jacket and forgetting that Chris had a set of her keys.

Within minutes, Chris called her room, still yelling. Caitlin hung up on him. He called again. She unplugged the phone. Using Caitlin's keys, Chris stormed into her room, fuming about how Caitlin didn't trust him.

"Damn it, Chris, listen to yourself!" He didn't usually get this drunk.

Chris threw Caitlin's keys at her, hitting her hard in the leg. "I want my fucking jacket!"

Caitlin, almost laughing at his belligerence, tossed his jacket into the empty hallway. Immediately Chris was up against her, pushing her into the wall, his elbow at her throat. "Chris?" She tried to stay calm, but he was hurting her. "You're drunk and nothing is getting accomplished by this. Just leave."

He let go of her neck and said in a low voice, "I want my hundred dollars back."

Caitlin had borrowed the money from him a few days before. "I only have eighty-two," she said.

"I want the rest."

"I don't have the rest."

"Well, find it!" Chris shouted.

"Whoa, Chris, I can't believe this got as far as it did," Caitlin said. "You say I blow things out of proportion? Look at where this has gone. You refused to listen to me. Just leave."

He wouldn't leave.

"If you don't leave," Caitlin said, her narrow eyes icy, "I'll call someone who will make you leave." Crying, she started to dial the House Mom. Chris came running to grab the phone from her, stepping on her foot on the way. She jabbed him with her elbow but he kept coming at her. She clocked him on the head with her lacrosse stick.

"Get out of here!" she shouted. Chris seized her wrists and tackled her onto the bed, pinning down her arms. "Get off of me!" Caitlin cried out. "Get out of here!"

Grace, who lived next door, was awakened by the noise and came rushing into Caitlin's room. "Get off of her!" Grace looked terrified. "Get out of here! You have no right to be here!"

Chris, easing up on Caitlin, looked from girl to girl. "You didn't see her hit me, did you? She hit me first."

Caitlin sat folded on the bed, crying as Grace shut the door behind him. Chris banged on the door, this time speaking more evenly. "I just want to talk. I just want to talk to you." The girls didn't move. He addressed Grace. "You have no idea what you're getting yourself into."

"Nobody's letting you in," Grace said. "Go away." She called the House Mom, who called the police.

It was three in the morning, but it was balmy enough for the girls and the House Mom to meet the police outside so the sisters wouldn't wake up. Caitlin didn't rouse Amy; she didn't want her to be involved in this situation. It was bad enough, in her opinion, that Grace had barged her way into the room and blown the argument out of proportion. She decided not to call

Sabrina, either, who was probably out with the professor. Caitlin was wary of the "weird adult effect" the professor was having on Sabrina, which gave Caitlin the impression that she wasn't mature enough to be good company. She had never met the professor, but his presence in Sabrina's life left Caitlin feeling inferior. When she would call Sabrina and ask her to hang out, Sabrina used a tone of voice that implied that the activities they used to have fun doing together were things only college students did—and that Sabrina was trying to get out of that world.

"Look, he didn't hit me," Caitlin told the officers. "I hit him really good with my lacrosse stick, but he didn't hit me. I'm not pressing charges."

"Caitlin," one of the officers said to her after hearing her story, "this is an abusive relationship and you should get out of it now."

Caitlin shook her head. The officers assumed that Chris treated her aggressively all the time, but it only happened when they fought, she told herself. She knew he could be obnoxious. But sometimes he was different.

"You two need at least a twenty-four-hour cooling-off period," the officer said. "If he comes back, call us. He's lucky he's not in cuffs."

The next day, Chris IMed her, "You called the cops on me! How did they get involved? They just fuck things up. I can't believe you called the cops on me."

She called him. "Grace is scared of you now. That was a dumb move, threatening her."

"Well, I'm glad you have someone looking out for you and protecting you," he said sarcastically.

"So why were you yelling at me?" Caitlin asked. Chris said he didn't know how the fight had escalated to that level.

"You've lost me, you know," Caitlin said. "It's over." Chris was quiet. "I'm not going to deal with someone who feels the need to restrain me," she said. "I'm not sorry for how I handled the situation. You say stuff and threaten things all the time." She hung up.

Later, Chris called her back on his way to class.

"Why are you calling me?" Caitlin asked.

"I'm really sorry for what happened. I don't know what got into either of us. But I know your mom would want us to talk this out, and I'm really sorry."

Caitlin relaxed. He didn't apologize often. "Me, too."

"What does this mean for us?" he asked her.

"I don't know. I don't know what it means," Caitlin paused. "But I do know I love you a lot and that we're worth fighting for. If you think it's a lost cause, that's fine. I'll love you regardless of what decision you make."

Later, she scrounged up $18 in quarters from her change jar, put it in an envelope with her $82, and asked a sister to bring it to Chris.

"I'll take it to him." Amy, who by now had been caught up on the situation, spoke gently and held out her hand.

That night, Caitlin, Amy, and Grace met quietly to talk about how to handle the incident. They agreed it was in Caitlin's best interest to keep it from the other sisters and from the Alpha Rho Disciplinary Board.

"I know it looks like I'm the girlfriend who keeps going back, but I'm not like that," Caitlin explained. "If anyone put their hands on me, it'd be over. But I don't blame him." The raised bruise on Chris's cheek would last for a week. "When Chris tackled me onto the bed, it was because I tripped and brought him down with me. I *know* he could never hurt me." The other girls looked unconvinced.

"He would never hurt me and I know that for a fact," Caitlin repeated, kicking off her Sambas and crossing her bare feet beneath her.

The group decided to have a secret meeting with the House Mom in a week. Meanwhile, they would consider their options: either Chris wouldn't be allowed in the house or he would be allowed only when others were around. "If he's not allowed in the house," Caitlin warned, "there would be resentment on my part, and I would consider getting an apartment. You guys shouldn't be able to dictate who I have in my room."

Exploiting the Rules

DECEMBER 10

SABRINA'S IM AWAY MESSAGE

Why can't this semester be over already?

SABRINA WAS IRRITATED. THERE WERE SO MANY OTHER things to worry about this time of the year, with the semester quickly coming to a close. She didn't need another house drama on top of it all. But this week was room draw, which perennially had the potential to be the second most stressful time of the year (next to January's rush). The Alpha Rhos had an unofficial agreement that every semester a new sister would get to move into "the Palace," the one single room in the house. Because Grace's three roommates were going abroad for the semester, the consensus was that Grace, a senior, should move into the Palace.

The logical option for Charlotte, who as president automatically earned the Palace in the fall, was simply to switch places with Grace for the spring. But Charlotte wasn't cooperating. She insisted that because of her seniority as president, she shouldn't have to move into a quad. Instead, she said she was going to pull Fiona from the Penthouse and the two of them would take the largest double in the house. The double, however, wasn't empty; Charlotte would have to kick out those sisters, whose room eviction would create a domino effect throughout the house. Charlotte had the power to do so, she said, referring to Article X of the chapter bylaws, which stated that if the outgoing president chose to switch to a new room, the girls in that room were required to move. There was nothing even Caitlin as vice president could do. Sabrina, who hated the bylaws, considered pointing out the hypocrisy of enforcing some bylaws and not others. Article XII, for example, stated that no boys were allowed upstairs, but that rule was broken on a daily basis.

When Charlotte hadn't arrived by the start of the house meeting for the preliminary room draw, the sisters who were present talked about her. Nobody wanted to live with Charlotte. She hadn't been elected president out of popularity; rather, she was elected because she was Little Miss Sorority, as some of the girls referred to her. The sorority meant everything to her, and she was always involved in every Alpha Rho activity. But as president she had focused so intently on the sorority that she had had no time for the sisters. They tried to come up with various alternatives to present to Charlotte. One solution was that Grace, who didn't want to cause trouble, could stay in the quad for a semester with new roommates and Charlotte could keep her bed in the Palace. But many of the girls thought Charlotte didn't deserve that privilege. "She's the main problem," they argued. "So she's the one who should move."

When Charlotte finally arrived toward the end of the meeting, a few girls presented the group's final recommendation: she should switch with Grace and move into the quad so that no one else in the house would be affected. Charlotte only smiled. Shortly afterward, she came up to the Penthouse to see if any Pents wanted to go to a frat party. The girls were still talking about the meeting.

"Charlotte," Sabrina said, "we're all sisters, so we're supposed to be friends. Why can't we all live together? Is it really that big a deal?"

Charlotte raised her chin. "Yes," she said. "There are certain people I could never live with, and people who could never live with me." She sat down on Fiona's bed, where the two conversed quietly.

"I guess we won't be rooming together," Fiona said within Sabrina's earshot.

Sabrina was startled to hear Charlotte's mocking laughter. "We still could," she said smugly, "if we really want to."

C.C., the vice president of House Affairs, was frantic. She told Sabrina in tears that the handful of girls who had spent the fall semester abroad had already sent word back that they refused to live in the house if they had to live in the quads or the Penthouse. In her elected position, C.C. was obligated by Nationals to make sure every bed was paid for, which was becoming an increasingly unlikely scenario.

Sabrina and C.C. had each gained enough merit points to move downstairs. C.C., Sabrina could see, wasn't going to move because it would make her job more difficult. Sabrina hated the Penthouse—living with twenty-five other girls was extremely difficult for a person who cherished her privacy—but she didn't want to cause C.C. additional grief (or draw her sisters' ire) by kicking girls out of downstairs rooms if it meant they would move out of the house rather than live in the Penthouse. Sabrina decided to keep her bed in the Penthouse. She was staying at Mike's three or four nights a week anyway.

Their relationship was progressing, but Sabrina was still uneasy with the fact that they were teacher and student, a sensation she attributed to her personal insecurities, not to him. The awkward part was the way he was treating her in his class. He didn't call attention to her, positively or negatively, in front of the other students—nothing like that—but he was grading her papers harder than he had graded them before they had started dating, and much harder than he graded the work of other students in the class. Instead of her usual As, Mike was giving her B+s, which were a slap in the face to a student who was used to 4.0 semesters. Before they began dating, she had received As on her last two quizzes. But on the quiz he handed back today, he took a point off because she had one spelling mistake, an error that had nothing to do with what Mike taught in class. While at Mike's house, Sabrina read some of her classmates' papers. Though the content was decent, the papers were fraught with grammatical and spelling mistakes, but Mike still gave them As. He told Sabrina that he had graded her harder than the other students because he could tell that she was much more talented than her classmates. He wanted her to "realize her potential." Sabrina was resentful but didn't want to say anything to him about it yet. She would wait to see what grade he gave her for the semester. She loved him, she thought, but wondered whether her visions of him as her husband had perhaps been too hasty.

Double Standard

DECEMBER 13

VICKI'S IM AWAY MESSAGE

i have the boys at state wrapped around my finger!

AFTER DANCING AND DRINKING WITH WILLIAM THROUGH-out the Beta Pi Winter Formal, Vicki was sorry to see it end relatively early, at 1 A.M. She would have preferred to stay the night at the hotel, but sorority rules required that sisters ride the chartered bus back to the house. Nonetheless, several seniors decided to stay at the hotel anyway. They told the juniors and sophomores and their dates to spread out on the bus so that it wouldn't be obvious that a handful of sisters were missing. William and Vicki spent the rest of the night smoking and sleeping in his room at the Iota house.

When Vicki got back to the Beta Pi house the next day, Dan called her.

"Do you want to go to a fraternity Formal with a fellow Californian this weekend?" he asked, so nonchalantly that he caught Vicki off guard.

"Okay," she said.

"You sure?"

"Um, yeah."

"Cool. Don't worry about paying for anything. I'll even cover breakfast," said Dan.

"Breakfast?" Vicki asked, startled.

"Vicki, it is a Formal." The Formals for the fraternities on campus were overnight affairs, including travel to faraway cities and anywhere from one to three nights in a hotel.

In the hotel room Vicki and Dan shared with another brother and his date, Vicki self-consciously put on a bit of makeup while the brothers watched curiously. At the dance, Vicki stuck close to Dan and the few Beta Pi sisters who were fellow dates. When Dan went outside for a cigarette, Vicki snuck into the lobby and checked her cell phone voice mail. William had called twice to tell her he was wondering where she was and that he was waiting for her to come over. Vicki hurriedly left a message for William so that he wouldn't think she had disappeared for the night. After the dance, when Vicki and Dan got back to their room, Dan passed out immediately on the bed. Relieved, Vicki curled up on the opposite side until morning.

The next afternoon William called. "Where were you?" he asked.

"Out with a friend," said Vicki.

"I'm a little jealous, I have to say," he admitted.

"Ha-ha, I made you jealous," Vicki teased. William was not the jealous type.

At William's Iota Formal the following weekend, Vicki was dismayed to hear William refer to her as his girlfriend. "I love everything about you," he kept repeating when they were in their hotel room after the dance. "You're fun, you're pretty, and you're smart." Hoping his effusiveness was merely prompted by alcohol, and wanting to avoid a serious relationship discussion, she didn't object. Instead, she changed the subject before he might try to say the three words she didn't want to hear. Olivia had warned Vicki that if she were to suggest to William that they act less like a couple, he wouldn't handle it well. He had already IMed Olivia that she and her sisters were going to have to do a better job of sharing Vicki with him in the spring semester.

In the morning, however, as they woke up sober, William kissed her and ran his hands through her hair, which now was long enough to brush her collarbone. "I love you so much," he murmured. Vicki tried not to gasp as he kept kissing her.

"I'm tired," she said when they pulled away.

"Why is this so weird?" he asked, sensing the change in tension.

"Um, I just got out of this serious relationship. I wasn't expecting you to say that to me. I don't want a boyfriend."

William spoke casually. "It's okay, Vicki, it's just an emotion. What I said isn't that important," he reassured her. "It's just something we have to get past so we don't wake up in the morning and it's weird." Vicki felt better.

Setting Boundaries

DECEMBER 14

CAITLIN'S IM AWAY MESSAGE

I am a prisoner here of my own device.

THE SECRET HOUSE MEETING ABOUT CHRIS, MEDIATED BY the House Mom, lasted an hour. Caitlin was surprised at how civil it was. Caitlin, Amy, and Grace agreed that Chris would be allowed into the house—after Winter Break. For the remainder of the semester, if Caitlin wanted to see Chris, she would have to meet with him at his apartment or elsewhere. The girls also set rules in place for the spring semester. When school resumed in early January, Chris would not be allowed in the house drunk, which meant that he couldn't sleep over after events like Formal or Crush Party. If Chris became violent again, he would be forbidden to enter the house entirely. And if the couple argued loudly enough to bother any of the sisters, the girls could vote again on whether Chris would be allowed back in.

"I don't think he should be allowed in if there are any arguments at all," said Grace.

"I just don't think that's reasonable," said Amy, shaking her dark curls emphatically.

"We shouldn't have to be woken up because they're screaming at each other," Grace said.

Caitlin hadn't known that their screaming fights throughout the semester had awakened the other girls. "Why didn't you guys just tell me, anyway?" she asked.

"If you got over whatever you were fighting about, we didn't want to drag up something bad," Grace said.

"Oh please," Caitlin said. "It's not like I didn't know what the fights were about or how they ended. It's not gonna offend me. If it were me, I'd say, 'Buddy, I could hear you last night so maybe try and watch that next time.'"

Caitlin despised the idea of treading on eggshells, but she felt worse about how the agreement would inconvenience her relationship. Fall semester lasted right up until Christmas, and she wasn't going to be able to see Chris at all over Winter Break. Chris was even angrier about the stipulations. "Why can't they just suck it up?" he asked her. "They don't know when I'm in your room half the time anyway."

It seemed ridiculous to Caitlin that, at nineteen, her relationships could be controlled by her sisters, who didn't understand that Chris hadn't meant to hurt her. After all, she was the one who had clocked him. And the couple had already made up. As a peace offering, Chris gave her a CD full of the love songs he believed characterized their relationship. Even Sabrina, Caitlin's voice of reason, was convinced that Chris wouldn't get violent again. Caitlin's mother blamed Caitlin's "hot temper." But the Alpha Rhos wouldn't listen to Caitlin. Caitlin's only comfort was that the tension with Amy over their fight about Chris had abated.

Ω Ω Ω

The Scope of Authority

NO MATTER THE LENIENCY OF A CHAPTER, IF IT IS AFFILI-
ated with a national sorority it is beholden to the sorority's national rules.
This is why C.C. panicked about not being able to provide Alpha Rho Nationals
with a report that all beds in the house would be paid for—and why Charlotte,
a stickler for the rules, knew that she would be able to exploit the Nationals'
established merit points system. National sororities impose extremely strict
rules on their chapters, usually stricter than those of campus Panhellenic
Councils and, according to most sorority girls, always stricter than those of
their fraternity counterparts. Sorority sisters at the University of Kentucky,
for example, told me about what they called a double standard. "When the
fraternities have a Formal, they can have it over a weekend and stay overnight
at a hotel in Canada," one said. "But we aren't allowed to get rooms at hotels,
and we can't have any event—even Date Parties or mixers—outside of a
fifteen-mile radius of Lexington."

I had expected to find rules designed by Nationals to protect collegiate
members from unsafe situations (and itself from potential lawsuits and insurance hazards); I had not expected, however, to find that national regulations
could command such a broad scope of behavior. One sorority guide, for
instance, explains, "Sorority girls have moral obligations that extend beyond
promising to follow sorority ideals during initiation. If a member does not
follow sorority morality guidelines, her pin may be *jerked*. If a girl's pin is
jerked, she is kicked out of the sorority." When I asked the National Panhellenic Conference chairman about these types of rules, she vaguely explained,
"Each sorority has its own standards—standards of behavior you'd expect of
anyone whom you'd like to think of as a nice person. It's just about how that's
interpreted at the local level." The fact remains that sororities are entrenched
in the traditions of their past. Over and over again at the NGLA Conference,
the leaders emphasized "going back to the basics" and returning to the ideals
and standards of the organizations' founders.

One point of contention here is that "sorority morality guidelines"
aren't being developed by religious, law enforcement, or university officials;

rather, they are formulated and passed down from the women who work for a sorority's national headquarters. These are women with dubious qualifications, for whom there may be no specific requirements save enthusiasm—certainly no degree requirements—who may be stuck in a time warp, from the era of their own active sorority membership. (Campus advisers sponsored by the university, by contrast, usually have a graduate degree in student personnel administration, counseling, or educational administration.)

Another troublesome aspect of these moral standards is that they leave room for interpretation by the girls who lead the chapter. For example, the sorority guide specifically states, "The most common reason a girl is kicked out of a sorority is that others feel she has a questionable reputation—QR. *Questionable reputation* is the term given to a girl whose conduct, behavior, or appearance is not acceptable according to her sorority's guidelines." In the same way that Charlotte was able to use the national rules to her advantage, so, too, could the "mean girls" described in November's chapter use "QR" to run a less popular girl out of their sorority.

The guide goes on to delineate certain types of behavior deemed morally unacceptable for sorority members (in these direct quotes, the emphasis is in the original):

▣ *Sorority girls do not have sex.* The easiest and most common way a member's reputation comes into question is for her to have sex indiscriminately and indiscreetly. Spending the night with a date is generally unacceptable for sorority girls. It is usually overlooked at least the first time a girl passes out (from drinking too much) at her date's place—unless he lives in a fraternity house, where it is *never* acceptable . . .

▣ *Any sleeping over is only accepted on weekend nights* . . .

▣ *Sorority girls don't do drugs.* Being caught smoking pot or partaking of other drugs is another way for a member to get her pin jerked . . .

▣ *Sorority girls do not dress inappropriately.* A sorority member may acquire a QR from something as innocent as the way she dresses. Although sororities do not dictate specific dress codes, there are definite dos and don'ts . . . The way you dress may express a loose moral attitude, which reflects on the entire sorority. Tight or revealing clothes must be avoided at all times.

The vagueness and contradictory nature of the latter rule in particular (no specific dress code, yet definite dos and don'ts) seems to reserve a sorority's right to apply the rules to unspecified guidelines, thus allowing for purely arbitrary enforcement. The guide admits, "She may not know that she has broken a standards rule because many are unwritten. For example, the sorority may not teach pledges how to dance . . . but if a pledge (or active) dances too suggestively at a fraternity party, her pin may be jerked. Girls are kicked out of sororities for even more minor 'standards problems,' such as wearing midriff tops or tight jeans."

Considering how many navels I saw at Date Dash, if this abridged list of rules still held true, there would be no Alpha Rho at State U. There would certainly be no Bitsy. But the guidebook, surprisingly, wasn't from an era all that different from the present day—or all that removed from, say, Madonna. It was published in 1985, and many sororities still expect their girls to follow the standards it describes. Similarly, Caitlin confided to me that as Alpha Rho vice president, she had heard of another sorority's national office that was currently debating instituting a countrywide rule that would mandate the specific items required for an official rush uniform—right down to the color of sisters' thongs. "It would make them look a lot nicer," Caitlin said.

"But the idea that they can mandate a thong?"

"Yeah." Caitlin explained, "Some people wear big, frumpy underwear and their butts don't fill it and when they bend over, their underwear comes out of their pants."

National offices manage to enforce their broad list of regulations in several ways. Before they can be initiated, girls in many sororities are required to sign an agreement promising to abide by the Nationals' rules. Even these written rules can be arbitrary. Kappa Delta warns new members, "Any promiscuous behavior on the part of a member or new member will result in National Probation or termination of her pledge . . . Kappa Delta expects each member and new member to conduct herself in such a manner that neither her activities nor the appearance of such activities would elicit unfavorable thoughts, judgements and comments about herself and/or the sorority."

To monitor chapters, Nationals regularly send representatives, who often stay in the guest bedroom of a house, attend meetings, and observe the active members. These representatives can include regional directors, local alumnae, or "traveling consultants." Known under names that vary by sorority, traveling consultants are alumnae dispatched by national offices to check up on a chapter and help it become more aligned with national standards. Usually a year or two out of college, these women can spend a week or more examining a chapter's notebooks, making sure their finances are satisfactory, and, occasionally, meeting with the campus Greek adviser. They then write a report on the chapter and deliver it to national headquarters. ("Employers look at this as valuable experience," the National Panhellenic Conference chairman explained to me. "They're getting around all of those airports by themselves.")

Nationals also control chapters by appointing a number of advisers, whose duty it is to make sure the chapter is following proper policy and procedure. In addition, Nationals keep in touch with campus Greek officials: there is usually a university Greek adviser or Office of Greek Life and/or an adult director of the campus Panhellenic Council. Using these representatives' reports, Nationals can inflict penalties on a chapter to keep its girls in tow, such as "social probation," which limits or prohibits chapter-sponsored social events. Moreover, a chapter's elected executive board is comprised of sisters supposedly willing to take on the extra responsibility of encouraging their chapter to adhere to Nationals' standards.

When Brooke was a junior, Eta Gamma Nationals sent a regional director to stay at the house for several weeks because, as Brooke put it, "our girls were just hellions." The director "turned the house around." She instituted mandatory study hours, streamlined the financial system, made sure meetings were run efficiently and with the proper rituals, and influenced executive board nominations so that the candidates for the administrative positions were known more for their responsibility than for their popularity. "If you're going to be a vice president, you have to work," the director told the chapter. "It's not all about smiles." The Ten, therefore, stuck to fun, prestigious positions such as social chair and rush chair.

This is how Brooke found herself on her chapter's Disciplinary Board. Many sororities have similar committees, also called "Standards," "Judicial

Board," "Hearing," or "Council," which are comprised of a specific number of girls from each pledge class in the chapter. The responsibility of enforcing Nationals' vague moral standards usually falls to these few sisters. The Disciplinary Board, which the girls called "D.B.," could call up a sister for anything from failure to pay a fine to wearing "slutty" clothing. D.B. met after every weekly chapter meeting and conducted its business in secret. During chapter meeting, a girl who was to "sit in front of D.B." would be surreptitiously handed a sealed note saying, "The Disciplinary Board asks that you meet with them at [such and such] time." The recipient would wait nervously outside the D.B. room without knowing why she had been "called." The D.B. could request to see a girl because she had committed an infraction, because she might have had information that could help the board's investigation of one of her sisters, or because she herself had requested a meeting in order, essentially, to rat on a sister.

"I saw Susie doing a line of cocaine at a party," Brooke heard at one D.B. meeting. The board then investigated by calling in other sisters who were at the party, including Susie's good friends in the house, who would be expected to confess to the board if they knew that Susie had indeed done a line of cocaine. The Disciplinary Board was expected to compile a sufficient amount of evidence before it was allowed to impose a penalty. Many girls referred to D.B. as "the goody-goody group," but Brooke told me it was a useful way to get rid of "bad seeds." The year that Brooke was on the board, one sister didn't attend chapter meetings and allegedly did drugs. The board couldn't obtain enough evidence to disaffiliate the girl on the basis of a drug habit. Instead, the committee members kept a close eye on the girl, waiting for her to do something egregious. A few months into the year, they found what they were looking for: a D.B. member spotted the girl, late at night, having sex on the lawn behind a fraternity house. She was called in front of the committee. "We couldn't get her on the drugs," Brooke said, "so we told her she was giving the house a really bad name and had her disaffiliated." Forced disaffiliation, Brooke explained to me, is a sorority mark of shame. Once a girl has been initiated into a national sorority, even if she is disaffiliated, she is barred from joining another for the rest of her life.

In other groups, sisters who aren't on the Disciplinary Board take it upon themselves to rein in girls who aren't properly representing their letters.

At an Alpha Phi house in Virginia, the sisters devised a way to let sisters or pledges know when they were out of line in public. When a sister drank too much and made a fool of herself, an older Alpha Phi sister walked by and loudly hissed, "TNP!" When a pledge hooked up with five other girls at one party, a few sisters angrily took the pledge aside and whispered, "TNP!" And continually, whenever a sister isn't behaving up to the sorority par, other sisters make sure to look her in the eye and say emphatically, "TNP!" That's Not Phi.

Ω   Ω   Ω

Breaking the Rules

DECEMBER 19

CAITLIN'S IM AWAY MESSAGE
When's it my turn to be the priority? Could ya throw me a frickin' bone please?

▣ *Sorority girls do not dress inappropriately.*

Amy, Sabrina, Caitlin, and René were hanging out in Amy's room as Beth helped Amy and Caitlin get ready for Formal. It was the first time this semester that René had ventured into the sorority house that had rejected her.

Professor Stone called Sabrina's cell. As the other girls chatted, Sabrina kept a furtive eye on them to make sure they weren't listening to her conversation.

"No, it's okay," she reassured him. "They know. They don't care . . . No, they're not even listening . . . I know, I just can't wait until the semester's over."

After Sabrina hung up, Amy asked her what she planned to wear that night. Instead of going to Formal, Sabrina would join Beth and René for dinner at an upscale restaurant.

"I don't know, just some nice pants, I guess."

"You can borrow one of my dresses if you want, honey. René's roommate, Traci, borrowed one last night for a fraternity formal," said Amy, who was wearing a dress that plunged so low in back that her rear cleavage was easily visible. "And what about makeup?"

"No makeup, thanks," Sabrina said. She never wore makeup. Sabrina went upstairs to a sitting room for a quick smoke.

Beth was flabbergasted. "She should have *some* makeup."

When Sabrina returned, Amy asked her, "Does Professor Stone know you smoke?"

"No. He doesn't know. Mike doesn't even drink, so I'm not going to tell him about my little marijuana habit. But, hey—" Sabrina brightened. "I haven't smoked in three weeks!"

Amy was delighted at her sister's breakthrough. "Sweetie, that's fabulous!"

Sabrina cocked her head, thinking. "Oh wait," she muttered, "except yesterday I got some for free."

Amy shook her head, paged through *Vogue,* and sipped from a "40"—a large bottle of malt liquor—she had been storing underneath her bed. She stopped at a picture of Brittany Murphy. "Oooh, she's emaciated now." The other girls peered at the picture, which Amy held up so they could see. "She used to have boobs. She looked fine in *Clueless.*"

"Traci's boob popped out last night," said René. The girls laughed.

"Bless her heart, she fell out of my dress?!" Amy giggled and leaned forward, almost falling out of her own dress as Beth yelled at her to keep her head back.

René fidgeted in the corner, as if working up the courage to speak. She took a deep breath. "Remember how we used to have breakfast in the mornings together to catch up?" she asked Amy and Caitlin, who were surrounded by makeup and hair appliances.

"I don't think I'm going to be up for breakfast tomorrow," said Amy, missing the point as René, looking down, blinked quickly. "Anyway, can't I please put makeup on you, Sabrina, please?" Amy implored, her speech lisped as she let a handful of breath mints dissolve on her tongue.

"Why?"

"Because it's fun!"

"But I'm just going to wash it off."

"We all do that eventually. Please? Just eye makeup then?"

"No way." Sabrina changed the subject. "Your dress is so pretty!" Amy, tipsy, curtseyed repeatedly in her gravity-defying stilettos, her breasts halfway heaving out of her braless halter dress.

Amy had waited months for Formal. She felt like a princess as Chad, who seemed like the perfect date, escorted her to the pre-game. She glanced at Caitlin in a two-piece ensemble that exposed her navel and much of her breasts. Amy thought Caitlin looked incredible, even if she didn't know much about designers. Earlier in the week Amy had vowed to buy a subscription of *Vogue* and force Caitlin and Sabrina to read it regularly. Amy had been carrying her Fendi purse that day and Caitlin had asked what the "F" stood for.

"Are you serious?" Amy had asked her. "You don't know what the F means?"

"Uh, no."

"It's Fendi!"

"Yeah, okay . . ." Caitlin looked at her skeptically. "Should I know that for some reason?"

"Everybody knows that!"

As they walked home, Amy stopped several friends on the way to ask them, "If you saw an F on a purse, what would it stand for?" They all answered correctly. But then, Caitlin hadn't even known what Gucci was until freshman year. She usually wore Adidas.

▣ *Sorority girls do not have sex.*

At the pre-game, the girls drank as quickly as they could so that a buzz would set in by the time they headed to the house. The Alpha Rho entry hall was packed with drunk girls snapping photos and squealing, "I love your dress!" and "Oh my God, you look so cute!" While the sisters raved over each other's dresses and makeup, the boys slapped each other fives in greeting. Chad looked around, mesmerized. "This is great!" he exclaimed. "A hundred drunk girls!"

On the short limousine ride to the hotel, Amy and Chad shared her thermos of Absolut and Seven-Up. The adjacent ballrooms rented out for the evening offered several banquet tables of food and a well-stocked bar that nicely complimented the Alpha Rho Winter Formal shot glass souvenirs. But Chad and Amy spent most of the night dancing alone, drinks in hand. She wasn't interested in paying attention to anybody but Chad. So Amy didn't notice when a crowd formed around the women's bathroom as girls laughed about a sophomore who was having sex in one of the stalls. And she didn't realize that before the night was over, a third of the girls had disappeared to take Ecstasy and have sex with their dates upstairs.

On the limousine ride home, Chris and Caitlin began kissing, foreplay to what they would finish once they returned to Chris's apartment. Amy, tired from the drinking and the dancing, leaned into Chad, who kissed her gently. Then he flipped out, for no discernible reason.

"What's going on here?" he asked.

"What?" Amy forced herself to wake up a bit. "You kissed me and I kissed you back."

"Do you know what you're doing?" He seemed to be patronizing her because she was so drunk, but he was drunker; Amy was sure of it.

"Yes, honey, I kissed you back." Annoyed that Chad was being so huffy, Amy fell asleep.

When they got off the bus, she tried to storm away, but it was a challenge to storm on four-inch heels. Chad helped her home, keeping her at arm's length. When Chad said he was going back to his dorm instead of staying over, Amy was surprised. She had expected to sleep with him that night. "You're drunk," she said. "At least just eat something before you go."

"No, I just want to go home," he slurred, and drove away.

A week later, when Amy still hadn't heard from Chad, she noticed his IM away message: "@ Louie's with a hottie, maybe somethin more." Amy was crushed. Things had been going so well. "What's wrong with me?" she wept to her Big Sister, who was friendly with Chad. "Why does it work for everyone else but me?" All of her sisters fell into relationships so easily, she told her friend. Why couldn't she?

"I think it's because you're too accommodating and guys are afraid of getting too comfortable," said her Big Sister. "Chad freaked out because he thought that if he started a relationship with you, it would get serious really fast."

Friends and sisters tried to console her but they weren't nearly as helpful as her twin would have been. Amy missed her terribly. These were exactly the kinds of issues she would have confided to her sister. As much as she wanted to treat her Alpha Rho sisters like real sisters, it wasn't the same—her sorority sisters weren't actually related and didn't offer unconditional love.

Amy vowed to get back on the Atkins diet and start a regular gym schedule immediately. If she could just lose five pounds, she told herself, that would make a difference. Maybe then someone would stick around long enough to like her.

◼ *Sorority girls don't do drugs.*

The day after the end of the semester, the House Mom, following national sorority rules, closed and dead-bolted the house, taking all of the sisters' keys until she returned from Winter Break. Sabrina and Caitlin, who were staying at a friend's apartment on campus for another day before going home, decided they wanted to spend the night tripping on mushrooms—the slight difficulty being that the mushrooms happened to be in Sabrina's dresser in the Penthouse. Accompanied by two non-Greek male friends, the sisters crept around outside the house, looking for a window inadvertently left unlatched. Undeterred by the police car that kept circling the block, the group lurked in the shadows while one of the boys jimmied the lock on the side door of Alpha Rho. After several minutes, he pried the door open and the group sneaked into the house, bumping into furniture on their way to Sabrina's room. When they found the mushrooms, they crept back out of the house. After a couple of hours at the apartment, where the group waited for the mushrooms to take effect, they returned to the house and smoked marijuana for hours on the back porch. "It was the most fun night ever," Caitlin told me later. Though she knew her mother would impose her regular 11 P.M. curfew when she returned home for Winter Break, she no longer believed that her mother was sending minions to monitor her behavior at school. Caitlin relished the way the drugs made her feel freed from her mother's influence. "It was like when you're a little kid and you're sneaking downstairs on Christmas Eve to see if Santa came yet. You're nervous but excited at the same time." She grinned and lay back on the floor, dreamily folding her hands behind her head. "That," she said, "was one of the greatest nights of my life."

JANUARY

———

When does Rush begin? You might not know it, but Rush begins during your freshman year in high school! Your grades, activities, and interests combine to make you the rushee of the future.

—Ready for Rush: The Must-Have Manual for Sorority Rushees! 1999

A smile is the sorority girl's most important accessory . . . In fact, actives put Vaseline on their teeth (just like beauty contestants) to make smiling easier. Rushees go home at the end of the day with sore muscles from smiling. *But it's worth it* . . . Some girls . . . should practice smiling in front of a mirror before rush.

—Rush: A Girl's Guide to Sorority Success, 1985

Ω   Ω   Ω

JANUARY 10

AMY'S IM AWAY MESSAGE

some people confuse the heck outta me . . .

AMY RETURNED FROM WINTER Break refreshed, relaxed, and excited for rush. All sororities at State U were required to come back from vacation a few days early to prepare for the formally structured process of recruiting and selecting new members. Alpha Rho held an annual Pre-Rush

Weekend, an in-house retreat intended to remind the sisters of rush protocol and to build a sense of solidarity.

In between general sessions run by Charlotte, as president, and Elaine, the recruitment chair, during which the girls practiced "rush conversations" and learned rush songs, the chapter divided into smaller groups for team-building activities. During one of the general sessions, the girls discussed what the executive board considered the biggest weakness of the chapter: cliques.

"We need to act more like one sisterhood than a lot of little sisterhoods," one board member said. "We need to break down the cliques." Most sisters agreed.

"But there are always going to be cliques anyway," said another. "We're not all exactly alike—that's one of the great things about Alpha Rho. We're not the kind of sorority in which everyone's the same and they're all best friends but they're also killing each other."

"Maybe if we stopped prioritizing people by their seniority, pledge class divisions wouldn't be so much of an issue," a sophomore sister offered. "Seniority is kind of petty anyway."

Whitney whipped around to face the girl. "I've been waiting four years to sit at the front of the meeting, so if you think that's petty, then you're mistaken," she snapped. But by the end of the session, the sisters had come to a consensus that they would actively try to dissolve the subgroups within the house.

After the meeting ended, the girls had a short break before the next session. They immediately dispersed into their usual cliques.

Amy, Caitlin, and Sabrina met up in the kitchen to catch up on their relationship gossip. Caitlin and Chris were stable. Sabrina was upset that Mike seemed to be making less and less time for her (though he did grade her the A she deserved). While at home over break, Amy had reconnected with her high school sweetheart, who proclaimed his love for her and asked her to try a long-distance relationship.

"Ew, why him?" Sabrina asked. "He's unattractive." Sabrina had met him the year before and disliked him immediately.

"I don't care!" Amy said, her dimples fading. "He doesn't have to be hot. He's like a teddy bear, and he's adorable to me. He's the only person I've ever been able to see myself with forever."

"You're just lovesick," Caitlin dismissed. "You're making him out to be perfect. No guy is perfect."

"He is!" Amy crossed her pale arms.

"The only reason you think he's perfect is because you only see him two weeks at a time," Sabrina argued.

Amy couldn't believe it. Finally, she seemed to be having a healthy, serious relationship, and her sisters couldn't be happy for her because the guy didn't meet their aesthetic standards. Amy decided her sisters were misguided because they didn't understand what a real relationship was. In her opinion, their boyfriends clearly didn't treat them properly, while her high school sweetheart treated her the way a girl should be treated, sending her roses and calling her almost daily. But she kept her thoughts to herself as the conversation shifted.

"Mike can't kiss," Sabrina complained.

"Chris can't appreciate sex the way it should be appreciated anymore," said Caitlin.

"I know. What's with these guys? They hardly ever slow down or do something lovey-dovey or in the moment."

"That's never been the case with my guy," Amy said. "I deflowered him!" This comment led to a debate over whether there were two or three classifications of intercourse.

"There are three categories: making love, sex, and fucking," said Caitlin.

"There's no difference between sex and fucking," Amy argued. "They're the same category."

"You are so sheltered," Sabrina said.

"The third one is just a yucky term for the second," Amy said.

"You live in your own little fantasy world," Caitlin said, exchanging a knowing look with Sabrina before she left to go to an exec board meeting.

An hour later, the exec board summoned the girls into the chapter room for the next session: "The Recruitment Runway," a fashion show instructing the girls on what they could and could not wear during rush.

Rush was a weeklong series of nightly events known as "rush parties," during which sisters would have short blocks of time to get to know the hundreds of candidates. On Monday, the "open house" party would be open to everyone. About twenty-five candidates at a time would be led into each sorority house for a fifteen-minute rush party, over a period of slightly more than five hours. All of the sisters had to be present for the entire duration.

A sister pranced in front of the room, wearing homemade letters on a tank top and a very short miniskirt. "This is an example of what you can't wear to open house," Elaine, the fashion-show emcee, said loudly. "No homemade letters. And you can't wear miniskirts because you have to sit down and the skirt will ride up."

Charlotte walked across the makeshift stage. "This is the ideal outfit for open house. On that first night," said Elaine, "you are to wear your letters on a nice shirt, neatly tucked into your cute khakis, which can't be cut up. You must wear cute shoes."

On Tuesday would be the first round, a Teal and Jade party celebrating the sorority and its colors for the girls who had been selected to come back to the house. Each rushee could attend parties at up to ten houses if the sororities invited her. The sisters were expected to wear their sorority colors for the first round.

Grace paraded across the front of the room wearing large blue sweatpants, sneakers, and a green sports bra. The girls laughed. "That is not how you wear our colors. Obviously, you are not to dress messily any night of rush week," Elaine said. "And your clothes should fit right—get a seamstress." Fiona strutted onstage wearing navy slacks and a crisp green J. Crew sweater. "That's more like it."

Wednesday would be the second round, or "skit night," during which some of the Alpha Rhos would perform a skit for the rushees, who could attend parties at four houses that night. The girls who were not in the skit were supposed to wear black capris and a brightly colored top.

Thursday would be the third round, or "Preference Night," the most solemn night of the week. The rushees, who could attend up to two Preference parties, would be told to dress up for the occasion. The sisters were supposed to wear white dresses. Bitsy walked onstage in a short white skirt, a tight white tube top, and flip-flops. "Notice how Bitsy isn't wearing any stockings," Elaine pointed out. "That's unacceptable. Stockings look nicer." Following Bitsy, another sister wore a long white linen dress with nude stockings and white heels. Amy took notes in her pink sorority binder.

"Dress Checks"

JANUARY 12

VICKI'S IM AWAY MESSAGE

this is boooshit

WHEN VICKI STEPPED OFF THE PLANE AT THE AIRPORT NEAR State U after Winter Break, Olivia and Ashleigh came running in their platform sandals to greet her, screaming her name as they careened through the crowd. The house in January seemed like a different place than it had been when Vicki first moved there in August. This time, instead of moving in with her parents' help, Vicki moved back into the house with her sisters. This time, with many of the juniors studying abroad, the sophomores were the dominant class in the house. Vicki walked into the entry hall, got her new room key from the House Mom, and started unpacking in the double she now shared with Olivia. She was neither excited nor apprehensive about moving back in for second semester. But she felt much more comfortable than she had the semester before. This time, the house actually seemed like the place where she lived.

That night, Vicki sat through her first rush practice. The exec board read through a long, confusing list of appropriate and inappropriate rush behavior. The sisters were forbidden, for example, to initiate discussions with the recruits about drinking and smoking. They were allowed to talk about these subjects, however, if they flowed naturally from the conversation. The sisters practiced talking about the sorority's philanthropy, so they wouldn't "forget and look stupid" if a recruit asked them about it. The meeting ended after the recruitment chair informed the girls what they were expected to wear for the week.

The night before rush began, the Beta Pi recruitment chair stopped in each sister's room for "Dress Checks." Every night this week, the Beta Pis were required to try on the clothes they planned to wear at the next day's rush events. The recruitment chair would look over each girl's outfit and veto it if she thought it was inappropriate. For open house, the Beta Pis were supposed to wear a shirt with their letters, khakis, and nice shoes or sandals.

Vicki and Olivia could hear sisters complaining after the recruitment chair left their rooms. "That's still not good enough," she said repeatedly, even after the sisters had changed their outfits. "That shirt doesn't look great. You need to change into something else."

Morgan came in and, without asking, tried on one of Olivia's shirts. The shirt hung off her gaunt frame. "Ugh," Morgan groaned as she twisted in front of the mirror, "I'm so fat."

"Leave now," said Olivia. Morgan skipped out, still wearing the shirt.

When the recruitment chair reached Vicki and Olivia's room, she glanced down Vicki's outfit and stared at her flip-flops.

"You can't wear those. You need to wear fancy shoes," the recruitment chair said.

"I don't have fancy shoes." Vicki owned only flats because she didn't want to emphasize her height.

"Vicki, you have to wear what you'd wear to an interview. Everyone has those kinds of shoes."

"I don't."

"What about nice sandals?"

"I don't have those, either."

"Borrow from Olivia."

"The only ones she has that I can walk in are the ones she's wearing." Olivia parodied a model pose, pointing a sandaled toe and tossing her bleached hair.

"Then borrow from someone else."

"But if I'm wearing shoes that I wouldn't normally wear, then that isn't my style and I'm not portraying the person I really am, right?"

"Oh, all right." The recruitment chair gave up. "Try to find something, but if you can't, then wear your flip-flops. Just don't tell anybody."

"Okay."

As the recruitment chair turned to leave the room she scrutinized Olivia, whose outfit she had already approved. "Get a belt, Olivia," she said, and walked out.

Ω   Ω   Ω

Practicing Conversations

FOR MOST SORORITIES, "RUSH"—THE OFFICIAL RECRUIT-
ment period during which members and candidates get to know each other
and narrow down the mutual selection process—is the most stressful time of
the year. Never is the image of a sorority more important than when the girls
are on display in an attempt to attract the best new members available. On
the one hand, Vicki disliked the superficiality of the rush atmosphere; she
said to me, "If this is the white shirt I'm comfortable in, then this is the
white shirt I should be wearing, to reflect who I am." On the other hand,
she also understood her sorority's perspective. "Beta Pi wants to portray a
certain image," she said, rationalizing Dress Checks. "The girls coming
through rush want to see you look put together." Sororities are driven by
fierce competition with the other chapters and pressure from Nationals to fill
their new-member quota with the right kind of dues-paying girls. The quality
of the girls who select their house (and whom the house selects) can drastically alter a sorority's statistics, such as its average GPA, its image, and its relationship with fraternities, depending on the looks and affability of the girls.
Rush is such a nerve-wracking experience, for both rushers and rushees, that
whenever I asked sisters what they liked least about sorority life, rush
inevitably was near the top of their lists.

Rush, which generally lasts for a week or two, ends on Bid Day, when
sororities give rushees "bids," or formal offers to join. Many Greek systems
run two rushes, a "formal" rush one semester—during which rules, quotas,
and protocol are stringent—and an "informal" rush the other semester, with
a more lenient structure and no quota. (Some sororities, especially those low
on numbers, also have "open rush," or "continuous bidding," which allows
them to induct new members throughout the year.) Several schools guaran-
tee that every rushee will be assigned to a house. Depending on how many
girls rush, the school divides that number by the number of sororities to
determine a quota that every house must reach (in some sororities the quotas are derived by a more complex formula).

For some sororities, a rushee must provide a photograph and a wealth of
paperwork, including recommendations from sorority members in her home
state. To get these recommendations, rush guides recommend that girls

wishing to join a sorority call or write the Panhellenic office at their college or university during the spring of their senior year in high school. "Any sorority alumna can send a letter to any chapter of her sorority or to a rec board, recommending that the sorority pledge a particular rushee," says *Rush: A Girl's Guide to Sorority Success.* "However, a letter of recommendation is not the same as the formal recommendation, which is a *rec.*" Sorority alumnae associations in cities and counties appoint official recommendation boards, though some sororities allow any alumna to write a formal recommendation.

These subjective evaluations, often written by complete strangers, carry great weight in the rush process. An alumna who knows that a rushee "has a bad reputation" can write a "no recommendation," or no rec, which outweighs a formal rec even if the no rec doesn't come from a rec board. "In some cities," says *Rush: A Girl's Guide to Sorority Success*, "board members drive by a rushee's home or run a check on her father's occupation to decide whether or not she should receive a recommendation." The guide further advises, "Knowing a member of a recommendation board helps you receive a recommendation. By the same token, if a rec board member does not like you, even for a silly reason (maybe you hurt her daughter's feelings last year) you may be denied a recommendation."

If a rushee doesn't know a rec board member, she is advised to prepare a résumé for the rec board and the sorority alumnae she will ask to write recommendations. The résumé is expected to include grades, honors, and activities, as well as talents, interests, and travel—to give sorority sisters material for rush party conversations. "Travel, especially abroad, indicates affluence and sophistication, which are always positive factors in the evaluation process," states the rush guide, which emphasizes the importance of presenting as upper-crust an image as possible. It stresses, *"You should not list previous blue-collar employment on your resume unless it is very exotic. If you served food at McDonald's don't mention it. If you served food at a restaurant on Martha's Vineyard, do."*

One of Brooke's friends was pressured to get into Eta Gamma by her mother, who lined up a staggering twenty recommendations from Eta Gammas. As domineering as stage mothers and as pushy as beauty pageant mothers, sorority mothers can be a strange breed. Perhaps because their sisterhood was a product of a different time, sorority mothers often pin their hopes for their daughters' future achievement both in college and in adulthood on their success or failure at rush. At one school in the mid-1990s, for example, a girl was courted by two houses; the campus considered one superior to the other. The girl phoned her mother to inform her that she had chosen the inferior one. The mother, appalled, hissed, "You just ruined your life," and drove down to see her daughter right away. After a heated conversation, the sobbing girl went to the campus's Panhellenic office at two in the morning to change her bid, but the officers still working there said it was too late. When a Texas sorority girl told her mother that she didn't get into Tri-Delt, her mother cried and moaned, "Now how are you going to meet a husband?" This incident also happened in the mid-1990s.

In Brooke's Texas hometown, mothers practically courted each other to lobby sorority daughters to help their own children. "Oh yeah, moms talked. They would get together for tea and go, 'What is Susie thinking?' 'Well, Cindy's just so happy in EtaGam.' 'We really wish Susie would go EtaGam,' " Brooke said. "They'd have lunch over it; it's a huge deal in Texas. Moms were definitely like, 'Oh, Susie really likes EtaGam; do we think she has a chance? Can Cindy help? Could you ask Cindy to get back to me on that? I'd like to know if Susie really has a chance.' "

According to author Maryln Schwartz, at universities in the South, mothers and grandmothers of rushees start sending sorority houses cakes, cupcakes, flowers, and other tokens in time for rush. They send pencils engraved with the rushee's name so sisters will remember to vote for her. Iced letters on the baked goods read versions of, "Just remember my daughter Jane Smith." Schwartz wrote, "This practice got so out of hand at the University of Mississippi that the dean of students . . . put an end to it, saying sororities would no longer accept these pre-Rush gifts." But an Ole Miss Kappa Kappa Gamma told Schwartz, "Those cakes still keep coming."

A legacy isn't necessarily automatically admitted to the sorority in which her relative was a member. But she will get special treatment. A chapter that doesn't automatically admit legacies will usually decide by the second night of rush parties whether or not it plans to extend the legacy a bid; if it does not want her, the group will give her the courtesy of letting her know early enough so that she can connect with another house. Occasionally out of competitiveness, other sororities will try to "steal a legacy" simply to lord one over another house.

Rush candidates are divided into groups and assigned a "rush counselor," or "Rho Chi": a sorority sister who, supposedly unbiased, cannot be involved with or disclose her sorority as she guides her group through the process. The Rho Chis are sometimes known to carry emergency packs including nail polish, mints, Band-Aids, and tampons. On the first night, the Rho Chis lead their groups to parties at every sorority on campus, where they mingle with the sisters. After open house, rush parties are by invitation only.

The last party of rush, called Preference Night, usually involves emotional speeches by seniors about what the sorority has meant to them, as well as a ceremony intended to make the candidates feel as if they are already a part of the group. But mostly, the purpose of Preference Night is to make girls cry. This way, if the rushees are led to believe that the sisters are so close that the sorority moves them to tears, then they will conclude, "I want friends like that, too." (Some sororities bring in a favorite rushee's older sister or aunt, if she is an alumna, to help persuade her to join. Others distribute tiny cakes with the rushees' names on them.) Between the parties, the sisters have five to ten minutes to write down anything they can remember about the girls they have met, in order to help them when they later vote to narrow the list of candidates.

After the Pref parties and before a specified deadline (usually midnight), each rushee submits to the campus Panhellenic office a card on which she ranks her top few (usually two or three) choices. The sororities, meanwhile, submit their final bid list of girls in the order that they would accept them into the sorority. Panhellenic staff members then feed the lists into a computer, which matches the girls to the sororities, depending on how high the names appear on each list.

On the first few nights of rush, sorority sisters will be expected to meet several hundred, if not more than a thousand girls, who are herded around the house to have approximately three-minute conversations with as many sisters as possible. This brief impression, crucial for both rushers and rushees, is what causes sororities to begin to prepare their members for rush several days in advance. Many sororities return to school early to go on a pre-rush retreat or rush "workweek" before formal rush (Alpha Rho and Beta Pi stay on campus). At one mid-Atlantic school, I observed a sorority's first pre-rush meeting of the year in order to observe its "practice conversations," the superficial small talk that sisters will have with candidates. Essentially the older sisters train the younger ones in how to respond to most recruits' questions with one goal in mind: "making every girl want us." This can entail spinning, flattering, and outright lying. ("Will you take my best friend if I pick your sorority?" "We love her! She'll probably get in anyway!") During the pre-rush meeting I attended, the girls were specifically instructed to lie. If a rushee were to ask if she would have to live in the house, the sisters were told, "Don't say yes because some girls get intimidated"—even though there was a one-year requirement. If a rushee asked how big the chapter was, a practice question-and-answer sheet suggested the sisters inflate the number.

As sorority sisters from around the country have described to me, the conversations at these parties are all about the same. A rushee is ushered to a sister, who will engage in something akin to the following conversation:

"So . . . where are you from?"

"New York City!" [Candidate reminds herself to smile brightly.]

"What's your major?"

"I'm a dance major!"

"Oh, my sister Tiffany is a dance major, too!" [Sister reminds herself to find something the rushee has in common with a sister.] "Here, I'll introduce you! Tiffany, come talk to [insert rushee's name]." [Sister thrusts candidate toward Tiffany.]

Meanwhile, the sisters have gestures to let the rest of the sorority know what they are thinking about the girl to whom they are talking. Some sororities cross their legs certain ways to indicate what they think of a rushee. Others put their hands behind their back in a silent plea for rescue, signaling, as one sorority girl explained, "Help—this girl can't talk."

Before the semester begins, many sororities have their sisters memorize names, faces, and details about the girls who have already sent in recommendations. State U sisters receive photographs of each rushee at the start of the term. Sometimes the rushees have extra help. According to *Ready for Rush*, Kappa Kappa Gamma alumnae from Vanderbilt University one year sent "Goo-Goo Clusters" to University of Virginia Kappas. The candy bars were wrapped with ribbons reading, "Vandy alumnae are Goo-Goo over Laura Smith and Cheryl Wood!" The manual says, "This not only fed the actives a tasty treat but also made everyone remember these two rushees. Needless to say, both Laura and Cheryl pledged Kappa Kappa Gamma."

At the pre-rush meeting I attended, the sisters were sitting in their chapter room on the floor, chairs, and couches, some having arrived straight out of the shower, still in thin bathrobes, wet hair, and bare feet. As they waited for the meeting to commence, they engaged in important preliminary conversations.

"I really need to change my underwear. Should I go change my underwear?" asked one.

"Did you guys see me do my mermaid dance last year?" asked another.

"Yeah, I have to change my underwear," affirmed the first, who briefly left the room.

The recruitment chair began to explain logistics. During the selection process, as the recruitment chair called each recruit's name, the girls could voice opinions about the recruits before the sisters voted.

The president interrupted. "Remember not to compliment them to their faces, like 'Oh my God, you have such a cute bag,' because then they think you're judging them by their appearance," she said. "But if their parents are generous and they fit the mold of this house, we want them. And if there's a cool girl but you're not sure what else to say about her and you want to get to know her better, call her an 'NGB': 'Nice Girl But.'"

"And if you really, really, really love a girl," the recruitment chair said, "you say, 'I would take her as my Little.'"

"Remember," the president interrupted again, "you want everyone to want you. You want *everyone* to want you."

A sign-in sheet was passed around the room as the meeting shifted to conversation practice. "You might think it's really easy to talk to someone, but it's really not and you could feel really stupid," the recruitment chair said.

"Girls are going to ask you the dumbest questions you've ever heard in your life," added the chapter's adviser.

The recruitment chair offered a few tips before the practice began in earnest. "Memorize our philanthropy. Last year someone asked a sister what our philanthropy was and she said, 'Uhhh . . .' And don't talk about drugs."

"What if someone comes up to you and says, 'I'm coked up out of my mind'?" asked a sister.

A junior piped up, dramatizing the typical rush introduction: "Oh, then you say, 'Oh, I have a sister who's coked up out of her mind, too! Here, I'll introduce you!' " The girls erupted with laughter.

The sisters in the room were paired up and assigned scenarios for practice conversations. The first pair sat on a couch in front of the room, one of them perched on an armrest.

"Okay, first, you should be sitting on the same level at all times," the recruitment chair pointed out. The perched girl hopped down to the cushions.

The girls introduced themselves and shook hands.

"No touching!" the adviser exclaimed.

"I thought there was just a 'no massage' rule," a sister said.

"No. Even if she's your friend, don't be stroking her head and stuff," the adviser said.

The girls resumed.

"So, are you excited?" asked the girl pretending to be the rusher.

"I've been waiting for this day my whole life!" said the sister who was acting as a rushee.

"What kind of classes do you take?"

"I'm an engineer and I'm trying out for band!" The room laughed.

"Oh, that's . . . nice. How many credits are you taking?"

"Twenty-three!" The audience laughed again as the rushee turned to them to explain, "You get to talk to a lot of dorks."

"So," the rushee turned back to her partner, "do you like veggie burgers?"

An older sister addressed the room: "Even if this girl is the biggest tool, you still have to say hello and smile. You don't know who she lives with, so you want her to go home and say we're awesome, because her roommate might be like our number one choice."

"Use the analogy that this is a guy who you know likes you," said a senior. "You're flirting and you pretend there's no one else in the room. Even if you're obviously not going to hook up with him, you still want to make him want you."

"Just remember," said the recruitment chair, "there should never be any more than two sisters on one potential new member and even two shouldn't be there for long. It's intimidating."

At the end of the meeting, the girls were handed a sheet entitled "Increase

Your Rush Vocabulary" to help them think of words to describe candidates. Among the vocabulary words were "shy," "attractive," and "loud."

Bump Groups

JANUARY 13

CAITLIN'S IM AWAY MESSAGE

Oh man, at the house for-ev-er.

OPEN HOUSE, CAITLIN'S FIRST RUSH EVENT AS A SISTER, was a disappointment. Eighteen times, a Rho Chi led a group of rushees past the beds of blue pansies and into the entry hall as the Alpha Rhos chanted, cheered, and clapped. Eighteen times, Elaine stepped forward from her position in the TV room and said, opening her arms wide, "Hi, I'm Elaine, the recruitment chair. Let me know if you have any questions. Welcome to Alpha Rho!" As the Rho Chi prodded the girls forward one by one, the next Alpha Rho in the long line snaked around the room stepped up to introduce herself and take the girl into either the dining room or the TV room to chat. For just over five hours (including four ten-minute breaks) Caitlin forced herself to have superficial conversations with girls who were "just okay." The only girl she liked was someone she already knew: Traci, who lived with René.

The sisters had decorated the TV room and the kitchen with posters, pictures, and T-shirts, as well as awards and trophies that Alpha Rho had won in recent years. The Greek Week trophy sat on a table in the center of the TV room. When girls weren't talkative and Caitlin couldn't think of anything to say beyond the usual trite questions she refused to ask ("Where are you from?" "Where do you live on campus?" "What's your major?"), she led them on a tour of the decorations and told them about the events associated with the props.

Caitlin couldn't believe how overconfident some of the rushees acted, even when they discovered they were talking to the Alpha Rho vice president. Midway through the evening, Caitlin was assigned to speak to a sophomore from Beverly Hills who opened the conversation by saying arrogantly, "I went through rush last year and didn't find a house I liked." Caitlin noticed right away that the girl carried a Chanel bag and wore a Tiffany bracelet and necklace. During pre-rush weekend, the older sisters had emphasized how important it was to make note of designer labels. The benefits were twofold: if the rushee could afford expensive items, then she likely had the money to pay dues and house expenses; and memorizing details about a rushee's outfit would help sisters to better remember her when they voted. Caitlin wasn't used to paying attention to these kinds of details, but she had been reading the issues of *Vogue* that Amy left out for her and was beginning to recognize various designers' logos. Her mother would be proud.

The Beverly Hills girl seemed to have the idea of a rush party backward: instead of trying to impress upon Caitlin that she would fit into Alpha Rho, she interrogated Caitlin, as if Caitlin had to sell Alpha Rho to her. "What sets your house apart from all the others?" she asked, eyeing Caitlin's nondesigner preppy top.

Surprised, Caitlin spoke carefully. "There isn't only one thing that defines our house and that sets us apart—we're not the blond house or the rich house or the smart house. A lot of our girls are really laid back and we have a lot of different personalities. We have people involved in all kinds of things."

The girl hardly seemed to listen before firing her next question. "What would you say is your greatest downfall as a house?"

"Well, our diversity can be good but it can also be bad because we have so many different kinds of personalities, and they can clash. But it's a house that lots of people can feel comfortable in," Caitlin said, trying to spin the answer into a positive trait. She made a mental note to give the girl poor marks for self-importance.

Caitlin dreaded Tuesday's first-round Teal and Jade party. Rush parties were choreographed practically down to the minute. The sisters were divided, according to a common sorority custom, into "bump groups" of three. Caitlin, as sister #1 in her group, would have to greet a rushee, give her a full tour of the house, and then take her to sit down and talk in the dining room. Sister #2 escorted a rushee in front of the fireplace to chat. Sister #3 gave a rushee a tour of the house and then led her to the chapter room to talk. After ten minutes, Caitlin would find #2 and "bump" her: she would take over the conversation with the rushee and then lead her on a tour of the house. Then #2 would find #3's girl and continue chatting with her in the chapter room. And #3 would find Caitlin's rushee and converse in the dining room. It disgusted Caitlin that the rushees, who rarely knew the nights were choreographed, would believe that they were randomly entering into a series of natural conversations.

In between each rush party, the sisters had five minutes to get to their designated spot in the house (Caitlin's spot was in one of the second-floor showers, for privacy) and write in their notebooks everything they could remember about the girls. The rushees didn't realize that anything they mentioned that the sisters remembered would form the basis of how they were "scored" in the voting process. Meanwhile, Caitlin and her Big Sister kept an eye out for potential new additions to their family, because Caitlin knew she wanted to take a Little Sister this semester. They joked that they were going "Little Hunting," as they discreetly appraised the rushees who walked by. But as the rounds went on they grew increasingly discouraged.

Skit Night

JANUARY 15
VICKI'S IM AWAY MESSAGE
vicki=rock star??

RUSH WAS TAKING OVER VICKI'S LIFE, ALTHOUGH AT FIRST she wanted nothing to do with it. She hadn't had a chance to open a textbook or to see William, who was still trying to convince Vicki to be his girlfriend exclusively. On Tuesday night, Vicki spent the first-round party giving the same speech over and over again to the girls whom her bump group met. "I didn't want to rush in the beginning, but as I went through it and met more people, I got more into it," she would tell the rushees. "When I got in and started pledging, I still wasn't even sure if Beta Pi was, like, something I wanted to do. It wasn't until I actually moved into the house and became a part of it that I realized I had made a good decision to join. It made the school smaller, but at the same time it made it bigger because I got to meet so many new people!" [She inserted a wide, welcoming smile here.] The girls seemed to believe her.

Several rushees tried to impress the Beta Pis by telling them how close they were with the brothers of Iota, the fraternity that the informed candidates knew was generally paired with Beta Pis.

"Oh, I'm like best friends with them!" several girls separately effused to Vicki.

"Really? Like who?" Vicki pressed.

"All of them!" The girls didn't realize that Vicki was dating William, the Iota president—and when they found out, they feigned nonchalance. But Vicki noticed that they treated her with more respect.

With some girls, Vicki had to work hard to move a conversation. When she saw that one rushee wore a shirt bearing a picture of a horse, she talked about how much she had loved horseback riding as a child. "Oh, no, I don't like horses," the girl said. "I just like the way it looks on my shirt." One of the longest conversations Vicki had with a rushee revolved entirely around the products they used to straighten their hair. But Vicki didn't make the "help signal"—putting a hand on her hip—until she met an overweight girl who was sweet but had terrible breath. A sister immediately came to bump Vicki, who left to find another rushee.

After the first-round parties, the Beta Pis scored the girls and announced their "rush crushes," the girls they most wanted to be their sisters. Then the recruitment chair told the sisters how they needed to improve their rush. "First of all, if you know you're not funny, don't make a joke," she said. "Also, don't slouch." Vicki blushed. "And don't give anyone dirty looks, because I saw some girls were doing that." During the first two parties, the recruitment chair greeted the rushees as they entered the house while the rest of the Beta Pis stood in lines behind her. "I don't know if you guys noticed, but when a girl who was ugly, fat, had no style, seemed dorky, or her clothes didn't fit her came up, instead of moving forward, you guys stepped backward. You can't be that obvious about it."

The recruitment chair also told the girls they needed to be more opinionated when they scored the rushees. After each rush party, the Beta Pis had to score all of the girls on a scale of 1 to 5, with 5 as the worst rating. Only executive board members were allowed to give 6s. Candidates given mostly 4s and 5s were automatically cut. "A lot of you gave threes to girls who were cute but you didn't know what to do with them," the recruitment chair said. "You need more ones and fives and fewer threes."

On Wednesday, Vicki skipped all her classes to rehearse and help build the sets for Skit Night. Beta Pi's skit was "Total Recruitment Pi," a play on the MTV show *Total Request Live*. The girls changed the lyrics to four songs so that they were about the Beta Pi sisters. The recruitment chair had asked Vicki and Olivia if they would sing a version of Christina Aguilera's "Dirrty" (with lyrics changed to "It's about time for Pi arrival"). Initially, Vicki had been horrified at the thought of singing in front of four groups of rushees. But Olivia put together a funny dance routine and Vicki warmed to the idea. She convinced herself that because she didn't personally know any of the rushees, she didn't care about the impression she made.

Vicki was self-conscious when she and Olivia ran out onto the makeshift stage wearing hot pants, bikini tops, and kneepads. But when she started slithering on the floor and mocking Christina Aguilera's lewd dance moves, it dawned on her that the crowd thought she was hilarious. By the final rush party, Vicki had lost all inhibitions, pouring the contents of a water bottle on her head as Olivia spanked her, while the rest of the rushees and the sisters doubled over in laughter and cheered uproariously for Vicki.

Ω   Ω   Ω

Rush Rules

MANY CAMPUS PANHELLENIC ASSOCIATIONS HAVE ENTIRE books full of rush rules with which sorority sisters are expected to familiarize themselves. For example, rush parties cannot go over their allotted time limit, and rushees cannot knock on a sorority house door, even when arriving for a rush party (Rho Chis must knock). During rush week, many schools put rushees "on silence," meaning rushees can speak only with each other and are discouraged from speaking even to their friends and families. This rule was established so that few people could influence a rushee's decision. At some schools, rushees aren't even allowed to speak with their biological sisters outside of rush events. In the 1980s, at schools that imposed silence rules, fraternities often harassed rushees on their way to rush parties—and occasionally, according to *Rush: A Girl's Guide to Sorority Success*, kidnapped them "just for fun. But this isn't always fun for the rushees, especially if they are late for a party or if frat boys vomit on their dresses. Friendlier girls write their phone numbers on the backs of their name tags and flash them at good-looking fraternity boys who pester them."

At Brooke's school, though the official rush week wasn't until second semester, sisters began lobbying the freshmen two or three weeks after they arrived on campus in the fall. Conversations were limited to twenty-five minutes with freshmen, who weren't allowed to enter a sorority house until rush week. At the first college football game Brooke attended as a freshman, she was shocked to see the reception waiting for rush candidates. As soon as she walked into the concession stand area, sorority sisters, wearing their pins and positioned in strategic places, immediately approached her as if they wanted her to be their best friend. Even if the girls merely had a friendly conversation about the weather, "they made you feel like you were a super-star and they were the paparazzi," Brooke told me. "You'd meet them at fraternity parties and they'd say, 'Oh my gosh! Can I get you a beer?'"

Because rush was so competitive, sisters would watch members of other houses intently to try to catch them in a rush infraction; they worked almost as hard to get other houses in trouble as they did to woo the recruits. Sisters carefully timed any rival sisters they saw talking to potential recruits. "This is so bad—you'd time somebody on a girl so you could turn that other house in, that's how petty we were," Brooke said. "I did it to my best friend once, because I wasn't best friends with her then. I was like, 'Mallory Jenkins has been talking to Christina for, oh my Lord, thirty minutes. I'm turning her in.'"

The sister would write down the details of the infraction and turn the document in to her sorority's rush chair, saying something like, "I saw Mallory Jenkins talking to a freshman for thirty minutes; I want to bring her up on charges." The rush chair would collect and save the violations. When she had enough ammunition to turn in to Panhellenic, the Panhellenic president and vice president of rush would hold a mediation session with the "rush teams" of both sororities: the rush chair and the rush adviser (an older alumna who would represent the house). "They would sit there as if at the U.N. and talk about it and try to come up with some kind of adequate punishment, like banning a sister from a rush party or lowering the number of girls a chapter could take," Brooke told me. "One house would say, 'Well, this is what I have on your 'house.' And the other would answer, 'Well, this is what I have on your house.' And then you'd say, 'Well, this is what I have on your house again.' It was like a poker game. They would show a card that had a written report of a violation and when they had decided on a resolution, that card would get crossed off so things wouldn't get regurgitated fifty thousand times."

Five top houses at Brooke's school competed ferociously for the same recruits. Most of them would try to come up with reasonable sanctions to rush violations; their rush advisers were known to meet in a car in a school parking lot at 2 A.M. to hammer out mutually agreeable punishments. But another top house would "do really mean stuff and go for the jugular" by trying to inflict the worst possible penalty on the other houses. "They were really bad," Brooke said. "They had a lot of really Texas girls whose mothers were big in society, like university parents' clubs, and, since they were really involved alumnae, they knew their girls wouldn't get into trouble."

Ω Ω Ω

Voting

JANUARY 15
SABRINA'S IM AWAY MESSAGE
Everything is different but nothing has changed.

BY WEDNESDAY NIGHT'S VOTE MEETING, SABRINA WAS thoroughly disgusted by the superficiality of the week. She had met some girls she liked, in particular Andrea, a sophomore with braces whom Sabrina had noticed immediately because she seemed relaxed and wore funky vintage clothes. When Sabrina talked to her, she found that Andrea, intelligent, studious, petite, and slightly irreverent, reminded her a little of herself. But Sabrina had also met girls she referred to as "shoot-me-in-the-head girls," who were so uninterested in the conversation that they wouldn't even look at Sabrina when she was speaking to them. The most frustrating part of rush week was Elaine's unwavering, dogged focus on "the image of the house."

Among other things, the rush chair wouldn't let Sabrina wear her capris more than once during the week, even though Sabrina didn't own more than two pairs of pants besides jeans.

"But you already approved these," Sabrina argued when she tried to wear them again on skit night.

"They saw you in those pants last night," Elaine said.

"No one cares."

"We want to make a good impression," Elaine said. She had even gone so far as to vacuum every bedroom in the house and hang teal and jade streamers above Sabrina's bed because Sabrina didn't display the Alpha Rho colors.

Sabrina didn't have the time or the patience for rush this year. On top of her usual waitressing schedule and course load, she had to deal with the constant complaints of her new bed neighbor, who had been forced upstairs to the Penthouse when Charlotte took her double room, and she was also busy struggling to keep Mike interested in their relationship. She had seen him once before rush started (there was no time once rush began), but the date hadn't gone well. As they watched a movie, she had asked him why he was so quiet.

"I feel like a dirty old man," he said.

"Is that why you seem so distant?"

"Yes. I feel more like your big brother than your boyfriend."

"Mike, I know we're at two different points in our lives, but it won't always be that way," Sabrina reassured him.

After the skit parties, the Alpha Rhos gathered in the basement for the most important vote of the week. The recruits who made it through this round of cuts would be invited to Preference Night. One by one, Elaine would put up a photo of each recruit on a slide projector screen, call out the recruit's name, give the sisterhood the chance to discuss her, if necessary, and then call for the Alpha Rhos to vote by holding up either a green card or a red card. After they had gone through the entire list, each sister would rank each of the girls who had accumulated more greens than reds.

Sabrina knew it was going to be a long night when sisters requested 2-2-1s for each of the first five recruits. The rush adviser had suggested that the girls make up their minds based on how the recruits would contribute to Alpha Rho. But the sisters grew weary and frustrated as one 2-2-1 after another was called, and the adviser spent the meeting yelling at the sisters for talking out of turn and having side conversations (they were supposed to remain quiet so as not to influence other people's decisions). The older sisters, meanwhile, were chiding the younger ones for not giving specific details about their conversations.

"I really hated this girl. I hope she doesn't come back," one sophomore said.

"I went to high school with that one. I don't want to be her sister," said another.

"Really, I had a great conversation with her," another offered. "She's from Highland Park."

Elaine practically exploded. "You need to tell me how she will contribute," she shouted. "It doesn't mean anything if she's from Highland Park, because she could live in the maid's quarters and not have the money for dues. You need to tell me more."

Sabrina bristled. It wasn't easy to get financial details out of recruits in the first place, but Sabrina didn't think they should be basing their decisions on financial considerations at all. "That sounds Big Brother. Why do you care? That's not what the process is all about," she said. "How would you find out that kind of specific financial information, anyway?"

"You can ask if the parents are financially supportive," Elaine said.

"But the parents could be doctors and still not want to pay for dues," Sabrina said.

During the next 2-2-1, the sisters tried to get more specific.

"She was wearing a Gucci sweater."

"She had white trash friends."

"She had a Kate Spade bag."

Sabrina remained quiet for the rest of the meeting. She, Caitlin, and Amy had already gone over how they were going to vote. If one of the trio hadn't met a recruit, she simply trusted the others' judgment and followed their lead. The meeting lasted until four in the morning.

Preference Night

JANUARY 16

AMY'S IM AWAY MESSAGE

recruiting some fabulous new Alpha Rhos!

ON THURSDAY MORNING, ELAINE CIRCULATED A SIGN-UP sheet with the remaining candidates' names. She instructed the sisters to write their names next to up to three of their rush crushes—the girls they most wanted to "pref," or lead around on Preference Night. When she noticed that no one had signed up to pref Traci, Amy enthusiastically marked down her name. Unlike the other rush parties, during the two Pref rounds, or parties, each rushee would be assigned to a sister, one-on-one, for the entire hour and a half. But, like the other rush parties, Pref was completely choreographed before it started.

That night at Pref practice, before the rushees arrived, the sisters rehearsed the ceremony, their Pref songs, and the choreographed movements and positioning that would take them and their recruits around the house in an orderly fashion. About ten minutes before the first party, Elaine handed each girl a card that said whom she was preffing each round and the room in which she was supposed to talk to the recruit. Immediately Elaine was mobbed by irate sisters. While she had assigned some girls to pref both rounds, she had arranged it so that others wouldn't pref at all. Elaine, like recruitment chairs at other houses, was attempting to influence the rushees by displaying the most beautiful and charming girls in the house as much as possible while hiding the less attractive girls by putting them on kitchen duty. Amy, figuring that although she was attractive, she hadn't bothered to charm Elaine, didn't mind that she was on kitchen and waitress duty for one of the parties, but she was furious that another sister had been assigned to pref Traci while she hadn't been given anyone to pref.

Because the other sister was one of the best-looking girls in the house, Elaine assumed that meant she was great at preffing, and had assigned her to pref both rounds. But the sister actually hated rush because she was incredibly shy.

Amy approached the sister. "We can just switch for that round," Amy said.

"I'd love to, but they're not letting us," the sister replied.

Amy went to talk to Elaine but stopped short when she saw Whitney screaming at her. "I'm a senior and this is my last Preference ceremony so I should get to pref!" Whitney was yelling. "I'm skipping my brother's birthday party for this!"

Elaine was bawling so hard she couldn't talk.

"There has to be one sister who will give her Pref to me. Other girls got two and I got none!" Whitney screamed. Getting no reaction from Elaine other than sobs, Whitney turned and stalked out of the house. "This is ridiculous. I'm going home!"

Amy quickly deduced that this wasn't the best time to approach Elaine. Instead, she found the rush adviser. "I love this girl and she's one of my closest friends. I really want to pref her and the assigned sister doesn't. I don't want to upset Elaine."

"That's fine," the adviser said. "Go ahead and switch."

After the first Pref ceremony, while the recruits and the sisters chatted softly in the TV and dining rooms, Amy, on waitress duty, tottered around on her Manolos every ten minutes asking girls if they wanted a drink. Her job wasn't taxing; sisters knew they weren't supposed to ask for a drink unless their assigned recruit asked first, and the rushees were too nervous to ask for anything. So Amy spent most of the round in the kitchen, listening to the complaints of the sisters whom Elaine had stuck in the kitchen for both rounds.

The sisters had been told they weren't allowed to eat from any of the lavish displays of food unless they were preffing a recruit and the recruit was eating, too. Amy routinely peeked out of the kitchen to see the sushi rolls, cheese platters, berry tarts, and fudge squares sitting untouched because the rushees were too edgy to eat. Amy waited for an opportune moment, then glided by one of the tables, quickly grabbed a handful of fudge squares, and, palming her snack, circled to the guest bedroom to eat them.

A recruit on her way to the bathroom saw Amy stuffing a piece of fudge in her mouth and sniffed. "Do you know how many calories are in that?" the recruit warned. "I mean, you're practically eating a cube of fat!" Amy made sure to remember the recruit's name to vote against her.

When it was time for the final Pref party, Amy went outside at the pre-scribed time, found an excited Traci, handed her a white rose, and said, "I am especially happy to invite Traci King to be my special guest this evening at Alpha Rho." Traci dropped her purse and her wrap in the pile in the entry hall. Rush rules forbade recruits from taking anything with them—even so much as a cookie—when they left a house so that sisters couldn't bribe them with gifts. Rushees had to leave their purses and any outerwear in the hall-way to prevent them from hiding any offerings. The rushees, many in short designer skirts and knee-high boots and carrying designer bags, quietly and reverently followed the sisters downstairs to the chapter room, where the sisters who weren't preffing stood in a semicircle facing a large bouquet of pansies and sang until all of the recruits arrived.

Elaine stood in the middle of the semicircle, holding a candle in front of her face. (Amy, Sabrina, and Caitlin whispered to each other that Elaine's seem-ingly glued-on fake smile made her look evil in the glow of the flame.) Char-lotte distributed candles to every girl in the room as the Alpha Rhos sang their candle-passing song. She lit the candle held by the first sister, who used her candle to light the candle next to her, and so on around the room. Several sis-ters read lines from a poem about sisterhood. Then Charlotte and another se-nior gave emotional speeches about the meaning of Alpha Rho, as sisters around the room wept. The ceremony ended after the two sisters with the best voices in the house sang the Alpha Rho version of "Amazing Grace." Amy watched Traci carefully.

Beth, a friend of Traci's, had confided to Amy that Traci had initially been torn between Alpha Rho and Beta Pi, where two sisters who were close friends of hers were pressuring her to join. But Traci didn't think she was "the right image" for Beta Pi, who were mostly blond, wealthy party girls. "She thinks the Alpha Rho girls are much more down to earth," Beth had told Amy. "She says in Beta Pi it would be too hard to stay perfect all the time." And now, at Pref, Amy could see that Traci was smitten with Alpha Rho.

After Pref Night, the girls had to fill out a form to rank the recruits who had attended their Pref parties. As the forms were passed out, some sisters were loudly campaigning: "If Mary's in this house, I'll kill myself!" "We want Janine—she'll be the coolest sister ever!"

At five-thirty on Friday, after a short ceremony during which each Rho Chi revealed her sorority, the recruits, in sundresses and heels despite the grayest weather of the year, filed into the student center to receive their bids. Meanwhile, the sisters waited outside their houses, blasting music and dancing on the lawn. They wouldn't know which recruits had made the cut until the new girls showed up at the house. Parents and students milled around with balloons and flowers. At six-thirty, the presidents of each sorority led their new pledges from the student center to the house. As they walked down the short path, the sisters cheered loudly and chanted from their lawns. Fraternity brothers bellowed and held up signs with numbers rating the attractiveness of each new pledge who passed by.

When the pledges reached Alpha Rho, the sisters—many of them drunk—hugged them and took pictures. They gave the pledges the same Bid Day jerseys the sisters wore: pink tank tops with glittered cursive script reading "There are two kinds of women in this world: Alpha Rhos, and those who wish they were." When they spotted her beaming in her new Alpha Rho jersey, Amy and Sabrina raced to hug Traci and told her how excited they were that she would be their sister.

After an hour of mingling, the Alpha Rhos led the pledges inside the house for a "cookie buffet": hundreds of sugar cookies arranged in the shape of the Alpha Rho swan. As they sat around the dining room, each pledge and sister said her name and told a funny story about herself. The Alpha Rho sisters looked around at each other and smiled. They had filled their quota with girls from the top half of their bid list. Now it remained to be seen how the new sisterhood would turn out.

Ω Ω Ω

Membership Selection

RUSH HAS BECOME SO COMPETITIVE AND ELABORATE A process that determined mothers have taken to hiring "rush consultants" to groom their daughters so they will be accepted by their desired sorority.

These consultants, who have sprung up in private companies not affiliated or endorsed by the National Panhellenic Conference, are a cross between beauty pageant coaches and college preparatory service counselors, training a rushee on everything from attitude to outerwear.

Furthermore, some sorority alumnae have published guidebooks to help lead aspirants through the process. *Ready for Rush: The Must-Have Manual for Sorority Rushees!*, the 1999 guide, includes an informative rush calendar that suggests that six to twelve months before rush begins, a sorority hopeful should:

- List your honors, achievements, and activities. If your fact sheet or résumé is not impressive, get involved now! . . .
- Start saving money for your Rush wardrobe.
- Get in shape. Establish an exercise program so you will look and feel your best when it comes time to leave for school.

Three months before rush begins:

- Have a flattering photograph of yourself made.
- Read a good etiquette book to brush up on your manners.
- Order personal tea cards.

One month before rush:

- Go on your Rush shopping spree . . .
- See a few current movies, which can serve as great conversation topics.
- Schedule an appointment at a beauty salon for two weeks before Rush begins.

Two weeks before rush:

- Have a dress rehearsal to try on all of your outfits for each round of parties. Make sure everything is altered appropriately and that you have the right lingerie and accessories for each ensemble.

- ▣ Go on a last minute shopping spree for things you need.
- ▣ Have your hair cut and highlighted if necessary. [The authors later recommend a "blunt," "crisp" cut and explain, "A good colorist can weave in hues of soft golds and gentle reds. If it takes the colorist three hours, it's well worth it."]
- ▣ Practice applying cosmetics in natural light.

And two days before rush:

- ▣ Get a manicure. ["Avoid too many rings. One on each hand is best."]

This kind of advice is hardly unusual. In a section of *Rush: A Girl's Guide to Sorority Success* titled "How Sororities Judge Rushees," the book states:

> The first significant evaluation sorority members make of a rushee is how she looks. It is important that you look your very best throughout rush week. If you're not attractive, you should play up your other strong qualities (for instance, background, money, or, more important, personality and accomplishments). Although every rushee is obviously not beautiful, each girl should make the best of what she has to offer. For example, if you are overweight, you must try to lose weight before rush. If you have acne problems, you should work on clearing up your face. Whatever problems you have, you must do your best to minimize them. Physical attractiveness plays a large part in the overall evaluation process.

Sororities will publicly argue that they do not choose members based on looks, and that a rushee's personality and achievement will best sway the Greek jury of her peers. This is about as likely as a Mississippi Delta Delta Delta chapter rejecting supermodel Heidi Klum in favor of, say, Jon Lovitz. Rushees are initially judged by their level of attractiveness, beginning with the early rush parties, when during breaks sisters frantically write down all they can remember about a girl to trigger memories of their conversation when they are voting. They also review the card before they next speak with the candidate, so they can flatter her by pretending they remember her. Usually these descriptions revolve around looks: "She had ugly red hair" and "She was a pig" are some actual examples. "I'd see a girl across the room, read her name tag, and make a mental note to vote against her because she looked like such a loser that I didn't want her to wear my letters," said Shannon, the West Coast Delta Zeta. "If some really fun, interesting girl came in and she was really fat, she wasn't going to be invited back, that's for sure. Ugly girls wouldn't make it. That would look bad for the sorority."

Many southern sororities blow up each girl's rush application photo onto a large piece of poster board to display during the rush meetings held weekly throughout the fall—a semester before rush actually begins. In sororities that use this method, girls told me, it is this photo, more than any other single factor, that essentially determines a sorority candidate's fate. When a rushee's photo is shown in front of the membership, the sisters' candid assessments are unleashed: true examples include "I don't like her clothes," "She's obnoxious," and "Ew, she's a total dog."

In many sororities, sisters are allowed to use only specific descriptive phrases. In some chapters in the Deep South, the good descriptions include, "She is just the most shining star and she can look so pristine and she went to such-and-such school." In these chapters, the worst description a sister is technically allowed to give of a rushee—and the phrase used most often when no one likes a particular candidate—is, in full, drawn-out southern drawl, "I think she would shine brighter in another house." (Conversely, Tri-Delts who think a rushee will fit in use the phrase "She has that Delta Sparkle.")

Nonetheless, another nonlist phrase that comes up often is "That girl's a real slut." In many chapters, when a sister has objections to a recruit, she can take her concerns to the chapter's Rush Council, a jury of sisters like the Standards Board. It is the Rush Council's job to dig up the secrets of rushees, using their sorority's network of alumnae across the country to unearth potentially damaging dirt. The Rush Council listens to every complaint about a freshman, such as, "I heard she's already slept with seven Pike brothers—and it's only September." The Rush Council then investigates the claim and the girl's reputation first by calling the alumnae chapter in the girl's hometown to ask those members to find out as much about the girl as possible. The members of the council then talk to people on campus (usually their boyfriends) to try to confirm rumors. In these chapters, it is up to the members of the Rush Council to weed out the undesirables, to ensure that the sorority doesn't accidentally admit a girl who would never belong.

FEBRUARY

———

Every once in a while one member's behavior negatively affects those around her. Her actions, which are inappropriate and unsisterly, lessen the quality sorority experience that Kappa Delta attempts to provide to all members . . . Acceptable reasons for placing a member on National Probation: 1. Disparaging remarks against the Sisterhood. 2. Refusal to cooperate with the chapter. 3. Violation of the principles of the Order, which make her uncongenial to the other members of the Sisterhood.

—*The Norman Shield of Kappa Delta, 2003*

Ω   Ω   Ω

FEBRUARY 26
SABRINA'S IM AWAY MESSAGE
I am simultaneously colorful and invisible.

IT WAS COMPOSITE DAY at Alpha Rho, the day when a professional photographer came to the house to photograph each girl for the Composite. The large, framed compilation of portraits of each sister—organized alphabetically and by pledge class, with the exec board and the older sisters on the top—hung in the chapter room with Composites from previous years. This afternoon, like every year at this time, the sisters were complaining that it took at least thirty minutes to put on makeup to prepare for a photo session that took only two. While one sister posed in the chapter room, the next five or six girls were crammed into the small bathroom across the hall, helping each other fasten black drapes around their bare shoulders. This was no easy task. Once the drape was on, a sister couldn't move her arms without disturbing the way the drape fell. Therefore, each girl had to do her makeup and fix her hair, have another girl close the drape, and then walk like a penguin across the hall for her photo.

"Can you help me with this cape thing?" a sister asked Sabrina. "Last year it was pulled down too much and showed way too much cleavage." Sabrina stood on her toes and raised the drape. "Wait, don't pull it too high— I still want to show a little!" Now surrounded by penguins, Sabrina was the only one in the room who hadn't preened. The sorority had instituted a new rule this year that required the girls to wear their hair down and unadorned for the Composite. (Caitlin had persuaded the exec board that Sabrina could keep her hair in braids.) This meant that Sabrina, who didn't wear makeup and therefore had nothing to primp, was assigned to drape-fastening duty as she waited for her turn. Most of the sisters passed the time gossiping about who was taking whom to the upcoming Date Party.

Sabrina wouldn't be going, again—this time because she was reeling from her relationship with Mike. After weeks of getting the runaround, she decided that she was tired of the way that Mike, who seemed always to be busy this semester, had been ducking out of possible dates. When they were together he would profess his love for her and bring her daffodils, but when she phoned him and left a message, sometimes it would take him days to return her call. When she finally reached him a few days before Composite Day, he said he would call her back at seven the next evening.

He called at eleven.

"Why didn't you call me at seven?" Sabrina asked.

"I had things to do," Mike replied.

"Why didn't you call me and tell me you had things to do?" she pressed.

In the ensuing three-hour discussion about his insecurities, the professor brought up his past girlfriends. "Every time we broke up it was because I was afraid to let them in," he said.

Sabrina loved him, she respected him, and she appreciated the way he had, as she put it, furthered her "intellectual development." But she was not going to be his lapdog. For the first time, she realized, she was more mature than her professor was.

"Okay, fine," she said to him. "Clearly this isn't working for you. But you're an adult, so you go figure out what you want. I'm done with this."

"Wait," he said. "I'll try harder."

"First you get your head straightened out, and you do it alone," she said. And hung up the phone and wept.

As the photographer told her to smile, Sabrina glanced at the walls full of Composites from prior years and wondered why she had ever thought she would truly belong. Alpha Rho was probably the most tolerant top-level white sorority at State U. And still, as Sabrina looked over the white back-drop, it pained her to confront a reality that she was nonetheless reminded of every day she spent with Alpha Rho: out of now 160 sisters, still only 2 of them weren't Caucasian.

The only reasons Sabrina had rushed Alpha Rho as a freshman was because Amy was rushing and because she liked the way the prestigious sorority promised access to a network. Not only had Sabrina not considered rushing a black sorority, but she also hadn't seriously pursued any sorority other than Alpha Rho. Only after her freshman year Bid Day, when as a pledge she was required to be at the house much of the time, did she notice how much she stood apart from her sisters. The veneer that had glossed the house during rush quickly wore thin, exposing the true politics and stereo-types of a sorority. Sabrina had almost dropped out. But when the sisters kept telling her, "Stick with it. It gets better," she believed them.

She questioned that prediction now. Sabrina loved a few of the girls in the house as individuals, but the baggage that came along with sorority life—the herd mentality, the materialism, the disproportionate wealth, the stuck-up attitudes—made the girls as a group inordinately more difficult to bear. She was unwilling to believe that her sisters' occasionally racist remarks were meant maliciously. Many of these girls had been raised to think a certain way, and Sabrina felt she couldn't blame them for that. These were girls who didn't understand what it meant to be poor and who certainly didn't understand what it meant to be black. Sabrina had noticed, for instance, that when the girls described white guys, they would say things like "He has brown hair with blond highlights and blue eyes." But when they described black guys, they would use descriptions like "Who's that big black guy downstairs?" Once, Sabrina had asked Caitlin about it.

"Why do white people always say stuff like that?"

Caitlin pondered. "Well, for me personally," she spoke slowly, "I don't know how to describe black people. They just seem to have less describable features. I know I sound like an asshole, but I don't mean it that way."

Sabrina brushed it off. She knew Caitlin wasn't racist—and that she didn't fully understand the underlying racial tension in the house, and in the country in general, because Caitlin had grown up in a mostly white neighborhood that didn't deal often with these issues. There was simply a level of ignorance among white Greeks that Sabrina assumed she couldn't hope to overcome. This would explain why Alpha Rho didn't offer bids to the non-whites whom Sabrina had given high marks. The sisters couldn't comprehend the value of diversity, which didn't make Alpha Rho—which at least did have black sisters—much more tolerant than the other sororities on campus. The year before, when Sabrina's friend rushed another sorority on campus, she asked a sister if there was diversity in the house.

"Oh, sure we're diverse," the sister told her. "We have blond girls, red-haired girls, and a lot of brown-haired girls. I think we have a Spanish girl, too."

A few days after Composite, Sabrina was playing games on her computer when she overheard some Pents talking about an attractive fraternity brother.

"Mmm, I would love to take him home with me," Bitsy said.

"Well," Fiona interjected, "he's black." State U's historically white fraternities were much more racially inclusive than the sororities.

A third Pent nodded. "My parents wouldn't be happy with me if I dated someone black."

Sabrina stood up. As she walked past them to go downstairs, they abruptly stopped talking.

Another night, well into pledge period, the exec board distributed to the sisters the list of pledges and the girls the execs had assigned to be their Big Sisters. Fiona was once again holding forth in the Penthouse, complaining to a large audience of Pents about why so many of the sophomores hadn't been given their first-choice Little Sister.

"They must have given the officers first pick," Fiona whined. She read aloud the list of Big–Little Sister pairs, commenting on each one. "That match makes sense," "That one's understandable," "That's a shady match." When she got to C.C. and C.C.'s newly assigned Little Sister—Andrea, the stylish sophomore with braces—she stopped. "This doesn't make sense," Fiona announced. "Other people like that pledge, too."

C.C., sitting unnoticed on Sabrina's bed on the other side of the Penthouse, quietly wept on Sabrina's shoulder. "Why is this an issue?" C.C. asked Sabrina. "Why don't they think I'm cool enough to be her Big Sister?" Sabrina was incensed. Fiona's implication was clear: why should a black girl get a white Little Sister if the white girls wanted her, too? The longer Sabrina lived in the house, the more she noticed how Alpha Rho seemed to be an elitist institution for people who had grown up believing they were privileged. Sabrina could have said something then, in the Penthouse, with all of the girls there and C.C. still crying in her arms. She could have confronted Fiona. But she said nothing.

Ω   Ω   Ω

"One Hundred Percent Apartheid"

THE MOST EMOTIONAL I EVER SAW SABRINA WAS IN EARLY March, a few weeks after Composite Day. She sought me out to rehash what I had initially assumed was the last straw for her. That afternoon in the TV room, Sabrina and other sisters were watching MTV when one of the girls talked about a skit she and her friends had performed at her private high school.

"For our talent, we dressed up like Busta Rhymes, with the pigtailed dreadlocks, muscle shirts, and bling bling [jewelry]," the sister joyfully recounted. "And we painted our faces black! It was so hilarious!"

Sabrina's stomach dropped. "Excuse me," Sabrina said politely, to make sure she had heard the girl correctly. "Did you just say you guys painted your faces black?"

"Yeah!" the sister said, as the other girls on the couch laughed. "We painted our faces black and it was the funniest thing!"

Sabrina couldn't believe that the girls would laugh about blackface right in front of an obviously black girl.

"Did you say anything?" I asked her.

"No," Sabrina sighed. "I was surrounded by a group of laughing white girls. Clearly I couldn't say anything."

"But if these are your 'sisters,'" I challenged her, "why do you feel you can't or shouldn't say anything?"

"Well, I'm not ready to say anything to them yet. I know a lot of shit, I just don't know how to articulate it in an effective manner yet," she said.

"But haven't there already been a lot of instances this year when white girls in your house have had racially insensitive conversations?"

"Ha," Sabrina said. "'Racially insensitive.' I don't know if that's the right term for it."

"Well, last time when we talked about Fiona's comments and I called her racist, you said she didn't mean to be and so you didn't know if you'd call it racist," I said.

"It's not like they're being 'insensitive' to racial issues—I don't think that people should speak about racial matters in a sensitive manner," Sabrina explained. "But some people just don't get it. My sisters are nice . . . for the most part . . . but most of them have grown up with privilege or in sheltered worlds, so they don't even think about worlds other than their own. So I just feel like they just have no idea."

"Have you thought about educating them?" I asked, having assumed that a sisterhood should naturally encompass a mutual learning experience. "Not that it's your responsibility, but maybe they'd get it if you clued them in that they're not the center of the universe. The sorority has eating disorder speakers and drunk driving speakers, but nobody can have a serious discussion about race?"

"But there are sooo many of them compared to little me. I would become this object of . . . I don't know," Sabrina said. "It would be very uncomfortable for me to say anything."

I asked what would happen if she did speak up.

"Most of my sisters aren't receptive to reality or to new ideas," she said. "I know from being in this house that if I were to say anything, number one: certain people wouldn't like me anymore because they would think I'm just bitter. They would refuse to listen. Number two: people would pity me. Number three: people would think I'm a hypocrite. Number four: people would constantly be asking me stupid questions about it. And number five: I'd just feel like even more of a token than I already am."

"Why would you be a hypocrite?"

"Because if I were to teach them some things about race and society, they may be like, 'Well, you're in a sorority and you're in college, so you have no right to speak about this,' or something like that. I feel like either all the girls see me as a token, or they don't even see me as black. They're color-blind or something."

"Even if you and C.C. were to stand up in front of the sisterhood together and start a dialogue?"

"We're two people out of one hundred and sixty," Sabrina said. "Things would be awkward, and then C.C. would have to defend me or maybe even dismiss me because she would have the other girls asking her questions all the time, or making comments about me or what I say."

"Have you discussed this with C.C.?"

"Not really. Just because you are brown doesn't mean that you think differently from white people."

"Then why do you stay?" I asked.

"I would have dropped out last semester but I don't have an affordable place to live."

"Is that the only reason you stay in Alpha Rho?"

"Basically. But while I'm here I try to make the most of it. It's a learning experience, I guess," Sabrina said. "I mean, I'm not really learning anything new, just getting more experience in how to deal with things. Because I'm in college, where people are supposed to be diverse and liberal and yada-yada-yada, but that's not really the case. So when I enter the working world, I know that I am going to find more of the same stuff that I find here. I might as well learn how to cope with it."

I was still wondering how such a "together" girl could take the kinds of abuse I watched her sisters inflict on her without giving any of it back. "So do you think that throughout your Alpha Rho career you're never going to confront anyone—not just about race issues, but also people like Fiona for treating you as an inferior?"

"Probably not," she said. "If I were able to remove myself from this situation, I probably would. But I have to live here and can't get away for the time being."

I was startled by the level of ignorance at Alpha Rho, supposedly the most racially accepting white sorority on a campus that was generally perceived to be tolerant and liberal. If a minority girl here at State U—a girl with more composure and awareness than the average college student—had to have such a large reserve of strength on hand simply to survive sorority life on a daily basis, I wondered how black girls fared in the Deep South, where sorority membership is a crucial part of both university culture and adult life.

In August 2000, the Alpha Gamma Delta house at the University of Georgia was voting to cut a few of the eleven hundred girls who had attended the first round of rush, when the sisters read the name of a particular candidate. Sophomore Ali Davis saw that some of her sisters had given the girl terrible scores. When she asked what the girl had done to deserve the scores, a sister responded, "She's black. I don't even know why she'd want to come to our rush." Another sister asserted that if Alpha Gamma Delta admitted a black girl, "none of the fraternities would want to do anything with us."

When the girls voted to cut the only black candidate who had braved rush, Ali, disgusted by her sisters' bigotry, decided to leave the sorority—and the university. Upon learning of Ali's reasons for leaving, the administration temporarily suspended the chapter until Alpha Gamma Delta agreed to promise that they would aim to be more tolerant of diversity. Ali, who transferred schools, has since heard from sorority sisters around the country who shared their own stories of sorority discrimination.

From 2001 to 2003 at schools across the country, there were numerous instances of Greeks exhibiting blatant racism, from students staging fake lynchings and donning Klan costumes to sororities taking pictures of fraternities in blackface. To better understand the ways African American students deal with this kind of atmosphere, I set up a visit with Melody Twilley, a junior at the University of Alabama, in Tuscaloosa.

Ω Ω Ω

TALL, BRIGHT, PRETTY, AND OUTGOING, MELODY TWILLEY is leading me on a tour of the University of Alabama's Sorority Row: two streets full of impressive Greek Revival houses framed by manicured lawns, meticulously pruned shrubbery, and flowers planted in each sorority's colors. Rocking chairs and wrought-iron tables line columned porches straight from a southern grandmother's dreams. The front of the Zeta house is festooned with a large banner proudly proclaiming, "Congrats! ZTA Gini Mollohan lavaliered to ΒΘΠ Jason Hudson."

Melody and I pass the Tri-Delt house. "Old money," she says, gesturing to the fountain in front of the house, surrounded by brick mosaic and orange flowers, and featuring a sculpture of a cherub. On the sidewalk leading up to the house the Tri-Delt letters are inlaid in metal. We pass the Pi Phi house, where broad windows reflect long Ionic columns tied with yellow ribbons. "New money," Melody points out. She sighs as we continue down Sorority Row. "Ah," she mutters. "Skid Row."

On paper, Melody Twilley is, by anyone's standards, prime sorority material. A graduate of the prestigious Alabama School of Math and Science, Melody won several awards and was chosen to speak at commencement. At the time that she rushed at the University of Alabama, she had a 3.87 GPA and sang first soprano in the campus choir. She was seventeen, having skipped two grades before arriving at college. Her father was known as the largest black landowner in the state.

In the fall of 2000, Melody signed up for fall rush. One of the main reasons she had backed out of going to Rice University at the last minute was that they didn't have sororities. At Alabama, by contrast, sororities practically controlled the student body. The University of Alabama, like many southern schools, runs a segregated rush process: white Greeks rush in the fall for the white organizations, while the black Greeks rush in the spring for the black organizations. Melody didn't think anything of joining white rush; she was used to navigating a mostly white community from her time in high school. Many of the more ambitious Alabama students—and a fifth of the campus— join the UA Greek system, which is expected to match them with appropriate future spouses and provide an entree into a powerful state network. Residents who aren't members of the UA Greek system, it has been said, rarely break into the state's political and economic elite. But Melody wasn't motivated by the promise of power and connections. She merely liked the idea of belonging to a sisterhood. It sounded like fun.

So Melody, optimistic and excited, began the year as the only black girl to enter white rush. "I thought I was the greatest. Stupid me. I didn't know they didn't take black people," she explains. The girls seemed nice and Melody looked forward to the social outlet a sorority could offer her. She was especially excited about the Thursday night "swaps," or Greek theme parties—"Pimps and Hos," "Saints and Angels"—in which pledges from sororities and fraternities were matched up. When seven of the sororities invited her back for the second round of rush, she was mildly disappointed that the other eight weren't interested, but didn't think anything more of it.

Only a small group of women were rejected from all fifteen white sororities. Melody was one of them. Over the next year, faculty members and administrators rallied around Melody as a way to encourage the university to desegregate its Greek system and unify its rush process. In the fall of 2001, at the insistent prodding of students, faculty members, and sorority alumnae, Melody rushed again, this time with letters of recommendation from scores of sorority graduates and endorsements from university officials.

"I was glad she was going back through," says Kathleen Cramer, the university's associate vice president for Student Affairs. Cramer, who had been the president of the Kappa Kappa Gamma house when she attended Alabama in the 1970s, gestures in her office with manicured nails and a crisp bob. "I was very optimistic the second time could work. I lined up recommendations, introduced her to alumnae, student, and Panhellenic leaders, and a faculty member and I had a talk with her about rush wardrobe and conversation. We thought we could help her."

Melody wasn't completely willing to believe that she had been rejected the first time around because of her skin color. She still wanted to join a white sorority, and she thought there was a good chance they might take her in. By the third round of rush, only one sorority, Alpha Delta Pi, still had her on its list. Sparkling in an indigo gown, a rhinestone cross necklace and earring set, and smart patent-leather pumps, Melody walked into ADPi, the first house on the corner of Sorority Row. Inside, sisters and rushees were talking one-on-one, mostly about the latest football game. A sister sat Melody down.

"There's a rumor going around that you're only going through rush just to prove a point," said the ADPi sister.

Melody was flabbergasted. "You've been through rush—why would anybody go through all of this twice just to prove a point?!" The sister seemed to understand. "I'm here to find sisterhood, fun, and good times, same as everyone else is," Melody continued. "Don't look at me as the black girl going through rush. Look at me as a girl going through rush." They couldn't do it. Once again, every white sorority on campus turned her down.

When I speak about this with Kathleen Cramer, she shakes her head with resignation. "This is a system steeped in tradition, and I think that's part of the problem. Chapters are afraid to go first. I think there's an unarticulated pressure toward sameness, which fosters racism and a homogeneity they'll never see the rest of their lives," she says. In May 2002, Cramer and the Alabama faculty senate sent to each of the twenty-six historically white national sorority presidents a letter requesting help "eliminating barriers to recruitment of diverse members for fraternity and sorority chapters" by de-emphasizing the letter of recommendation requirement. Only Tri-Delt responded. (The Tri-Delt president thanked Cramer and said she would work on this issue.) "Most Nationals don't want to talk about it," Cramer tells me. "Nationals have other priorities. These are women who had a very different sorority experience and are struggling with change. They're more worried about the media attention than they are about doing a progressive thing."

The University of Alabama remains the only Greek system in the country never to knowingly admit an African American. (One sister with a white mother and a black father came forward in 2001 to defend the Greeks, but because she looked like a white girl with a tan, her sorority hadn't known—and she hadn't confessed—her background.) This is a school where many of the alumni, who comprise the largest university alumni association in the world, opposed integration. This is a school where, in the late 1980s—when the campus chapter of Alpha Kappa Alpha, the country's oldest African American sorority, was about to move into what had until then been an all-white Sorority Row—two white students burned a cross on the front lawn of the new house.

"We have one hundred percent illegal segregation here, and the president, vice president, and board of trustees lie about it," says Pat Hermann, a professor at Alabama who has been fighting this issue for twenty years as the liaison to the faculty senate on Greek diversity and the chair of the Student Coalition Against Racism. When I meet with him in his out-of-the-way office on the English department floor, I don't have to prompt him with any questions. He calmly leans forward, eyes flashing through his thin-framed glasses, pale fists clenched in the sleeves of his checked blazer. "There have been a dozen whites in the black system, but there have been and are zero blacks in traditional sororities. This is our third century of total segregation. The administrators would rather support racism and a one hundred percent apartheid policy than take any real steps, steps they claim to be taking."

He points to the current issue of the student daily newspaper, which ran an article about a vice president who had just announced her resignation. "She was one of the very worst vice presidents we ever had. She took no steps. This problem could have been solved in ten minutes, but there is an extreme reluctance to polarize the racist element," he says. "The older Greek alumni are racist and the Panhellenic group here is hard-core racist. They want to make sure there is no desegregation under their watch. They are not going to allow a breaking of that line."

Hermann has been an explosive force on the segregation issue on a campus that he says hosts "the most powerful Greek system in America," a system that the sororities control, while the fraternities are "appendages." Hermann has been so vocal that the national office of a white sorority flew in a lawyer from Colorado to discuss cultural diversity with him. "She privately indicated that she supported me, but that her professional obligations required that she represent the other side of the argument." The national president of the sorority, Hermann says, "was very hostile to me simply because we suggested integration. She reacted in a way that, I felt, showed lack of breeding and a cold-hearted commitment to her local chapter's racist policies rather than a civilized, open-minded 'liberal' attitude toward the inevitable integration."

Hermann is disgusted with his university. "I'm pro-Greek, but hard-line racist sororities like all of ours should be disbanded. This is the only social group we allow to discriminate on the basis of race. It's illegal, it's immoral, it's imprudent," he says. This is a school where, Hermann tells me, his tone incredulous, "one of the members of our board of trustees said, 'We're not going to turn our fraternities and sororities into places where just any nigger could get in.'"

Ω   Ω   Ω

"I GUESS THERE WERE TOO MANY OTHERS SAYING, 'NO, you're not letting that black girl in my sorority,'" Melody tells me now as we continue down Sorority Row. I silently wonder if Hermann ever told her what the trustee said.

"But why would you try again when it seemed those girls didn't want to be your sister?" I ask her.

"That's not what it was," Melody says. "It wasn't that the members didn't want to be my sister. It was pressure from the alumnae saying, 'I don't want a black girl wearing my sorority letters.'"

I give her a skeptical look.

"For the most part I blamed the alumnae, after the second time," she adds. "I can't think that the girls, even after all the pressure, would still not want me. I'm sure it was hard for some of them to agree to turn me down. At least, I would like to think that."

An Alpha Omicron Pi sister who works at the library reference desk under Melody's supervision calls out to Melody and crosses the street to greet her. The girls talk about upcoming Formals. "She's a sweet girl," Melody tells me as we walk away. "But we're not allowed to talk about what happened. Rush is a forbidden topic with me. Sorority sisters always change the subject, even my good friends."

I ask her why she didn't consider joining any of the black sororities on campus, one of which expressly told her she'd be welcome. With one exception, the black sororities are housed across campus, far from the venerated Sorority Row. "I didn't know a whole lot about black sororities," Melody says. "And I wouldn't fit in at all. DST, AKA—they'd put me out in two days."

"Why?"

"Because they'd be like, 'You're really a white girl. You're on the wrong row.'"

We watch as, at about ten minutes to the hour, white girls come streaming out of the sorority houses with backpacks and sorority T-shirts, ponytails bouncing as they walk each other to class in small groups. Melody glances at one of the houses, then looks down. "Sometimes I wonder what could have been," she says softly. "It's hardest to see the girls who would have been in my pledge class. Life would have been so much easier if they had just let me in."

Chasms Between Black and White

FROM THEIR INCEPTION, HISTORICALLY BLACK SORORITIES differed greatly from white sororities. Alpha Kappa Alpha began in 1908; Delta Sigma Theta split from AKA in 1913; and Zeta Phi Beta and Sigma Gamma Rho were founded in 1920 and 1922, respectively. One of the main purposes of these organizations, which emphasized service and scholarship far more than the white sororities did, was to improve the social status of African American women. According to the National Pan-Hellenic Council (NPHC), the black sororities' (and fraternities') umbrella group, the sororities specifically grew out of "racial isolation" and "a need for African Americans to align themselves with other individuals sharing common goals and ideals." The black Greek organizations subsequently "took on the personae of a haven and outlet, which could foster brotherhood and sisterhood in the pursuit to bring about social change through the development of social programs that would create positive change for Blacks and the country."

It wasn't as though black aspiring sorority sisters had a choice. Until the 1960s, most white sororities were contractually obligated to their national organizations to refuse membership to nonwhites. White author Rita Mae Brown wrote, "My sorority sisters were horrified by my civil rights activities. I was dismissed via a little handwritten envelope in my mailbox, silver, gold and blue border, Delta colors." But since 1963, when federal law prohibited Greek groups from discriminating based on race, black sororities have grown exponentially. Black Greek-letter organizations estimate that 75 percent of black leaders in business, government, science, and the arts are members of NPHC sororities or fraternities. Membership has included such popular women as Star Jones and Maya Angelou (Alpha Kappa Alpha), Aretha Franklin and Lena Horne (Delta Sigma Theta), Zora Neale Hurston (Zeta Phi Beta), and former congresswoman Gwendolyn Cherry (Sigma Gamma Rho). Patricia Roberts Harris, the first black woman to be appointed dean of the Howard University School of Law and the former secretary of housing and urban development, was the first executive director of Delta Sigma Theta. The night President Lyndon Johnson appointed her ambassador to Luxembourg in 1965, she said, "While there are many things in my life which have prepared me for what I am about to do, it is largely the experience of Delta Sigma Theta which gives me the most security."

Much of the success of black sororities can be attributed to their primary purpose. While white groups are largely college social organizations, black sorority sisters sign up for a lifelong pursuit of common service and cultural ideals. Unlike the white sororities, black sororities offer graduate and alumnae chapters that members are expected to join after college; prospective members need not even be undergraduates to join in the first place. According to the NPHC, graduate chapters expect each member to "attend regular chapter meetings, regional conferences and national conventions, and take an active part in matters concerning and affecting the community in which he or she lives."

At one of these conventions—the 2003 Alpha Kappa Alpha North Atlantic Regional Conference held at the Baltimore Convention Center—I attended the opening event, a public meeting. During that session, devoted to speeches from sorority officers and the presentation of "Spirit Awards" to Montgomery County, Maryland, Police Chief Charles Moose (who could not attend) and Maryland Lieutenant Governor Michael Steele, I was surrounded by women swathed in salmon pink and apple green—the AKA colors—from their hats to their sneakers. From the start, I was struck by the main difference between this opening session and that of the white Greek Leadership Conference in Pittsburgh. Here there was no talk about boosting numbers to fulfill a quota, no side discussions about mandating specific types of clothing. Rather, the vast majority of this meeting was devoted to talking about community service. (There was also a short discussion of public service; Maryland State Senator Gloria Lawlah noted that of six African American senators on the Maryland floor, three of them were AKA women.) Speakers addressed the sorority's efforts to improve health care and literacy and strengthen the family bond of African Americans. "Always giving back to the community," said the sorority's international president. "This is the foundation of the heart of Alpha Kappa Alpha."

This theme encapsulated one of many differences between white and black sororities. Sabrina and Melody, it turned out, had good reason to think that the black and white sororities were not interchangeable. These are not organizations that are born from the same beast; they embrace entirely different meanings of the idea of being pledged to a sisterhood. As Irene Padavic and Alexandra Berkowitz revealed in their aptly titled study "Getting a Man or Getting Ahead: A Comparison of White and Black Sororities," all of the black sorority sisters they interviewed said that community service consumed the majority of their sorority time. By contrast, the white groups were focused on date events and romantic relationships—something that black sororities, which don't have lavaliere and candlelight ceremonies, are not concerned with. Meanwhile, the researchers pointed out, the white sororities in their study had elaborate ceremonies to celebrate when sisters achieved various stages in their romantic relationships, but one white group's award for the sister with the highest grade point average, unaccompanied by ceremony, was a bag of potato chips.

I spoke about these issues with Mary L. Bankhead, a Sigma Gamma Rho and Eastern Illinois University graduate student who was working on a thesis about whites in black sororities. She described three additional major differences between black and white sororities. First, she said, "I'm in Sigma Rho for life. If I choose not to pay my dues, I'm not active but I'm still a member. In [national white sororities], if you don't pay you're not a member."

Second, black sorority candidates, who aren't allowed to join as first-semester freshmen, are expected to learn about the sorority before they choose which group to rush. "You can't join when you're seventeen or eighteen and don't know what you're getting into. We get a chance to know each other beyond the superficial crap so the people who join really know they want to be in that particular group," Bankhead said. "Whites are about what they can learn about the organization as a pledge instead of before accepting. Their attitude is, 'Whoever picks me I'll go from there.' "

Third, Bankhead told me that in the black sororities the continuity of a chapter and the recruitment process—which black sororities call the "Membership Intake Process" (MIP)—rely on far less bureaucracy than in white groups. A chapter of a black sorority begins MIP with an interest group meeting (not necessarily the same week as the MIPs of other black chapters on campus) during which the sisters give a presentation about their organization, explain MIP, and distribute application forms. Interested candidates are discouraged from applying to more than one chapter and, in some sororities, are interviewed by undergraduate and/or graduate members. And that's it— no rush parties, no open houses, no Preference ceremony, no ranking. Candidates are judged on criteria that include their GPA, community service experience, leadership roles, and the way they mesh with the members. If a candidate is rejected, she is welcome to apply again, both as an undergraduate and/or after she graduates. "In my sorority, as long as you're in good standing financially and not in trouble, you can go through the Membership Intake Process," Bankhead said. "White sororities are based on money. They're *forced* to take people or get shut down. My undergraduate chapter now has six people and it's functioning." (It must be said that black sororities are much less likely to have houses, which can affect the number of women that Nationals believe are necessary to maintain the chapter's bottom line.)

These varying emphases lend black sororities a much different aura from that of white chapters, beginning with a sense of inclusivity. Unlike white sororities, black sororities generally hold events that are open to the campus and the community, instead of emphasizing the kinds of closed parties that are supposed to be one of the main perks a girl can gain by joining a white group. Parties, in fact, are not emphasized nearly as much as service and networking opportunities. Furthermore, attention to scholarship is not merely lip service: a 2002 study found that black and other minority Greeks achieved higher GPAs than white Greeks. And the network that is available both within and among these sororities is far more perceptible than with white sororities. As a former national president of a black fraternity told Virginia Tech professor Elizabeth Fine, active black Greeks are "the best trained, most highly experienced, and most influential people in the black community [and belong to a] network that cannot be matched anywhere in the black community. The NAACP can't match it; it doesn't have the highly trained and sophisticated people you'll find in a fraternity or sorority. Even the black church doesn't have it."

This is not to say that black sororities are flawless. Agendas of the sororities' national organizations are similar to the "Message from Delta Sigma Theta Sorority, Inc.," a mission statement from the late 1990s: "The future vision of Delta Sigma Theta Sorority, Inc., simply stated, is to raise its voice and its volunteer service commitment to assist African Americans in our search for racial, social, and economic parity." Some black sorority sisters I spoke with said they wished the chapters would focus on the community as a whole, rather than on a specific African American demographic.

Additionally, some of the drawbacks of white sororities pertain to black sororities as well. Although black groups generally don't base their membership selection on looks, some black sisters have admitted that their chapters use "the paper bag test": rushees with skin darker than the bag don't get in. Moreover, in 1990 the presidents of each of the black national sororities and fraternities banned pledging, replacing it with an educational process lasting between three days and three weeks, during which time new members perform community service projects and attend meetings about their sorority's history, structure, and values. But the transition hasn't necessarily gone smoothly. Student and nonstudent members have since divided into "old school" and "new school" camps, with the old schoolers charging that non-pledging sisters haven't earned their letters.

Some chapters have continued not only to pledge girls, but also to haze them. In 1998, a Western Illinois University Delta Sigma Theta pledge told police that during her pledge process, sisters kicked and pushed her, ripped her hairpiece from her head and stuffed it in her mouth, and forced her to eat whole raw onions, hot peppers, and a concoction of vinegar and hot sauce until she vomited. She also claimed that sisters ordered her to do one thousand sit-ups until the skin on her behind cracked. Additionally, she was allegedly forced to use her elbows to grind cornflakes until she bled into them—and then to eat the cereal. In 2003, Virginia Union University suspended its Zeta Phi Beta chapter when several sisters were fined and convicted of misdemeanor hazing for paddling a pledge; after being struck approximately thirty-five times, the pledge was taken to the hospital for her severe bruises.

In many chapters that abide by the ban on pledging, the step show has become more important as a way to prove and publicly display devotion to the group. The NPHC recommends that step shows "convey positive political, social justice, and moral messages." New sisters are now taught their soror-ity's signature steps as part of their initiation process and are encouraged to participate in shows. "Step shows," Professor Fine wrote in her book on the topic, "have become a key venue for displaying and asserting group identity as well as for negotiating the status of each group within the social order."

Latina groups, too, have adopted stepping as a dominant expression of group loyalty. More similar to the black groups than to the white groups, the fourteen national Latina sororities belong to the National Association of Latino Fraternal Organizations, which formed in 1998. Latina sororities are easily identifiable because their pledges can often be spotted marching silently around campus in a line that moves only at right angles. They step in time, expressionless, refusing to acknowledge the friends they pass and the spectators who inevitably heckle them.

A 1999 alumna of the Sigma Lambda Upsilon/Señoritas Latinas Unidas sorority explained to me the meaning behind "lining," which white Greeks, who traditionally have not lined, are quick to define as a militant form of haz-ing. "The line is about unity because you're walking in unison. You're there for each other—literally someone is behind you. Sometimes people try to harass the line, but the line does not respond. It teaches you to focus academ-ically and prioritize your life. When you spend your day stopping and chat-ting with people, you waste two or three hours on nonsense. We're cutting out the extraneous social stuff," she said. "People are curious. Some people are nice enough to ask about the line, but other people walk up to the pledges and harass them. When people see blacks and Latinos pledging, they're quick to say that that's hazing. Meanwhile, we see white pledges with black-and-blue eyes. In our sorority, if you don't want to do something, you don't have to do it." The pledge process for many Latina sororities is public and "like a cross between the military and the Girl Scouts," the Sigma Lambda Upsilon said. "It's to teach self-discipline. You fight for things in the community."

Members of Latina sororities described to me a scene that differs markedly from that of their white counterparts. Latinas don't generally stray far from home when they are growing up—no overnight summer camps and few sleepovers, a Latina sorority member told me. "So when you go to school in the boonies, with trees everywhere, it's a culture shock. You're lonely and far from home, so we consider the sorority to be family." For these girls, the sisterhood, or *Hermandad*, is said to last *hasta la muerte*—until death—and exists so that the girls can support each other in an unfamiliar environment. "Our sisterhood doesn't look like any of the white sororities," the sister said. "A lot of our girls came from poverty and had to fight for scholarships. Some of them are single mothers. And they all work hard."

Some sororities do not limit membership to a specific ethnic group. Mu Sigma Upsilon, founded in 1981 at Rutgers University, was the first multicultural minority Greek-letter organization in the country, with a goal of "unity among all women." A senior sister at one of MSU's nineteen chapters told me it has succeeded. "I have been asked many times why I, a white Jewish girl from East Brunswick, New Jersey, would join a 'minority' organization rather than a mainstream sorority," she said. "It's true that I get looks sometimes when I'm wearing the letters or when I'm surrounded by my sisters. I have sisters of all nationalities and religions: Latina, African American, Filipino, Italian, Egyptian, African, Asian, Christian, Muslim. People can't figure us out when we are all together. There have been many instances in my life when I have been criticized or penalized for being different. What I loved most about MSU was that the differences between each person are celebrated."

Ω   Ω   Ω

WHEN MELODY TWILLEY FOUND HERSELF WITHOUT A Greek affiliation, she began researching MSU and dozens of other national multicultural sororities with the aim of founding her own nondiscriminatory multicultural group. At the first open meeting she held on campus for students interested in joining a multicultural sorority—an entity foreign to the University of Alabama—fifty girls showed up, many of them white. In January 2003, Melody and eight of the girls officially started their own sorority from scratch. For reasons they keep secret, they picked a mascot (the sea horse), colors ("real blue," blush, and silver), a flower (Stargazer Lily), and a jewel (pearl). They came up with a secret group purpose and the letters to stand for it: Alpha Delta Sigma. They wrote rituals, put themselves through an induction ceremony, a pledge period, and initiation, and a sisterhood was born.

Now, as Melody—in jeans, flip-flops, and a T-shirt commemorating a community service event—and I lounge on couches in a student center, coincidentally across from the university's Greek Life Office, she tells me what it's like to be a sister. "We had an ice cream social Tuesday night, Friday night we had a dinner, and we have to fulfill our community service requirement," she says. "We'll rush in the fall. We're trying to be as close to Panhellenic as possible, but there are some differences."

"Like what?" I ask.

"Well, during Panhellenic rush, [rushees] wait in front of each house and suddenly the doors fling open and the sisters do their 'door songs.'"

"They have door songs?"

"Oh, yes!" Melody puts on a phony wide smile and, in a cheesy little-girl voice, sings and claps the chirpy Phi Mu door song. Then she says, "We can't do door songs because we have no door."

The Panhellenic Association, the university's governing body for the white sororities, has yet to reach out to Alpha Delta Sigma. Melody plans to apply for her group to be accepted as a campus Panhellenic sorority; if Panhellenic rejects ADS, Melody will consider suing them.

A thin white girl passes by and taps Melody. "I'm going to come to one of y'all's things, I promise. It's just finals and everything," she says before moving on.

"Potential New Member," Melody explains to me, her face lit up as she uses one of the terms newly instituted by the national white sororities (it is supposed to replace the word "rushee").

I ask her why it is so important to her to be part of a sorority. "Why not just have friends?"

She tells me that sisters are more than friends. "We want to leave a legacy, perpetuate this. We'll be seniors and then the next year all of us are gone," she says. "I wanted to start a sorority so my future daughter can join it. All the other little girls would get to say, 'My mama was a Tri-Delt,' or 'My auntie was a Pi Phi.'" Melody laughs as she mimics the you-go-girl gesture of snapping in the shape of the letter Z. "My daughter will be able to say, 'My mama *founded* Alpha Delta Sigma.'"

MARCH

———

Hazing activities are always mandatory unless a girl is physically unable to take part, gets sick during the activity, or is terribly upset about the hazing. Girls who are unable or have the courage to refuse to participate in hazing are less a part of the pledge class.

—Rush: A Girl's Guide to Sorority Success, 1985

Your pledge educator, the chapter's Vice President of Social Advancement, will outline specific requirements in the areas of Moral, Mental, and Social Advancement.

—Pi Phi Forever, 1990s

Ω   Ω   Ω

Revolving

MARCH 1

VICKI'S IM AWAY MESSAGE

you'll never remember class time, but you will remember the time you wasted hanging out with your friends. downstairs in the tv room

THE CONSENSUS AMONG BETA Pi sisters was that the 2003 rush had been extraordinarily successful: the current pledge class was the best overall group the sorority had recruited in many years. Granted, the sisters still commented to each other about some of the pledges' flaws. "Oh, that one's not as cool as we thought she was," the Beta Pi sisters said about a girl they had persuaded to come to their house instead of going to Alpha Rho. Even Vicki got into it, making fun of a "dorky-looking" pledge with Ashleigh and wondering aloud why they had accepted her. But the Beta Pis were largely satisfied: they heard from the Rho Chis who returned to Beta Pi that many of the rushees had ranked Beta Pi as their favorite house.

The officers were determined to take full advantage of this opportunity. Now that they had an impressive collection of pledges, the sisters' job was to mold them into a unified pledge class. During the first Saturday night sleep-over of pledge period, the pledges had to listen to the insufferably repetitive Kylie Minogue song "Can't Get You Out of My Head" over and over again, for the entire night. On the second Saturday, the girls participated in a mandatory scavenger hunt that sent them scrambling into various other Greek houses to coerce members into giving them the desired objects, and when that failed, to steal them. During the third sleepover, the sisters got the pledges drunk and forced them to serenade and dance at several fraternity houses.

Meanwhile, the pledges were expected to find time during the eight-week pledge period to interview every sister in the sorority. They recorded the interviews in their "pledge books," which the pledgemaster reviewed periodically. This was a way to force the pledges to spend time at the Beta Pi house and participate in activities, such as planned pre-games with fraternities, so they could get to know the sisters. Each day, the pledges were also required to carry a different item around with them everywhere—a box of Lucky Charms, a fork, corduroy pants, bright pink azaleas in their hair—and to be prepared to present the item whenever a sister requested to see it.

For the fourth sleepover, the sisters decided to celebrate the halfway point of pledge period. Beta Pi officers lugged several handles of vodka upstairs to the fourth floor "pledge room"—a large, cold, loftlike room where the pledges were already beginning to curl into their sleeping bags—and told the girls they had to finish the alcohol. Vicki and a few other sisters smuggled away one of the handles for themselves and hid in Vicki's room to empty it. At the preapproved time, when the pledges were sufficiently drunk (and Vicki was practically keeling over), the Beta Pi sisters entered the pledge room. The president waited until the room was full, then came barreling upstairs.

"The campus police heard we were having a party and are coming to check it out!" she yelled. "You have to finish the alcohol right away!" The pledges drank faster. Vicki generously helped them. When the doorbell rang and the president hurried downstairs, the girls screeched; when she returned with a uniformed police officer by her side, the screeching subsided until the officer flicked on a stereo and started dancing. Now the girls screamed in delight, continuing to drink as the officer, blond and chiseled, stripped. Later, Vicki spent the rest of the night throwing up in William's bathroom. William held back her hair.

Vicki, Olivia, and Morgan thought that the pledges—who often went out of their way to be extra nice to Vicki and her friends—were "cute." They tried to spend time with the pledges when they came to the house to do interviews or for their weekly pledge meetings. Vicki and her friends also helped some of the pledges acquire fake IDs. Gradually, a new division emerged in the house: the girls who had IDs and went out to the bars (on average about five times a week), and the girls who didn't and stayed home. The first group would learn about the evening's social activity by finding Vicki or Olivia, both of whom could now usually be found holding court in the television room. The pledges, some more nervous than others, would peek into the room and ask in a deferential tone, "What are you guys doing tonight? Are you going out?"

Vicki was euphoric about the changes in the house this semester. Her bedroom was calm, lacking the tension and drama of last semester's room. Morgan seemed more tolerable. When Vicki ran into Laura-Ann, Vicki was outwardly kind and inwardly remorseful that their friendship had been ruined because they had roomed together. Laura-Ann, who lived in a world of her own, felt differently. A sister had informed Vicki that Laura-Ann said how happy she was that she and Vicki could be "best friends" even though they didn't live together anymore.

Sometimes during the Saturday night sleepovers, Vicki and Olivia would stride into the pledge room, their long hair flowing, to say hello to pledges. During one of these visits, a pledge asked Vicki for advice.

"Vicki," she whispered, "I can't stand one of the other pledges. What do I do?"

"Just give it time," Vicki said. "Going through pledging together will really help you learn to appreciate her."

"It's so weird," the pledge said. "You and I are the same age, but I look at you like you're so much older." Like most of the other pledges, as she spoke to Vicki, her voice became higher pitched and more unsure.

That night, the pledgemaster had the pledges name the fraternity brothers they had hooked up with so that the older sisters could tell them whom they were and weren't "allowed to touch."

"I hooked up with Dan in Theta Theta after the last pre-game," said one pledge.

"Wait a minute," said a sister, "*Vicki's* Dan?!"

The pledge looked mortified. "Oh my God, I didn't know," she said, her tone rising. "Oh my God oh my God oh my God!" The room hushed.

Vicki, who liked this pledge, hadn't seen much of Dan this semester. She saw William regularly, and (unbeknownst to William) had also gotten together once with a friendly Epsilon Chi brother. Vicki and Olivia, who was now dating one of William's fraternity brothers, had gone to the Epsilon Chi house, made out with their dates there, then moved on to Iota together to be with their supposed boyfriends.

With all of this other action, Vicki was surprised to find that she cared that Dan had recently hooked up with, of all people, one of her pledges. Nevertheless, she reassured the now-hyperventilating pledge that she wasn't currently involved with him.

One night soon thereafter, Vicki flirted with Dan at Louie's, not noticing that William was staring at them from his seat on the other side of the bar. Olivia walked in, saw William first, and asked him where Vicki was.

He gestured with his chin, his goatee neatly pointing to Vicki, who was flicking her bangs out of her eyes. "Over there," he said, "all over that sketchy guy in the baseball cap."

When Vicki spotted William and came over to talk to him, she noticed Dan pacing back and forth, watching her from a distance.

Ω   Ω   Ω

A FEW NIGHTS LATER, MORGAN, WHO WAS DATING ONE of Dan's Theta Theta brothers, told Vicki that Dan had found out about William. Dan had admitted to his brothers how much he liked Vicki, and how hurt he was that she had a boyfriend. Vicki immediately called him and arranged to meet him at Louie's.

"Okay, so I've been seeing William on and off now for a couple months," said Vicki, shaving the time period.

"I heard he was your boyfriend," Dan said.

"No. I don't want a boyfriend," Vicki said. "I've been seeing him but I don't feel that way about him."

"Were you seeing him when we went to my Formal?" Dan asked.

"I had so much fun with you at Formal," Vicki dodged. "I thought William was playing me—that's when I started talking to you. You're the best Formal date ever. William's not my boyfriend. I'm just hooking up with him." Vicki left the bar after promising to see Dan again soon.

When she got back to the Beta Pi house, Vicki changed into a pair of capris. "Ugh," she remarked aloud to herself. "I look fat."

As if on cue, Morgan suddenly popped into Vicki's room. "Really?" she said, standing on her toes to inspect Vicki's body. "Let me see!"

Vicki rolled her green eyes and distracted Morgan by telling her about her discussion with Dan. "I don't like how weird he and I are," Vicki said. "I don't know how long it's going to be before we talk again."

"Come on," said Morgan, who was planning to see her boyfriend anyway. "We're going to the Theta Theta house."

Dan was overjoyed to see Vicki. The foursome were lounging in his room when Ashleigh repeatedly called Vicki's cell, crying hysterically and hanging up. When Vicki called Ashleigh back, Ashleigh didn't pick up her phone. Morgan returned home to Beta Pi, leaving Vicki and Dan kissing on the couch.

Ten minutes later, Morgan called Vicki. "Ashleigh's going crazy. The guy she asked to Date Party said no," Morgan said.

Five minutes later, Olivia called. "Oh my God, you have to come back to the house," she said. "She's drunk and talking about killing herself."

Vicki hurried to Ashleigh's room, where Olivia and Morgan were trying to console her. Ashleigh's drunken panic had passed, and now she was curled in her hot pink comforter muttering, "I just want to go to sleep. I want to wake up in the morning and not be here." As Ashleigh drifted off to sleep, Vicki, Olivia, and Morgan sang "I Will Survive" to her and told Ashleigh how much they loved her.

Vicki and Olivia went downstairs to the dining room to recap the night's events. As Vicki was updating her on the latest developments with Dan, Olivia sneaked to a sink and mischievously poured a tiny cup of water over Vicki's head.

Vicki sat still for a moment, dripping. "Oh no, you did not just do that," she said, then made a beeline for the nearest water pitcher and dumped it over Olivia. As the girls dashed around the room collecting all the liquid ammunition they could find, a thought struck Vicki. This spontaneous fun was exactly the kind of thing she wanted to remember about college—not the obligation to call William, not her tendency to stay over at his house instead of cavorting around hers, and not even William himself.

The next night, Vicki and Olivia returned to the boys in Epsilon Chi. Again, they fooled around with their dates, then went to the Iota house to be with their supposed boyfriends. But Vicki couldn't muster up enthusiasm for William. Too tired to stay up with him, she immediately fell asleep in his bed.

When Vicki woke up the next morning, William was looking at her strangely. "What's with you? You can't tell me something's not wrong," he said.

Vicki inhaled deeply before she spoke. "I realized that you and I have been hooking up for several months now," she said. "The reason I wanted to break up with my boyfriend at the beginning of the year was to be single, and I'm not. I want my freedom. I don't want the obligation to call you after the bars. I want to do what I want and then go home with my girls. We have to break up."

Tears welled in William's eyes.

Ω Ω Ω

From Pricking Fingers to Hard-Core Porn

IN MAY 2003, TELEVISION VIEWERS INTERNATIONALLY WERE transfixed by a video taken of Chicago high school seniors—most of them girls—punching and kicking juniors and covering them in urine, feces, pig intestines, fish guts, coffee grounds, and mud. The incident, a hazing rite that was part of an annual Powder Puff Football tradition, sent five girls to the hospital, one with a broken ankle and one with a head wound needing ten stitches. Seniors shot juniors with paintballs and forced meat down a vegetarian's throat. The school district expelled more than thirty seniors, and prosecutors pressed charges against sixteen students and two parents. While this case is extreme, similar types of hazing are par for the course in Greek life.

As the producers of Girls Gone Wild and MTV can attest, there are many things college girls will do for attention or money. There are few organizations, however, that can persuade this demographic to masturbate with salt shakers and drop trousers or fake orgasms while humping doorknobs and ski poles in front of a room of cheering fraternity brothers—merely so that they can belong. But sororities can.

The pledge period, which lasts about five to nine weeks, occurs in between the time a rushee has accepted a bid and the time she is initiated. Traditionally the pledge period serves as a proving ground; the new members are supposed to show their devotion to the sisterhood and to their fellow pledges as they deprioritize the individual in favor of the collective group. In the chapters across the country that still haze (some chapters have stopped the practice entirely), pledges often have to wear their sorority's colors. Some sororities also force their pledges to wear similar hairstyles so they look as much alike as possible.

Every week, there might be a different greeting that a pledge must use whenever she sees a sister: "Hi sister so-and-so, I'm a happy pledge of Alpha Alpha Alpha, Zeta chapter, Zeta class!" If a pledge messes up the greeting, she must stand there repeating it over and over again until the sister is satisfied. Pledges are often expected to know the name of every sister, which in some cases can entail committing two hundred names to memory. (Other sororities expect the pledges to know specific details about sisters' lives and test them on this obscure knowledge.) Pledge books like Beta Pi's are another widely used pledge tool.

Throughout the pledge period, many houses hold pledge exams on the sorority's history, the Greek alphabet, names of sisters and alumnae, and details about the exec board officers. In Brooke's house, these tests were given nightly during the week leading up to initiation. When girls did not take these tests seriously, there were measures in place to bring them into line. If all of the girls did not pass a test, then all of them had to take it again—at increasingly inconvenient hours. After the first test, Brooke's pledgemaster awakened each pledge at 4 A.M. the next day to drag them to the house to take the test again. After the second test, the pledgemaster graded the exams, came back into the room, and said, "Girls, three of you did not pass. All of you will be at the house at two-thirty tomorrow morning to take the test again." The pledges had to make sure that their fellow pledges were present. When one night a pledge failed to show, Brooke and her group had to find her. Eventually, they located her in her boyfriend's bedroom in one of the fraternity houses, which the group had to break into at 3 A.M. to seize their future sister. These sorority exams sometimes occur during midterms, but there are no excuses allowed. If a girl has an 8 A.M. midterm and is trying to study or get a decent rest the night before, she still must attend her 2:30 A.M. sorority test. The practice isn't unusual. At her school, Laney, the Alpha Sigma Alpha, said, "We were always quizzing them. We put X's on their arms with a marker when they got answers wrong. It was very stupid when I look back, but at the time it seemed really important."

In some houses, pledges can also generally be "on call" nearly every night of the pledge period. This means sitting by their phone in case a sorority sister wants something—for example, a Slurpee at 3 A.M., a ride, her dishes washed, or her room cleaned—or a spontaneous activity is about to start: "*Find a dress and a date and be at the house in thirty minutes.*" As one recent Phi Mu said, "We were essentially slaves to the sisters." Other activities are intended to promote team-building and pledge loyalty, though they often consist of useless, time-wasting arts and crafts as pledges must stay up late into the night decorating posters, writing songs, and drawing pictures. In 2001, Northeastern University suspended its Alpha Epsilon Phi chapter after two pledges quit the sorority and complained of abuse. They said they were forced to mark their stomachs to prove they hadn't showered for a week, and to stay awake throughout the night completing jigsaw puzzles or separating candy with their noses.

Many sororities also put pledges in lineups during which the sisters scream insults at them, sometimes even individually critiquing pledges' weight or the size of their nose, breasts, or dress. "*You're nothing!*" "*You're a bunch of sluts!*" Usually a few girls cry. Some drop out. "They tear you down," I was told, "so they can build you back up again." But those who attempt to drop out are met with resistance in the form of sudden kindness from the sisters. One girl who tried on three occasions to quit her pledge class told me why she ultimately stuck with the process. When she told the sisters she wanted to leave, they immediately acted as if they were her best friends. "When a sorority claims you as a pledge, it has to report that to its national organization. If I quit, my dues go with me, but the money they have to pay the national organization remains the same, so everyone else's dues would go up," she explained.

For this reason, many houses, such as Brooke's Eta Gammas, have as one of their elected positions the role of sorority "chaplain." One of the chaplain's duties is to make sure the hazing doesn't make the pledges so uncomfortable that they drop out. During Brooke's junior year, for example, a pledge became distraught and angry during an activity that forced the pledges to watch hard-core pornography while the sisters watched them. As the sisters determined that the pledges, who were not allowed to crack a smile, were focused solely on the television screen, the sisters made comments and laughed at them. When the distraught pledge shouted, "This is awful! I don't want to do this!" it was the chaplain's job to calm her down.

Pledging mostly involves mental games, as sisters from houses across the country told me over and over again. But, although fraternities are better known for their physical hazing rites, a surprising number of sororities also make bodily demands on their girls. One sorority made its pledges call fraternity brothers and read pornographic material (*You make me so hot! I want to suck on your . . .*) before telling the brothers they were coming over. A Phi Mu at Widener University has said that sisters stuck coasters down the back of pledges' pants. "We were told to squeeze our butt cheeks together to keep them up." The same chapter also regularly commanded pledges to stand against a wall with the words, "Nose, tits, and toes!"

Brooke described a custom in her sorority known officially as "Boob Ranking." When Brooke was a pledge, her group was taken to an upstairs room in the house and told to take off their shirts and bras. Shivering, the pledges nervously glanced at each other as they wondered what new activity would follow. Then the sisters informed the girls that they were going to line them up in order of breast size. As the sisters told the pledges where to go in the line, the pledges were unaware that they were actually being lined up according to attitude. If a pledge, for instance, thought she had large breasts and tried to insert herself at the large end of the lineup, the sisters would loudly tell her that she should go to the opposite end. Eventually, the sisters marched the pledges downstairs to the dining room, told them they were not lined up correctly, and then, as they laughed and heckled, demanded that the pledges put themselves in the correct order.

Often, sisters who were treated badly as pledges were more likely to continue the cycle by treating the next class of pledges even worse. "We were just mean," Brooke said. Why, I asked Brooke—a kind and reasonable person—would she not only subject herself to this embarrassment but also inflict it on others? "It was disgusting," she admitted. "But it was like a cere-monial ritual. Everyone before you did it, so you have to do it, too."

This sentiment—the bedrock of organizations that rule by tradition—can motivate girls to participate in dangerous activities. Esther Wright, a pledge in the late 1980s, has written about how her pledge class was told to prick their fingers with the same needle and let their blood commingle in a shot glass. "You must be willing to put your sisters first and sacrifice for us, bonding with us in every way," the sorority president intoned. The pledges were then ordered to put some of the mixed blood on the sorority's flower and rub the bloody petal onto their cut fingers (as they prayed the blood wasn't contaminated).

In 1997, in accordance with a tradition that had been in place at the house for four years, pledges of Kappa Kappa Gamma at DePauw University (a campus that is more than three-quarters Greek) were strongly encouraged to drink alcohol at a fraternity party and then taken to a room full of soror-ity sisters who held them down despite their screams, pulled their jeans down to expose their hips, and branded them with a lit cigarette. (Other sororities have used hot metal stamps of the sorority letters.) They were sev-enteen and eighteen years old. "That night, they took it from me—my bub-bliness, my personality, my trust. They took everything from me that night," one of the pledges said to the media. "When you leave home for the first time and you're naïve and you're eighteen and you think you know and you don't, when you're put in a room like that with people that you trust and you look up to and you follow—and to be put in a situation like that, you don't know what you're going to do." Other pledges in the class were made to kiss a skull adorned with two racquetballs and material simulating pubic hair and to pretend to castrate a sister wearing a fake penis.

Other sororities practice a branding of a different nature. Before I began investigating sororities, I had been under the impression that pledging practices such as "circle the fat" and "bikini weigh" were the stuff of urban legend. I was wrong. During circle the fat, pledges undress and, one by one, stand in front of the entire sorority membership. The sisters (or, in some chapters, fraternity brothers) then use thick black markers to circle the fat or cellulite on a pledge's body. The purpose is to help the pledge learn what parts of her body she needs to improve. For many sororities, thinness, as the pledges discover, is a priority. During bikini weigh, or "weigh-in," pledges are weighed in front of either the sisterhood or a fraternity; the audience yells the number displayed on the scale.

A version of circle the fat was described in a 1999 article written under a pseudonym by a sorority sister who feared dire consequences if her sorority discovered that she had written the piece. A few days after the writer and her fellow pledges were forced to sing and dance on tables "while fraternity guys let their eyes and hands crawl up our skirts," sisters told them to come downstairs in single file, wearing only their underwear. Sisters in white robes stood in the living room, in which the furniture and windows were covered with white sheets, and handed out strips of white sheets. The sisters told the pledges to blindfold themselves with the sheets and to lie facedown on the cold hardwood floor. "And that's when the men entered the room, whistling and howling," she wrote. "The men circled us . . . I was becoming disoriented and felt nauseated. Something smelled toxic. Then something cold came into contact with my thigh. I gasped. 'It's okay, baby,' said one of the men. 'I'm just helping to make you look good.' The cold moved to my inner thigh."

"You missed a spot!" the pledge heard a fraternity brother say.

Another responded, "Yeah, that's a pretty nasty one."

After the men finished, sisters led the blindfolded pledges upstairs to the "education room." When the blindfolds were removed, each pledge was standing in front of a mirror. "There was a moment of confusion as each of us noticed that circles and 'X's' had been drawn on our bodies in permanent marker," the sister wrote. "These were areas that 'needed some work,' the pledgemaster said. Some of the girls began to sob . . . 'Don't be a ninny,' one of the members scolded. 'It's just going to make you a better person.' "

Another dangerous but relatively common pledge activity involves survival of abandonment: sisters abandon pledges in a remote place and expect them to find their way back to the house. In 1970, Alpha Gamma Deltas from Eastern Illinois University dropped Donna Bedinger on a back road three miles from school. As the sisters drove away, Bedinger tried to launch herself onto the car's bumper—and died of injuries sustained to her head. In 1993, Sarah Dronek pledged a local sorority at Minnesota's Concordia College. The sisters drove Sarah and her fellow pledges, blindfolded, across the river into Fargo, North Dakota, left them in the woods in knee-deep snow, and drove away. When the pledges returned to campus the next morning, Sarah's foot was so frostbitten that it was too swollen to fit inside her shoe. At the sorority house, the sisters stood her up in front of the entire sorority, screamed at her about being a wimp, and, mocking her monstrously puffed blue foot, made her cry "moo." When Sarah objected to the hazing, the sisters told her, "This is tradition. This is what we do." After initiation, Sarah finally saw a doctor, who told her that she needed an emergency amputation. Instead, Sarah endured months of painful procedures and was able to save her toes.

If pledges think that the first few weeks are tough, they are in for great disappointment when they learn that the last week of pledging—the week before initiation—is usually known as "Hell Week," in which the humiliation, subordination, and sleeplessness of the previous weeks are magnified. (In the 1990s, some sororities officially started referring to Hell Week with the euphemism "Inspiration Week," but the hazing occurred nevertheless.) As Paige, a recent Phi Sigma Sigma, remembered, "They don't tell you 'Welcome to Hell Week,' but you basically figure it out. We weren't allowed to bathe or wear makeup, hair products, or contact lenses. They wanted us to look ugly, to 'purify' ourselves, to get rid of all of the extra fluff in our lives and concentrate on getting into the sorority. But did I sneak hair spray? Of course I did. You can look disgusting only for so long."

Generally, missing one pledge activity can invite screaming and humiliation in front of the entire sorority but won't necessarily prohibit a candidate from becoming a member. If she misses several activities, however, she is out.

"Then they would say you didn't have what it takes to be a sister, that you're not giving enough of yourself to the sorority," Paige said. "They'd say you're going to be a 'deadweight,' and they didn't want any deadweights. So you pretty much had to do all the activities and just trust that they wouldn't make you do something you'd die from."

These power games, these exaggerated Greek versions of Simon Says, inevitably grant the sisters more perceived influence over their new members. "When you're pledging, you really think the older girls have so much power over you," said Laney of Alpha Sigma Alpha. "At my school, all pledges had to participate in a campus-wide lip-sync contest. We'd see the sisters standing on chairs cheering for us and think, 'They really *do* like us!'"—one reason girls continue to endure the strange and sometimes cruel treatment of pledging. After initiation, the pledges are suddenly expected to cozy up to the girls who have been tormenting them for two months. As Laney said, "They treated me like shit for nine weeks, and then at nine weeks and one day I was their sister. But you think, 'I'm doing what everybody else had to do.'"

Pledging is one of the most controversial aspects of sorority life because of the ways girls compromise themselves to earn membership into the group. Why do so many girls willingly undergo the pledge experience? I asked this of most of the women I interviewed. "I questioned that all the time. It's true, you look back and say, 'Why did I have to do all that stupid crap to be able to sit in these stupid meetings every week and pay several hundred dollars a year for a few extra parties?'" Paige mused. "But it gave me a sense of belonging. Everyone needs someplace where they can mesh with people. And I wasn't an athlete or an artist, or active in the student association. I'd feel comfortable walking up to every girl out of a hundred in that room and striking up a conversation. You had people to study with in the library. Odds were there were sisters who had taken your classes and could guide you. So the benefits outweighed the steps that it took to get in."

Ω   Ω   Ω

"Close Contact and Deep Friendship"

MARCH 3

AMY'S IM AWAY MESSAGE

i know people change . . . it's just mighty hard when people
we care so much about drift so far away

ON BADGE DAY, SABRINA AND CAITLIN WERE NOWHERE TO
be seen. The National Panhellenic Conference had declared March 3 "Badge
Day," a day during which all sorority sisters across the country were expected
to wear badge attire and proudly display their pins (manufactured by one of
two national sorority–approved "official jewelers"). At night, the Panhellenic
Councils at college campuses nationwide were supposed to run a mandatory
Badge Day Ceremony. As Amy stood with her arm around her Big Sister in
the cramped room in the student center among sisters from all of State U's
sororities, she craned her neck, searching for Caitlin and Sabrina. Hundreds
of sisters in sundresses and heeled sandals, clustered with their respective
houses, listened quietly as a few Panhellenic Council officers stood at the
front of the room reading the "Panhellenic Creed," the mission statement of
the National Panhellenic Conference:

> We, as undergraduate members of women's fraternities, stand for
> good scholarship, for guarding of good health, for maintenance of
> fine standards, and for serving, to the best of our ability, our college
> community. Cooperation for furthering fraternity life, in harmony
> with its best possibilities, is the ideal that shall guide our fraternity
> activities.
>
> We, as fraternity women, stand for service through the develop-
> ment of character inspired by the close contact and deep friendship
> of individual fraternity and Panhellenic life. The opportunity for
> wide and wise human service, through mutual respect and helpful-
> ness, is the tenet by which we strive to live.

After the ten-minute ceremony, the sisters dispersed.

Amy wondered if Caitlin and Sabrina were off smoking again. The two had become much closer to each other, particularly since Sabrina had broken up with the professor. But as they became increasingly inseparable, distancing themselves from other sisters and from Alpha Rho, they were also drifting away from Amy. Part of the rift, Amy knew, could be attributed to the fact that Caitlin and Sabrina regularly smoked marijuana with non-Greek friends and she did not—and it frustrated her that something like pot could drive the friends apart. But there was more to it than that. On several occasions, Amy saw Caitlin and Sabrina leaving the house to go shopping or to the movies without inviting her. Amy wondered how much her friction with Chris had contributed to the way the Alpha Rho trio had shrunk to a duo.

Amy had been used to hearing daily updates, and now she didn't know what was going on in her friends' lives anymore. She didn't even know their plans for the following week's Spring Break. But though she missed her sisters terribly, Amy didn't raise the issue. As hurt as she was that Caitlin and Sabrina were excluding her, Amy still didn't want to cause conflict. She wanted to tell them that they had been right about her high school sweetheart, who had been a fantasy after all: he had called her at three o'clock one morning to tell her that he couldn't handle a long-distance relationship. She wanted to tell them that she had gone back on her intense-exercise-and-cabbage-soup routine and had lost four pounds already. And she wanted to tell them that Hunter, a cute baseball player, had not only kissed her but also practically invited himself to escort her to Alpha Rho's upcoming Date Party.

Instead, she confided in Traci, the new pledge who was René's roommate. René was another friend who had disappeared—but Amy suspected her snubs were more deliberate than Caitlin's and Sabrina's. René had been furious when Alpha Rho offered a bid to her roommate. For several days, she was aloof whenever Amy or Sabrina tried to talk to her. Traci relayed conversations back to the girls.

"Not another Alpha Rho," René groaned when she heard about Traci. "Why does everyone we know go to Alpha Rho?"

This year's rush had dredged up René's own bitter feelings about her experience with the process. "If all my friends could get in, why couldn't I?" she said. Amy could understand why René was angry back when she had rushed. She remembered the bitter fight they had when Amy got into Alpha

Rho and René didn't get in anywhere. "All of you are the same," René had accused then, including Amy in the same group of girls that had just rejected her as a friend. René got over her rejection much more quickly than she seemed to be getting over her roommate's acceptance.

"She's having a really hard time," Traci confided to Amy. "All of her friends got in and she didn't. She feels like she isn't good enough."

Even several weeks into the pledge period, René still wouldn't accept Amy's frequent invitations to go out. René finally called Amy the afternoon of Date Party.

"Do you like the Alpha Rho pledgemaster?" she blurted when Amy answered the phone.

"I get along with her but she's not one of my best friends. Why?"

"Do you think she's being very fair?" René pressed.

"What are you getting at?"

"Traci doesn't think she likes her. She told the pledgemaster, 'I don't drink. Is that going to be a problem?' and the pledgemaster acted like it was."

"Oh honey, the pledgemaster is a party animal," Amy said. "She has a problem understanding why everyone doesn't want to party. And now she's on a power trip."

"Traci has tried to engage her in conversation but the pledgemaster doesn't care. You know Traci needs validation from people—but the pledge-master won't give her the time of day," said René.

Amy promised to say something to Charlotte about making sure the pledgemaster wasn't forcing the pledges to do things they didn't want to do.

Actually, this year the Alpha Rhos were being extra careful to have as uneventful a pledge period as possible. Many national offices had cracked down hard on hazing, warning that any chapter caught hazing could lose its charter. Traditionally on Bid Day, the sisters would take the pledges out to the theater or a fancy dinner. Throughout the pledge period, the sisters would send the pledges on scavenger hunts, set up various games during which the pledges received presents, and assign rotating "Swan Pals," or temporary Big Sisters, to help them through the pledge period. But under this year's national rules, it seemed that all of those activities could be construed as hazing. Because they were so confused about the rules and afraid of possible repercussions, the Alpha Rhos decided they were safer not doing anything to or with the pledges at all. So they planned nothing. The only items the pledges received were a Bid Day jersey, the usual "new member guide" (a binder full of rules and regulations sent down from the national office), and the "pledge pin"—a cheap, tiny pin that would be replaced by the gold Alpha Rho pin during the initiation ceremony. The only pledge activities were "Clue Week"—the week leading up to the assignment of Big Sisters—and a weekly pledge test on Alpha Rho history to prepare the pledges for the national Alpha Rho exam they would have to pass before they were initiated.

About a week before initiation, however, the sisters realized that eliminating pledge activities had caused a more urgent problem than violating national rules. Several of the older girls complained to the pledgemaster that initiation was around the corner, yet they still didn't actually know their soon-to-be-sisters. Usually each new pledge class took care to buy sisters lunch, send them cards, or invite them to coffee in an effort to show the sisters they cared enough to meet them. "This year the pledges aren't doing anything," the sisters griped. "It's their job to go out of their way to get to know us and they haven't done that." The pledgemaster agreed to yell at the pledges, who arrived together at the house the next day, cleaned the sisters' bedrooms thoroughly, and left adoring notes on each sister's pillow.

"And now, since the pledges got in trouble," René told Amy, "Traci feels really bad. She knows you, Sabrina, and Caitlin had to do pledge things and be at the house and stuff, and Traci doesn't have to do anything. Traci doesn't feel like she belongs."

"Everyone just loves Traci," Amy reassured her. "The sisters were sweating her like no other. People were like, 'I wanna be her.'"

René was silent.

"Anyway," Amy said, "do you want to go to the bars tonight?"

René's answer was the same as it had been all semester, even though Amy was careful to invite her to activities that had nothing to do with the sorority. "Nah," she said. "I have stuff to do."

That night, Amy got ready for Date Party alone.

Revelation

MARCH 22

CAITLIN'S IM AWAY MESSAGE

Only child, my ass. Scha-wing!

EXCITED BUT NERVOUS, CAITLIN WAITED IN THE CHAPTER room with the other sisters on Revelation Night, the night before initiation when each pledge learned which sister would be her Big Sister. On Monday, the pledgemaster and her assistant, who knew the pledges the best, matched up pledges with the sisters who wanted to be Big Sisters and informed each Big Sister who her Little Sister would be. Caitlin wasn't surprised that she didn't recognize her Little Sister's name. She didn't know the names of most of the pledges, unlike Sabrina, who had quickly bonded with Andrea, C.C.'s Little-Sister-to-be. But Caitlin, who was an only child, didn't care whom she was assigned to. She just wanted to be a Big Sister.

Once Caitlin realized who her Little Sister was (she had to have the pledgemaster surreptitiously point her out one night before a pledge meeting), she was pleased. She knew that the girl was quiet and not annoying, like some of the other pledges, and that she was a fellow athlete who played on State U's club soccer team. Caitlin spent the next few days shopping for her Little Sister. Every day that week, she was supposed to give the pledgemaster a box of presents to pass on to her Little Sister. Each box contained clues to the Big Sister's identity, as well as some Alpha Rho items. The Big Sisters had been told not to spend more than $200 on gifts for their Little Sisters, but Caitlin couldn't help spending more. She wanted to make sure that her Little Sister's boxes were filled to the brim and that her Little Sister wasn't one of the pledges—there were some every year—whose boxes were dinky and halfhearted compared to those of the other pledges. Caitlin packed her boxes with Alpha Rho clothes, mugs, picture frames, and a stuffed swan, the sorority mascot. For clues she included apple-flavored candy and apple pastries (representing her hometown, the Big Apple), a key chain with a pair of miniature running shoes (representing her athleticism), and a collection of scrunchies (representing the ponytail Caitlin wore nearly every day, to her sisters' amusement).

Now Caitlin stood in a circle of sisters, waiting anxiously for the Revelation ceremony to begin. Caitlin pelted herself with what-if questions. What if she and her Little Sister didn't have much in common? What if her Little Sister didn't like her? Finally, the pledgemaster led the eager pledges into the darkened chapter room and hooked them into the circle. One by one, the pledgemaster called out the name of a pledge, who stood in the middle of the circle. The girls on the perimeter passed around a lit candle and sang a syrupy song about families. When the candle reached the pledge's Big Sister for the second time, she blew out the candle and stepped forward to hug her new Little Sister.

As Caitlin's Little Sister stepped to the center of the circle, Caitlin was overcome with a sense of warmth. When Caitlin had first joined Alpha Rho, she didn't know anything about Greek life. She didn't even know if she would remain a part of it. A year later, she was proud to have stuck with her sorority, proud that she had been able to get so much out of it, such as the leadership skills she had gained as vice president. Caitlin wasn't close with her Big Sister or Grand Big Sister—what with her mother's constant harping, she didn't desire guidance and control from any more females. But now, as she was about to receive a Little Sister, Caitlin thought about how that meant that instead of being one of the youngest girls in the house, she now knew enough to be able to guide a new girl through the process. She could teach her Little Sister how to experience sorority life without getting caught up in the superficialities, and how to navigate sorority politics while keeping her outside life intact. But the most important advice Caitlin planned to give her Little Sister was that if she gave Alpha Rho the chance, it might introduce her to her new best friend, as it had for Caitlin and Sabrina. This was her Little Sister's night, Caitlin knew, but she couldn't help feeling that this was a special night for her, too. Caitlin decided that this was the defining moment of sorority life for her, the moment that affirmed that joining Alpha Rho had been the best decision she had made in college. She couldn't wait to assume the role of Big Sister.

After the ceremony, the new Big Sisters took their Little Sisters to an assigned bedroom, where the rest of the family awaited them. Caitlin, her Big Sister, and her Grand Big Sister chatted with their newest addition, who was enthusiastic about meeting her family. They gave her "Welcome to the Family" cards and a sweatshirt on which they had hand-sewn the Alpha Rho letters in their "family pattern": a blue and green tartan. Some families made their new members undergo a family-specific initiation, which usually consisted of drinking a shot of the family's traditional drink, but Caitlin's family didn't do that. Instead, before they drove her home for the night, they presented Caitlin's Little Sister with the "family lavaliere," which had been passed down from Big Sister to Little Sister for several years.

During the following weeks, however, Caitlin and her Little Sister hardly had time to see each other. They settled for catching up online whenever they could. With her lacrosse schedule, her obligations as Alpha Rho vice president, and a heavy course load, Caitlin wasn't even able to make much time for Chris. Despite his distaste for Greek life, Chris, who understood that Alpha Rho had given Caitlin both a support system and a leadership role, hadn't complained in recent months. In fact, he had treated Caitlin on more equal terms since December's fight.

When Caitlin did manage to find spare time, inevitably she spent it with Sabrina. Now that Sabrina was no longer dating the professor, she and Caitlin were constantly together. When Caitlin had lacrosse practice, Sabrina watched or read at the field beneath rows of Bradford pear trees so white and puffed they looked like clouds. When Sabrina crammed for a biology exam or worked the late shift at the restaurant, Caitlin studied alongside her. When Caitlin prepared to give a presentation on rape to the sisterhood, Sabrina helped her rehearse. Sabrina introduced Caitlin to her non-Greek friends, who welcomed her into their group and provided free marijuana when they got together several times a week. Sabrina and Caitlin smoked much more than they had the previous semester. It was tough to turn down free weed.

By the end of March, Sabrina and Caitlin were spending so much time together and talking so frequently that they joked they were dating. When anyone asked either of them to do something, they checked on plans with the other first. A non-Greek friend remarked to them that they had become a collective unit. "You two make group decisions," he told them. "You have a hive mentality." Caitlin and Sabrina knew this observation was true. They reasoned that because they preferred a few close friends to many acquaintances, it made more sense to spend time with each other than to nourish relationships with other sisters who weren't as much fun.

This included Amy. Caitlin had been impressed with Amy's continued cordiality toward Chris, but increasingly she was coming to the conclusion that she and Amy had completely different personalities. Amy exuded so much energy that sometimes it made Caitlin tired simply to be with her. Nearly every morning, Caitlin woke up early to the sounds of Amy laughing loudly as she told some sister a story. Her mother considered Amy a bad influence anyway, because she shopped more than she studied. As much as she still occasionally enjoyed Amy's company, Caitlin thought, it wouldn't be terrible if they began to drift apart.

Ω   Ω   Ω

The Pledging Paradox

IN THE 1990S, NATIONAL GREEK ORGANIZATIONS AND SCHOOL administrators, facing threats of civil lawsuits, cracked down hard on hazing, to which several dozen Greek deaths had been attributed. In May 2002, Alfred University banned Greek life from the school following an investigation of the February death of a fraternity brother that allegedly was because of a beating during pledging. Other schools, including Bowdoin and Colby, had previously also terminated their Greek systems because of hazing violations. By mid-2003, forty-three states had passed antihazing laws that rendered hazing a crime. In March 2003, congressional lawmakers, supposedly sparked by the September Alpha Kappa Alpha drowning deaths, introduced the Hazing Prohibition Act of 2003, a bill that would withhold federal student financial aid from students caught hazing. (As of this writing, the bill was referred to the House Committee on Education and the Workforce).

Meanwhile, the Greek definition of hazing expanded from focusing mainly on physical violence to the current National Panhellenic Conference definition: "Any action or situation with or without consent which recklessly, intentionally or unintentionally endangers the mental or physical health or safety of a student, or creates risk of injury, or causes discomfort, embarrassment, harassment or ridicule or which willfully destroys or removes public or private property for the purpose of initiation or admission into or affiliation with, or as a condition for continued membership in a chapter or colony of an NPC member fraternity." The way to avoid these situations, as moderators at the Northeast Greek Leadership Association Conference explained, was to prohibit all activities that differentiate pledges from sisters. "Hazing is anything that distinguishes one member from another," the moderators said.

Despite Nationals' vocal derision of hazing, the National Panhellenic Conference has not sent the strongest message that it could. The NPC has two levels of policies: resolutions, which require a majority vote of the delegates of the twenty-six sororities, and Unanimous Agreements, which "must be incorporated into College and Alumnae Panhellenic procedures and are binding upon all chapters of NPC member groups." Currently, the NPC's stance against hazing is only at the resolution level. "It might have been more powerful if it were a Unanimous Agreement," NPC chairman Sally Grant conceded when I asked. "It would be tougher on students."

The new definition has led to debate and bewilderment among sisters such as the Alpha Rhos, who didn't understand why their previous year's activities—which included scavenger hunts and other pledge-only games—qualified as hazing. Several sisters felt they had lost the ability to relate to the pledges because their pledging experience was so different. "We never really hazed in the first place. I was disappointed we couldn't do things the way we've always done it. It's weird changing it after years of doing it a certain way. I didn't understand why we couldn't do some of the stuff—no one got offended by it and the girls seemed pretty comfortable," Amy said. "This year's pledges didn't have to do anything. They said it was really easy, and they didn't understand why the activities we canceled were considered hazing. We felt bad because we had to do all this stuff and they didn't. We knew the older sisters better because we were given more of a chance to be involved."

Beta Pi defied hazing rules much more egregiously than Alpha Rho by using pledge books, holding mandatory sleepovers, and forcing pledges to drink and carry around silly items. When I asked Vicki if she and her sisters were afraid they would get caught hazing, she replied, "I didn't think it was really hazing because it was fun. We're not a hazing house."

Between sorority girls' confusion over the rules and their disregard for or unawareness of them, the hazing crackdown has hardly eliminated sorority hazing. When Arika Hover pledged Alpha Chi Omega at Arizona University in

November 1998, the sisters repeatedly reassured her that the chapter was opposed to hazing and that Arizona was an antihazing campus. But one night, sisters divided Arika's pledge class into groups of five and separated them into different rooms in the house. In one room, the pledges had to answer questions and drink straight shots of vodka when they answered incorrectly. The girls consumed several shots in a fifteen-minute span before they were hustled to another room. The sisters in this room smugly gestured to a table that displayed a black permanent marker, a knife, a hammer, and a dildo.

"We are going to ask you questions," the sisters told the anxious pledges. "And if you get them wrong, we will violate you with your weapon of choice."

"Who were the founding mothers of this sorority?" a sister asked one of the pledges. That was an easy one; the pledges had been memorizing sorority minutiae for a month. The sisters turned to Arika, whom they had picked on throughout the pledge period. "How far is it from here to Wisconsin?"

When Arika thought they were kidding and made up a number, the sisters told her to choose a weapon. She picked the marker, and the sisters made her write the correct mileage number all over her face. Then Arika grew angry. "This is bullshit!" she yelled. "You told us when we pledged that you guys were against hazing and that this was a nonhazing campus. This is going to stop tonight. I'm leaving." She led the pledges in her group out of the room and through the hallway, where they saw other pledges crying and cowering in the corners. Sobbing at home, Arika called her mother, who called the campus police. The sorority's national officers came to Arizona to "take control and start the reformation," Arika told me. "And then I got kicked out."

Here I interrupted Arika's story. "Wait a minute," I said to her. "You're saying that you were so upset with the hazing that you walked out, called your parents, and cooperated with the police, but despite everything these girls did to you, you didn't willingly drop out of their sorority?"

"Nah," she replied. "I thought about dropping out but my whole family was Greek. They're like, 'That's just what happens.'" Not long after the national officers arrived on campus, the adults instituted a random room check for alcohol—and found a bottle of alcohol that had mysteriously appeared in Arika's closet. Allegedly framed, Arika was tossed out of the chapter.

Compared to other hazing stories I heard, Arika's experience seemed fairly run-of-the-mill. What surprised me, however, was that after all the supposed torture that the older girls had put her through, she still wanted to be their sister. Throughout my interviews I discovered that girls just arriving at college, seventeen and eighteen years old, lost and lonely among thousands of strange faces, will often do just about anything to belong to something larger than themselves; to find fast friends and a long-term affiliation. "They've actually done studies in which they've found that those people who have been hazed . . . actually feel that they want the group even more. They are more determined to be in. They're more dedicated," Dr. Joyce Brothers has said on television. The tightness of the group and its aura of secrecy lead these dedicated members to succumb more easily to peer pressure. "Whenever you have a group . . . it becomes a mob after a while when it's secret, when there's no light there, when you don't let other people know. So the very worst part of the worst person in that group begins to do something, and then the others are afraid to pull away, so you get behavior, mob behavior, which is the very lowest common denominator." (When I asked Brothers, a sorority member herself, for further comment, she told me she would not participate in "somebody else's book.")

Clearly, lowest-common-denominator behavior, such as the California sisters leading their pledges to their death in the ocean, is deplorable. But the new national sorority interpretation of hazing, which essentially says that a group can't make pledges do anything the sisters don't do, is confusing and frustrating to today's sorority girls. Many upperclassmen have difficulty understanding why their current pledges are not allowed to share the experiences they had. In their eyes, punishing a sorority for hazing because it asked the pledges to wear sorority colors is akin to suspending a fifteen-year-old under a high school zero-tolerance drug policy because she carried Tylenol for a headache. As Amy explained, the panic over the new rules led to a rift between sisters and pledges instead of a slowly strengthened bond. "Part of the problem was that there was no pledging," Amy said. "I know it's different now with all the rules, but we were trying to come up with a happy medium and couldn't find it."

The moderators at the Greek Values Institute I attended in Pittsburgh reluctantly allowed a brief group discussion about hazing after students kept raising the issue. When the moderators explained that the rule forbidding pledge-only activities extended to the mandatory pledge study hours—that the sisters would have to be in the room studying with the pledges—many students objected. "The reason why national policies are so comprehensive is because someone screwed up and you guys have to pay the consequences," explained the moderator. Hands immediately waved in protest.

"The hardest pledging makes you care about your house so much," said one student. "I feel like it has to happen."

"Not hazing means not pledging," said another. "Without it you're not considered 'real' brothers and sisters."

"It's tradition," said a third. "It is a rite of passage and a necessary evil."

Nationwide hazing debates repeat these sentiments, particularly the need for a pledge to "earn her letters" before being allowed to become a full-fledged sorority sister—to prove her worth and devotion to a sorority and to learn to subordinate herself to the group. A 1980s study found that 77 percent of then-current Greek members and 63 percent of alumni believed that hazing was important to Greek life. In the same vein, in 2000, a sorority president posted on stophazing.org, a leading antihazing web site, a defense of hazing. "Wherever you go you are going to be hazed to some extent, at work, at school, even at home," she wrote. "I have been hazed, and I now haze our pledges . . . There is a purpose. It teaches the pledges togetherness, communication, respect, courage, and a huge sense of accomplishment. I can't tell you the feeling I got when at the end of hell week I was able to take off my blindfold and all of the sisters were gathered around us and a banner saying congratulations was there. I had earned something. I had accomplished something. And for that I am a much stronger person."

A 2003 post expressed the argument that college students face risks regardless of whether they are hazed. "People can be harmed or even die doing almost any activity. It seems silly to say that scavanger [sic] hunts present a real threat to the life and limb of students," the person wrote. "I assure you more people have died at concerts, skiing, hiking, crossing the street, or climbing ladders. Should we therefore ban greeks (or better yet all college students) from latters [sic], crossing streets, rock climbing etc.?"

The flaw in this approach is that just because any situation can be risky doesn't mean we shouldn't try to prevent risks. Should we remove lifeguards from beaches and pools because some swimmers have died while lifeguards were on duty? At the same time, however, it's clear that the current catchall policy—apparently designed to shift as much liability as possible away from the sorority national offices—isn't working. In December 2001, Michael V. W. Gordon, a former longtime executive director of the National Pan-Hellenic Council, stated, "There's no question that hazing in sororities is increasing in frequency as well as severity."

This failure may have to do with the ambiguous and subjective nature of the current sorority hazing definition. Representatives of the national sororities say that anything chapters do that distinguishes a pledge from a sister is hazing. But these same Nationals still call for a mandatory pledge period between rush and initiation—unlike the African American sororities, which eliminated official pledging entirely in 1990. Moreover, under the hazing definition, chapters would be vilified for doing to pledges what sororities are already allowed to do to rushees, such as suggest they wear certain outfits, herd them around in groups, or make them wait outside the house until the end of a "door song." Further, by banning all ways to distinguish pledges, Nationals have pushed more dangerous forms of hazing underground. Because they aren't even allowed to send pledges on scavenger hunts or other activities they consider benign, many sorority sisters figure that if they are going to do anything to the pledges, then they might as well revert to the forced drinking and fat-circling of the 1980s.

It is difficult to see how asking pledges to wear a particular color could injure or kill them. There is a line drawn between demanding color-coded dress and forcing pledges to wear bikinis in the snow. And with all of the local advisers at a sorority's disposal, it seems reasonable to expect that an adult could be present at all pledging activities. Regardless, if sorority national officers respond that these suggestions would lead such activities down a slippery slope, one could direct them to their own hypocrisy. Nationals claim that pledges aren't supposed to be distinguishable from sisters. Funny then, that these same Nationals require pledges to wear a "pledge pin" distinguishing them from sisters, don't allow pledges to wear the sorority's crest, exclude pledges from ritual ceremonies, and refuse to initiate pledges until they pass a pledge-only test.

TRADITIONS AND SECRET RITUALS
From Spring Breaking to Breaking Oaths

Our Ritual and ceremonies, those things which symbolically bind all Pi Phis together, are also to be shared only with other Pi Phis. It is a sign of your loyalty to the Fraternity, that you treat these things with confidentiality as well as respect. In turn you will find your entire lifetime fraternity experience and accompanying Pi Phi friendships take on deeper and more beautiful meaning when you know they are shared only with those who bear the name of Pi Beta Phi.

—*Pi Phi Forever*, *1990s*

Only sisters of your sorority know this confidential information, and you must promise never to reveal it to anyone.

—*Ready for Rush: The Must-Have Manual for Sorority Rushees! 1999*

Ω   Ω   Ω

Girls Gone Wild

SOMETHING THAT BROOKE SAID about her chapter's "Boob Ranking" continued to resonate with me throughout the year. She said, "Everyone before you did it, so you have to do it, too." This creed is the linchpin of sororities. Tradition binds sisters to each other, to their national organization, and to their organization's history. For some sororities, tradition is embedded in their strict adherence to their group's ritual. Others gain a sense of continuity through yearly repetition of specific activities. At one large Virginia school, chapters of Alpha Phi and Zeta Tau Alpha translate tradition to mean holding Naked Parties.

Once a year, these sororities hold what are officially called "Sister Parties" but are commonly referred to as "Naked Parties," for which the pledges dress up the sisters in outfits as unattractive as possible (a recent year's theme was "rednecks"). Naturally uncomfortable in their laughable outerwear, the sisters last only an hour or so before they end up stripping off their clothes until they are running around in the nude. While many of the girls continue the usual party activities (drinking, talking, and dancing), others take the now racy function in a different direction: the girls hook up, sisters and sisters, pledges and pledges. By the time boys are allowed to walk in the door, they are thrilled to find naked girls kissing.

This is not to say that these sororities condone lesbian activity at any other time of the year. An Alpha Phi at this school recounted an instance when a sister's boyfriend said, "I'd like to see you kiss your sister"—and she did. "But then," the Alpha Phi told me incredulously, "the boy left, and the sisters were still kissing in their room with the door closed! We couldn't believe it!" Sisters are free to simulate sex by freaking on a dance floor, but nonheterosexual activity outside of Naked Parties sparks shocked looks and snide remarks.

There is an exception to this contradiction, a time when sorority girls hope to shed their pearls and escape from under the shadow of their letters. This annual tradition—Spring Break—sends them with hordes of other college students to warm climes with lax rules, such as 2003 hot spots Cancun, Acapulco, and Panama City Beach. To study these migratory patterns, I spent several days at another popular 2003 Spring Break destination.

Negril's Seven Mile Beach, on the western tip of Jamaica, is a long stretch of powdery white sand bordered on one side by tranquil, aqua waters and on the other by bars, restaurants, and, during my stay, a constant series of Spring Break parties. Theoretically, Spring Break is a time to unwind, a time to relax with sorority sisters away from the pressures of campus life and in a setting whose breathtakingly exotic splendor encourages bonds that transcend pledge class. Theoretically, Spring Break is a calming escape from the hubbub, a time to regroup and collect one's sorority self in order to return to campus refreshed and composed after a week or so away from the stresses of purchasing partywear and maintaining fraternity relations. But who's kidding whom? In reality, Spring Break usually degenerates into one long wet T-shirt contest during which sorority sisters onstage (fed volumes of alcohol by a bar or restaurant's hired party hosts) comply with the request repeatedly chanted in unison by hundreds of fraternity brothers and other college men: "Show us your titties."

At Jimmy Buffett's Margaritaville, dubbed "Spring Break Headquarters 2003," I intercepted four southern Delta Phi Epsilon girls as they exited the stage of a similar contest. Flushed and breathless in their bikinis, they glanced around furtively to make sure a conservative faction of their chapter wasn't watching them. "We're outgoing and they're dorky," one DPhiE explained. "They're wearing their letters, and I was wasted and high as soon as we got on the bus at the airport. By the time we got here I was friends with everybody on the bus. They look down on that."

Margaritaville was a frequent highlight on the pink Spring Break calendar distributed to the throngs of student arrivals each week. Nightly parties offered all-you-can-drink specials, a water trampoline, and themes ranging from "Earn Yo Beads Mardi Gras Party" to "The Foam Hook-Up Party" ("Free Bongs for All Party Patrons!!"). Signs at the bar read "Help Save Negril Water. Drink Beer" and "Shirt and Shoes Required. Bra and Panties optional."

The DPhiEs took these messages seriously. The night before, one of them, a small, perky girl with large breasts, stripped onstage at Margaritaville and let her sorority sisters paint her nipples and other parts of her body with their hands. "When she took her shirt off, everyone went crazy," one of her sisters said.

"I was wasted," said the petite girl. "The Travel Channel was there. Apparently, I signed the release form."

"But legally, contracts don't count if you're drunk when you sign them, right?" a sister asked me.

The small DPhiE shrugged. "Whatever. We leave in two days, and I promised the fraternity guys they'd see my boobs by the end of senior year."

After spending time at several campuses at which sorority sisters were easily distinguishable because they constantly wore sorority clothing, I went down to Negril expecting to find sorority girls to interview by spotting their letters. But I remembered once I got to the beach that sorority sisters don't wear their letters when they drink, and students on Spring Break tend to drink all day. With the exception of a few teetotalers' T-shirts and one set of blue and pink Delta Gamma flip-flops (the bottoms are engraved with the sorority letters backward so that when the girl steps into the sand, she stamps her letters), I was on my own.

Gradually, it became easier to pick sisters out and I was able to interview nearly a hundred sorority Spring Breakers. Sorority sisters came to Negril in groups of six, ten, twenty-six, or forty. They walked the beach in small, close-knit packs that strode together, unlike the non-Greek girls, who fanned out on their walks, one or two stopping to pick up a shell or cool her feet in the water. The sorority groups had similar hairstyles, wore makeup to sunbathe, or blow-dried their hair straight before coming to the beach. Also in contrast to their Independent counterparts, the sisters were less likely to wear shorts, sarongs, or towels to self-consciously cover their behinds. They didn't need to. As a person wary of gross generalizations, it is mind-wrenching for me to write this paragraph. But based on these observations, as I canvassed the beach and the bars asking, "Are you in a sorority?" by the end of my trip I was batting .800.

"It's unrealistic here," an attractive brunette Alpha Chi Omega said as she surveyed the beach outside Margaritaville. She either meant surreal or unreal; I wasn't sure which. The beach was dotted for miles with students holding rum, Red Stripe, Smirnoff Ice, Corona, or the popular mixed drink "Dirty Banana." At most of the bars, Spring Breakers could not get into the evening party unless they paid for the all-you-can-drink wristband. This meant that even the students who weren't planning to drink had to pay between about $20 and $50 just to join their friends; and once they paid, they often decided they might as well drink. Pulsating reggae or dance music throbbed from enormous speakers at intermittent beach bars every hundred feet or so. Jamaicans wove around the sunbathers, offering pineapple or cigarettes, and looking around surreptitiously before whispering, "You want ganga?" or "I got som't-ing for you," or "MARLBORO! MARLBORO! Marijuana. MARLBORO!"

"A few of us came here to escape the drama bullshit in our house," the Alpha Chi Omega continued. Her sister sunbathed topless nearby. "We stick together. Even if one of us hooks up with a fraternity guy, the rest of us just wait for her."

"Do the rest of you hook up with his fraternity brothers while you're waiting?" I asked.

"If the guys want to!"

The sorority girls were here because they could be anonymous. They were here to break the rules. "We're here to be wild and crazy because we're not allowed to be wild and crazy at school," said a group of midwestern Tri-Delts. "We're doing the all-inclusive," remarked a Pi Phi surrounded by six of her sisters. "That means we drink from ten to ten." An Alpha Sigma Alpha who was with several dozen sisters packed four or more to a room, listed the group's Spring Break achievements: "One of us won a hardbody contest, two girls came in second in a 'pimp and ho contest,' where they had to collect money to do things," she said. "Every year we all go somewhere. It's crazy. I wouldn't go with anyone else."

"Why did you come to Negril?" I inquired.

"We wanted to come back with a tan. That was the big issue."

Many sorority Spring Breakers are relieved that with some of their more conservative sisters staying home, they can let loose without fear that news of their behavior will travel back with them to school. Others aren't so lucky—or careful. While Spring Breaking on South Padre Island in 2003, two Southern Methodist University Tri-Delts agreed to expose their breasts for a Miss Girls Gone Wild pageant, during which contestants were encouraged to kiss each other, eat bananas, and be covered in whipped cream and chocolate syrup. The pageant was broadcast live on pay-per-view television. When Bridgette Wies, eighteen, and Reanae Sath, nineteen, left for South Padre Island, they said their Tri-Delt sisters told them, "Don't do anything stupid." After the contest, Wies told a local paper, "I thought I'd regret it. At first I thought I was lowering myself. But I'm really glad I did it."

Thanks to the wonders of mass media, however, by the time the girls returned to Dallas, so had the news of their adventure. When their chapter held a vote to determine whether to disaffiliate them, their sisters voted to keep one girl and drop the other, for popularity reasons. Dissatisfied with the results, the national office and chapter officers had not made a final decision on the girls' sorority fate by the time of this writing.

This was the kind of consequence feared by some of the girls I found in Negril. On my last day in Jamaica, I met two Alpha Delta Pis who told me about how they had placed in a wet T-shirt contest and hooked up with several men. "I had sex on the floor of the Jungle dance club with a Jamaican!" exclaimed one, a sophomore.

"We've been making fun of her the whole time," said the other. "She doesn't know his name."

"If our whole sorority were here, it'd be a big problem," the sophomore said. "They'd send me to 'Hearing,' the group we have to see if we do something against the code of conduct. They can't fine me for doing what I did, but they could talk with me."

"We hope the Jungle doesn't come back with us," said her sister, who then repeated what seemed to be the motto of the sorority Spring Breakers on the island: "What happens in Jamaica stays in Jamaica."

Sorority Secrets

SORORITIES' MOST SACRED TRADITIONS, OF COURSE, HAVE nothing to do with Spring Break. The crux of each organization is its "ritual," a set of members-only secrets that supposedly bind all chapters of a sorority to the national organization. Ritual, according to Mari Ann Callais, a National Panhellenic Conference–approved expert on the topic, is "a symbolic and often emotional expression of the organization's myths, values and identity, and, as such, forms the metaphorical bridge between the individual and the organization." Sorority ritual most often refers to the ceremonies and traditions at initiation and at formal meetings. Sisters swear by oath in front of the sisterhood to keep these customs secret.

In the last few years, sororities' national organizations have tried to emphasize a return to the ritual values as a way to try to right a Greek system that seems to have strayed from its founding ideals. In 1999, the national president of Alpha Sigma Alpha wrote in the ASA magazine, "As an organization, we clearly articulate our values through our ritual. Of all the documents, handbooks, policies and procedures, nothing replaces 'The Ritual of Alpha Sigma Alpha.' In fact, we could toss all of those other items out an open window and we would never lose our way." An Alpha Delta Pi document entitled "History Workshop I" explained, "Our Motto, Constitution and Bylaws and Ritual have withstood the test of time . . . The basic components of Alpha Delta Pi Ritual remain unchanged. The ideals remain unchanged."

It is generally accepted that Kappa Alpha Theta was the first university Greek-letter fraternity for women, and therefore the first sorority as we know it. In 1870, Bettie Locke, a student at Indiana Asbury University (now known as DePauw), tried to become a full-fledged member of her brother's fraternity. When the men refused to initiate her and told her that she could wear their badge only if she agreed to be their mascot, she declined. At her father's suggestion, she instead formed her own women-only fraternity with three friends. Originally, Kappa Alpha Theta served as a support network to the female students, who were treated poorly by male students, faculty, and friends at a school that had only begun to admit women three years before. Sororities were also expected to monitor girls' behavior. In her 1907 book *The Sorority Handbook*, Ida Shaw Martin argued that sororities provided a college girl "with family affiliations and with the essential elements of a home—sympathetic interest, wise supervision, disinterested advice . . . There is a danger, and a very grave danger, that four years' residence in a dormitory will tend to destroy right ideals."

Sororities considered it their duty to train their members in etiquette; in return, the women "were reminded not to disgrace themselves, lest they bring shame on their sorority," according to hazing expert Hank Nuwer. Traces of this purpose still thrived throughout the twentieth century as sororities took it upon themselves to advise their members of proper dress and comportment. A Phi Sigma Sigma who graduated in 1953 remembered the pressure to adhere to certain etiquette commands. She showed me a photograph taken of her sisterhood in which the sisters all wore loafers or saddle shoes, straight calf-length skirts, jewel-neck sweaters ("preferably cashmere"), similar tidy brown hairstyles, and pearls. "The word came down: Wear pearls," the Phi Sig said.

The Phi Sig, a Jewish woman, also recalled the exclusive divisions that still exist, either subtly or otherwise. When she rushed, she said, it was known that Jewish girls "were either in a Jewish sorority or none"—not accepted into even the groups that were not founded on Christian values (Chi Omega and Kappa Delta began as Christian-based groups). "There was no crossover. We had to rush all the sororities, but everyone knew which ones you'd really be eligible for. That's just the way things were." Several other graduates of the 1950s and 1960s shared stories about their sororities' blackballing of Jewish rushees.

By midcentury, despite a spate of state laws prohibiting sororities, fraternities, and secret societies at the high school level as "inimical to the public good," college sororities were flourishing. In the 1960s, many women viewed sorority sisterhood as a way to meet eligible men. When one woman was invited to become a Sigma Delta Tau in 1962, her parents said she "absolutely had to do it. They felt it was important for social status." Her experience doesn't sound all that different from that of sorority girls forty years later. She didn't like the looks-based snap judgments of the rush process, so she regularly volunteered to work in the kitchen instead. But the sisters wouldn't let her. "There was a necessary order of those sisters who were acceptable to meet other people in public and those who were shuttled into the kitchen," she said. "They told me I was 'not a kitchen person.'" She said that her sorority's main criteria for rush candidates were fairly shallow: "The big question we asked ourselves during the voting process about rush candidates was 'Would you want to brush your teeth next to her in the morning?'" Pressure was also intense to date only fraternity boys and to befriend only sorority girls; others were often viewed as outcasts. Hazing was almost as commonplace as it was in later years.

One major difference between sororities then and now, however, is that when the Sigma Delta Tau was a student, sororities were viewed in many schools as a necessary stepping-stone for women to achieve anything of merit. It was considered a given that women needed sororities to get anywhere. At the Sigma Delta Tau's midwestern school, where the majority of the student body was Greek, if a woman wasn't a sister, classmates assumed that it was because she wasn't good enough—not because she didn't want to join. But when I sent inquiries to several successful sorority graduates from that era and others, none of them was willing to discuss attributing any part of their accomplishments to sorority membership. Mega-author Sue Grafton, whom the National Panhellenic Conference advertises as a famous sorority woman, put it bluntly: "My sorority membership hasn't contributed anything to my success."

Nonetheless, sorority women from several generations still insist on keeping their sorority rituals secret—even if they can no longer remember what the codes actually mean. Usually gregarious women in their seventies and eighties, far removed from their college days, immediately clammed up when I asked them about their sorority experience. "I can't say anything about sororities, for reasons I can't talk about," one said.

The first members of sororities developed rituals to reflect the values and standards of their organization. "As sororities developed, a need for structure and continuity emerged," wrote Mari Ann Callais in a dissertation that does not reveal secrets of her sorority or any others. "As sororities expanded from their founding campus to other colleges and universities, it became important to keep each sorority's individuality and to establish what made the group special and unique." This often involves reminding sisters of the group's symbols. The symbols on a sorority's crest, whether Kappa Delta's dagger, Chi Omega's skull and crossbones, or Theta Phi Alpha's esquire helmet, mean something specific to the members. For example, the crest of the national sororities' umbrella organization, the National Panhellenic Conference, breaks down this way, according to an NPC document:

> The shield is a protective influence for our entire membership. A lamp denotes leadership, scholarship and enlightenment. The laurel wreath signifies victory, or achievement of ideals. The sword piercing the wreath indicates willingness to fight for ideals, symbolizing, too, penalty of obligation; also bravery, achievement and discipline. The mantling surrounding the shield is the protecting cloak that education gives us, and a protective influence of organization. Thus, there in the mantle is inscribed the name of the National Panhellenic Conference.

Nationals often remind their sisters to "live the ritual," meaning that they should reflect on and live by the values of the sorority expressed at its ceremonies. As a speaker at the Greek leadership conference proclaimed to his ballroom audience, "Am I living it better today than yesterday and tomorrow than today? That's what being Greek is all about. The pursuit of trying to live up to that oath." In a Kappa Kappa Gamma publication, a sister wrote in 2000, "What is really exciting is that part of your story is shared by every woman of Kappa Kappa Gamma, past and present. Our experiences differ, but despite chapter location, number of members, housing situations, and varied campus life, we do have a shared experience—our Kappa ritual. We all participated in ritual saying the same words, wearing the same clothes and on a higher level, naming the same dreams and the ideals of goodness, truth and beauty and then we endeavored together to seek the finest in life, thought, and character. This is when our Kappa stories became one."

Today's sisters still perform these rituals, which, according to Callais, encompass formal readings of passages, Greek letters on clothing, symbolic colors, "hymn-like Greek songs, and occasionally even drinking rites involving the use of loving cups." These rites occur at initiation, formal meetings, and special events (such as candlelight ceremonies). Initiation ceremonies, which often include themes of truth, justice, love, and honor, can involve symbolic "ritual equipment," such as flowers, jewels, candles, specific clothing, a ritual book, an altar, or other items reflecting ancient Greek mythology or religion. Sorority initiations are intended to transform pledges into sisters by teaching them the secrets of the sorority—such as passwords and mottoes—and having them pledge to keep these secrets within the membership. In the Greek community, it has been said if a sister chooses not to obey the oath throughout her time in the sisterhood, she should be asked to leave.

These oaths, however, are not necessarily steadfast. Many sisters I spoke to participated in rituals only because if they did not, the sorority imposed individual fines of up to several hundred dollars. Some women just a few years out of school had already forgotten the meanings behind their sorority's phrases and symbols. Others shared their secrets. Most sororities, for example, have secret handshakes that are used in meetings. For Chi Omega's secret handshake, sisters shape their right hand into a two-fingered gun (or the sign language letter "h") and clasp hands. One sister taps the other's wrist twice and says, "Chi Air"; the other taps twice and responds, "Offilimus." "Chi Air

Offilimus," the secret meaning behind the letters Chi Omega, represents a "helping hand." Delta Zeta has a sorority whistle, though it is rarely used anymore. Delta Zetas whistle two short tones, then two long tones ("Del-ta Ze-ta") to the notes G, G, high E, high C.

Other sororities have secret knocks. In some Alpha Phi formal chapter meetings, the girls line up by pledge class in alphabetical order. The first girl in each class knocks on the closed meeting room door three times—to stand for "A-O-E." An officer on the other side knocks back. When the first sister says "Alpha," the door opens a crack. The officer replies "Omicron" and opens the door further. The sister responds "Epsilon" and the class is allowed inside. The letters stand for Alethia Orno Eteronis, Alpha Phi's secret motto, signifying love. Alpha Xi Delta uses "TFJ" as a motto, which some chapters interpret as "Thanks for Joining." Sigma Kappa's "closed," or secret, motto is "Thus we stand, heart to heart, hand in hand." Alpha Sigma Tau's closed motto uses its letters as an acronym for "All Sisters Together." As part of Kappa Alpha Theta's ritual, sisters begin meetings by reading aloud "The Love Verse," 1 Corinthians 13. Some sororities find inspiration in the signifi-cance behind their symbols. For Alpha Sigma Alpha, the pearl represents growing beauty from ugliness (the oyster). Pi Phi's official flower, the wine carnation, represents many aspects of the sorority. According to Pi Phi *Forever*, the publication given to pledges,

> The roots of the flower are the Founders, for from them the whole plant grew, . . . the stem represents the Grand Council. It gives to us what was received from the roots. It gives us height and strength . . . The leaves of our flower are the alumnae. They stand nearest the stem and assist it in its work. They are in communication with the world and breathe in for us the best of the world's ideals . . . the petals are red for the girls are loyal. As it is the rich, wine color which makes the flower attractive, it, too, is the warm fervent loyalty of its members which makes Pi Beta Phi beautiful in the eyes of everyone . . . The pistil is the spirit and the stamens are ideals of Pi Beta Phi. The petals stand closely united around these to defend and protect them.

Many sororities also have specific names for their chapter presidents, such as "Grand Hierophant" (Chi Omega), "Lady Superior" (Alpha Phi), and "Archon" (Phi Sigma Sigma).

Some sororities still use secret passwords. Kappa Kappa Gamma's is "Adelphe," Greek for "sister." To get into chapter meetings, Tri-Delts greet their chaplain at the door to the meeting room by saying "Este laethes," Greek for "Be true." Phi Sigma Sigmas base their password on the pyramid, one of their symbols; their secret phrase is "LITP," or "Love in the Pyramid." Delta Zeta's password is "Philia," Greek for "friendship," and its motto is "Let the flame endure forever." Delta Phi Epsilon's password, "jusilove," is meant to remind sisters of the symbolism of the equilateral triangle on their sisterhood badge: the three points represent justice, sisterhood, and love. For Pi Beta Phis, the secret word is "worra"—the backward spelling of "arrow," their symbol. When a Pi Phi sees a woman who she believes might also be a Pi Phi, she is supposed to say "W." If the other woman spells the rest of the password, the Pi Phis know they're sisters. Chi Omega's secret dialogue is called the "watch":

"What is it?"

"A good thing."

"To be elected."

"Can all be elected?"

"Hardly."

In earlier days, the Kappa Kappa Gammas also allegedly had a procedure to ascertain whether someone was a fellow member. If a Kappa spotted a potential sister, she would rest her chin on the palm of her hand and stick up her index finger. If the target was a Kappa, she would respond by putting her chin on her palm and pointing up her middle finger. For obvious reasons, that practice has since fallen out of favor.

Initiation ceremonies for the various sororities are fairly similar. Many groups drape the initiation room in white, and most require sisters and pledges to wear only white. Called "The Temple," the initiation room in some houses is intended to replicate the house of the Greek gods. In one chapter's Kappa Alpha Theta initiation script, the initiates are to follow the lead of the "High Priestess," who carries a ceremonial cup. Girls in some Sigma Kappa chapters must purchase specific white dresses (described by one recent graduate as "long-sleeved with a slightly dropped waist, heinously ugly, and very shapeless"). For Sigma Kappa, wearing white is mandatory and inflexible. In one Sigma Kappa chapter, when a national representative came to oversee a ritual meeting, a sister entered the room wearing white shoes with black toes. The national representative "had a conniption. She said, 'You have to go home and change them,'" a participant said. Zeta Tau Alphas also "wear their whites" for initiation—"we couldn't even have a button on them that was another color, all the way to our stockings and our shoes," a Zeta said. During initiation, Zetas receive a blue ribbon representing their ties to the sisterhood; sisters are told to hide the ribbon, to let no one see it, and to keep it forever.

During the Delta Phi Epsilon initiation, the sisters and initiates form concentric circles according to pledge class. When Pi Phi pledges enter the initiation room, they are each handed candles—wine-colored or silver blue, if possible. Inside the room, the neophytes stand in a circle and sing songs. They must repeat an oath that includes the line "I pledge myself to Pi Phi." Sororities consider these vows crucial to the bonds of sisterhood. As the National Song of Alpha Delta Pi proclaims,

> We pledge once more allegiance now
> With hearts as true and high
> As when we took the sacred vow
> For Alpha Delta Pi.

Both Chi Omega and Kappa Delta include songs with religious overtones, which some non-Christian girls refuse to sing. Chi Omega has initiates kneel on cushions in front of an "altar," place their hand over a Bible, and pledge themselves to Chi Omega. In "hard-core" Chi Omega chapters, pledges are dropped into a coffin, pronounced dead, and then reborn as sisters.

Many sorority initiations occur in stages over the course of the pledge period. At Kappa Delta's First Degree Ceremony, pledges receive their pledge pins and pledge themselves "to Kappa Delta and her ideals," according to *The Norman Shield of Kappa Delta*, a publication for new members. After a retreat and a six-week education program (with sessions entitled "KΔ—Simply the Best!" "Being Your Best!" "Becoming Your Best!" "Best of the Best" "Giving Our

Best!" and "The Best Is Yet to Come!"), pledges reach the Second Degree, which is the First Phase of Initiation. The Second Degree Ceremony grants pledges a Second Degree pin and teaches them more about "the bonds of Kappa Delta." The period between the Second and Third Degree ceremonies is known as the "White Rose Celebration," "a meaningful time of reflection where you and the chapter prepare for the beauty of the Third Degree Ceremony and the true meaning of Kappa Delta." At the Third Degree Ceremony, "the full significance of our sisterhood is revealed. You will learn . . . all of the other secrets of the ritual, which has remained virtually unchanged since 1897."

After initiation, sororities give the new sisters a certificate and, eventually, access to everything from sorority ID cards to credit cards emblazoned with the sorority crest. The sisters also must purchase a pin, or badge, given to them at an official pinning ceremony; in some groups, a girl cannot be initiated until she has purchased this pin through the sorority. It is crucial that the pin not "fall into the possession of a nonmember," according to *The Key*, Kappa Kappa Gamma's magazine for the membership. The magazine includes a form that advises members to fill out and enforce with the assistance of a lawyer. The form's "Kappa Kappa Gamma Badge Disposition Instructions" direct members to indicate whether upon their death they would like their one-inch golden key buried with them, returned to KKG headquarters, or left to a legacy, chapter, or alumnae association.

Now that the new sisters have been initiated, they are privy to secrets held supposedly only by their sisters and the sisters before them, secrets so sacred that at the National Panhellenic Conference Centennial Celebration and Interim Session in the fall of 2002, the delegates stressed, "Fraternity secrets must be maintained to maintain intimate association."

Some of the girls I interviewed would disagree. "It's kind of cool that the ceremonies have been going on since Beta Pi was created," said Vicki, who laughed as she then espoused a view I encountered among many of the girls I spoke with. "But ritual doesn't mean anything to me. It's a hassle."

APRIL

———

Most of all, "Kappa Delta" is the feeling you will now have when you drive down the highway, and see a Kappa Delta decal on the car in the lane next to you and try to speed up so you can wave to your new "sister"!

—Norman Shield of Kappa Delta, July 2003

Practically every girl looks better with some makeup. Just because you didn't wear any in high school doesn't mean you shouldn't now . . . Do not wear bright-colored eye shadow. Do not wear too much dark blush applied in rectangles. Do not affect a tan with a dark makeup base. Do wear mascara, blush, and lip gloss at the least.

—Rush: A Girl's Guide to Sorority Success, 1985

Ω   Ω   Ω

Rock Bottom

APRIL 7
Amy is not logged on

A FEW WEEKS AFTER Date Party, Amy was still aglow from what seemed to be a burgeoning relationship with Hunter. This was the first time that a date had wanted to continue seeing Amy after an Alpha Rho function. Hunter showed up at the house every few days and usually joined her at the bars, where once he happened to kiss her passionately right in front of Spencer, her old crush. Amy bloomed, putting her diets and her self-doubt aside. Several other girls had crushes on Hunter, who was increasingly in the campus public eye as a rising-star shortstop. But Hunter had chosen her.

Amy was so excited about the upcoming Alpha Rho Parents' Weekend that she hardly noticed when Hunter hadn't called in several days. Alpha Rho annually planned its Parents' Weekend for the end of the first week of April, when the dogwood trees lining the streets were in full pink-and-white bloom. Amy's mother had to stay home with Amy's brothers, but her father was flying in to spend the day with her and escort her to the Alpha Rho Tulip Dinner at an expensive restaurant near campus. Amy, who rarely had the opportunity to spend time alone with her father, was so geared up she was practically bouncing off the walls. She couldn't remember the last time she had spent a day with him.

Friday morning, Amy's father picked her up in a rented convertible to take her shopping near campus. In Saks Fifth Avenue, Amy's father stopped short at a shoe display. "Those are excellent shoes!" he said, pointing to a pair of pastel mules with kitten heels. "If I were a girl, I'm sure I would want those shoes." Amy thought the shoes were somewhat impractical, and a little too low-heeled for her taste, but they fit and were comfortable. Her father looked so pleased that he had found something to buy her that she graciously accepted them and pecked a thank-you kiss on his cheek.

When they walked into the restaurant lobby, Amy was dismayed to find that of the eighty-five Alpha Rho sisters attending the dinner, Amy and her father were only the third family to arrive—and the first two sisters were Fiona and Whitney. Amy and her father leaned awkwardly against a wall while Fiona and Whitney and their parents studiously ignored them. Every now and then, they eyed Amy's father up and down, smirked, and returned to their conversation, folding into a circle that excluded Amy and her father. Amy, who was used to funny looks when people first met her dad, stood close to him and put her hand on his arm protectively. While most sorority girls' fathers, like those attending tonight, wore jackets and ties or sweaters and khakis, Amy's father, his hair in a ponytail, was dressed in his usual Hawaiian shirt, gold chains, white pants, and loafers without socks.

When the hostess led them to the private party room with two long tables, Fiona and Whitney and their parents sat at one end of one table, while Amy and her father made their way to the opposite end of the other. Eventually, other sisters arrived to fill the uncomfortable gap.

"Daddy, they're my least favorite two in the house," Amy whispered, offering her father a mint.

Her father smiled. "I could tell you didn't like the first two right away, and you get along with everyone. So there must be something wrong with them."

Amy and her father spent the dinner chatting with Traci and her parents. While the parents inquired about jobs and majors, Traci started talking about Formal. Amy and her father stiffened, deliberately not looking at each other until the topic had passed. She had already informed him that she hadn't yet asked Hunter to Formal and that she would be Jake's date for the Mu Zeta Nu Formal two weekends later. Ever since their autumn argument about her inability to keep a boyfriend, Amy and her father had avoided the topic of boys. Amy didn't understand why her romantic life mattered so much to him in the first place.

That night, after her father dropped Amy off, her mother called. "It meant a lot to your daddy that you invited him to spend time with you tonight," she said in a velvety voice that matched Amy's. "Don't tell him I told you this, but you just need to understand. Honey, the only reason he's pushing for a boyfriend is because he hates to see you alone. When your sister died, it broke his big heart to see you walking through the world without a partner. He's just afraid you're so lonely you're like the last pea at pea-time." Touched, Amy resolved to try even harder to find—and keep—a boyfriend.

A FEW NIGHTS LATER, AMY AND HUNTER STOPPED AT Hunter's dorm on their way back from bar-hopping. Hunter introduced her to his roommate, who was thumbing through a textbook on the couch. The roommate chatted affably with Amy before turning to Hunter.

"Hey, Hunter, your girlfriend called again," he said. Hunter's head jerked up. "So when are you two getting married, anyway?" the roommate teased.

"What?" Amy said. She glanced at Hunter, who wouldn't meet her eyes.

"Oh yeah, Hunter has fallen really hard for this girl," the roommate said, evidently assuming that Amy was just a friend.

"Really," said Amy, trying to mask the shock that pierced her drunken fog. "That's news to me." She looked again at Hunter, who couldn't conceal his embarrassment. Amy left the dorm, already worrying about Formal. At least she had had the forethought to line up Jake as a backup Formal date in case a straight guy didn't work out.

Back at her room, as soon as Amy took down her IM away message, Nathan, the Mu Zeta Nu brother who had date-raped her, IMed. "Hey, are you staying up for a while? You want to come over?" he wrote.

"No, I'm not coming over," Amy typed back.

"Can I come to your place? I promise I'll make it worth your while," Nathan wrote.

"Try me." As Amy typed back to him she wondered what on earth she was doing.

Five minutes later, she opened the door to the house and Nathan zoomed in, kissing her hard on the lips the second he was in the entry hall. He rushed her up the stairs and shut the door to her bedroom. Amy, still drunk, let him take off her clothes, still berating herself for letting him come over. She didn't even like him.

When he was finished, satisfied where Amy wasn't, she let him out of the house so that none of her sisters would see him. "It was a stupid mistake," she told herself. "I'm an idiot." When she woke up the next morning, the evening's events suddenly hit her, and, disgusted, she buried her head in her pillow and cried.

$$\Omega \quad \Omega \quad \Omega$$

The Gender Role

OF THE FOUR SISTERS I FOLLOWED, AMY WAS ALWAYS THE most enthusiastic about the Greek experience. She loved the trimmings of sorority life—songs, rituals, bonding sessions, sorority-themed decorations—and she proudly wore her letters around campus. Unlike the other girls, she attended nearly every event the sorority sponsored throughout the year.

For Amy, sorority sisterhood was an opportunity to try to re-create a bond she had lost when her biological sister passed away. She craved the support system that she believed Alpha Rho could provide. As she learned, however, no institutionalized sisterhood could come close to filling the void left by her loss. Sororities do not offer unconditional love. Nonetheless, Amy was grateful for the connection she said she had with her sisters. "There's a common bond through all of us," she said at the end of the year. "Even with the girls I don't get along with, we still share something special. If they heard something really good or really bad about me, even Fiona and Whitney, they'd tell me congratulations or be comforting." I asked her what she meant by the "something special" they shared. "We all joined the same organization and whether they're my best friends or not, we all love Alpha Rho," she replied. "That's the building of a sisterhood."

It made sense, then, that Amy participated in so many sorority activities: she thought that the more time she spent with the sisters, the stronger their bond would be. But of the four girls I followed, Amy was also left the most heartbroken. The confidence she might have gained from belonging to a sisterhood was not enough to outweigh rejection from the boys she believed she needed in order to keep up with her sisters.

Therein lies the contradiction of these all-girl groups. As much as sororities extol the value and virtue of a single-sex group, these sisterhoods are not necessarily designed to concentrate on sisters' relationships with one another. The sisterhoods revolve around men. This was evident at State U, where semesters were divided between Crush Parties, Date Parties, and Formal, all of which required a date, and mixers—which existed essentially to find dates for those other events. This was also obvious at several other chapters, such as the sorority that held a lavish ceremony to celebrate the achievement of a sister who had acquired a steady boyfriend but gave only a bag of chips to the sister with the highest GPA. Lisa Handler, a professor at Temple University who studied sororities in the 1990s, told me that she found that "sisterhood is not as strong as brotherhood." Sisters told her that "a brother would never give up a brother for a girl, but a sister would give up a sister for a guy. That's a difference between sisterhood and friendship. A friend doesn't sleep with your guy, but it was held up as a constant that in the sisterhood, women were going to stab your back. Sisterhood is not more powerful if boys can *pierce* it."

But what if boys are part of it? In the last thirty years, several national and local coed fraternities have sprung up across the country, groups that model themselves after fraternities rather than sororities. In order to discover whether female members of these groups find sisterhood, I visited Zeta Delta Xi, a coed fraternity at Brown University in Providence, Rhode Island.

At Zete, Paul, the secretary, ushered me downstairs to a lounge where some undergrads and fraternity alumni—Zete alums return frequently, even years after graduation—were sitting on tables, chairs, and each other, girls on guys and girls on girls. These were friendly, unpretentious students, proud of their alternative status on campus and the way none of them, appearance- or personality-wise, was ever mistaken for a mainstream Greek.

Like all-male fraternities, Zetes have rituals, weekly meetings, social and service activities, and rush. "In the process to decide who gets a bid, unless someone doesn't seem interested or really pissed us off, they're considered," said Faye, Paul's girlfriend and a Zete brother—both male and female Zetes are called brothers. During Brown's Spring Weekend in April, the Zetes host "Spag Fest," an all-you-can-eat-and-drink party for members of the Brown community. The thirty Zetes stay up all night slicing bread, making garlic butter, and cooking more than a hundred pounds of dry spaghetti. The Zetes provide table service for the usual turnout of five hundred people.

Sometimes the girls in Zete have "girls' nights": female-only slumber parties to which they each bring a pint of Ben and Jerry's ice cream. Although they don't often break off from the rest of the brotherhood, the girls believe that Zete women have "something special," Faye said. "When I'm with women in Zete, I feel comfortable and relaxed. We have an intense, unique bond in common, along with the same underlying characteristics that made us want to become Zetes."

On a tour of the house, which is actually a wing of a dormitory building, the brothers pointed out the unisex bathrooms and the "damned" spots in the house. The damned spots were the items on which a brother had had sex (sex defined in Zete terms as "two or more people, one or more orgasms"). So far, the only items that were not damned, meaning nobody thought twice before sitting on them, were the pool table and a cooler. "Incest" is inevitable in a coed fraternity, many Zetes told me; in fact, several of them had experimented sexually with Zetes of the same gender. Faye, who wrote a paper on "fraternity girls" for a class project, said that sexual tolerance is a characteristic of many coed fraternities. When she interviewed female members of seven coed fraternities across the country, she found that many of the groups encouraged experimentation. The Zetes were the first fraternity at Brown to elect as president an openly gay man.

Intrafraternity relationships led to a rumor among Brown's sororities that in order to be fully initiated into Zete, pledges had to sleep with every brother. The Zetes were hurt by the falsehood but also at the same time seemed to be a little bit proud—there had been half a dozen marriages within the fraternity in the past decade. And some of the activities in the house were games involving nudity or a college version of Spin the Bottle. "We do more after two A.M. than most people do in a day," a Zete officer told me. "Our motto is 'Have a good time all the time.'" The officer, a self-described "Zete manwhore" who looked like an exotic, better-looking version of *Sesame Street*'s Ernie, had worked his way through both genders of many of the brothers in Zete. For the entire night he wore an expression of constant, unbridled delight.

With the exception of 1998, the year when Zete females outnumbered the males, the fraternity's ratio is usually two guys to one girl. This is evident in the Composites hanging on the walls, which blatantly differ from traditional sorority composites. There are few photographs of girls wearing family pearls and obedient smiles. Rather, the Zetes, prioritizing character over composure, wear props and strike poses that one imagines could be captioned the Thinker, Blues Brothers, or Pimp Daddy.

The Zetes originally were affiliated with the national male fraternity Zeta Psi, which organized a chapter at Brown in 1852. In 1982, the Zetes at Brown decided to accept female members. When the national office found out, it sent word that it refused to recognize the female Zetes and that national rules prohibited the women from becoming Zeta Psi officers. Instead, Nationals suggested that the chapter consider the female Zetes only as fraternity little sisters. In response, the Brown chapter rebelled, electing women as fraternity officers in 1986. When Nationals threatened to revoke the chapter's charter if the women were not removed from office, the chapter voted unanimously to withdraw from the national organization because it refused to recognize all of the chapter members. Nationals promptly declared the chapter defunct and sent over movers, who took most of the house's furniture and the old Composites.

A month later, the chapter resurrected itself as Zeta Delta Xi, "an independent, co-ed fraternity founded on principles of equality." Since then, the Zetes have continued to refer to their female members as brothers—as Paul said, "leaving no question about the full and legitimate membership of women members." Zete is now an open-minded house under the guise of a fraternity. Like any other fraternity, during my visit the brothers played beer pong, a popular fraternity drinking game during which a team tries to bounce Ping-Pong balls across a table into the other team's full cups of beer—a quick way for brothers to get drunk from beer tasting like sweaty Ping-Pong balls. (The brothers were careful to play at an off-campus location, given that drinking games are prohibited at Brown houses.) The brothers who surrounded us, however, were a mix of races, genders, and clothing styles. A Zete in a wheelchair explained, "This was a fraternity that would accept me as a person."

"It just felt different here," Faye said. Although her mother was in Alpha Epsilon Phi, Faye said she never considered rushing a sorority because it would be "unnatural" to isolate herself in an all-woman house when the rest of society isn't that way. "I couldn't stand to live only with women. I think I'd go nuts," she said. "Zete is a very accepting, not exclusive house—there aren't cliques. Zete women are liberated and aren't afraid to be themselves."

When I asked Faye if she believed she had missed out on a sorority experience, she said she found something better than a sorority sisterhood: she found a pressure-free place to belong. "I definitely feel like I belong to something. That's new for me because I felt like I didn't belong for so long. And it doesn't put pressure on me to live with the girl-group power kind of thing," she said. "I don't need a sisterhood because I have a brotherhood, a peoplehood, a siblinghood. I have a supportive, gender-nonspecific family."

Going "local," as the Zetes did, is a popular alternative for women seeking a sisterhood outside of the twenty-six national sororities. At schools across the country, dozens of local single-sex sororities wear Greek letters and gather, hold meetings, and live in off-campus houses. The members of the local sororities with whom I spoke were just as involved in and enamored of their sisterhood as the national members were. "Being in a local is better because there are no national dues and we can pledge girls whenever we want," said a local sister at a New Hampshire university. A local sister at a Pennsylvania school explained that she preferred a sorority that did not have to follow Nationals' rules—a double-edged sword that lets the local girls evade, say, dress codes, but also leaves them unsupervised during events that may involve hazing. "In a local you don't have to answer to national reps. It makes us unique," she said. Locals, she said, escape the way people try to apply stereotypes of one campus's national sorority to every chapter, even though the chapters vary by campus. "We're more independent. It's more intimate."

Melody Twilley's sorority at the University of Alabama is also a local. Given the intolerance she experienced within the Greek system, I wondered why she would want to model her organization after the white sororities on her campus—and, for that matter, why she needed to institutionalize her relationships at all. Why did she need a sisterhood rather than a club?

"Well, that's not as much fun. You don't get to keep secrets from everyone else! It's like being in a gang, but not illegal. You have stuff that identifies you as part of a group," she said. "We knew we were going to be a Greek sorority. You can't be recognized by the university if you don't take men unless you're part of a Greek organization."

Keeping in mind that her group had not yet been officially accepted into the Panhellenic community on campus, I asked if Melody considered her fellow Alpha Delta Sigmas sisters. "Oh my God, yes. If we're not sisters, I don't know what we are. We have gone through more than any of the sororities on campus could understand. We're sisters because we're friends. I don't have any friends who are like family here who aren't in my sorority. These guys are like my family on campus."

"What does sisterhood mean to you?" I asked.

"It means having a family that you don't have to love," she replied, "but you do anyway."

Ω   Ω   Ω

Advice Dispensed

APRIL 11

SABRINA'S IM AWAY MESSAGE
Gettin' mah hair did

SABRINA AND CAITLIN WERE SITTING ON THE BATHROOM counter at Louie's, their favorite bar, drinking and chatting with a few sisters when Bitsy walked in.

"Bitsy," Caitlin asked, "where exactly did you get pierced?" The other sisters circled Bitsy with interest while she cleared her throat. Several sisters had gotten similar piercings since Bitsy had done it in September, but Bitsy was widely considered the Jedi Master of nether-region rings.

"Well. So I didn't get my clit pierced. I got my hood pierced." Bitsy rounded her thumb and forefinger and held up her hand so everyone could see. "This is your clit." She pointed. "This is your hood—it's this little piece of skin. One ball goes here and one goes here, and since this ball sits on your clit, it's called a clit ring."

"How long did it hurt for?" asked Caitlin.

"Not long. Every time you pee, you clean the wound, so it healed quickly," Bitsy said. "I'm getting my nipple pierced tomorrow."

"Can I come get my hood pierced?" Caitlin asked, to Sabrina's horror.

"Definitely."

"Do you guys want to do it, too?" Caitlin asked the other sisters. Several were enthusiastic.

"Why would you do that?" Sabrina said, though she already knew. Caitlin was struggling to prove her growing independence from her mother's control. In Sabrina's opinion, it was a bizarre way, but at least it was something Caitlin wanted to do for herself that her mother would never discover. Caitlin's mother probably didn't even know it was possible for a girl to get pierced down there. "I'll just keep you company," Sabrina said.

The next day, the other sisters (now sober) all conveniently had something else to do.

At the piercing salon's front desk, the receptionist brought out a mold of a vagina spiked with various rings. "Point to the area you want pierced," she said to Caitlin.

"Bitsy!" At Caitlin's call, Bitsy stepped forward and pointed to one of the rings.

When they got to the piercing room, the man with the needle told Caitlin to strip. She handed Sabrina her denim shorts and underwear, and put her feet in the stirrups. Bitsy rushed around the chair to Caitlin's feet, where she watched the proceedings intently. Noticing how tense Caitlin was, Sabrina began to sing an old Prince song to her; Caitlin always laughed when Sabrina sang because she couldn't carry a tune. As Caitlin squeezed her hand so tightly it hurt, Sabrina tried not to think it strange that her friend was lying half naked next to her while a strange man was piercing her hood.

Afterward, Caitlin and Bitsy turned to Sabrina. "Do you want one, too?" they asked her.

"Hell, no."

ON A WARM MID-APRIL EVENING, CAITLIN AND SABRINA joined Amy and Beth to prepare for Spring Formal. This time, Sabrina planned to attend. Sabrina hadn't spoken to her professor since she broke up with him in February. She wasn't angry with him—he was just another guy whom she had dated, and from whom she then moved on. She had forced herself to stop thinking about him by going to Greek parties, drinking more, and telling herself that she would do fine on her own. Gradually she found that she was happier when she was with people her own age. Over the last six weeks, Sabrina had hooked up with a fraternity brother and two non-Greek friends with whom she and Caitlin often smoked. Because none of the boys were Formal-worthy, Amy had convinced Sabrina to go to Formal with Jake. Amy would take one of Jake's gay friends instead.

"Hey! What are y'all wearing tonight?" Amy asked when Caitlin and Sabrina walked in wearing T-shirts and boxers. Amy was sitting in her Victoria's Secret robe watching MTV as Beth pinned up her curls.

"I don't know. I don't like my dress anymore. I gained weight," said Sabrina.

"Honey, it's only Jake," Amy smiled. "He'll be more concerned about everybody's dates anyway."

"It's not the boys I'm worried about," Sabrina said.

"Oh, yes." Amy realized Sabrina was referring to the Alpha Rhos, who were far more critical of each other's looks than any male would be. "And the photos." Amy started to sing "Sweet Home Alabama" into her flatiron.

"Head back!" Beth yanked Amy's shoulders. As she lurched backward, Amy grabbed a protein bar from the table. "What's with you and the protein bars?" asked Beth. "There are four boxes in your room."

"I can eat only protein bars this week because I ate so much last week," Amy said, taking a bite.

"I think this is the first time I've participated in my sorority all year," Sabrina said as she handed out "pre-pre-game" drinks.

"No, you did Homecoming stuff," Amy pointed out.

"I'm talking about fun party stuff," Sabrina said.

Beth finished Amy's hair and abruptly stood up from her perch on the couch, screaming, "Agh! There's a bra on me!" A lacy black bra was hooked to the back of her sweater just far enough out of reach that she couldn't swat it off. The girls doubled over in hysterics.

"Hey, that's mine!" Sabrina gasped.

"How'd it get there?" Beth asked.

"I put it there!"

"On my back?"

"No, on the couch. I was wondering what had happened to it." Sabrina plucked the bra from Beth's back. "Do you have a clippy thingy?" she asked Beth shyly. "I wanted to put my hair half up today." She turned to Caitlin. "And could you maybe give me a little makeup?"

As Caitlin led Sabrina into her bedroom, Amy said to Beth, "Can you believe Sabrina's getting her makeup done?"

"Tonight I want to be pretty, too," Sabrina said.

"Put on a little shimmer stuff," Amy suggested before muttering to herself, "I need to fix my 'boobage.'"

Sabrina settled on Caitlin's bed and closed her eyes, opening them just in time to see Caitlin about to poke at her eyelid with an eye pencil. Sabrina flinched. After several more attempts to introduce Sabrina to eyeliner,

Caitlin applied subtle hints of eyeshadow, mascara, blush, and lipstick. When she was finished, she handed Sabrina a mirror. Sabrina's eyes widened in disbelief. "Hey, I look pretty!" she said, surprised at her first foray into cosmetics.

Amy came in wearing a resplendent plum gown and heels that matched her eyes. "We're going to be late for pre-game, girls. Let's go," she said.

Caitlin looked at her plastic cup. As she and Sabrina followed Amy out the door to a satellite house, Caitlin muttered, "What's the point of getting to pre-game on time if we're already pre-pre-gaming?"

At the pre-game, Sabrina stayed close to Andrea, the newly initiated sophomore with the funky wardrobe. The two of them watched from the periphery as Alpha Rhos glided around the room in Armani and Chanel dresses, with their "Louies" and "Kates"—Louis Vuitton and Kate Spade handbags—on their arms.

"I don't know about this sorority thing," Andrea whispered, rattled by her sisters' phony tinkling laughter and the judgmental way they eyed each other's outfits.

"I was really skeptical after I was initiated, too," Sabrina told her. "I know you're intimidated by the older sisters, but you shouldn't be. Since there are so many girls in the house, it's going to be hard to fit in the moment you walk through the door."

"But what if I have to miss a bunch of meetings?" Andrea asked.

"Don't sweat it. You have to keep your priorities straight. A sorority is a good experience, but you don't have to let it take over your life," Sabrina said. "Over time, you'll be more confident about being in the sorority. I am."

After that conversation, Sabrina felt more connected to Andrea. Simply having another confidante gave Sabrina herself greater strength in the house—not enough to confront the more ignorant sisters, but enough to make her sense that she remained in Alpha Rho for reasons other than a living space. This year had taught Sabrina both that she could survive in a sorority without taking it very seriously and that she was not in Alpha Rho for all 160 girls. She remained a sister because of the ten or so girls who meant something to her and reminded her that though the real world, like many of her sisters, may not be kind, she would always have allies to help her succeed.

Ω Ω Ω

Sisterhood without the Sorority

BY THE END OF THE YEAR, SABRINA'S FEELINGS ABOUT sorority life hadn't changed much. She didn't believe that the concept of a sisterhood squared with reality. "Sisterhood is a form of structure, drama, and friendship. It has given me some structure in my life, with regular meetings and events that help me plan my schedule. It's an organization that I met my best friend through," she said. "But it's also a thing where you have a lot of people 'there' for you only superficially. That really hits home for my situation. I don't think people really care about each other wholeheartedly or make an effort to be 'sisters.' I've noticed that many people in this house are so selfish. For them, being friends with another person depends on how that person can fit into their lives or benefit them."

For Sabrina, the value of belonging to a sorority wasn't in the sisterhood. She was grateful that Alpha Rho had introduced her to Caitlin and Andrea. But after a year of living in the sorority house, she had to grasp to find a reason that made her time in Alpha Rho seem worthwhile. "I feel ambiguous about it. It's an elitist institution. I know that I would have had an awesome college experience had I not joined. I've had a lot of negative experiences in Alpha Rho and in that sense it sucks sometimes, but it's teaching me more patience. At least it's a way for me to learn about people," she said. We talked about the ways some of the sisters had treated her and about how the extensive sorority commitments took both time away from her studies and money from the funds she used to pay for her education by herself. "The way I see it, [these negatives are] just a part of life. I feel like from now on, I'm always going to have to juggle commitments and somehow you have to make them work out. So this is practice, I guess," she said. "Maybe once I'm in the real world I'll have an easier time being independent than my sisters."

Ultimately, sorority membership held little more for Sabrina than a learning experience. This was the only way that she could justify loyalty to an organization in which some sisters mocked her culture (with racist remarks), treated her meanly (by eating her birthday chocolates and rummaging through her things), and talked down to her ("go down there right now"). It was the only way that Sabrina could rationalize remaining in an environment in which she did not feel comfortable enough to stand up for herself. "If I don't look at Alpha Rho with a positive spin on the negative things, then I'd just be miserable," she said.

Caitlin, whom I talked to separately about sisterhood, felt that life in a sorority held similar lessons for her. "Alpha Rho taught me some stuff, like some people never change. There's always going to be that group of girls who think they're better than you—not just in high school—and they don't always grow out of it. Some people don't understand there's no point in being mean. I wonder what kind of people Fiona and Whitney will grow up to be," she said.

By the end of the year, however, the sorority had become a bigger part of Caitlin's life than Sabrina's. The strength, independence, and confidence that Caitlin sensed she had gained between August and April she attributed in part to her leadership role as Alpha Rho's vice president. "My mother was wrong about sororities. Greek life in general has been supportive for me, something to motivate myself, to be involved in, to care about. It's been a grounding," she said.

When I asked Caitlin what sisterhood meant to her she said nothing about her sisters as a support network or a collective unit. Instead, she talked about Sabrina. "I'm not best friends with anyone in the house except Sabrina. I couldn't just call up anybody and say, 'Wanna hang out tonight?' But Sabrina and I became a lot closer. We've never had girl best friends before and it's weird. Now we actually tell each other about stuff that happens when usually we would just keep it in," Caitlin said. "I think of sisterhood as a one-on-one bond. It's a strong bond you share with another female, and a building on that bond based on common experiences. We might be sisters but not have a strong sisterhood unless we go out and do things like retreats, where we really get to know each other. I'm looking forward to next year in Alpha Rho."

While Sabrina managed to stay ambivalent about sorority life and Caitlin was appreciative of it but took the Greek system with a grain of salt, Vicki's attitude toward her sisters changed dramatically through the year. I was particularly curious about whether Vicki believed the speech that she gave rushees in January. "I guess I exaggerated a little bit, but I think basically it's true. It was a good decision that I did this. It opened up a new world where I've met so many people I wouldn't otherwise have met," she said. "I never used to want to come back to my room. Now I get sad when nobody's here. It took a semester to warm up to it, but now this feels like my house and I'm ten thousand times more comfortable. I'm sad to be leaving for the summer. I have a much bigger social thing going on over here than at home. I drink more, smoke more, I'm more into trying new things, meeting new people . . . My friends at home"— she paused, perhaps realizing the dramatic change in her attitude since her first days in the Beta Pi house—"aren't cool anymore."

As an observer, it was evident to me that Vicki had gone from being a wallflower who watched the sisterhood from its fringes to one of the "popular girls" around whom the sisterhood revolved. I asked her what had changed besides her room situation that had so radically altered her attitude toward Beta Pi. She said that the older girls who moved out of the house after first semester were the sisters she didn't know well. The girls who remained, by contrast, were people she wasn't afraid of. During second semester, Vicki was a constant fixture in the television room she had shied away from before. "There are only so many of us who go downstairs and talk in the television room. I didn't do it last semester. But I finally realized that if I wanted to be friends with these girls I would have to hang out in the television room and make the effort. Now I talk to anyone who's sitting down there and that's how the friendships are made, you know?" she said, laughing self-consciously to signify she recognized the triteness of her words.

The factor that most turned Vicki's experience around was that she found a close circle of friends who cared about her—Olivia, Ashleigh, and even Morgan insulated her within the sisterhood. "I definitely feel so much better now that I have a group," Vicki told me at the end of the year. She was careful, however, to add a caveat: it was friends, not sisterhood, that improved her year. "I have my friends but I still think the concept of a sorority is weird. It could be seen as we're all friends because we're in the same sorority, but there are definitely girls here who I'm not friends with," she said. Vicki viewed the sorority as a series of inconveniences that were necessary to tolerate so she could live with and get to know the girls who became her close friends. Many times throughout the year, she said, Beta Pi's rules, rituals, activities, and commitments left her thinking, "This is so stupid. Why do I have to do this?" By the end of the year, although her attitude toward some of her sisters had changed, she still would not volunteer to non-Greeks that she was a sorority sister—and in public she never wore her letters.

Vicki separated the "concept of a sorority" from the friendships she had made within it. Watching her distinguish between friends and sisters caused me to wonder whether it was possible to have an organization that separates sisterhood from what the girls characterize as the frequently silly trappings of sorority life. For these girls, the ideal organization would have Amy's common bond, Sabrina's structure, Caitlin's home base, and Vicki's friendships—but without sororities' pressure to conform, focus on fraternity dates, overwhelming number of obligations, emphasis on alcohol, imposed rules and values, superficial recruitment system, disdain or reluctance toward true diversity, and hierarchical environment conducive to hazing. Was it possible to find sisterhood outside of a sorority?

With this question in mind, I attended a Subrosa meeting at the University of Pennsylvania. At Penn, Subrosa is a women's community service organization that is unaffiliated with any national group (some other schools also have local Subrosa chapters). Like sororities, Subrosa has initiation, Formals, Big and Little Sisters, mixers, regular meetings, and sisterhood bonding activities such as Bowling Night and Screw Your Sister. Unlike sororities, Subrosa has no dress code, rule book, fines, or mandatory events, and most of its activities involve community service.

Because Subrosa does not have a house on campus, its forty-five sisters meet weekly in a private lounge in one of the on-campus high-rise apartment buildings. Like most of Subrosa's meetings, this one was run informally, with sisters leaning on couches or sitting cross-legged on the floor. The sisters varied in looks, race, clothing, and hairstyle. As the meeting began, a co-social chair distributed tickets to the following week's Formal; 100 percent of the sisters had signed up to attend the end-of-the-year activity. As it did every semester, Subrosa rented out a bar/restaurant with money raised from the girls' seventy-dollar-per-semester dues. Subrosa, which doesn't believe in hierarchies, refers to its leaders not as presidents but as calyxes, "the part that holds a flower together." In a soft, unassuming tone, the co-calyx explained that after addressing this week's business the girls would assemble "care baskets" and cards to deliver to women at a nearby hospital.

After discussing the group's web site, "senior send-off" social event, bake sale, and "Hunger Walk," the sisters caught up on each other's lives as they assembled items such as mugs, scented candles, and pastel photo albums into the care baskets. I took the opportunity to talk to some of them about the strength of the Subrosa sisterhood. "In many ways our sisterhood is stronger than a sorority because we're not forced to be with each other or live with each other," said one of the co-calyxes. "It's more by choice that people want to be a part of this, so our bond is stronger."

I sat next to Darcy and Jessica, two of several Subrosa sisters who joined the group after giving up sorority life. The former Phi Sigma Sigmas told me that their Penn Phi Sigma Sigma chapter did community service activities only once a semester. If a sister didn't want to participate, she could buy her way out of the requirement for ten dollars. "We had to force girls to come to events at Phi Sig. Here, everyone wants to come," Jessica marveled. "Everything here is *more* optional than sorority activities and Subrosa gets better attendance."

"This is better for me. I'm kind of bitter about sororities. I'd kill myself before I'd go through that again," Darcy added.

Jessica and Darcy joined Subrosa after their Phi Sigma Sigma chapter was shut down in the fall. They said that Phi Sigma Sigma's national office informed the sisters at a meeting at Penn in October 2002 that because several girls had deactivated in the spring, the chapter wasn't at full capacity. Informal rush had already ended, but Nationals gave the sisters just three weeks to find new members, give them bids, initiate them, and get them to pay dues. In 2002, the Phi Sig chapter had the highest sorority GPA at Penn and a Phi Sig sister was voted the campus's "Outstanding Greek Leader." The chapter was one of the few sororities on campus that hadn't broken rules in recent memory; meanwhile, at the time the girls told me their story, three other sororities at Penn were under investigation for alcohol violations. But Phi Sig Nationals, the sisters said, "didn't care unless you gave them the seven hundred dollars." If the chapter didn't make quota, Nationals would shut it down.

When Nationals told the sisters of their plan to "re-colonize"—or reestablish the Penn Phi Sig chapter with new women—in 2004, the girls balked. The sisters didn't even try to recruit new members. Instead, when Nationals gave the sisters the option to deactivate from the sorority or take on alumna status (thus maintaining their Phi Sigma Sigma affiliation), nearly all of the seventy-five sisters resigned. In a campus press release, the Phi Sigma Sigma Penn chapter president stated, "the bureaucracy of Phi Sigma Sigma has caused the organization to forget what sororities and Greek life are created to promote, and the former sisters no longer want to be associated with such an organization."

Meanwhile, since they gave up their letters, the sisters haven't made an effort to keep in touch. "When everything fell apart, the older girls didn't come ask about us at all," Jessica said. "But Nationals keeps sending us e-mails asking for money." When I asked Darcy and Jessica if anything symbolic or meaningful from the sorority had stayed with them despite the demise of a sisterhood that became so easily fractured, they laughed. The one thing they could remember was that in keeping with their national ritual, the Penn Phi Sigs, like all Phi Sigs, ended every meeting with the words, "Once a Phi Sigma Sigma, Always a Phi Sigma Sigma."

The "Special Bond of Sisterhood"

My daughter will make friends in her residence hall and classes. What would be different about sorority friends?

—A question in the 2001 National Panhellenic Conference publication
Women's Fraternity Membership: A Perspective for Parents

A special bond of sisterhood is developed among chapter members—a bond that extends to all who share the same heritage, traditions and ritual and who wear the same sorority badge. These friendships last beyond the college years and are nurtured by alumnae activities and networking programs that provide opportunities for continued camaraderie, service, and personal development.

—Answer, from the same publication

WITH THE EXCEPTION OF A FEW CHAPTER ADVISERS, MOST of the graduates I spoke with had distanced themselves from their sorority after college—or after sophomore year. They rarely attended alumnae activities, if at all, and knew of few networking programs available. They did not think of sororities as a source of "continued camaraderie, service, and personal development." Several women did keep up with a few of their closest friends from their sorority and told me that those friends were the best things to come out of their sorority experience. Others continued old rivalries. Some of the Delta Zetas, for example, managed to get revenge on one of their "mean girls" a few years after graduation. A girl who had played a role in bullying Mary out of the chapter had job interviews set up at a well-known marketing company in New York City. Her first interview was with a woman in the human resources department who turned out to be one of her sorority sisters. The minute the bully left the room, the sister ripped up her résumé, laughing as she said to herself, "You should have been nicer in college."

Just as Penn's Phi Sigma Sigma illustrated that institutionalizing friendships couldn't keep a sisterhood from cracking, Brooke discovered after graduation that an affiliation is not the same thing as a support system. After college, the Ten settled in the same suburban area. Beginning with the week after graduation, they each got married on successive weekends, with the other nine as their bridesmaids. They now attend the same church and country club together and still try to discourage Eta Gammas from keeping in touch with women from other sororities. Three years after graduation, they still e-mail each other about how they cannot believe that Brooke continues to date Johnny, her Mu Zeta Nu boyfriend.

The Eta Gamma label clearly helped Brooke in her first year out of college. Sorority networks are especially powerful in the South—and can get a sister far in Texas. As the interviewer at one of the most prestigious entertainment agencies in the country looked down Brooke's résumé, she stopped and gasped. "You're an Eta Gamma?" she asked. "So was I! You've got the job." Brooke also believed that the experience of learning how to get along with difficult women prepared her well for her position in a company known for its corporate backstabbing. "I don't know if I'd do the sorority all over again if it meant being with my pledge class," Brooke said. "But it made me so ready for this company because otherwise I'd never have been with so many bitchy girls in one setting before. This is a walk in the park compared to Eta Gamma." Once the Ten found out she was working for some of the industry's most famous names, they suddenly began to call her. Finally, in their eyes, Brooke was worthy.

But that didn't mean she was a friend. Nine months after graduation,

Brooke was driving home from work on a highway when her convertible was broadsided by a truck. When she regained consciousness after several hours of surgery, she learned she had broken her neck and hip, fractured her femur, and sustained other injuries that would leave her in the hospital for weeks. One of the most difficult things Brooke had to do in her life was to talk to her parents after the accident without letting on that she was terrified. Sobbing, her mother told her she wanted to fly to Texas and take care of her long-term, but Brooke thought that with Johnny and her large number of friends in the area she would be able to take on her additional surgeries and massive rehabilitation with strength, grace, and gumption. And she did—but not with as wide a support network as she had expected. When word spread quickly through the Eta Gamma grapevine about Brooke's accident, she received care packages and regular visits and calls from four of her sorority sisters. A few other sisters e-mailed short notes. But the rest of the sisterhood, including the Ten, were silent. "It was very strange. They all knew about it," Brooke said. "It made me realize who my friends were and weren't, and it clarified what's important and what's really not." Over the next year, as Brooke struggled to walk again, only the four sisters offered help and compassion. "The other girls, it just wasn't in their makeup. They're really out for themselves. They might have been supportive if this had happened in college, but now that we're out of the group, it's just not how they work," Brooke said.

I asked her what sisterhood meant to her now, three years after college and nearly two years after her accident. "I gained four really great friends. Eta Gamma was a good experience for that time in my life. During college, while I was getting adjusted, I had a group of girls who would support me outside the house, even if they were destructive within it. If I argued with a girl from another sorority or got drunk and needed a ride home, my sisters were there for me. We kind of looked out for each other," Brooke said. "But after school, life is different. Some women get very involved as adults and at football games they all go back to the Eta Gamma house to hang out. But not me. For me, Eta Gamma is just not a big thing anymore."

$$\Omega \quad \Omega \quad \Omega$$

Becoming

APRIL 19

CAITLIN'S IM AWAY MESSAGE
It's going to be a good summer

WHEN CHRIS HAD ASKED CAITLIN IF IT WOULD BE ALL right if he went to another sorority's Formal with a friend, Caitlin said that she wouldn't forbid him to go but that she would be uncomfortable with it.

"So it's okay?" he asked.

"Well, I'm not going to be the person who tells you no," Caitlin replied, hoping he would reach his own conclusion that he shouldn't go. He went.

Two nights later, as they walked into the marble-columned reception hall for the Alpha Rho Formal, Chris wearily sunk into a chair near the buffet table, which displayed a lavish spread of vegetable and marinated steak brochettes, jumbo stuffed shrimp, and baked brie in phyllo with toasted almonds and raspberries.

"I was up working last night," Chris said, wrinkling his suit as he slouched.

"Don't fuck with me. You're still tired from the other Formal," said Caitlin.

"Wait a minute, you told me it was okay, so I went."

"I only said it to be nice."

Caitlin dragged him to the dance floor teeming with stilettoed Alpha Rhos gyrating to the DJ's fast-paced pop selections. Yawning, Chris remarked on the differences between this Formal and the one he had just attended.

"At the other Formal, the newest sisters weren't allowed to dance closely with guys because they were just initiated," he said.

"Can we please stop talking about that other Formal and enjoy ours?" Caitlin grumbled.

"I was just telling you about it, that's all," Chris said, raising his voice.

"This is my Formal and I don't want to hear about the other one."

"I've been invited to a lot of other Formals and Date Parties, but I didn't go," said Chris.

The blood rushed to Caitlin's head. "You never told me that! It seems really sketchy that you didn't tell me."

"It was just some people from class."

"Not telling me is like you were trying to hide something," said Caitlin.

"Well, I knew it would make you upset," Chris said.

"Then you shouldn't have told me ever." Caitlin stalked off. For the next two hours, she wandered around beneath the arches of teal and jade balloons, wondering if Chris had cheated on her. She tried to distract herself by dancing with Jake and by making fun of drunken sisters with Sabrina and Andrea. When she had cooled down, Caitlin returned to Chris, who was sitting alone in a corner with his arms crossed.

"I'm sorry," she said. "Let's just enjoy the rest of my Formal. There's still an hour left."

Chris wasn't appeased. "I didn't come here to get walked away from. The girl at the other Formal didn't leave me."

"Look, I'm sorry it's a big deal to me, but I didn't want to spend my Formal talking to you about other people's Formals," Caitlin said.

"My other Formal date is my friend. Why should I have to put her on the back burner for you? Why should I put *you* in front of my friends?"

Caitlin shook her head sadly. "You know what?" she said. "Just get out of my life." She hurried out of the reception hall and sneaked into another sister's limousine, where she hid until Formal ended and the driver took the girls back to the house.

A FEW DAYS AFTER CAITLIN TOLD HER MOTHER THE relationship with Chris was over, Caitlin called again to tell her mother the fall semester classes she had preregistered for. When she informed her mother that she had signed up for two art classes instead of political science courses, her mother went ballistic.

"That's hardly worthwhile," she yelled. "I'm not paying for those classes."

Later that night, Caitlin's father e-mailed Caitlin to assure her that he would find a way to slip her the tuition money without her mother's knowledge.

Throughout the next several days, Caitlin's sisters tried to distract her from her anguish. They praised her for how well she delivered her rape presentation and gave her high marks as vice president on their executive board evaluation forms when her term ended. Sabrina and other sisters took her out to the bars and tried to convince her that it was fun to be single. The other sisters told her that she shouldn't be upset, that Chris wasn't worth her energy. But that didn't console her. Only Sabrina came up with something that finally made Caitlin start to feel better.

"I like Chris as a person," Sabrina said, "but as a boyfriend he needs a lot of work."

When one of Jake's Mu Zeta Nu brothers asked Caitlin to go with him to the MuNu Formal, Caitlin's sisters persuaded her to go. After double-checking with Jake, who assured her that his brother had only asked her as a friend, Caitlin decided the Formal would be a good opportunity to escape for the weekend. The fraternity Formal was at a hotel in a city a few hours away.

Caitlin was dancing with her date and chatting with Jake and Amy when she spotted a familiar profile across the room. After not having seen Taylor since he had given her the tulip bouquet in November, Caitlin was surprised at her twinge of jealousy: he looked good, and he was with another girl. "Whatever," Caitlin told herself, "I'm prettier than she is." She vowed to make it seem like she was having the time of her life, in case he saw her. When Amy suggested the group go upstairs to their hotel room to do some shots, Caitlin quickly agreed.

Jake and Amy lined up their alcohol on an ironing board, setting up an impromptu bar. After a few Kamikazes, Caitlin cut herself off. She had already pre-gamed with her date in their hotel room before the dance and had finished a whiskey sour downstairs. Back in the ballroom, Caitlin was feeling the effects of the alcohol when she spotted Taylor again. She turned to Amy. "You gotta help me seduce Taylor," Caitlin said.

"Really?!" Amy beamed, excited about her sister's unexpected interest. "That is so great. You should totally go for it! I'll go distract your date." She disappeared. Caitlin didn't know how Amy engineered it, but all of a sudden,

Amy was dancing flirtatiously with Caitlin's date across the room, and Taylor and Caitlin were face-to-face on the dance floor.

"Hey," said Caitlin, "long time no see." She lightly punched his shoulder.

Taylor grinned. He gestured toward her date. "Why are you here with him?"

"Chris and I broke up. Who's your date?" Caitlin asked.

"Just a friend." They danced for a few minutes before he kissed her. This, Caitlin realized, felt right.

"Do you want to go upstairs?" Taylor asked. They tried to slide off the dance floor and out of the room without other people noticing. In Taylor's hotel room, as they fooled around, Taylor acted tentatively. When Caitlin began unbuttoning his shirt, he hesitated.

"We're in a hotel room," Caitlin whispered. "What did you expect?"

An hour later, as they put their clothes back on, Caitlin suggested they see what everyone else was doing. But when they got downstairs, Formal was over. Caitlin spotted her date at the bar and went to join him while Taylor left to find his friend. Caitlin acted as if nothing had happened. When her date fell asleep in their hotel room, Caitlin returned to the bar, where a few people suggested they change into their swimsuits and reconvene in the hot tub. As Caitlin sat in a lobby chair and waited for the elevator, Taylor walked by.

"What are you up to?" he asked.

"We were going to go hot-tubbing."

He leaned on the chair directly in front of her and looked her straight in the eyes.

"Please don't go," he said quietly.

"What do you mean?"

"Come hang out with me."

"What about your date?" Caitlin asked.

"She passed out in someone else's room."

Back in Taylor's room, they moved toward having sex again. "Can we slow it down and do it at my pace now?" he asked. Afterward they talked for hours. He told her how frustrated he was that an entire semester had passed when they could have been getting to know each other better. And Caitlin, who had until then merely been enjoying the moment, abruptly became aware that Taylor genuinely liked her. For Taylor the Player to be talking sincerely about seeing her again, Caitlin realized, she must have unknowingly made a tremendous impression on him.

Early in the morning, Caitlin slipped back into her hotel room so that no one would ask any questions. In the limousine on the way home, Jake and Amy corralled her.

"So," Jake asked, in a wink-wink-nudge-nudge tone, "how's it going?"

"Fine," Caitlin said, amused.

"Did you guys have fun?" he pressed.

"Taylor and I? We just talked."

"Seriously?" asked Jake, disappointed.

"Yeah," Caitlin repeated. "We just talked."

Amy, Jake, and Caitlin's date fell asleep quickly. Caitlin was glad she had been able to spend some quality time with Amy—who was genuine and a good friend—even if it hadn't come until the end of the semester. Caitlin leaned against her window and watched the scenery whiz by, smiling at last night's memory. Caitlin doubted that she and Taylor would embark on a serious relationship, but who knew? It didn't matter to her, anyway. What mattered was that even just six months ago, with her world centered on Chris, she never would have entertained the thought of being with another guy—especially a fraternity brother of whom her mother would disapprove even before knowing anything about him. And now, what seemed like eons later, she was finally realizing that there were so many other people out there who would think that she was terrific that there was no reason to hold her breath waiting for someone who couldn't decide.

Caitlin concluded that she had changed more this year than any other year in her life. She had finally learned that at some point she simply had to give up her futile efforts to please her mother. It had taken an extraordinary amount of turmoil for her to feel like she was finally growing up, and now that she had successfully wrestled with so many issues, it dawned on her that she was gradually starting to become what she had always pretended to be on the outside but was not truly until now. She was becoming—she thought—strong.

Saying Good-bye

APRIL 25

VICKI'S IM AWAY MESSAGE
gangs so tight they call us virgins!!!

ON THE LAST SATURDAY IN APRIL, BETA PI HELD ITS END-of-the-Year Banquet, which was simultaneously a semiformal date function and a farewell dinner for the seniors. Beta Pi rented out a local restaurant and decorated it with candles and tablecloths in burgundy and cream, the Beta Pi colors. At each senior's place setting rested a Tiffany sterling silver mesh bracelet nestled in a blue box—a parting gift purchased by the rest of the sisterhood.

Vicki arrived straight from pre-game with Olivia, Ashleigh, Morgan, their dates, and William. Beneath sidewalks framed in creamy white magnolia trees, the girls walked in a tight group together, their dates practically afterthoughts. Having been escorted to her Formal by Dan, Vicki chose to invite William to the banquet as a gesture of friendship.

After dinner, Vicki was dancing with her friends in a circle of long blond hair when Morgan tapped her on the shoulder and told her that Ashleigh was crying in the bathroom. Vicki followed Morgan to the women's lounge. When Ashleigh saw them, she cried even harder, blubbering about how the Iota brother William had set her up with didn't like her.

"I never bring someone to these things who actually cares about me," Ashleigh bemoaned, sniveling as she dug into her hot pink purse for a scented tissue. "You can find love and Olivia can find love and Morgan can find love but no one's ever going to love me."

"Ashleigh, yes they will," said Vicki, hugging her friend.

"If I could change one thing about myself it would be everything," Ashleigh wailed.

"Ashleigh, who's ditching her date to spend time with you in the bathroom for like half an hour? I love you so much, obviously," Vicki said.

When the girls emerged, the seniors were passing out the Superlatives

Booklet, an annual tradition during which the Beta Pi sisters wrote "Most Likely to" jokes on the designated page for each Beta Pi.

"Nobody get offended!" the seniors shouted as they distributed the stapled pamphlet. "We tease because we love!"

"If you don't have a sense of humor, don't read this," muttered another senior.

When Vicki got her copy, she and Olivia ran to a corner to peruse it together. They laughed hysterically, both because of the booklet and because Olivia was drunkenly repeating everything that Vicki read aloud.

"Here's Morgan's Page: Most Likely to Vote for Herself as Most Beautiful, Most Likely to Marry a Senior Citizen at Age 25, Most Likely to One Day Model Clothing Lines for Sticks and Poles," Vicki laughed.

"Ha-ha, sticks and poles!" echoed Olivia.

Vicki continued down the list. There was a Most Beautiful, Most Likely to Have a Sexual Position Named After Her, Most Likely to Need Her Stomach Stapled, and Most Likely to Lose a Car While Still in It. Ashleigh was labeled Least Likely to Be Able to Hold an Aspirin Between Her Knees and Most Likely to See Titanic Too Many Times. Laura-Ann was tagged Most Likely to Be Put in a Mental Institution and Most Likely to Be an Old Woman Who Talks to Her Cats, Which Will All Be Named Beta Pi. Olivia was voted Most Likely to Miss Class for Pre-Pre-Pre-Game and Most Likely to Wake Up Still Drunk. And Vicki's page read Most Likely to Be a Player for Life and Least Likely to Sleep in Her Room. Upon reading their pages in the booklet, some of the sisters, offended, ran out of the room.

As Vicki and her friends resumed dancing, she spotted William walking by and caught his arm. "Come dance!" she said. After a few minutes, Vicki turned around, saw Olivia, and danced with her for a while. When she turned back around, William was gone.

Vicki found him sitting alone, hiding beneath his blond curls at a table across the room.

"What's wrong?" she asked.

"You haven't been treating me like your date," he said.

"Okay, first Ashleigh needed me. She was really upset. Then we had the superlatives . . ."

"I don't know how to act with you," William cut her off. "We went from so much to absolutely nothing. Do we act like we're friends? We've never been friends. Do we act like we're together? We're not together."

"This couldn't wait until after Banquet? I mean, you couldn't just dance and have fun and we could talk about it later?" asked Vicki.

As they squabbled, the sisters grouped together on the dance floor, put their arms around each other, and sang two senior farewell songs, the first one dirty and the second one sad. Vicki ached to join them, but William wouldn't let her. All she wanted to do was have a good time with her sisters. Half an hour into their argument, the DJ played the song the girls had used for their Delta Lambda Homecoming serenade. The sisters ran to the dance floor again and joyously shouted their raunchy Beta Pi lyrics. Vicki, who couldn't pull away from the argument in time, grew increasingly upset that this was the seniors' last Beta Pi event and she couldn't fully participate.

After she and William had been arguing for nearly an hour, Vicki saw Ashleigh and grabbed her arm. "I'm going to the bathroom," she said, dragging Ashleigh with her. In the bathroom, Vicki retreated into a stall and wept, something she hadn't done since September. This was the first real fight she had had with anyone all year.

"I can't go back in there," Vicki whispered hoarsely to Ashleigh, who wrapped her arms around her. "I can't deal with him anymore."

"What happened?" Ashleigh asked. "Whatever it is, it's going to be okay."

"Don't cry, Vicki," Morgan said as she opened the door to the stall and came in. "There's no point in crying."

Olivia came rushing into the bathroom and dashed into the stall. "Vicki!" When the sisters updated Olivia, she knelt and looked Vicki in the eyes. "Oh my God, Vicki. Screw him. You shrug it off, take a couple of shots, and get out there on the dance floor and have a good time." She spritzed Vicki with a tiny perfume bottle from her purse. "This is your banquet. And we love you."

There in the bathroom stall, Olivia began to belt out the Delta Lambda Homecoming serenade that Vicki had missed. Ashleigh and Morgan joined in and shimmied to the tune, their hips banging against the sides of the stall. Laughing, Vicki looked around at her closest sisters, singing and dancing, missing their banquet to spend time with her in the bathroom. "This is what really matters—not the guys out there," she thought to herself, getting up and standing tall in her heels. "These are my girls. And they're here for me."

CONCLUSION

———

Young women today still are looking for a place to belong.

— *The Trident,* Delta Delta Delta's magazine, Summer 2001

There is a beauty queen house on every campus . . . Beauty, bathing suit mea-
surements, and wardrobe go a long way.

—*Ready for Rush, 1999*

Ω   Ω   Ω

IN MAY, AFTER VICKI, Sabrina, Amy, and Caitlin went home for the
summer, I returned to my hometown, where I happened to pass a nearby
Greek boutique. This time, as I gazed at the lettered jewelry, bottle openers, and
baby tees, their meanings were no longer foreign to me, from the pre-gaming
equipment of Pi Phi shot glasses and Kappa water bottles, to the wooden pad-
dles pledges would decorate for their Big Sisters, to the Δ on a blue stuffed
Delta Phi Epsilon lion, representing justice, sisterhood, and love. It was strange
to be well versed in the lingo of a world that I barely knew existed one year
before. But it was stranger still to have to step back and analyze it as an outsider
turned insider turned outsider again. This book was largely intended to spark
discussion of women's treatment of women; I did not write it to argue either a
pro-Greek or anti-Greek point of view. As the academic year ended, however,
I found I had deeply mixed feelings about sororities.

On the one hand, Vicki and Caitlin had overall positive experiences, as sorority membership gave them what many members told me were the biggest benefits of joining: girlfriends and confidence (though validation from boys played a large role in their confidence boost, which makes an interesting statement about the effect of sororities' emphasis on males). According to a National Panhellenic Conference brochure, recent studies have concluded that Greeks are more likely to graduate from college than unaffiliated students. Furthermore, a two-year survey conducted by the Center for Advanced Social Research at the University of Missouri found that Greek graduates are more likely to participate in community activities and religious and civic organizations and to "show stronger inclinations to give financial support to non-profit agencies." (This study was commissioned by the National Panhellenic Conference and the National Interfraternity Conference.) Some sorority chapters do make a point of emphasizing community service or raising money for good causes.

On the other hand, for every girl who emerges from a sorority with improved self-esteem, there are numerous others whose confidence has been crushed—like Amy, for whom the pressure to find dates so crumbled her self-image that out of unhappiness and desperation, she slept with the boy who had date-raped her. In addition, sisters' intolerant, conformist attitudes left Sabrina feeling helpless and alienated from the group. Within the sorority, the girls found a competitive environment in which they were constantly being judged by their sisters; this is what Amy and Sabrina referred to when they discussed Sabrina's Formal dress. ("It's not the boys I'm worried about," Sabrina said. Amy responded, "Oh, yes, and the photos.") My observations and interviews also supported several studies revealing the darker side of sorority life. Research has linked Greeks to higher occurrences of binge drinking and academic cheating and weaker levels of "principled moral reasoning." Further, a 2003 Penn State survey disclosed that students who belong to social fraternities and sororities are more likely to encounter "problem behaviors," including being assaulted or humiliated, engaging in a serious argument or quarrel, or experiencing unwanted sexual advances.

Moreover, the National Panhellenic Conference, which has an Academic Excellence Committee that distributes a seasonal newsletter, holds up scholarship as a reason to join sororities. "All NPC groups . . . encourage high scholarship as a priority," the NPC assures parents in its pamphlet, *Women's Fraternity Membership: A Perspective for Parents.* But the multitude of mandatory nonacademic sorority obligations can leave little time for studying (and more incentive to use house "class files" to cheat). Lisa Handler, the Temple University professor who studied sororities in the mid-1990s, said that as a professor she can tell which of her students are Greek. "When they're pledging, for instance, solid students suddenly aren't doing so well—the young women more than men. They start being irregular: skipping classes, falling asleep in classes. It's strange. You notice the ones who are slacking off," she said. "Sororities can't claim to be about the academics and then ruin them."

The NPC also emphasizes leadership, another one of the "four pillars," as a central benefit of sororities. But the leadership opportunities available in a sorority don't necessarily translate to a vast career network; sororities often encourage the sisters who show initiative to seek out a career in sorority administration. While some girls may get job opportunities from employers who play sorority favorites, none of my alumnae interviewees suggested that historically white sorority membership provides access to a wider, better-connected network than that which is available to unaffiliated students. Sororities promote the organizations as groups that enrich life experiences and further the development of women, yet at the same time they enforce regressive standards and strip sisters of their sense of self-empowerment. This conflict breeds an attitude that I call "fake feminism." Under the guise of propelling women forward, sororities also tug them backward—with dress codes, male-centered activities, ideas of proper comportment, and a subjugation of self to the group—so that the constant contradictory pulls lead to a stagnancy that is slow to accept any change at all.

In 1994, a study in the *Journal of College Student Development* found that Greeks, compared to unaffiliated students, "had significantly less independence, liberalism, social conscientiousness, and cultural sophistication than the independent students, and tended to be higher in sociability, hedonism, self-confidence, and social conformity." That research echoed the results of a study of the values of four sororities at the University of Colorado in the 1960s, which found that sorority sisters valued independence less and loyalty to the group more than non-Greek women. They also scored lower when rated on the value of kindness.

Not only does it appear that sororities haven't changed much over the last forty years, but it has also become evident that they remain unwilling to change with the times. This revulsion to change, euphemized as a devotion to tradition, is what keeps the sororities ignorant and intolerant—it's what allows University of Alabama Greeks to blame their mortifying race statistics on the stubbornness of alumni. If there is a single reason that sororities must change in order to survive it is that their unwillingness to prioritize diversity as a value comes across as racism. "We aren't diverse," a national sorority's traveling consultant wrote in an official report to and about a southwestern chapter. "Our ritual makes us the same." That is a superficial rationalization. Sororities must rework their recruitment policies so that their membership becomes more diverse, which does not mean "blond girls, red-haired girls, and a lot of brown-haired girls." Instead of referring to themselves as "historically white," these sororities should be proud to call themselves "multiculturals."

Experts have offered several reasons why it has been so difficult to force Greek organizations to evolve. Author Hank Nuwer pointed out that college administrators who belonged to Greek groups might be less willing to make demands on chapters and more willing to condone behaviors by looking the other way. Some administrators also "protect their institution's reputation by blocking the disclosure of particulars to the press when members of student organizations commit offenses such as criminal hazing." Another obstacle has been the power of university Greek alumni. G. Armour Craig was acting president of Amherst in 1984, the year the school abolished its Greek system. "The reason fraternities don't get abolished in smaller schools is that the trustees are generally terrified of offending the alumni and cutting off large, essential contributions," Craig told The Nation. But for university administrations to let alumni control the reins of these groups simply because they don't want to lose the coffers seems like bribery.

Greeks tap into resources for a couple of reasons, said Daryl Conte, Alfred University's associate dean of students and the administrator in charge of Greek life until the university shut down the system in 2002. "Greek organizations present a higher liability to the institution, so they have to be monitored. And they give more. In terms of giving in groups, they blow away the average Joe Shmo student. So you can get a higher return on your investment if it's handled correctly," Conte said. "In our case, the liability imposed was no longer equal to the return on the investment. No money was worth having to pick up a phone and tell a parent that, for example, your daughter fell off a roof and won't walk again. Alumni like to say that universities don't do anything for Greeks, but that's crap."

In order to begin to reform sororities, one should look at these groups for what they truly are. The twenty-six historically white sororities are not service groups, they are not organizations based on intellectual development, and they are not vehicles of women's empowerment. They are, purely and simply, social groups. Girls join sororities to make friends. They join them to meet guys. They join them to have parties. They join them to belong. It is easy to see the initial allure of sororities to lonely or bewildered freshmen floundering in a large student population. Among my interviewees, the most common catalyst for rushing was to belong to a smaller community within the campus. For girls who don't have the skills or interest to play on an athletic team, the drive to run for student office, or the voice to join a singing group, sororities offer a niche—a smaller segment of the community that purportedly helps to make college life more manageable. But within the hierarchical structure of sororities, even once a girl is in the group, she still does not necessarily belong. As noted in the previous chapter, at the end of the year, Vicki told me, relieved, "I definitely feel so much better now that I have a group," referring to her tight clique of friends. This sentiment defeated the purpose of joining a sorority in the first place, because Vicki was uncomfortable in the sorority's smaller community until she could assemble an even smaller group-within-a-group.

"There [is] a significant need at the undergraduate level for affiliation," the National Panhellenic Conference asserts. Unlike the early days of sororities, however, colleges are now doing more to help freshmen fit in. The residential college system and the wealth of orientation programs help funnel students into ready-made affiliations to use or not use at their discretion. At their core, sororities insist that the special bonds of sisterhood transcend those of ordinary friendships. But in fact what is sisterhood beyond friendship? Temple's Lisa Handler calls sisterhood a "fictive kinship," a "vowed allegiance to a collectivity" utilizing a language that institutionalizes friendships. Sisterhood is an institution supposedly bound by secrets, which we now know in many cases come down to nothing more than backward-spelled passwords or trite expressions. One must consider the extent to which this fictive kinship did anything for Brooke at the time in her life when she needed her sisters the most.

On the surface, sororities are labels. In some areas of the country, they are considered the most important life-defining tags a girl can have. In Mississippi, for example, girls who are determined to get into a particular sorority at Greek powerhouse University of Mississippi are known to matriculate at Millsaps College in Jackson, Mississippi, where sorority rush is not as competitive. Once the girls accept their bids, they then transfer to Ole Miss, where the Ole Miss chapter of their sorority must accept them as sisters. In Texas, some die-hard sorority mothers send their girls to an out-of-state school to pledge a particular sorority and then have them transferred to a Texas school after initiation.

Why should sorority membership still mean so much even in twenty-first-century America—so much that girls throw themselves fully clothed and blindfolded into fatally dangerous riptides merely for the privilege? "Fraternities and sororities are the best thing on a college campus, without a doubt," the opening speaker at the Northeast Greek Leadership Association Conference said to his audience. Currently, that's not true. There are too many negative features of sorority life that outweigh the positives. But the point that struck me as I finished out the year was that sororities have the potential to be something more. Today, the National Panhellenic Conference includes at least 3.5 million initiated women in nearly three thousand collegiate chapters, with numbers generally holding steady and increasing in Texas and the Southwest. In 2001, the NPC added eighty thousand sisters, a 9 percent increase from 1999. The potential power of these groups as collective social units is phenomenal. What if these groups snubbed the fraternities that condoned the behavior of rapist brothers? What if sororities fought for political or cultural change on issues they cared about? What if, as a young Kappa Kappa Gamma alumna suggested to me, sororities boycotted companies using ads that demean women? (The Kappa was incensed in particular by an ad featuring young girls in bathing suits or sportswear with the caption "Don't just take the scenic route. Be the scenic route.") What if sororities focused their energies on something more than mixers and Greek Week floats?

Sororities shouldn't have to wield political power in order to defend their existence, of course. But if they are primarily social groups, then they do not deserve preferential treatment on university and college campuses. They do not deserve their own university-funded Greek adviser, Office of Greek Life, portions of student activity fees, and other resources that are not equally allotted to any student club. In fact, if they are to continue to receive any university assistance at all, then they must be willing to make some compromises. They must be willing to change.

What Nationals and Sorority Sisters Can Do

▣ Reform rush

Most important, sororities need to change their rush policies because the sorority recruitment system is in desperate need of an overhaul. National offices have a range of possible options. One is to model the rush system after the historically black sororities' Membership Intake Program. Instead of condensing rush into a short series of superficial events during which a recruit must visit every white chapter, chapters could hold recruitment periods at different times throughout the year. Recruits could spend time getting to know the sisters and the sororities they are most interested in before they decide to make a commitment. Because sororities wouldn't compete for the same recruits at the same time, there would be less pressure on both parties. Another option is to have continuous open bidding for all sororities throughout the year instead of rush—a practice that a few sororities already encourage as a supplement to the rush period. As girls get to know each other naturally rather than through forced three-minute conversations, they could introduce potential new members to the rest of the group at any time during the year, invite the candidates to spend time with them, and choose at a less hurried pace whether to offer a bid. Interested candidates could observe and participate in sorority events and meet sorority sisters in something other than a cattle-market setting.

The recommendation process also needs to be reformed, if not eliminated outright. Alabama's associate vice president Kathleen Cramer has rightly called for a de-emphasis of some sororities' recommendation processes, which help to ensure that sorority demographics remain virtually the same year after year—something that Nationals may appreciate but students, university officials, and concerned members of the public should not. In addition, Nationals should repudiate the current volumes of rush rules putting girls "on silence" and separating recruits from sisters outside of proscribed rush events so they can't be "influenced" in their decisions. Refusing to allow girls to get to know each other outside of the choreographed rush parties doesn't allow them to meet friends in a more casual way.

All of these options would create simpler and fairer ways to widen a sorority circle rather than choosing new members on shallow grounds at a hectic pace and then praying after Bid Day that the girls turn out to be decent people.

In any event, there is no doubt that rush—both informal and formal—should be postponed at least until after the first semester of freshman year. Representatives at the Leadership Conference said they preferred fall recruitment so sororities could "get 'em early." The earlier they lure the girls, the sooner they get their money. But expecting already overwhelmed first-semester freshmen to choose an affiliation before they even settle into a college routine makes little sense. Seventeen- and eighteen-year-olds just entering college—vulnerable, impressionable, away from friends and parents for perhaps the first time—often know virtually nothing about sorority life yet are expected to navigate the complex and intimidating rush process and decide within days which girls they most want as "sisters." In general, they are too young to know what they will be pledged to. How can sisterhoods transcend friendships if potential sisters don't know any more about each other than their favorite purse designers?

Another necessary reform is that every girl who rushes must get into a sorority. College literary and debate societies began by assigning every interested student an affiliation; sororities should as well. There is no reason that a girl who wants to be in a sorority shouldn't have the opportunity to join one, whether it's her first or fourth choice. Nationals complain about low numbers yet are unwilling to accept girls who don't fit a certain "type." Assigning every rushee to a chapter would improve both numbers and diversity. Once the sisters get to know—and accept as a fellow sister—a girl whom they otherwise might have dismissed, their understanding of and tolerance for girls who don't fit the previously prescribed sorority mold would improve. Further, if sorority demographics were to shift enough so that sisters did not look the same—with different races and different body types—then perhaps there would be less pressure to conform to one image, and therefore fewer peer-pressure problems (such as eating disorders). Speakers at the Leadership Conference emphasized the point of being Greek (to such an extent that they exhibited an air of superiority over non-Greeks). As one moderator said, "We all wear different letters but we're all the same. We're Greek." If that's true, it shouldn't matter which girls receive which labels. The kinds of girls who would no longer rush sororities because they would no longer feel an elite superiority are not the kinds of girls who would keep sororities honorable and with noble purpose anyway.

▣ *Define hazing and reduce or eliminate pledging*

Nationals also need to present a consistent message about hazing. They should begin by formulating a clear definition of exactly what is proscribed and then support it with a Unanimous Agreement, the strongest measure possible in the National Panhellenic Conference. Currently there is no Unanimous Agreement prohibiting hazing, yet there is one concerning the media: "It is in accord with the dignity and good manners of fraternity women to avoid negative publicity on Panhellenic matters." This imbalance teaches college students to prioritize image over action, and spin over safety.

Once a hazing definition is in place, Nationals should not have contradictory policies. If they define hazing as anything that distinguishes pledges from sisters, then Nationals cannot differentiate pledges from sisters with different pins and pledge-only exams—and cannot exclude them from ritual ceremonies and the revealing of sorority secrets. Some Greek groups have begun to transition their pledge program to a "Membership Development Program," which is intended to educate and include all members. This is a step in the right direction.

Nationals recently began referring to pledges as "new members," because for some, the term "pledge" suggests a period of having to earn membership. "Something as simple as changing terminology can assist in changing a culture of hazing in an organization," according to an educational resource called the *Greek Gazette*. In fact, Nationals might consider forgoing the pledge (or new member) period entirely. If recruits were to have the opportunity and the time to learn about the sororities before they accepted a bid, then they wouldn't need the interim time as a pledge to decide whether or not they truly wanted to become a part of the sisterhood. They could be initiated the day after Bid Day.

What's more, sororities have a large number of local advisers who are expected to assist the chapter. If Nationals insist on having a pledge period, they could at least reduce it to one week and have an adult supervisor on site for the full period. With all of these adult volunteers, it makes great sense to utilize them by requiring adult supervision and oversight at any time during which hazing might occur.

▣ Emphasize supervision and de-emphasize the house

Along similar lines, if sorority Nationals, unlike fraternities, are going to serve a role in loco parentis, then they should make certain that the adult supervision they advertise is not only present but also influential and effective. At the sorority house that would not allow me access, the adviser knew very well that her house—which openly displayed drug paraphernalia and what appeared to be cocaine—had a drug problem. But when she heard the sisters discussing drugs, she laughed it off and looked the other way. At other houses I visited, the house mothers were nonentities, rarely venturing from their private apartments, not serving as supervisors in the least. Chapters do not allow a house mother to supervise meetings, rituals, or other closed activities if she isn't a member of the sorority; as an uninitiated woman she is not entitled to know the sorority's secrets. Given the nature of sorority secrets, however, it seems unreasonable to forgo adult supervision merely out of a fear that an unaffiliated adult might be privy to the sorority's secret knock.

But for the adults at both the national and regional levels, acting in loco parentis does not need to translate to micromanaging girls' lives, dictating whom they can speak to or what they can wear. Sororities can have strong sisterhoods even if the girls are allowed to be individuals.

Moreover, Nationals should not have quotas. If they truly believe their own ideals and in the notion of sisterhood, then numbers shouldn't matter. The Phi Sigma Sigmas at the University of Pennsylvania should not have lost their chapter simply because they didn't have a specific number of sisters. If they don't have the money to maintain their house, so be it. A house isn't necessary for a sisterhood. I spoke with sisters in non–historically white sororities who had no house and fewer than ten members, but they still had strong sisterhoods they were proud of. I also heard from girls without houses in historically white sororities who were relieved they could have sisters without living with them.

Nationals should also consider abolishing rules that require sisters to live in the sorority house for a certain number of years. It is one thing to welcome girls into a club but quite another to force them to reside with each other. Many girls told me that they would rather have had the choice to live off campus, with nonmember friends, or on their own so that they could have an escape from the sorority and a life outside of it. Vicki, in particular, would have preferred to live outside the house. Requiring girls to live in the house forces them to live under the kind of constant scrutiny that encourages conformity and discourages independence and initiative. If Nationals need to fill rooms in a house to maintain it, they could rent rooms to nonaffiliated boarders or share the house with another sorority—both scenarios that currently exist at some universities today.

▣ Adjust activities

Sisters, too, could take the initiative to make some changes. If the pledge period remains, instead of having pledges perform useless crafts and nonproductive errands for the sisters, pledges instead could be required to spend their "bonding time" performing community service activities together with sisters. Further, sorority policies of fining sisters who can't attend events or refusing to allow them into social events are counterproductive, particularly when the sisters in question, like Sabrina, work one or more jobs merely to pay for their dues. An Ivy League sister I spoke with said that after two years in her sorority, her financial situation deteriorated so that she could no longer afford to pay dues. She wrote a letter to her sorority's national office asking if it could reduce her dues or assign her alumna status so that she wouldn't have to disaffiliate. The national office refused. If Nationals are so fixated on the financial bottom line that they prioritize money above sisters, then it is up to the sisters to look out for their fellow members. When a friend can't make it to certain events because she has to work, sisters could attend extra events for her and assign her their points.

Sisters could also decrease the number of fraternity socials and replace them with sister activities; after all, sisters aren't in fact joining all-girl groups if the activities all hinge on men. (And not every girl is as lucky as Amy to have a willing gay backup date.) They could also encourage the girls to bring friends rather than dates to events, if the girls so choose. In the same vein, if sororities are going to continue to have rituals like candlelights to celebrate relationship milestones (or hang banners announcing a lavaliere, as did Alabama's Zetas), they are inevitably going to alienate sisters who don't find steady boyfriends. These rituals ought to be expanded to address achievements that have nothing to do with sex. Furthermore, historically white sororities are known to have closed parties while historically black sororities open events to all students. There is no reason why white sororities need to be so insular. Some schools have at least worked out a compromise: sorority parties are closed for two to three hours before they are opened up to a guest list that includes nonmembers.

▣ Strengthen the sisterhood

No girl should be so uncomfortable with her sisters that she cannot stand up for herself. Sabrina's alienation could have been prevented if any of the other sisters who observed the situation had said to the girls making racist comments, "That's racist, and that's wrong," or "That's unacceptable. We won't tolerate that." Or suggested to the exec board that they have a speaker come in to discuss race issues. Or even just shown the compassion and consideration to ask Sabrina how she was doing. Perhaps sororities should use their speaker budget to invite someone who specializes in team-building exercises and can help sisters open the lines of communication within the chapter.

The current arbitrariness of sorority rules is troubling—particularly involving such notions as "questionable reputation" and similar ideas. Sisters should not be able to oust a fellow sister unless they not only have involved responsible adults in the process but also have done everything they reasonably could to help the sister in question. Rather than disaffiliating a girl for drug use, the local advisers, the house mother, university personnel, and sorority sisters should help to get her into a rehabilitation program. Instead of rejecting a girl for public sexual antics, sisters should address the deeper insecurity and self-esteem issues that the girl may be experiencing. Advisers and house mothers should be trained to recognize problems and, at the least, to make appropriate referrals when necessary. If sisterhoods were truly stronger than friendships, then, like real sisters, sorority members wouldn't cast someone out merely for making a mistake.

What Universities and Graduates Can Do

▣ *Establish authority*

In the 1980s, colleges and universities shied away from direct responsibility of Greek houses because of stricter host-liability laws regarding student drinking. Among the sometimes conflicting rules of national sorority offices, campus Greek administrators, and local advisers, students have slipped through the gaps between the various levels of authority. Consequently, so many people try to impose rules that the rules are often never enforced. There are things that universities can do to try to turn sororities into more positive and useful campus groups. And graduates, whether or not of the Greek system, have a strong voice that can persuade universities to make the right decisions.

Universities must assert that they still hold the ultimate power over sororities. "Sororities need to realize that they are part of an institution—the university—and the institution is not part of them," said Alfred University's Daryl Conte. Any of the recommendations in the previous section could be demanded by universities; in fact, some schools are already taking steps to move rush from first semester to second, when freshmen are more accustomed to campus life. School administrators have the capacity to tell sororities that if, for example, they actively exclude minorities, encourage bulimia, or prevent members from going to class and doing homework, they will no longer be recognized by the university. By providing resources and, in some cases, housing to Greek groups, universities imply that they condone those groups' behavior and standards. It is well within an administration's discretion to withhold or limit those resources if a sorority does not comply with university policies.

Universities cannot continue to let Greek alumni dictate the composition and comportment of these campus groups. Nor should universities allow sorority national offices to insist that students answer first and foremost to them. Whereas university administrators are trained officials with degrees, national officers aren't necessarily qualified to counsel or supervise students. As Kathleen Cramer said, these sorority volunteers are stuck in the past, "struggling with change." If universities could wrest greater control of sororities from the national offices, then perhaps individual chapters on a campus would be more on a par with each other, with less elevation of one sorority above another, less Chanel over Kmart.

In addition, adult representatives at the NGLA Conference suggested that Greek advisers are young and underpaid and therefore should have some flexibility in the time and energy they put into supervising students. That is no excuse. There will usually be some trustworthy adult who would be willing to serve as mentor and adviser to these students despite low pay and long hours. If a university furnishes a Greek adviser, then the university should at least find someone who is willing to take on the full responsibility of the position.

▣ Offer other options

University administrators should understand that one of the main reasons girls join sororities is to find a more intimate community within the larger student body. Universities could offer a range of less exclusionary alternatives that could achieve the same result, such as the residential college system. The residential college system distributes students equally among a number of smaller living communities, which in many schools have their own publications, student government, social committee, and intramural athletic teams. Students have a more personal home base—and the opportunity to transfer affiliations if they choose. Furthermore, Alfred University has for years offered "First Year Experience," which provides social, academic, counseling, and health programs to freshmen. To make up for the loss of its Greek system, Alfred has also increased the number of social programs it offers students. The student activities office holds events such as dances or coffeehouses every weekend. On Fridays and Saturdays Alfred keeps the recreation center—with a gym, pool, and movie-viewing area—open until 2 A.M. and brings in free pizza for the students. Whether or not a school maintains its Greek system, these are creative ways to offer students alternative entertainment and bonding opportunities.

What Parents, Siblings, Friends, Advisers, and College-Bound Girls Can Do

▣ *Learn about the system*

Individuals who want to help prepare a girl for college should educate themselves about the sorority system—and about other alternatives, such as Subrosa—before the girl decides whether to rush. This learning process should not be limited solely to National Panhellenic Conference promotional materials, many of which proclaim only the platitudes the NPC thinks parents and advisers want to hear. Sororities might not be what a seventeen- or eighteen-year-old believes them to be, and she could be further misled during rush—a time when, as I learned, sorority sisters are prone to exaggerating and outright lying. It is important for a girl to know what she is getting into before rush and to be prepared for the level of commitment.

It is also crucial for a parent/sibling/friend/adviser not to allow a girl to go "on silence" during rush. That rule is intended to prevent girls from being influenced by others as they make their sorority decision. But parents, especially, should be able to counsel and to serve as a sounding board for this decision just as they have with many of their daughter's decisions up until college. Additionally, "on silence" sets a dangerous precedent: girls need to feel that they can talk to their parents openly about sorority life—otherwise parents like those of Kristin High and Kenitha Saafir, the 2002 drowning victims, don't find out what is going on until it is too late.

EPILOGUE

IT IS BID DAY at Southern Methodist University in 2003. On Sorority Row, party rental and moving trucks slowly wend their way through a parking lot lined with BMWs, Mercedes, Accords, and Jeep Wranglers sporting sorority stickers and vanity plates reading DG—SMU, A CHI O, SMU 05, and IM KEG. The houses are festooned with bright, professionally made banners: "Deep in the heart of DG" on the Delta Gamma house, "Sweet Home Kappa Gamma," and "True to Tri-Delt." Middle-aged women—house mothers or advisers, perhaps—fuss with decorations, arrange chairs on the lawns, and scrutinize the movers hefting helium machines and elegant fountains into houses already dripping with fancy chandeliers.

The night before, on Preference Night, girls in black coats and high heels walked solemnly toward the sorority houses led by heavily made up Rho Chis in blue RC SMU sweatshirts and jeans. The rushees lined up on the sidewalks and waited patiently for sisters to come out of the houses and escort them inside. They had been instructed only to wear "cocktail dresses," but they looked as if in uniform, draped in black, filmy dresses with short, uneven hemlines. When the Pref parties ended at seven, the rushees were shepherded to the ballroom of the Hughes-Trigg Student Center, where they were required to stay until midnight so that they could not communicate with sorority sisters. The Panhellenic Office showed them movies—*Girls Just Wanna Have Fun* and *When Harry Met Sally*—to keep them occupied. Several girls quietly sneaked out of the ballroom to be alone for a few minutes or to call their mothers and cry because of the stress of the recruitment and elimination process.

This morning the rushees, with long straightened hair shining, anxiously return to Hughes-Trigg, wearing tight jeans and snug white turtlenecks or long-sleeved tees. A few brave or stubborn girls are in stilettos, the rest in sneakers because they know they will have to run. The Panhellenic Office has made some changes since the late 1990s to cut down on charges of hazing, but the Bid Day uniform and Pigs' Run still remain in force. Reluctant to go into the ballroom alone, the girls shiver outside, most without jackets despite the bitterly cold thirty-degree bleakness. Hugging themselves for warmth, they call fellow rushees on their cell phones, meet up with them, and enter the ballroom in pairs, fours, and sixes. Inside the ballroom, guarded by Greeks with clipboards so that only rushees can enter, they wait for their names to be called. A Rho Chi at one of the tables in the room adjacent to the ballroom hands them their small, cream-colored Bid Card (if they receive one), and watches them carefully for their reaction.

[Name]
IS CORDIALLY INVITED TO BECOME A MEMBER OF THE
[Name] Sorority

IN ACCEPTING SHE IS REQUESTED TO COME TO
[Address]

IN DECLINING SHE WILL PLEASE SIGN AND
RETURN THIS INVITATION.

If the girl is distraught, the Rho Chi takes her aside, murmurs words of consolation, and hands her tissues. Otherwise the girl takes her Bid Card and waits in the ballroom, where in the chaos girls are shrieking, screaming, hugging, or crying quietly in the corners.

Upstairs in Hughes-Trigg, mothers in long leather jackets and fur-trimmed coats—their hair done, their clothes designer—pace the main floor, fidgeting and glancing at the staircase their daughters descended an hour ago.

Two mothers perch on stools near the top of the staircase, strangers chatting to pass the time. Their cell phones keep interrupting.

"Yes, I saw her this morning," one says to her husband. "She was just about in tears. Three girls in her rush group asked me if I could buy them white turtlenecks. It was all she could do to keep from crying." She hangs up and explains to the other mother that she has been here for days to monitor her daughter throughout rush. "She was ecstatic one day and terrified the next day," she says.

"I heard SMU is cutting this year because there are more girls rushing than in years past," responds the other. They watch as a lone girl, weeping, dashes up the stairs and toward a dormitory.

"I saw another girl heartbroken because she didn't get into any. She was crying, too," says one of the mothers.

"Oh, this is just horrible," the other clucks.

"This is a cruel, cruel thing."

"Do you have any other kids?"

"I had a boy who went to a college without a Greek system, thank God."

A cell phone rings repeatedly. The mother whispers to the caller that there has been no news. "They're calling me and saying, 'Do you know yet? Do you know yet?'" she explains to the other mother. "I should call my mother. She's anxious."

"Is your mother in your sorority also?"

"Yes." The mother cocks her head. "You don't seem nervous."

"No, I know she got in."

"How?"

The mother waves a manicured hand dismissively. "Oh, one of the sisters told me yesterday, 'Don't worry, she's in.'"

The other mother bites her lip and looks relieved when her phone rings again. "You did? Oh!" She begins to cry. "Oh honey, thank you, Lord. Oh darlin', I'm so happy for you. You know who you need to thank, don't you? I need to say a prayer first."

The mothers make their way outside to the crowd of hundreds waiting in front of the sorority houses. Police officers stationed on corners hold maps highlighting the path of Pigs' Run. When all of the nearly five hundred girls have learned their fate, they come bursting out of the doors to Hughes-Trigg. The first pledges to leave the building are exuberant, holding hands and laughing as they sprint. Fraternity brothers pack the crowd, holding red plastic cups of beer. They are forbidden to spray water this year; in fact, a Panhellenic missive on the Student Center Bid Day calendar orders "Men must stay behind the barracades [sic] or in the parking lots at all times."

"I almost brought ground beef to throw at my girlfriend instead," says one brother.

"I just came here to watch girls run," says another.

The last girls out of Hughes-Trigg walk slowly, trying to compose tear-streaked faces before they disappear into the waiting throngs, swallowed by a Burberry sea of high-heeled boots, roses, and fur. Within minutes, professional photographers snap group picture after group picture of the pledges, the sisters, then the pledges and the sisters, while DJs at many of the houses blast music from elaborate sound systems. Kappa Kappa Gammas and Delta Gammas pose under balloon arches. At the Theta house, First Lady Laura Bush's old haunt, sisters line-dance on the lawn and the porch, doing the "Theta Shuffle" as they cheer. On the next block, Pi Phis dance for the crowd to Abba's "Dancing Queen," which competes with strains from other porches of Nelly's "Hot in Herre" and Ludacris's "Roll Out."

In the Hughes-Trigg Student Center, the ballroom is now empty. A few Bid Cards are strewn on the floor, and boxes of tissues still lie in their strategic spots on small couches and behind the Rho Chi tables. The girls have been judged and dispersed, assigned letters and labels signaling their new affiliations. Signaling that they belong. The pledges' anonymous, blank white shirts are now covered by lettered jerseys identifying them forever—as long as they adhere to proper standards. They were not drenched on their way to their new homes, as sisters were in years past. They did not have to sit on the sealed envelopes bearing the name they still believe will play a critical role in the rest of their lives. But as before, girls peeled off from the pack, unlabeled and crest-fallen, veering away from the houses in tears. And again, the exhibitionism, the preening and dancing for the boys, the painstakingly chosen clothing and diamonds, appropriately conformed, PradaGucciChanel with designer sunglasses on their heads as accessories. Again the rush toward the upper echelons of a scene that one SMU sister calls "90210 Goes to College," a sphere in which Greek administrators dictate to whom the girls can and cannot speak, a world that, the sister tells me, holds for them such a penetrating pressure to fit in that it currently hosts an "eating disorder epidemic." And it becomes clear that in the realm of the pledged, nothing much, really, has changed.

For further information on sororities and
for updates on
Vicki, Sabrina, Caitlin, and Amy,
please visit
www.alexandrarobbins.com

GLOSSARY

Alumna: A sorority member who has graduated or is no longer active in the organization.

Badge (also called Pin): The symbolic, distinctive jewelry worn by initiated sorority members.

Bid: An official written invitation to join a sorority.

Big Sister: An initiated sorority member who is assigned to serve as a mentor to a new member. The new member is called the Little Sister.

Chapter: Also referred to as a house, a college branch of the sorority's national organization.

Disaffiliate: To give up (or be forced to give up) sorority membership.

Grand Big Sister: The Big Sister of a Big Sister.

House Mom: A woman who is hired by the sorority to manage house affairs. Usually lives in a private apartment within the sorority house.

Local: A campus sorority that is unaffiliated with a national office.

National Panhellenic Conference (NPC): The umbrella organization for the twenty-six national "historically white" sororities. (Panhellenic means "all Greek.")

National Pan-Hellenic Council (NPHC): The umbrella organization for the four national "historically black" sororities and the five national "historically black" fraternities.

Nationals: Sorority sister slang for the central office, or sorority headquarters, that governs every chapter of the sorority. Some groups call these headquarters Inter/nationals because sororities have chapters in Canada.

Panhellenic Association / Panhellenic Council: Sometimes just called Panhellenic, the college organization or office that governs the NPC chapters on campus.

GLOSSARY

Pledge: A new member who has accepted a bid but has not yet been initiated.

Pledgemaster: The sister in charge of preparing the new members for initiation.

Pledge Period: The time between Bid Day and initiation when a new member prepares to become a sorority sister.

Rush: The period designated by the Panhellenic Association during which the sororities and interested candidates (rushees) participate in a mutual selection process.

ENDNOTES

PROLOGUE

2 *Southern Millionaires University*: See Fiske, Edward B., with Robert Logue. *The Fiske Guide to Colleges, 2001*. New York: Three Rivers Press, 2000.

2 *"college in country club clothing"*: The Insider's Guide to Colleges 2000, compiled and edited by the Yale Daily News. New York: St. Martin's, 1997.

2 *such as "Running of the Bulls" or "Squeal Day"*: Running of the Bulls—Oklahoma State University. See Saucier, Heather. "Crushed by the Rush: When Perfect Matchmaking Doesn't Work, Sorority Rejection Can Be Painful." Tulsa World. August 24, 1997. *Squeal Day*—at the University of Alabama, among other schools. See Zengerle, Jason. "Sorority Row: Alabama's New Schoolhouse Door." *The New Republic*. February 4, 2002.

INTRODUCTION

5 *"Delta, Delta, Delta, Can We Help Ya, Help Ya Help Ya?"*: This was the line sisters used to answer the telephone in a sorority skit on *Saturday Night Live*.

6 *"Old Blue" and "Café Au Lait" (Sigma Delta Tau)*: See Thornton, Bonnie, and Debbie Thornton. *Ready for Rush: The Must-Have Manual for Sorority Rushees!* Nashville: Hamblett House Inc., 1999. See also http://www.sigmadeltatau.com/info/pmfc.html.

6 *"Olive Green" and "Pearl White" (Kappa Delta)*: See Thornton and Thornton. *Ready for Rush*. See also *The Norman Shield of Kappa Delta*, an intrasorority publication given to new members, last revised in July 2003.

6 *sorority emery boards, money pouches, picture frames, bottle openers, and refrigerator magnets . . . "Sorority Lip Balm" . . . sorority air freshener . . . sorority bath crystals . . . sorority tissue:* All of these were actual items for sale on tables and in bins at a Greek boutique.

8 *sorority's national office:* Because several sororities now have chapters in Canada, they are beginning to refer to their offices and headquarters as "Internationals" or "Inter/nationals." The current college sisters whom I spoke with still call them "Nationals"; for this reason, I refer to headquarters as Nationals throughout this book.

8 *MTV had just aired a show called* Sorority Life: MTV's *Sorority Life* tracked a local sorority at the University of California-Davis. *Sorority Life 2,* which followed a local sorority at the University of Buffalo, aired in spring 2003.

9 *The twenty-six member groups of the National Panhellenic Conference . . . established in 1902 to oversee the historically white national sororities:* See *100 Years of the National Panhellenic Conference.* Published by the National Panhellenic Conference, which is headquartered in Indianapolis, Indiana, to celebrate its century anniversary. Within Greek communities, groups in the National Panhellenic Conference are often referred to as "historically white" sororities, or "NPC" sororities, as opposed to the "historically black" sororities or "NPHC" groups overseen by the National Pan-Hellenic Council. Because in all of the sororities I came into contact with, the "historically white" sororities were indeed heavily majority-white and the "historically black" sororities were heavily majority-black— and because the NPC and NPHC designations can be confusing—I sometimes refer to the groups as "white" or "black" groups.

9 *claim to instill within their sororities . . . whose motto is "Many Hearts, One Purpose":* See www.aephi.org; www.aephi.org/story/phacts.asp.

9 *goals such as Delta Delta Delta's, to ". . . assist its members in every possible way":* See www.deltadeltadelta. org/about/about.htm.

9 *They foster, like Kappa Kappa Gamma, "friendship rooted in a tradition of high standards":* See www.kappakappagamma.org/new_about.htm.

9 *when one school's Panhellenic adviser attempted to blacklist me on her campus for writing this book, she insisted she must "protect our women":* The adviser, who oversees the sororities on her campus, included in an e-mail the line ". . . we would like to do what we can to protect our women and our Greek community." I refer to this letter again in December's chapter.

AUGUST

25 *Sorority "types" are inevitable . . . "Klan's Daughters":* Sorority sisters told me about these stereotypes in interviews.

26 *Ready for Rush: The Must-Have Manual for Sorority Rushees! . . . "hotbed for controversy":* See Thornton, Bonnie, and Debbie Thomton. *Ready for Rush. The Must-Have-Manual for Sorority Rushees.* Nashville: Hamblett House, 1999.

29 *In the spring of 1996 . . . "It was surreal"*: See Hubbard, Kim, Anne-Marie O'Neill, and Christina Cheakalos. "Out of Control; Weight-Obsessed, Stressed-Out Coeds Are Increasingly Falling Prey to Eating Disorders." *People*. April 12, 1999.

29 *A 1990s study . . . self-induced vomiting were sorority sisters*: See Meilman, Philip W., Ph.D, Frank A. Von Hippel, and Michael S. Gaylor, M.D. "Self-Induced Vomiting in College Women: Its Relation to Eating, Alcohol Use, and Greek Life." *Journal of American College Health*. Vol. 40 (July 1991).

29 *Turned to plastic surgery to better fit in*: See, for example, Wright, Esther. *Torn Togas: The Dark Side of Campus Greek Life*. Minneapolis: Fairview Press, 1996.

35 *There are three stages . . . alumna*: This information is in basic sorority guides and glossaries. See, for example, Rose, Margaret Ann. *Rush: A Girl's Guide to Sorority Success*. New York: Villard, 1985.

35 *These elected officers . . . a philanthropy chair, and others*: In addition to learning about sorority structures through interviews, I gleaned information from copies of chapter bylaws given to me and from sorority manuals such as *Pi Phi Forever*, the guide distributed to new members by "The Grand Council."

37 *According to a private investigation . . . pledging activity*: See "Sorority Accused of Hazing in $100 Million Suit." CNN.com. September 24, 2002.

37 *with at least three AKA sisters and two other pledges*: See "Sorority Accused of Hazing in $100 Million Suit." CNN.com; Banks, Sandy, and Jill Leovy. "Drownings Raise Hazing Questions." *Los Angeles Times*. September 14, 2002; and Hayasaki, Erika. "Victim's Mother Starts Anti-Hazing Group." *Los Angeles Times*. October 13, 2002, reported two other pledges and at least three sisters on the scene. Fields-Meyer, Thomas, and Susan Christian Goulding. "A Sea of Pain Eager to Join a Sorority, Two Women Die in the Surf. Was It a Hazing Gone Wrong?" *People*, October 14, 2002, noted there were five witnesses.

37 *After running . . . jogging clothes and sneakers*: See "Sorority Accused of Hazing in $100 Million Suit." CNN.com; Ayres, Chris. "Sisterhood Initiation Rite Blamed for Drownings." *London Times*. October 19, 2002; Associated Press, "Sorority Hazing Is Blamed in 2 Deaths." *San Diego Tribune*. September 11, 2002.

37 *had lost sleep . . . paint over them*: See Ayres. "Sisterhood Initiation Rite Blamed for Drownings"; Fields-Meyer and Goulding. "A Sea of Pain Eager to Join a Sorority."

38 *When police officers . . . fifty yards from the beach*: See Ayres. "Sisterhood Initiation Rite Blamed for Drownings"; Banks and Leovy. "Drownings Raise Hazing Questions."

38 *Kristin's family . . . $100 million wrongful-death lawsuit*: See "Sorority Accused of Hazing in $100 Million Suit." CNN.com.

38 *The national AKA office . . . were missing*: See Ayres. "Sisterhood Initiation Rite Blamed for Drownings."

38 *forced calisthenics are a common ritual . . . West Coast pledge periods*: See Banks and Leovy. "Drownings Raise Hazing Questions."

38 Kristin's mother, who, following Kristin's death, founded the group Mothers Against Hazing: See Hayasaki. "Victim's Mother Starts Anti-Hazing Group."

38 "stop these savage acts of passion in the name of sisterhood": See "Sorority Accused of Hazing in $100 Million Suit." CNN.com.

SEPTEMBER

42 Song lyrics available on www.greekchat.com.

58 rape and sexual assault are particularly prevalent at Greek events and houses: See, for example, Binder, Ron. "Changing a Culture: Sexual Assault Prevention in the Fraternity and Sorority Community." Sexual Violence on Campus: Policies, Programs, and Perspectives. Springer Series on Family Violence. Ottens, Allen J., and Kathy Hotelling, editors. New York: Springer Publishing Company, 2001; Copenhaver, S., and E. Grauerholz. "Sexual Victimization among Sorority Women: Exploring the Link between Sexual Violence and Institutional Practices." Sex Roles. Vol. 24, Nos. 1/2 (1991).

There have been multiple accounts of fraternity gang rapes. See, for example, Weiss, Kenneth R. " 'Animal Houses' Try to Sober Up; A Fledgling Temperance Movement Is Struggling to Take Hold at Some Fraternities Chastened by Bad Binges and Hijinks Gone Wrong." Los Angeles Times. April 6, 1997. The Los Angeles Times reported, "Of 110 gang rapes reported on campuses in a seven-year period, 80% occurred at frat functions." See also Schmich, Mary T. "Gang-Rape Accusations Scar Fraternities." Chicago Tribune. May 13, 1988.

58 At one university . . . parties anymore: See Collison, Michele N. K. "Although Fraternities Bear Brunt of Criticism for Hazing, Activities of Sororities, Too, Stir Concerns on Campuses." The Chronicle of Higher Education. October 10, 1990.

59 rules that seem to discourage sex . . . strict bylaw: See, for example, The Norman Shield of Kappa Delta, which stipulates in its policy section, "There shall be no male visitors permitted in the sleeping quarters of any Kappa Delta house, apartment or suite or any property designated as 'Kappa Delta' by the institution unless the chapter has a male visitation policy that has been approved by the National Council."

60 In 1997 . . . and depledged: See Rivera, Geraldo, host; Pretlow, Jose, executive producer. "When Hazing Becomes Torture; Panelists' Experiences with Hazing, the Ramifications of It and Problems It's Given Them." The Geraldo Rivera Show. August 8, 1997.

60–61 the late 1970s . . . sleeping with strangers: See Weingarten, Paul. "Media Step Warily on SMU Story." Chicago Tribune, March 29, 1987; Associated Press. "S.M.U. Acts on Sex Report." New York Times. March 25, 1987; Associated Press. "SMU Allegedly Provided Sex for Recruits." Los Angeles Times. March 24, 1987; Rossi, Rocco. "Money the Root of Evil in U.S. College Sports." Toronto Star. April 7, 1987.

61 *the NCAA to impose its first "death penalty"* . . . *1987:* See Lane, Wendy E. "SMU Will Find Out If There's Life After NCAA's Death Penalty." *The Record.* August 30, 1987.

61 *"Ponytail Gate":* See Weingarten. "Media Step Warily on SMU Story."

61 *in 1988 . . . dropped out of school:* See 20/20. "They Never Call It Rape." ABC News. April 13, 1990.

61 *Fraternity chapters started the little sister programs . . . in the 1960s:* See "Campus Life: California; Fraternities Phase Out 'Little Sister' Groups." *New York Times.* September 17, 1989.

61 *by the late 1980s . . . sexually exploiting the girls:* See, for example, "Campus Life: Missouri; 'Little Sister' Program Stopped After Assaults." *New York Times.* October 22, 1989; Volland, Victor. " 'Little Sister' Auxiliaries Dying Out; Fraternities Under Pressure to Stop; Practices Called Sexist." *St. Louis Post-Dispatch.* October 18, 1989.

61 *In 1988 . . . "second-class' status":* See "Campus Life: California; Fraternities Phase Out 'Little Sister' Groups." *New York Times.*

61–62 *At the University of Missouri-Columbia . . . before meeting their "big brothers":* See "Campus Life: Missouri; 'Little Sister' Program Stopped After Assaults." *New York Times.*

62 *The University of South Florida . . . complaints of sexual harassment:* See Harper, James. " 'Little Sisters' Abolished at USF." *St. Petersburg Times.* December 7, 1990.

62 *1994 report . . . breasts were too small:* See Hill, John. "Abolish frats, sororities, Rhode Island Report Says." *Providence Journal-Bulletin.* April 3, 1994.

62 *little sisters are generally defined . . . little sister meetings at the fraternity house:* See Rose, Margaret Ann. *Rush: A Girl's Guide to Sorority Success.* New York: Villard, 1985; *often pay dues:* See, for example, "Campus Life: California; Fraternities Phase Out 'Little Sister' Groups." *New York Times.*

62 *cheerleaders at athletic events:* See Harper. " 'Little Sisters' Abolished at USF."

62 *to cook for them, to clean up after parties:* See Stombler, Mindy, and Irene Padavic. "Sister Acts: Resisting Men's Domination in Black and White Fraternity Little Sister Programs." *Social Problems.* Vol. 44, No. 2 (May 1997).

62 *help them recruit new brothers by flaunting their sexuality:* See Harper. " 'Little Sisters' Abolished at USF." See also "Campus Life: Missouri; 'Little Sister' Program Stopped After Assaults." *New York Times.*

62 *Fraternity brothers use pictures . . . access to these girls:* See Stombler, Mindy. " 'Buddies' or 'Slutties': The Collective Sexual Reputation of Fraternity Little Sisters." *Gender & Society.* Vol. 8, No. 3 (1994) 297–323.

62 *charts explaining the number of beers it took to seduce each little sister:* See, for example, Lord, M. G. "Frats and Sororities; The Greek Rites of Exclusions; Racism and Sexism." *The Nation.* July 4, 1987; Wright, Esther. *Torn Togas: The Dark Side of Campus Greek Life.* Minneapolis: Fairview Press, 1996.

62 *"good care of the brothers":* See Stombler. " 'Buddies' or 'Slutties.' "

62 *little sisters . . . a distinct possibility:* See, for example, Binder. "Changing a Culture." See also Abbey, Antonia. "Alcohol-Related Sexual Assault: A Common Problem among College

Students." *Journal of Studies on Alcohol.* March 1, 2002, which reported, "One fraternity man stated that at parties, 'We provide them [little sisters] with "hunch punch" and things get wild. We get them drunk and most of the guys end up with one' . . . With no remorse or guilt, this fraternity man described his plans to get one particular woman drunk by serving her punch without letting her know it was spiked for the challenge of having sex with a 'prim and proper sorority girl.' "

62 *Studies of these programs . . . sister in the first place:* See, for example, Binder. "Changing a Culture."

62–63 *"had their jersey pulled" . . . too promiscuous:* See Stombler. " 'Buddies' or 'Slutties.' "

63 *touch their breasts . . . brothers' approval:* See Wright. *Torn Togas.*

63 *Some fraternities auction . . . baking, cleaning, and driving:* See Stombler and Padavic. "Sister Acts."

63 *When a fraternity selects a little sister . . . "almost fell over":* See Stombler and Padavic. "Sister Acts."

63 *"Something that made me . . . power to do that":* See Stombler. " 'Buddies' or 'Slutties.' "

OCTOBER

68 *At Syracuse . . . "large disposable income":* See "2002–2003 Advertising Information." *Hermes: The Greek Community's Independent Student Newspaper.* Syracuse, NY.

68 *sorority dues . . . to $2,500 a semester:* I encountered a range of sorority dues, some of which include room and board for the time period a girl is required to live in the house. See, for example, Esther Wright's *Torn Togas* (Minneapolis: Fairview Press, 1996), which cites dues of $2,500, or Vendela Vida's *Girls on the Verge: Debutante Dips, Gang Drive-bys, and Other Initiations* (New York: St. Martin's Press, 1999), which states that sorority dues at UCLA ranged from Kappa Alpha Theta's $1,895 to Alpha Delta Pi's $2,237.

68 *Sorority dues cover the costs . . . chapter's national office:* This is generally available information, which was also confirmed by chapter finance documents.

71 *community service . . . revolves more around donations than actual service:* The discussions I heard at the Northeast Greek Leadership Association's Conference supported this statement (see December's chapter). Many sororities claim to have a designated philanthropic cause. These "philanthropies," also called causes or visions, are listed on the web sites for the national organizations.

79 *Is it worth it? . . . Missy Elliott:* Warner Brothers music granted permission to reprint these lyrics.

85 *governed by parliamentary procedure:* Many sororities follow *Robert's Rules of Order* and in the manuals given to pledges, specify the meetings' parliamentary procedure. *Pi Phi Forever,* for example, instructs when to request a "point of information," "point of order," "amend the amendment," "division of the house," and so on. The book also lists the order of business for weekly meetings: call to order, opening ritual, roll call, reading and adoption of minutes of previous meeting, reports of officers and committees,

unfinished business, new business, election and installation of officers, closing ritual, and adjournment.

86 *known as the "candlelight" . . . she is engaged*: See, for example, Rose, Margaret Ann. *Rush: A Girl's Guide to Sorority Success*. New York: Villard, 1985. Conklin, Ellis E. "Fraternities Are Back, Seeking a Better Image." *The Record*. October 15, 1985. *The Record* reported that at the University of Georgia after an engaged sister's candlelight ceremony, "then she has to go rescue her fraternity boyfriend who has been tied to a tree by his frat brothers, stripped naked and squirted with shaving cream."

87 *Attendance at chapter meetings . . . "get a note from the teacher"*: Some sororities, such as Kappa Delta, specify these obligations in their national rulebook. Kappa Delta's *Norman Shield* states, "Attendance at all chapter meetings, ritualistic services, membership recruitment activities and all other required chapter functions: An unexcused absence from one of these events puts a member on bad standing for one calendar month. Excused absences are permitted only for illness; unavoidable absence from town; night classes, if needed for graduation and the class is not scheduled at any other time; or because, out of necessity, a member has to work. Except in the case of an emergency, excuses are due in writing prior to the meeting to be missed. Special permission to miss a chapter meeting because of work may be given only in rare cases and, then, only for a temporary period of time."

91 *"Not on the bed . . . shave my chacha."*: Warner Brothers Music granted permission to reprint these lyrics.

96 *A sister at another sorority canceled a meeting . . . "have your priorities out of order"*: See Soos, Margaret J. "With Friends Like These." *OC Weekly*. August 27, 1999. "Margaret J. Soos" is the writer's pseudonym.

97 *sororities have thorough "class files" . . . exclusive use of their sisters*: See, for example, Zwilling, James. "Greek Test Files Necessary, Beneficial Say Some Texas Christian U. Students." *Daily Skiff*. (Texas Christian University.) Via University Wire. October 26, 2001; Henley, Tim. "Oklahoma State U. Profs Using Technology to Battle Plagiarism." *Daily O'Collegian*. Oklahoma State University. March 25, 2002.

97 *Class files . . . "we pay to be Greek"*: See Zwilling. "Greek Test Files Necessary, Beneficial Say Some Texas Christian U. Students."

NOVEMBER

107 *At the University of Missouri . . . triple bunk beds*: Interviews; confirmed with the Office of Greek Life at the university.

107 *houses at the University of Washington . . . pledges must sleep*: Interviews; confirmed with the Panhellenic Office at the university.

107 *At half the houses at Purdue . . . windows left open at all times*: Interviews; confirmed with the Greek adviser.

107 *At Indiana University . . . in order to be considered an active member:* Interviews; confirmed with the Student Activities Office.

108 *The houses are usually owned . . . covers parties and similar expenses:* Interview with Sally Grant, chairman of the National Panhellenic Conference.

117 *This movement . . . elementary through high schools:* Among the intriguing works on this issue are the important books *Queen Bees and Wannabes: Helping Your Daughter Survive Cliques, Gossip, Boyfriends and Other Realities of Adolescence,* by Rosalind Wiseman (New York: Crown, 2002), and *Odd Girl Out: The Hidden Culture of Aggression in Girls,* by Rachel Simmons (New York: Harcourt, 2002). Laura Sessions Stepp of The *Washington Post* wrote about Alphas and Betas in her widely cited article "Alpha Girl; In Middle School, Learning to Handle the ABCs of Power" (February 23, 2002).

118 *"natural . . . popularity and social status":* See Wiseman. *Queen Bees and Wannabes.*

126 *"girls' social hierarchy . . . one of the consequences of girls' social hierarchies":* Ibid.

126 *others have called the Alphas:* See Stepp. "Alpha Girl; In Middle School, Learning to Handle the ABCs of Power."

128 *the current popularity of "mean girl" books . . . who turn out just fine:* See Meadows, Susannah. "Meet the Gamma Girls." *Newsweek.* June 3, 2002; Kantrowitz, Barbara. "Selling Advice—as Well as Anxiety." *Newsweek.* June 3, 2002.

129 *"social manipulation on the playground" or "relational aggression":* See Lamb, Sharon. *The Secret Lives of Girls: What Good Girls Really Do—Sex Play, Aggression, and Their Guilt.* New York: The Free Press, 2001.

GREEK WEEK

137 *A 1996 Harvard University College Alcohol Studies Program report . . . "powerless to do anything about it":* See Wechsler, H., G. Kuh, and A. Davenport. "Fraternities, Sororities and Binge Drinking: Results from a National Study of American Colleges." National Association of Student Personnel Administrators. Summer 1996; 33(4). I am grateful to the Harvard School of Public Health's Department of Health and Social Behavior for providing me with a copy of this article.

Several other studies have linked Greek membership to heavy drinking. One particularly thorough report is Sher, K., B. Bartholow, and S. Nanda. "Short- and Long-Term Effects of Fraternity and Sorority Membership on Heavy Drinking: A Social Norms Perspective." *Psychology of Addictive Behaviors.* Vol. 15, No. 1 (March 2001): 42–51. Their findings included both that "Throughout the college years, Greeks consistently drank more heavily than non-Greeks. Statistically controlling for previous alcohol use did not eliminate this effect" and that "Greek status did not predict postcollege heavy drinking levels."

In its most recent report on the topic, the Commission on Substance Abuse at Colleges and Universities found that "Students living in fraternities and sororities report drinking an average of 15 drinks per week, compared to only 5 drinks per week by other students." *Rethinking Rites of Passage: Substance Abuse on America's Campuses.* June 1994.

137 *In 2003 . . . 81 percent of non-Greeks:* See Freyvogel, Colleen. "Survey Finds Penn State Sororities, Fraternities Drink More. *Daily Collegian.* Pennsylvania State University. Via University Wire. March 4, 2003.

137 *in 1992 . . . nearly half used marijuana or cocaine within the thirty-day period preceding the study:* See Goodwin, L. "Alcohol and Drug Use in Fraternities and Sororities." *Journal of Alcohol and Drug Education.* Vol. 37, No. 2 (Winter 1992).

138 *Six years later . . . "escalating on college campuses within the Greek community":* See Strickland, Mary. "A New Look: The Changing Role of Greek Letter Organizations on American College Campuses." *KUDZU: The Journal of Higher Education Management.* Vol. 1 (Spring 1998).

138 *In 1985 . . . three times the legal limit:* See Nuwer, Hank. *Wrongs of Passage: Fraternities, Sororities, Hazing, and Binge Drinking.* Bloomington and Indianapolis: Indiana University Press, 1999.

139 *In a review of twelve hundred . . . "or automobile accidents":* See Weiss, Kenneth R. " 'Animal Houses' Try to Sober Up." *Los Angeles Times.* April 6, 1997.

139 *the University of Missouri in 1989 . . . alcohol-education program:* See "Campus Life: Missouri; Now, Fraternities Must Check Ages of Party Guests." *New York Times.*

139 *Other schools also prohibited . . . prevent open parties:* See Weiss. " 'Animal Houses' Try to Sober Up."

139 *Violation . . . "Greek Community Board":* See "Campus Life: Missouri; Now, Fraternities Must Check Ages of Party Guests."

143 *Snap back to reality . . . vomit on his sweater already:* The boys were misquoting Eminem's "Lose Yourself," from the soundtrack of the film *8 Mile.* The actual lyrics are:

> Yo, his palms are sweaty, knees weak, arms are heavy
> There's vomit on his sweater already, mom's spaghetti
> He's nervous, but on the surface he looks calm and ready
> To drop bombs, but he keeps on forgettin'
> What he wrote down, the whole crowd goes so loud
> He opens his mouth, but the words won't come out
> He's chokin', how everybody's jokin' now
> The clock's run out, time's up over, bloah!
> Snap back to reality, oh there goes gravity . . .

8 Mile Style granted permission to reprint these lyrics.

148 *Stepping originated . . . "performance traditions":* See Malone, Jacqui. *Steppin' on the Blues: The Visible Rhythms of African American Dance.* Urbana and Chicago: University of Illinois Press, 1996.

149 *It is marching . . . and slapping in one:* Ibid; See also Fine, Elizabeth C. *Soulstepping: African American Step Shows.* Urbana: University of Illinois Press, 2003.

149 *Each of the four . . . "Sweat":* See Fine. *Soulstepping.*

149 *each sorority has a "sign" . . . to encourage the performers:* See Malone. *Steppin' on the Blues.* I also learned a great deal about step during an interview with Dr. Walter Kimbrough, widely considered to be a leading expert on African American Greek life, and the vice president of Student Affairs at Albany State University.

149 *Alpha Kappa Alpha's call . . . "ee-i-kee":* See Ross, Lawrence C., Jr. *The Divine Nine: The history of African American Fraternities and Sororities.* New York: Kensington Books, 2000.

149 *Black sororities . . . at casual parties:* Interview with Dr. Walter Kimbrough.

149 *"salutes" or tributes . . . culture through dance:* See Fine. *Soulstepping.*

149 *step shows are to black Greeks what Greek Week is to whites:* Black Greeks traditionally have not been major Greek Week participants, although they have begun to get involved on some campuses. See, for example, Whipple, E. G., J. L. Baier, and D. L. Grady. "A Comparison of Black and White Greeks at a Predominantly White University." *NASPA Journal.* Vol. 28, No. 2 (Winter 1991). The *NASPA Journal* reported, "There is little or no participation by black Greeks in the traditional rush activities or Greek Week programs of white Greeks."

149 *As one sister has explained . . . "partying together":* Elizabeth C. Fine cites this quote; she credits Rita Harris for obtaining the quote at the 1999 Philadelphia Greek Picnic.

DECEMBER

166 *Northeast Greek Leadership Association Conference . . . Northeast region:* See the NGLA's conference web site at http:/greeklife.drexel.edu/ngla/annual_conference. More information about the NGLA can also be found at that site. The NGLA's mission statement is "The Northeast Greek Leadership Association exists to promote the founding principles and positive traditions of all Greek letter organizations through opportunities that encourage learning and leadership for the Northeast region."

168 *the "worst" things . . . dance sexily with each other:* See MTV's original *Sorority Life,* which aired in summer 2002.

168 *One sorority official . . . "protect our women and our Greek Community":* The adviser sent this letter to the professor and to me via e-mail on November 22, 2002.

169 *the professor wrote back . . . "on all matters that concern them":* The professor sent me a copy of her response, which she e-mailed back to the adviser slightly more than an hour after receiving the adviser's letter.

169 *lecture at the NGLA Conference entitled "The Greek PR War Room":* This lecture ran from 2:15 to 3:15 P.M. (Educational Session Block III) on the first full day of the conference. The Conference Guidebook listed the following description of the session: "The Greek public relations battle has reached the national level. The media condemns Greeks for failures, but fails to praise when chapters raise money for worthy causes or volunteer

in the community. This presentation takes participants inside the 'PR war room' and discusses professional techniques and their application to the Greek dilemma."

169–171 *"Pay close attention"* . . . *"every paper in town is there"*: The quotations in this section refer both to the presenter's statements and to the statements he posted on his slide show.

171 in October 1998 . . . Greek activity: See Nuwer, Hank. *Wrongs of Passage: Fraternities, Sororities, Hazing, and Binge Drinking.* Bloomington and Indianapolis: Indiana University Press, 1999, which notes that "an autopsy later turned up a trace of a date-rape drug in Courtney's system" and that Cantor's blood-alcohol level was, at .059, below the Michigan standard for intoxication.

171 *"The Values Institute"* . . . *plenary and breakout sessions on the four pillars:* These sessions ran from 9:00 A.M. to 4:45 P.M. on Saturday, February 29.

172 The theme of the conference, *"Values-Driven Leadership: Back to Basics"*: See, for example, 2003 NGLA *Annual Conference: Conference Guidebook.*

172 from Maryland to Maine: I confirmed that participants from these states attended in an interview with a member of the National Greek Leadership Association board.

174 that commercial . . . while fiddling with her pearls: The promos for MTV's *Sorority Life 2* aired in late winter 2003 in the weeks before the show debuted.

174 In her book . . . voted to drop the pledges: See Wright, Esther. *Torn Togas: The Dark Side of Campus Greek Life.* Minneapolis: Fairview Press, 1996.

187 No matter the leniency of a chapter . . . beholden to the sorority's national rules: See, for example, the Statement of Obligation in *Pi Phi Forever.* A pledge cannot be initiated until she signs this statement, which asserts, among other items, "I am knowledgeable of and in agreement with the Constitution and Statutes, Policies and Standing Rules and procedures of the Pi Beta Phi Fraternity and of _____ chapter's bylaws and house rules, and I promise to abide by them."

187 One sorority guide . . . *"kicked out of the sorority"*: See Rose, Margaret Ann. *Rush: A Girl's Guide to Sorority Success.* New York: Villard, 1985.

187 *"Each sorority has its own standards . . . at the local level"*: Interview with Sally Grant, chairman of the National Panhellenic Conference.

188 certainly no degree requirements: In an interview, Sally Grant confirmed that there are no degree requirements to work in a sorority national office.

188 who may be stuck in a time warp . . . own active sorority membership: For this reason, University of Alabama Associate Vice President for Student Affairs Kathleen Cramer, a Kappa Kappa Gamma alumna who regularly works with sororities (see February's chapter), said that the national office volunteers are "struggling with change."

188 Campus advisers sponsored by the university . . . educational administration: See Jones-Hall, Jennifer. "The Role of the Fraternity and Sorority Professional." *Advising Fraternities and Sororities,* a manual put out by the Association of Fraternity Advisers.

188 *"The most common reason . . . questionable reputation . . . sorority's guidelines"*: See Rose. *Rush: A Girl's Guide to Sorority Success.* The phrase "questionable reputation" also surfaced in the 1999 book *Ready for Rush.*

188 *"Sorority girls do not have sex. . . . revealing clothes must be avoided at all times"*: Ibid.

189 *"She may not know that she has broken a standards rule . . . tight jeans"*: Ibid.

189 *Kappa Delta warns . . . "judgements and comments about herself and/or the sorority"*: See *The Norman Shield of Kappa Delta.*

190 *To monitor chapters . . . "traveling consultants"*: See, for example, Delta Gamma's description at http:/www.deltagamma.org/cdc.html. The National Panhellenic Conference also has a consulting team that can visit and evaluate any chapter of a national sorority. See http:/www.npcwomen.org/college/c_consulting.php. See also McKee, C. William. "Understanding the Diversity of the Greek World." *Fraternities and Sororities on the Contemporary College Campus.* San Francisco: Jossey-Bass Inc., 1987. According to a recent Kappa Kappa Gamma brochure, KKG's consultants, called Kappa Trainers, "are able to present any existing *Pathways, Kappa's Continuous Education Experience* program or custom design one just for you. Kappa trainers are a wonderful resource for chapter and association officer training, providing educational programming for your Province Meetings and all leadership training needs."

189 *Known under names that vary . . . "airports by themselves"*: Interview with Sally Grant.

JANUARY

203 *determine a quota that every house must reach:* This is the simplest description of quotas, which can get complicated. For more information on quotas, see the "NPC Quota, Release Figures and Quota Additions" thread in the Rush Forum on www.greekchat.com.

203 *To get these recommendations . . . "the formal recommendation, which is a rec"*: See Rose, Margaret Ann. *Rush: A Girl's Guide to Sorority Success.* New York: Villard, 1985.

204 *appoint official recommendation boards . . . "may be denied a recommendation"*: Ibid.

204 *If a rushee doesn't know a rec board member:* Marilyn Schwartz points out that in order to get to know girls who don't know sisters or have recommendations, alumnae and sisters in cities visit candidates over the summer. "These are sometimes called Trash or Treasure luncheons because alums and members get to know an upcoming rushee and report back if she is trash or treasure," Schwartz writes. " 'If I had known what goes on during those sessions when they pick the girls, I never would have gone through Rush,' says one girl who did get in. 'We had one party that was Japanese and everyone had to take off her shoes when entering the house, which was decorated like a Japanese tea room. At the follow-up session that night, members were even discussing the cheap labels on some of the shoes and who was wearing the expensive labels." See Schwartz, Marilyn. *A*

Southern Belle Primer: Or Why Princess Margaret Will Never Be a Kappa Kappa Gamma. New York: Doubleday, 1991.

204 *advised to prepare a résumé . . . "at a restaurant on Martha's Vineyard, do"*: See Rose. *Rush: A Girl's Guide to Sorority Success.*

205 *According to author Maryln Schwartz . . . Ole Miss Kappa Kappa Gamma:* See Schwartz. *A Southern Belle Primer.*

205 *special treatment . . . "steal a legacy"*: See Rose. *Rush: A Girl's Guide to Sorority Success.*

206 *emergency packs including nail polish, mints, Band-Aids, and tampons:* See Vida, Vendela. *Girls on the Verge: Debutante Dips, Gang Drive-bys, and Other Initiations.* New York: St. Martin's Press. 1999.

206 *bring in a favorite rushee's older sister or aunt:* See Thornton, Bonnie, and Debbie Thornton. *Ready for Rush: The Must-Have Manual for Sorority Rushees!* Nashville: Hamblett House Inc., 1999.

206 *each rushee submits . . . how high the names appear on each list:* Ibid. (among other sources).

207 *"Will you take my best friend . . . get in anyway"*: This example was announced at the mid-Atlantic pre-rush meeting I attended.

207 *Kappa Kappa Gamma alumnae . . . "both Laura and Cheryl pledged Kappa Kappa Gamma"*: Ibid.

209–210 *At the end of the meeting . . . "shy," "attractive," and "loud"*: The girls were also given a handout that contained a list of suggested sentences for sisters to say to rushees on Pref night, including, "You've seen all our other sides, friendly, casual, outgoing, and now you can feel our sisterhood" and "We'll still be friends but there's a big difference in being a friend and being a sister—Friends are now and sisters are forever." Other dittoes in their packet of instructions reminded sisters of the following: look at rushees when they sing on Pref night, "Don't waste good sisters on Rushees already sold," and "SELL LIKE HELL—NEVER QUIT!!!"

214 *rush parties cannot go over . . . "good-looking fraternity boys who pester them"*: See Rose. *Rush: A Girl's Guide to Sorority Success.*

214 *At some schools . . . speak with their biological sisters outside of rush events:* See Thornton and Thornton. *Ready for Rush.*

222 *determined mothers have taken to hiring "rush consultants" . . . not affiliated or endorsed by the National Panhellenic Conference:* Confirmed in an interview with Sally Grant.

222 *six to twelve months before rush begins . . . "one on each hand is best"*: See Thornton and Thornton. *Ready for Rush.*

224 *"How Sororities Judge Rushees" . . . "Physical attractiveness plays a large part in the overall evaluation process"*: See Rose. *Rush: A Girl's Guide to Sorority Success.*

225 *"I think she would shine brighter in another house"*: Less southern-influenced houses might simply say a girl would be "happy elsewhere." See, for example, Thornton and Thornton. *Ready for Rush.*

FEBRUARY

234 In *August 2000, the Alpha Gamma Delta house . . . stories of sorority discrimination:* See Auchmutey, Jim. "Ali Davis Loved Her Life in Alpha Gamma Delta at the University of Georgia. Then a Black Student Came Through Sorority Rush and Everything Changed; The Sister Who Spoke Up." *Atlanta Journal and Constitution.* February 10, 2002.

234 From *2001 to 2003 . . . fraternities in blackface:* See, for example, Elliott, Debbie, reporter. Noah Adams and Robert Siegel, anchors. "Two Auburn University Fraternities Suspended after Wearing Racially Offensive Costumes at Halloween Parties." *All Things Considered.* National Public Radio. November 9, 2001; Jubera, Drew. "Racist Internet Photos Linked to Auburn University Fraternities." *Cox News Service.* November 7, 2001; Wertheimer, Linda K. " 'They Just Don't Feel Welcome.' Students Demand Answers after Racial Incidents at UT, A&M; School Presidents Hear Minorities' Concerns, Fear Lasting Damage." *Dallas Morning News.* February 19, 2003; Banerji, Ruma. "Blackface Bestirs Gray Area of Rights, Correctness—No Action by UT Against Students." *The Commercial Appeal.* December 10, 2002; Altamirano, Natasha. "National Chapters Suspend 2 U. Virginia Fraternities." *Cavalier Daily.* Via University Wire. November 19, 2002.

235 *graduate of the prestigious Alabama School of Math and Science . . . black landowner in the state:* All details confirmed with Melody Twilley in interviews. See also, for example, Jonsson, Patrik. "South Wrestles with Segregated Sororities." *Christian Science Monitor.* September 18, 2001; Gordon, Tom. "Bid Day for UA Sororities: No Blacks Taken by White Greeks." *Birmingham News.* September 11, 2001 (Gordon wrote several articles on this issue); Gettleman, Jeffrey. "The Nation; Sorority System in No Rush to Integrate." *Los Angeles Times.* September 10, 2001.

235 *a fifth of the campus—join the UA Greek system:* See Zengerle, Jason. "Sorority Row; Alabama's New Schoolhouse Door." *The New Republic.* February 4, 2002.

235 *Residents who aren't members . . . rarely break into the state's political and economic elite:* Ibid.

236 *"I was glad she was going . . . We thought we could help her":* Interviews, Dr. Kathleen Cramer.

237 *"This is a system steeped in tradition . . . doing a progressive thing":* Ibid.

237 *University of Alabama remains . . . never to knowingly admit an African American:* Interview, Pat Hermann; Associated Press. "All-White U. of Ala. Sororities Again Fail to Pledge Minority." *The Commercial Appeal.* September 12, 2001. Also, the *New Republic*'s Jason Zengerle reported, "When Melody Twilley stood in front of the Delta Zeta house last September, it was believed that no white fraternity or sorority at the University of Alabama had ever offered membership to a black student."

237 *One sister with a white mother . . . her background:* Interviews with a University of Alabama faculty member and with Melody Twilley.

237 *in the late 1980s . . . burned a cross on the front lawn of the new house:* See Zengerle. "Sorority Row; Alabama's New Schoolhouse Door."

237 *"We have one hundred percent illegal segregation here . . . 'just any nigger could get in'"*: Interviews, Pat Hermann.

240 *Alpha Kappa Alpha began in 1908 . . . were founded in 1920 and 1922*: See, for example, Ross, Lawrence C., Jr. *The Divine Nine: The History of African American Fraternities and Sororities.* New York: Kensington Books, 2000.

240 *One of the main purposes . . . the social status of African American women*: See, for example, Nuwer, Hank. *Wrongs of Passage: Fraternities, Sororities, Hazing, and Binge Drinking.* Bloomington and Indianapolis: Indiana University Press, 1999.

240 *National Pan-Hellenic Council*: For more information on the National Pan-Hellenic Council, see http://www.nphchq.org.

240 *grew out of "racial isolation" . . . "positive change for Blacks and the country"*: See the National Pan-Hellenic Council's web site at http://www.nphchq.org/about.htm.

240 *Until the 1960s . . . national organizations to refuse membership to nonwhites*: See McKee, C. William. "Understanding the Diversity of the Greek World." *Fraternities and Sororities on the Contemporary College Campus.* San Francisco, Jupsey-Bass. Inc., 1987. Whipple, E. G., J. L. Baier, and D. L. Grady. "A Comparison of Black and White Greeks at a Predominantly White University." *NASPA Journal.* Vol. 28, No. 2 (Winter 1991).

240 *author Rita Mae Brown . . . "Delta colors"*: See Brown, Rita Mae. *Rita Will: Memoir of a Literary Rabble-Rouser.* New York: Bantam Books, 1997.

240 *1963, when federal law prohibited Greek groups from discriminating based on race*: See Whipple, et al. "A Comparison of Black and White Greeks at a Predominantly White University."

240 *Black Greek-letter organizations estimate that 75 percent . . . NPHC sororities or fraternities*: See Fine, Elizabeth C. *Soulstepping: African American Step Shows.* Urbana: University of Illinois Press, 1996.

240 *women as Star Jones . . . Gwendolyn Cherry (Sigma Gamma Rho)*: See Ross. *The Divine Nine.*

241 *Patricia Roberts Harris . . . "Delta Sigma Theta which gives me the most security"*: See Giddings, Paula. *In Search of Sisterhood: Delta Sigma Theta and the Challenge of the Black Sorority Movement.* New York: William Morrow and Company, 1988.

241 *graduate chapters expect each member to . . . "affecting the community in which he or she lives"*: See the National Pan-Hellenic Council's web site at http://www.nphchq.org/about.htm.

241 *the presentation of "Spirit Awards" to . . . Maryland Lieutenant Governor Michael Steele*: See the event brochure, *Alpha Kappa Alpha Sorority, Inc. 72nd North Atlantic Regional Conference Public Meeting: Spirit of AKA.* April 10, 2003.

241 *salmon pink and apple green—the AKA colors*: See, for example, Thornton, Bonnie, and Debbie Thornton. *Ready for Rush: The Must-Have Manual for Sorority Rushees!* Nashville: Hamblett House Inc., 1999.

242 *"Always giving back to the community . . . foundation of the heart of Alpha Kappa Alpha"*: The international president at the time was Linda Marie White.

242 *all of the black sorority sisters they interviewed said . . . was a bag of potato chips*: See Berkowitz,

Alexandra, and Irene Padavic. "Getting a Man or Getting Ahead: A Comparison of White and Black Sororities." *Journal of Contemporary Ethnography*. Vol. 27 (1999): 530–557.

242 *thesis about whites in black sororities . . . "has six people and it's functioning"*: Interview with Mary L. Bankhead. Her thesis is entitled "A Qualitative Exploration of White Women in Historically Black Sororities: at predominantly white institutions in the Midwest."

242 *"Membership Intake Process" . . . as an undergraduate and/or after she graduates*: I learned about the Membership Intake Process primarily from interviews with Mary L. Bankhead and Dr. Walter Kimbrough.

243 *attention to scholarship . . . achieved higher GPAs than white Greeks*: See Binder, R., M. B. Seiler, W. Schaub, and T. Lake. *Greek Academic Achievement Update: Gamma Sigma Alpha and Bowling Green University Partnership*. Paper presented at the 2002 Conference of the Association of Fraternity Advisers. Columbus, Ohio. December 7, 2002.

243 *active black Greeks are "the best trained . . . black church doesn't have it"*: See Fine. *Soulstepping: African American Step Shows*.

244 *"Message from Delta Sigma Theta Sorority, Inc." . . . "racial, social, and economic parity"*: Cited in Ross. *The Divine Nine*.

244 *chapters use "the paper bag test" . . . skin darker than the bag don't get in*: See Wiseman, Rosalind. *Queen Bees and Wannabes: Helping Your Daughter Survive Cliques, Gossip, Boyfriends and Other Realities of Adolescence*. New York: Crown, 2002.

244 *in 1990 the presidents . . . history, structure, and values*: Interview, Dr. Walter Kimbrough.

244 *"old school" and "new school" camps . . . nonpledging sisters haven't earned their letters*: See Fine. *Soulstepping: African American Step Shows*.

244 *In 1998 . . . bled into them—and then to eat the cereal*: See Nuwer. *Wrongs of Passage*.

244 *In 2003, Virginia Union University . . . taken to the hospital for her severe bruises*: See Williams, Michael Paul. "VUU Sorority Chapter suspended for Hazing." *Richmond Times-Dispatch*. April 3, 2003.

244 *In many chapters . . . the step show has become more important as a way to prove and publicly display devotion to the group*: See Fine. *Soulstepping: African American Step Shows*.

244 *The NPHC recommends . . . "social justice, and moral messages"*: See the National Pan-Hellenic Council's web site at http://www.nphchq.org/about.htm.

245 *New sisters are now taught . . . "the status of each group within the social order"*: See Fine. *Soulstepping: African American Step Shows*.

245 *fourteen national Latina sororities . . . National Association of Latino Fraternal Organizations, which formed in 1998*: See NALFO, Inc. Update. NGLA 2003. For more information, see the National Association of Latino Fraternal Organizations' web site, at http://www. nalfo.org.

246 *Mu Sigma Upsilon . . . "unity among all women"*: See, for example, http://www.geocities.com/msu_anansichapter/MSUinfo.html and http://www.geocities.com/CollegePark/Stadium/2583/MSU.html.

247 *Panhellenic . . . has yet to reach out to Alpha Delta Sigma:* Interview, Melody Twilley. This was the case as of summer 2003.

MARCH

254 *In May 2003 . . . fish guts, coffee grounds, and mud:* See, for example, Black, Lisa, and Courtney Flynn. "Students' Mothers Charged in Hazing; 2 Northbrook Parents Accused of Providing Beer." *Chicago Tribune.* May 22, 2003.

255 *The incident, a hazing rite . . . one with a head wound:* See Black, Lisa, and Courtney Flynn. "School Will Try to Expel Girls in Hazing Fracas." *Chicago Tribune.* May 13, 2003.

255 *needing ten stitches:* See, for example, Black, Lisa, and Courtney Flynn. "5 Juniors Suspended Over Hazing; Students Refused to Sign Waiver." *Chicago Tribune.* June 3, 2003.

255 *Seniors shot juniors with paintballs and forced meat down a vegetarian's throat:* See Black and Flynn. "School Will Try to Expel Girls in Hazing Fracas."

255 *school district expelled more than thirty seniors . . . two parents:* See Black, Lisa, and Courtney Flynn. "Former Students Link Teachers to Hazings; Grease Supplied, Court Papers Say." *Chicago Tribune.* June 5, 2003.

255 *masturbate with salt shakers:* See Rivera, Geraldo, host; Pretlow, Jose, executive producer. "When Hazing Becomes Torture." *The Geraldo Rivera Show.* August 8, 1997.

255 *drop trousers . . . in front of a room of fraternity brothers:* See Broadbent, Lucy. "Dangerous Liaisons—The Hidden Perils of America's Secret Societies." *Cosmopolitan UK.* January 2003.

255 *Some sororities also force their pledges to wear similar hairstyles:* Interviews; See also Nuwer, Hank. *Wrongs of Passage: Fraternities, Sororities, Hazing, and Binge Drinking.* Bloomington and Indianapolis: Indiana University Press, 1999.

256 *As one recent Phi Mu said, "We were essentially slaves to the sisters":* Ibid.

256 *In 2001, Northeastern University . . . separating candy with their noses:* See Abel, David. "Campus Hazing Reportedly Increasing—in Sororities." *Boston Globe.* December 15, 2001.

257 *One sorority made its pledges call fraternity brothers . . . they were coming over:* See Wright, Esther. *Torn Togas: The Dark Side of Campus Greek Life.* Minneapolis: Fairview Press, 1996.

257 *A Phi Mu . . . "Nose, tits, and toes!":* See Nuwer. *Wrongs of Passage.*

258 *pledge class was told to prick . . . prayed the blood wasn't contaminated:* See Wright. *Torn Togas.*

258–259 *In 1997, in accordance with a tradition . . . wearing a fake penis:* See Vargas, Elizabeth, Diane Sawyer, and Sam Donaldson. "Sorority Hazing: Tales of Abusive Initiation Rituals." *ABC 20/20.* April 28, 1999; See also Nuwer. *Wrongs of Passage.* After the pledges complained to the school, DePauw issued one-semester suspensions and social probation to the branders, put the chapter on social probation, and cut its quota in half for the next two years. The chapter voted to keep the offending sisters. A sister who wanted to expel the hazers moved out of the house after other sisters ransacked her room. (Branding is hardly new to sororities. In 1988, a sorority at the University of Maine blindfolded six-teen pledges at a cemetery and branded them on their lower backs with a hot metal stamp of the sorority's letters.) See "No Charges in Sorority Pledge Branding." UPI October 13, 1988.

259 circle the fat was described . . . " 'It's just going to make you a better person' ": See Soos, Margaret J. "With Friends Like These." OC Weekly. August 27, 1999.

260 In 1970, Alpha Gamma Deltas . . . died of injuries sustained to her head: See Nuwer. Wrongs of Passage.

260 In 1993, Sarah Dronek pledged . . . able to save her toes: See Vargas, Sawyer, and Donaldson. "Sorority Hazing: Tales of Abusive Initiation Rituals."

260 started referring to Hell Week with the euphemism "Inspiration Week": See Wright. Torn Togas.

262 The National Panhellenic Conference had declared March 3 "Badge Day": For more information on Badge Day, see the description on the National Panhellenic Conference's web site, at http://www.npcwomen.org/newsevents/n_badgeday.php.

262 the "Panhellenic Creed" . . . "tenet by which we strive to live": See, for example, Speaking of Sororities: A Guide to Understanding the Privileges, Responsibilities, and Benefits of Sorority Membership. First edi-tion, 1961. Revisions by NPC Publications Committee, 1989, 1995, 2001; see also the National Panhellenic Conference web site, at http://www.npcwomen.org/about/an_creed.php.

269 In the 1990s, national Greek organizations . . . Greek deaths had been attributed: See, for example, Yee, Kelly T. "Fraternity, Sorority Hazing Under Increased Scrutiny." Times-Picayune. September 11, 1994.

269 In May 2002, Alfred University . . . because of a beating during pledging: Interview, Daryl Conte, Alfred University's associate dean of students and formerly the administrator in charge of Greek life. For more on the issues that led Alfred to abolish its Greek system, see Goetschius, Sue. "Greek Life at Alfred: Proud Tradition, Uncertain Future?" Alfred: The Magazine for Alumni and Friends of Alfred University. Spring 2002.

269 Other schools . . . terminated their Greek systems because of hazing violations: See, for example, Macpherson, Doug, reporter; Simon, Scott, host. "Controversy Over Faculty Proposal to Abolish Greek System at Dartmouth College." All Things Considered. National Public Radio. May 18, 2001.

269 forty-three states passed antihazing laws . . . House Committee on Education and the Workforce: See, for example, Hank Nuwer's web site www.stophazing.org, a clearinghouse for informa-tion on the subject. See also Haynes, V. Dion. "Across U.S., Hazing Lives Despite Laws." Chicago Tribune. May 26, 2003.

269–270 "Any action or situation . . . in a chapter or colony of an NPC member fraternity": See, for example, the definition available on the National Panhellenic Conference's web site, at www.npcwomen.org/policies/p_resolutions.php.

270 "Hazing is anything that distinguishes one member from another": Many of the students at the Northeast Greek Leadership Association Conference were grappling with this defini-

tion, while some current sorority sisters whom I interviewed outside of the conference (like Vicki) were unaware of it.

270 *NPC has two levels of policies . . . "tougher on students"*: I gleaned this information from the National Panhellenic Conference web site, specifically from www.npcwomen.org/ policies/ p_agreements.php, and confirmed the details in an interview with Sally Grant.

270 *When Arika Hover pledged . . . Framed, Arika was tossed out of the chapter*: Interview with Arika Hover. I originally learned about Hover's story from: Mahoney, Erin. "Ex-Sorority Member Alleges Harassment." *Arizona Daily Wildcat*. August 26, 1999.

272 *"They've actually done studies . . . lowest common denominator"*: See Rivera, Geraldo, host; Pretlow, Jose, executive producer. "When Hazing Becomes Torture."

272 *when I asked Brothers . . . "somebody else's book"*: Telephone conversation with Dr. Joyce Brothers.

273 *A 1980s study . . . hazing was important to Greek life*: See Blair, John L., and Patrick S. Williams. "Fraternity Hazing Revisited: Current Alumni and Active Member Attitudes toward Hazing." *Journal of College Students Personnel*. Vol. 24, No. 4 (1983): 300–305. Cited in Wright. *Torn Togas*.

273 *In 2000, a sorority president posted . . . "crossing streets, rock climbing etc."*: See www.stophazing.org.

274 *In December 2001, Michael V. W. Gordon . . . "hazing in sororities is increasing in frequency as well as severity"*: See Abel. "Campus Hazing Reportedly Increasing—in Sororities."

274 *require pledges to wear a "pledge pin" distinguishing them from sisters*: The pledge pin tradition was general knowledge among the sorority girls I interviewed; I confirmed this in an interview with Sally Grant.

274 *don't allow pledges to wear the sorority's crest*: Interview, Sally Grant.

274 *exclude pledges from ritual ceremonies*: This was general knowledge among the girls I interviewed; also, the purpose of initiation for most sororities is to finally introduce the pledges to the sorority's rituals and secrets. Sally Grant explained to me that pledges cannot wear the sorority crest because they do not know the meaning of it (and won't know until they are initiated).

274 *refuse to initiate pledges until they pass a pledge-only test*: See, for example, *Pi Phi Forever*, which states, "A Pledge Shall Be Initiated Into Pi Beta Phi Only After . . . She has passed the pledge test."

TRADITIONS AND SECRET RITUALS

277 *"Earn Yo Beads Mardi Gras Party" . . . "Free Bongs for All Party Patrons!!"*: This information was printed on brochures handed out to partygoers, as well as posted on signs in the area.

279 *While Spring Breaking on South Padre Island . . . "I'm really glad I did it"*: See Ovaska, Sarah. "Girls Gone Wild Holds Competition; Not Everyone Is Wild about the Nudity on the Beach." *Valley Morning Star*. March 15, 2003.

280 *Dissatisfied with the results . . . had not made a final decision on the girls' sorority fate*: I learned this

from SMU sorority members. The Delta Delta Delta national office did not return repeated calls for comment.

280 *"a symbolic and often emotional expression . . . between the individual and the organization"*: See Callais, Mari Ann. "Sorority Rituals: Rites of Passage and Their Impact on Contemporary Sorority Women." A dissertation submitted to the graduate faculty of the Louisiana State University and Agricultural and Mechanical College in partial fulfillment of the requirements for the degree of Doctor of Philosophy in Educational Leadership, Research, and Counseling. May 2002.

281 *In 1999, the national president of Alpha Sigma Alpha . . . "we would never lose our way"*: See Kilgannon, S. M. "The Ritual Provides Direction for Alpha Sigma Alpha." *The Phoenix of Alpha Sigma Alpha.* Fall 1999. Cited in Callais. "Sorority Rituals."

281 *An Alpha Delta Pi document . . . "The ideals remain unchanged"*: See Hensil, K. *Alpha Delta Pi History Workshop I–III.* Atlanta: Alpha Delta Pi Fraternity, 1994–1997. Cited in Callais. "Sorority Rituals."

281 *Kappa Alpha Theta was the first university Greek-letter fraternity for women*: See Kappa Alpha Theta's web site, at www.kappaalphatheta.org. Several sororities like to claim to be the "first." In 1851, women at Wesleyan Female College in Macon, Georgia, founded the Adelphean Society—the country's first secret society for college women—which later became Alpha Delta Pi. (See, for example, MacDonald, Jessica North, editor. *History of Alpha Delta Pi: From the Founding of the Adelphean Society in 1851 at Wesleyan Female College, Macon, Georgia, to the Establishment of the Fifty-fourth Chapter of the National Organization at the University of South Carolina in 1928.* Ames, Iowa: The Powers Press, 1929; See also *100 Years of the National Panhellenic Conference.*) The following year, Wesleyan women formed the rival Philomathean Society, later known as Phi Mu. (See, for example, Nuwer, Hank. *Wrongs of Passage: Fraternities, Sororities, Hazing, and Binge Drinking.* Bloomington and Indianapolis: Indiana University Press, 1999, for the rivalry.) In 1867, I. C. Sorosis (eventually Pi Beta Phi) was established at Monmouth College as the first women's college secret society to be modeled after men's fraternities. (See *Pi Phi Forever;* see also Pi Beta Phi's web site, at www.pibetaphi.org.)

In 1882, Gamma Phi Beta at Syracuse University was the first to call itself a "sorority," at the urging of the members' Latin professor. (See Owen, Christopher Kent. "Reflections on the College Fraternity and Its Changing Nature." *Baird's Manual of American College Fraternities.* Menasha, Wis.: The Collegiate Press, George Banta Primary, 1949–, 15th ed.; *100 Years of the National Panhellenic Conference;* Callais. "Sorority Rituals;" Gamma Phi Beta's web site, at www.gammaphibeta.org.) "Soror" is Latin for sister, but many sororities still officially continue to refer to themselves as fraternities. See, for example, Thornton, Bonnie, and Debbie Thornton. *Ready for Rush: The Must-Have Manual for Sorority Rushees. Nashville:* Hamblett House, 1999.

281 *In 1870, Bettie Locke . . . wear their badge only if she agreed to be their mascot, she declined*: See Kappa Alpha Theta's web site, at www.kappaalphatheta.org.

281 *At her father's suggestion . . . only begun to admit women three years before:* See Johnson, Clyde Sanfred. *Fraternities in Our Colleges.* New York: National Interfraternity Foundation, 1972. Cited in Benjamin, Faye. "Fraternity Girls" [a Brown University term paper]. December 2002.

281 *Ida Shaw Martin argued that . . . "residence in a dormitory will tend to destroy right ideals":* See Martin, Ida Shaw. *The Sorority Handbook.* Boston: privately printed, 1907.

281 *"were reminded not to disgrace themselves, lest they bring shame on their sorority":* See Nuwer. *Wrongs of Passage.*

282 *state laws prohibiting sororities . . . as "inimical to the public good":* See Oklahoma State Legislative Council Research Department. *States with Anti-Fraternity and Anti-Sorority Laws: A State Legislative Council Compilation.* Oklahoma City, Oklahoma, March 24, 1953.

283 *Mega-author Sue Grafton . . . "hasn't contributed anything to my success":* Grafton included this statement in a response to a set of written questions I faxed her.

283 *sororities developed rituals to reflect the values . . . "made the group special and unique":* See Callais. "Sorority Rituals."

283 *the crest of the national sororities' . . . "inscribed the name of the National Panhellenic Conference":* See *100 Years of the National Panhellenic Conference.*

284 *"What is really exciting . . . Kappa stories became one":* See Strength, D. W. "These Are Our Stories." *The Key of Kappa Kappa Gamma.* Summer 2000. Cited in Callais. "Sorority Rituals."

284 *encompass formal readings . . . she should be asked to leave:* See Callais. "Sorority Rituals."

284 *These oaths, however, are not necessarily steadfast:* I learned about most of the secret rituals in the following section from interviews with scores of sorority sisters.

285 *Delta Zeta has a sorority whistle . . . G, G, high E, high C:* See Miner, Florence Hood. *Delta Zeta Sorority 1902–1982: Building on Yesterday, Reaching for Tomorrow.* Columbus, Ohio: The Sorority, 1983.

285 *"The roots of the flower are the Founders . . . petals stand closely united around these to defend and protect them":* See *Pi Phi Forever.*

287 *National Song of Alpha Delta Pi . . . "For Alpha Delta Pi":* See MacDonald, editor. *History of Alpha Delta Pi.*

287 *In "hard-core" Chi Omega chapters . . . pronounced dead, and then reborn as sisters:* According to the web site www.chiomegasecrets.com, run by Kristin Verzwyvelt, the former Chi Omega who alleged her sisters arranged her date rape, a Chi Omega initiation song entitled "Unto Persephone" goes as follows:

> Unto Persephone
> Maiden now we yield thee
> Rest thou in deepest dream
> Til comes the wak'ning gleam
> Spirits attend thee

Light and love to lend thee
In Chi Omega
(pause)
To a new life rise
Blest by Demeter wise
In these bonds to find
Strength in friendship kind
Sister, we greet thee
Ever one with us to be
In Chi Omega

287 *Kappa Delta's First Degree Ceremony . . . "virtually unchanged since 1897":* See *The Norman Shield of Kappa Delta.*

288 *crucial that the pin not "fall into the possession of a nonmember" . . . or alumnae association:* See Isbell, Lila A. "Deep the Sweet Significance . . . What You Should Know About Your Kappa Badge." *The Key: A Kappa Kappa Gamma Publication.* Vol. 120, No. 1 (Spring 2003).

288 *at the National Panhellenic Conference Centennial Celebration . . . "secrets must be maintained to maintain intimate association":* See Letitia Fulkerson, Chi Omega Fraternity, 1st Alternate Delegate. NPC Summary 2002. "Celebrating 100 Years of Leadership, Values, and Friendship": the National Panhellenic Conference Centennial Celebration and Interim Session. Held at the Marriott Oak Brook in Oak Brook, Illinois, October 10–12, 2002.

APRIL

293 *Sisterhood is not as strong as brotherhood . . . "boys can pierce it":* Interview, Lisa Handler.

294 *I visited Zeta Delta Xi . . . Brown University in Providence, Rhode Island:* I am grateful to the brothers of Zeta Delta Xi for allowing me to use their actual names and affiliation.

294 *Faye, who wrote a paper . . . encouraged experimentation:* See Benjamin, Faye. "Fraternity Girls" [a Brown University term paper]. December 2002.

295 *The Zetes originally were affiliated . . . "fraternity founded on principles of equality":* See the Zeta Delta Xi web site at www.zete.org.

297 *"Well, that's not as much fun . . . you do anyway":* Interview, Melody Twilley.

305 *I attended a Subrosa meeting at the University of Pennsylvania:* I am grateful to the women of Subrosa for allowing me to use the name of their club and school.

306 *joined Subrosa after their Phi Sigma Sigma chapter was shut down in the fall:* Phi Sigma Sigma's national office did not return repeated calls for comment on the closing of the chapter.

306 *In 2002, the Phi Sig chapter had the highest sorority GPA . . . "Outstanding Greek Leader":* See the chapter's web site, at http://dolphin.upenn.edu/~phisig/awards.htm.

306 *one of the few sororities on campus that hadn't broken rules in recent memory:* See, for example, Tam-

ber, Caryn. "Phi Sig Troubles Due to Low Numbers; Nearly All Members of Penn's Chapter of the Sorority Resigned Wednesday." *Daily Pennsylvanian.* November 8, 2002.

306 *three other sororities at Penn were under investigation for alcohol violations:* See Dulberg, Andrew. "OSC Concludes Investigations into Six Greek Houses." *Daily Pennsylvanian.* April 10, 2003.

307 *option to deactivate . . . seventy-five sisters resigned:* See Tamber. "Phi Sig Troubles Due to Low Numbers."

307 *chapter president stated . . . "no longer want to be associated with such an organization":* See Maak, Jamie. "Phi Sig Sorority Members Resign; The Group's National Organization May 'Reestablish' at Penn." *Daily Pennsylvanian.* November 7, 2002.

307 *My daughter will make friends . . . opportunities for continued camaraderie, service, and personal development:* See the National Panhellenic Conference publication *Women's Fraternity Membership: A Perspective for Parents,* 2001.

CONCLUSION

320 *Greeks are more likely to graduate from college than unaffiliated students:* See the National Panhellenic Conference publication *Unlocking the Secrets to Success in College: Words of Wisdom from Sorority Women.*

320 *two-year survey . . . "show stronger inclinations to give financial support to non-profit agencies":* See *Women's Fraternity Membership: A Perspective for Parents;* Thornton, Bonnie, and Debbie Thornton. *Ready for Rush: The Must-Have Manual for Sorority Rushees!* Nashville: Hamblett House, 1999.

320 *higher occurrences of binge drinking:* See Wechsler H., G. Kuh, and A. Davenport. "Fraternities, Sororities and Binge Drinking: Results from a National Study of American Colleges." National Association of Student Personnel Administrators. Summer 1996; 33(4).

320 *academic cheating and weaker levels of "principled moral reasoning":* See Callais, Mari Ann. "Sorority Rituals: Rites of Passage and Their Impact on Contemporary Sorority Women." Ph.D. dissertation, Louisiana State University. May 2002.

320 *a 2003 Penn State survey . . . experiencing unwanted sexual advances:* See Freyvogel, Colleen. "Survey Finds Penn State Sororities, Fraternities Drink More." *Daily Collegian.* Pennsylvania State University. Via University Wire. March 4, 2003.

320 *which has an Academic Excellence Committee that distributes a seasonal newsletter:* See, for example, *The Scholar: Academic Excellence News.* Vol. 10, No. 1 (February 2003).

320 *"All NPC groups . . . encourage high scholarship as a priority":* See *Women's Fraternity Membership: A Perspective for Parents.*

321 *as a professor she can tell . . . "can't claim to be about the academics and then ruin them":* Interview, Lisa Handler.

321 *sororities often encourage the sisters . . . a career in sorority administration:* See, for example, "I Majored in Sorority . . . Now What Do I Do?" ph factor: *A Service of College Panhellenics Committee.* National Panhellenic Conference. March 2002. The publication's suggested

career paths include "becoming a professional staff person for Fraternity/Sorority Life," Greek Adviser, Coordinator of Fraternity/Sorority Life, Panhellenic Adviser, Traveling Chapter Consultant, and Chapter Adviser, among others.

321 *promote the organizations as groups that . . . further the development of women*: See, for example, *Women's Fraternity Membership: A Perspective for Parents.*

321 *In 1994, a study . . . "higher in sociability, hedonism, self-confidence, and social conformity"*: See Atlas, G., and D. Morier. "The Sorority Rush Process: Self-Selection, Acceptance Criteria, and the Effect of Rejection." *Journal of College Student Development.* Vol. 35 (September 1994).

321 *a study of the values . . . lower when rated on the value of kindness*: See Scott, William A., with the collaboration of Ruth Scott. *Values and Organizations: A Study of Fraternities and Sororities.* Chicago: Rand McNally & Company, 1965.

322 *"We aren't diverse . . . ritual makes us the same"*: A sorority sister I met on Spring Break showed me a copy of this report.

322 *"protect their institution's reputation . . . commit offenses such as criminal hazing"*: See Nuwer, Hank. *Wrongs of Passage: Fraternities, Sororities, Hazing, and Binge Drinking.* Bloomington and Indianapolis: Indiana University Press, 1999.

322 *G. Armour Craig . . . "terrified of offending the alumni and cutting off large, essential contributions"*: See Lord, M. G. "Frats and Sororities; The Greek Rites of Exclusions; Racism and Sexism. *The Nation.* July 4, 1987.

322 *"Greek organizations present . . . universities don't do anything for Greeks, but that's crap"*: Interview, Daryl Conte.

323 *"There [is] a significant need at the undergraduate level for affiliation"*: See *100 Years of the National Panhellenic Conference.*

323 *"fictive kinship" . . . utilizing a language that institutionalizes friendships*: See Handler, Lisa. "In the Fraternal Sisterhood: Sororities as Gender Strategy." *Gender & Society.* Vol. 9, No. 2 (April 1995): 236–255.

324 *In Mississippi . . . Ole Miss chapter of their sorority must accept them as sisters*: I first learned of this in an interview with Lisa Handler and have since heard of other examples at other schools in the South. According to Margaret Rose, "Chapters that are particularly difficult to pledge often get applicants from girls who pledged at another school with the intent of transferring to these chapters. Girls who are afraid that they will not be able to pledge a sorority on a large Greek campus go to a smaller school where it is easier to pledge and then transfer."

324 *In Texas, some die-hard sorority mothers . . . Texas school after initiation*: See Schwartz, Maryln. *A Southern Belle Primer: Or Why Princess Margaret Will Never Be a Kappa Kappa Gamma.* New York: Doubleday, 1991.

324 *National Panhellenic Conference . . . 3.5 million initiated women in nearly three thousand collegiate chapters*: See *100 Years of the National Panhellenic Conference.*

324 with numbers generally holding steady and increasing in Texas and the Southwest: Interview, Sally Grant.

324 In 2001, the NPC added eighty thousand sisters, a 9 percent increase from 1999: See La Ferla, Ruth. "How to Move Up? The Sorority Track." New York Times. July 13, 2003.

325 university assistance: For example, before Santa Clara University decided in spring 2001 to phase out its Greek system, it was providing approximately $30,000 each year in in-kind services and funds to the campus Inter-Greek Council. See "Santa Clara U. to Shut Down All Fraternities and Sororities." The Chronicle of Higher Education. April 6, 2001.

325 a practice that a few sororities already encourage as a supplement to the rush period: See, for example, www.alphachiomega.org.

325 Alabama's associate vice president Kathleen Cramer . . . de-emphasis of some sororities' recommendation processes: Cramer sent me a copy of the letter recommending this de-emphasis that she and the University of Alabama faculty senate sent to sororities in May 2002.

326 College literary and debate societies began by assigning every interested student an affiliation: See, for example, Bagg, Lyman Hotchkiss. Four Years at Yale (by a Graduate of '69). New Haven: Charles C. Chattfield, 1871.

327 "It is in accord with the dignity . . . to avoid negative publicity on Panhellenic matters": See "A Lesson in Public Relations." ph factor: A Service of College Panhellenics Committee. National Panhellenic Conference. Fall 2002. The publication specifically emphasizes, "All Panhellenic Associations should remind their members [of] the NPC Unanimous Agreement IV, Standards of Ethical Conduct #6" and reminds students to contact headquarters if they are approached by the media.

327 Some Greek groups . . . "Membership Development Program": See Greek Gazette. Vol. 1, No. 5 (September 23, 2001).

327 "Something as simple . . . changing a culture of hazing in an organization": See "Terminology: Pledge Versus New Member." Greek Gazette. Vol. 1, No. 4 (September 16, 2001).

328 serve a role in loco parentis: See Risman, Barbara J. "College Women and Sororities: The Social Construction and Reaffirmation of Gender Roles." Urban Life. Vol. 11 (July 1982). Reprinted in Deegan, Mary Jo, ed. Women and Symbolic Interaction. Boston: Allen & Unwin, 1987.

331 In the 1980s . . . stricter host-liability laws regarding student drinking: See, for example, Goetschius, Sue. "Greek Life at Alfred: Proud Tradition, Uncertain Future?" Alfred: The Magazine for Alumni and Friends of Alfred University, Spring 2002.

331 "Sororities need to realize . . . the institution is not part of them": Interview, Daryl Conte.

331 in fact, some schools . . . move rush from first semester to second: See, for example, Johnson, Michelle. "ASU Bans Freshmen Greek Pledging in the Fall: Hope Is for the Students to Start College Life with Studying, Less Partying." Winston-Salem Journal. July 24, 2002; George, Maryann. "University of Michigan Delays Fall 'Rush.'" Detroit Free Press. November 20, 2001.

332 adult representatives . . . flexibility in the time and energy they put into supervising students: The NGLA session was entitled "So, You Think You Hate Your Greek Advisor?" For more information on

the demands placed on Greek advisers, see Colgan, Susan, and John H. Opper, Jr. "Using Organization Development Techniques to Enhance Chapter Functioning." *Fraternities and Sororities on the Contemporary College Campus.* San Francisco: Jossey-Bass Inc., 1987.

332 *Alfred University . . . brings in free pizza for the students:* Interview, Daryl Conte.

333 *sorority sisters are prone to exaggerating and outright lying:* Besides learning this through interviews, I also was made aware of it when I observed the "practice conversation" meeting, during which the chapter adviser and the recruitment chair instructed girls on ways to misrepresent the sorority in front of rushees.

EPILOGUE

336 *"[Name] . . . she will please sign and return this invitation":* 2003 Bid Day Card, Southern Methodist University.

338 *At the Theta house, First Lady Laura Bush's old haunt:* See, for example, Schindehette, Susan, Jane Sims Podesta, Bob Stewart, Laura Calkins, Anne Lang, Hilary Hylton, Gabrielle Cosgriff, and Chris Coats. "The First Lady Next Door." *People.* January 29, 2001.

ACKNOWLEDGMENTS

I am profoundly grateful to Missy and Dave, without whom I could not have accomplished the reporting for this book. Both of them went extraordinarily far out of their way to assist me, sometimes on extremely short notice, and I thank them from the bottom of my heart. I also deeply appreciate the input and patience from the rest of my family and from my grandfather, all of whose support and encouragement carried me through the arduous days and nights that typified my work life throughout the year. Their comments and critiques, as well as those from Ellie, Vicki, and Andrea, proved invaluable.

The four girls who allowed me to observe and report on their college lives over the course of a year were gracious in manner, generous with time, and candid in interviews, even when their year became much bumpier than they had expected. I am overwhelmed by the way these girls risked their sorority membership to help a stranger, never once complaining about the hassle of dragging around an undercover reporter. I could not have found better sports, and I will always consider myself fortunate to have gotten to know them.

I am indebted to the other sources who allowed me to visit them and interview them at length on multiple occasions, especially "Brooke," my Texas representative, whose charm and courage are magnetic. Melody Twilley, the women of Subrosa at the University of Pennsylvania, and the Zetes at

Brown University made me feel welcome and kindly took time from their busy schedules to meet with me. Thanks also to Walter Kimbrough, Lisa Handler, Mindy Stombler, Kathleen Cramer, Pat Hermann, and Mary L. Bankhead for sharing their expertise.

Ruth Davis and Sebastian Rupley constantly help me to refine my writing and were patient and compassionate when I disappeared to write this book. I also appreciate Beth Dickey's enthusiasm and Elisa Lee's, Hannah Slagle's, and Catherine Mayhew's attention to detail. I cannot thank author Pamela Paul enough for suggesting that I tackle the topic of sororities. It is humbling to have such a talented and magnanimous friend in the field. Bill Parkhurst and Jane Mayer continue to drive me with their enthusiasm for my work, and Andrew, Amy, Andrea, Melanie, Nick, Beth, and the men and women on my soccer teams continue to distract me happily with their contagious spirit and post-game victory gatherings.

At Hyperion, I thank Will Schwalbe and Jennifer Lang for championing this project. I am inordinately lucky to have been paired with Mary Ellen O'Neill, a gem of an editor, whose sharp, thoughtful insights and thorough critiques turned this into a much better book than it was. Her good cheer and great sense of humor made every step of the process a true delight. And Paula Balzer, agent and friend, continues to be, in my newly acquired sorority speak, "clearly fabulous" and "just the most shining star." She definitely "has that sparkle."

Most of all, I thank my father, more than I've told him and more than he knows. Since the days of third grade fractions, I've turned to him to look over my work, a practice that I've continued in my professional life. With this book he outdid himself, offering crucial reporting ideas and spending weeks meticulously poring over the manuscript to provide stellar edits, critiques, and polish. This acknowledgment can't come close to conveying the admiration and the deep gratitude I feel with all my heart. He is my hero.

Finally, I would like to thank the readers, many of whom have contacted me with questions, comments, and suggestions. I will continue to respond to your e-mails regularly at www.alexandrarobbins.com.